MW01129058

THE JEWISH SOUTH

The Jewish South

AN AMERICAN HISTORY

Shari Rabin

PRINCETON UNIVERSITY PRESS

PRINCETON & OXFORD

Published by Princeton University Press
41 William Street, Princeton, New Jersey 08540
99 Banbury Road, Oxford OX2 6JX

press.princeton.edu

All Rights Reserved

ISBN 978-0-691-20876-3
ISBN (e-book) 978-0-691-26951-1

British Library Cataloging-in-Publication Data is available

Editorial: Fred Appel and James Collier
Production Editorial: Jenny Wolkowicki
Jacket design: Katie Osborne
Production: Erin Suydam
Publicity: Alyssa Sanford and Kathryn Stevens
Copyeditor: Maia Vaswani

Jacket image: Temple Mickve Israel, Savannah, Georgia, William A. Rosenthall Judaica Collection - Postcards, College of Charleston Libraries, Charleston, SC, USA

This book has been composed in Arno Pro

Printed in the United States of America

10 9 8 7 6 5 4 3 2 1

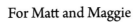

For Matt and Maggie

CONTENTS

Prologue   ix

PART I: 1669–1840   1

Chapter 1: Jews, Heathens, and Other Dissenters   3

Chapter 2: House of God   17

Chapter 3: The Cause of His Country   29

Chapter 4: Blessings and Privileges   39

Chapter 5: Faith of Our Fathers   48

PART II: 1840–1878   59

Chapter 6: Peculiar Institutions   61

Chapter 7: Unhappy Contest   72

Chapter 8: Infernal Crusade   87

Chapter 9: Scattered Nation   100

Chapter 10: Holy Cause   113

PART III: 1878–1967 125

Chapter 11: Subtle Ostracism 127

Chapter 12: The Alien Hebrew 139

Chapter 13: No Peace 153

Chapter 14: Port and Dock 168

Chapter 15: Trembling Tribes 183

Epilogue 198

Acknowledgments 203

Notes 207

Index 263

PROLOGUE

This book had three beginnings. The first was the day after my bat mitzvah in June of 2000, when I moved from Milwaukee, Wisconsin, to Marietta, Georgia, just six miles east of the site of the 1915 lynching of Leo Frank, perhaps the most infamous incident in American Jewish history. Marked by a modest commemorative plaque, it lies across the street from a local landmark known as "the Big Chicken," a large wooden bird that stands astride a KFC fast food restaurant. The second was in July 2015, a month before the Leo Frank centennial and just weeks after a white gunman massacred a Bible study group at Emanuel African Methodist Episcopal Church in downtown Charleston. As a newly minted PhD in religious studies, I moved into a carriage house on the Charleston peninsula to begin a faculty position focused on southern Jewish history. The third was in August 2019, after I left South Carolina for Ohio and began to put pen to paper; the words flowed easily. I had been brought to the South twice, the first time by family and the second time by work, and both times found myself in some sort of proximity to expressions of the region's—and the country's—most violent impulses. And yet, in both my teenaged and adult sojourns I was also embedded within dedicated Jewish communities, filled with warm and complicated people from all over the country and the world who were committed to the places that they lived and to commemorating pasts that often surprised their Christian neighbors and their coreligionists elsewhere.

While the origins of this book are easily traceable, those of southern Jewry are shrouded in mystery. No one knows when the first Jewish person came to the region we now know as "the South." Some thought that Native Americans *were* Jews, or at least lost tribes of Israel. With respect to actual Jews, European countries were ambivalent to say the least. Centuries of Christian doctrine had condemned them as shameful deniers of Christ, and England had expelled them altogether in 1290. Spain did the same in 1492, and Portugal in 1497, propelling large numbers of Jews to places around the world, including the Americas. England's American colonies were explicitly motivated by the goal of "propagating the Christian religion," but in practice they focused their attentions on economics. One result of this was widespread exploitation of Indigenous Americans and enslaved Africans; another was a desperate need for the mercantile skills that many Jews had come to possess after centuries of marginalization in Europe.[1]

As they entered this volatile maelstrom, Jews found that their status was negotiated along multiple, intersecting axes: the centuries-old distinction between Christians and Jews; the brutal system of labor that distinguished freedom from enslavement and, eventually, Black from white; and the imperial competition over territory that brought Protestant England and Holland, Catholic France and Spain, and diverse Native societies into contact, competition, and conflict. This complex beginning would have long-standing implications for those who lived and sojourned on southern lands. In the pages that follow, I trace how Jews contributed to and navigated emerging systems of inequality and hierarchy across four centuries in the territory that would briefly—but significantly—become the Confederate States of America. I chose this definition of the South not because it is the only legitimate one but because I take the government(s) under which Jews lived to be of central importance. The history I unravel here begins with peripatetic Jewish merchants pursuing the promise of toleration alongside "heathens and other dissenters" in the Carolina colony and ends with upper middle class professionals watching neo-Nazis march through the streets of Charlottesville, Virginia.

For many years, the history of southern Jews lived within these communities, shared among individuals and in obscure local studies. Those who told it were motivated by an understandable enthusiasm for documenting their travails and those of their friends and relatives, and by a strategic interest in highlighting their long residence and ample contributions to specific places. Then, in 1973, Eli Evans, the son of a former mayor of Durham, North Carolina, published a powerful memoir, travelogue, and popular history called *The Provincials: A Personal History of Jews in the South*, which opened the floodgates for professionally trained historians and newly organized historical societies. Together, these researchers studied southern Jews in order to counter what they saw as an inordinate emphasis on the northeast in histories of American Jewry.[2] Among themselves, they debated whether southern Jews were like their coreligionists elsewhere or whether, as American Jewish leader Rabbi Isaac Mayer Wise had already put it in the 1880s, "the descendants of immigrant Jews in this country are typically Americans, *according to the section of the country where they live*" (emphasis added).[3] Wherever they stood on this question, they produced an impressive body of scholarship attending to economics, gender, politics, religion, and other facets of Jewish life in diverse southern towns, cities, congregations, and families.[4]

In writing this book—the first narrative survey of southern Jewish history—I am deeply indebted to these foundational works. And yet, as I read across different generations of historical writing and undertook archival research, my interpretation developed in new directions. By drawing connections across southern communities, I was able to obtain a bird's-eye view of Jewish mobility as well as homemaking, and of both commonality and variation across many Souths: small town and big city, coastal and mountain, upper, mid, and lower. In writing Jewish history from these southern locales, I found that I was not only adding data or a regional analysis to existing narratives but, like the southern intellectual historian Michael O'Brien, exploring "modernity's provincial emergence, trajectory, and impact."[5] Although they varied in their place of origin, their religious proclivities, and in many other ways, all southern Jews were faced with fundamental modern Jewish questions: whether and how should they enact their identities as Jews.[6] While there were those who abandoned Jewish beliefs and practices, for most the answer was to reshape them; in the words of religious studies scholar Thomas Tweed, they "made homes and crossed boundaries," drawing on Jewish and other resources to "intensify joy and confront

suffering."[7] What the southern context makes clear is that these practices were inextricable from material conditions. Indeed, a focus on the
American South makes it impossible to ignore what narratives centered
on northern places might elide: namely, the centrality of race and violence to American Jewish history.

In his influential 1941 tome *The Mind of the South*, W. J. Cash described the region as a distinct entity, "almost a nation within a nation,"
shaped by its agricultural history and inhabited by people imbued with
Protestant theology, including a "sense of sin" and a faith "of primitive
frenzy and the blood sacrifice." Over eighty years later, this in some ways
remains the dominant image of the South, and it is one in which Jews
would seem out of place. Cash, for one, discussed Jews only in the context of prejudice: "[The Jew] is everywhere the eternal Alien; and in the
South, where any difference had always stood out with great vividness,
he was especially so."[8] To be sure, Jews were never more than a tiny
minority of the region's population, and they mostly dwelled in the region's cities and towns, rather than its iconic rural spaces. Not only were
they not Christian, but they differed from the majority in ways that went
beyond belief and worship, the categories typically granted respect and
the vaunted protections of American religious freedom. Jews were embedded within a system of religious law and a transnational community, which together encouraged exclusive kinship ties and a mercantile
economic orientation. And yet these idiosyncrasies, which have in the
past rendered Jews "alien," can also help us to uncover a different and
more dynamic South.[9]

Crucially, they make visible the pervasiveness of Protestant Christianity, not only inside churches, revival tents, and individual hearts but
in the structure of public life. As Flannery O'Connor, a Catholic, so
powerfully put it, the South has been "Christ-haunted," a condition of
especially profound consequence for those beyond the pale of Christianity altogether.[10] Writing in a different register, scholar Henry Goldschmidt has argued that "there are no such things as race, nation, or
religion, per se—only race, nation, and religion as they are constructed
in and through each other, and through other categories of difference."[11]
So too has *region* been "co-constituted" with religion and race. In other

words, the history of the South has not been defined by race alone but by religio-racial dynamics.[12] Religion and power, Christianity and whiteness, remained intertwined long after the colonial period. The Black-white binary was central, but the contours of white southern belonging also shifted in relationship to Jews, variably expanding and contracting. Their acceptance as white southerners was often achieved, through legal rights, through alliances with white Christians, and at the expense of Native and African-descended peoples.[13] It seemed most likely when Judaism appeared to be a Church like any other, but it was never guaranteed.

The lives of southern Jews bore the marks of this knowledge and the feelings of confidence, ambivalence, and even fear that it could engender. Across the centuries, they worked to claim their place within southern communities as white settlers and as Jews. There is a saying—Jews are like everyone else, but *more so*. One might say that the American South is like everywhere else, but more so. Both subjects have inspired forms of exceptionalist thinking, and have been seen as special "problems," and yet the story of this people in this place also sheds important light on the broader possibilities and challenges of American democracy.[14] At a time of increasing racial and religious diversity, southern Jews remind us that even the region of the United States seen as the most provincial and isolated has never been uniformly so, despite the fervent wishes, loud proclamations, and violent actions of some of its denizens and leaders. Jews were present in what would come to be known as the South almost from the beginnings of European colonialism, and they helped to define it.

Most Jews persisted in their difference and they occasionally contested aspects of the Protestant-dominated society they lived in. Again and again, as Jewish migrants settled in new places, they founded societies and congregations, bestowing upon them names that reflected their values and giving of their time and treasure to ensure a Jewish presence on the southern landscape. And when they felt they had been slighted or excluded—for instance, through the enforcement of Sunday closing laws—there were those among them who spoke up. At the same time, places can change people, in ways both self-conscious and totally invisible.

Cash ascribed to the Jews a "universal refusal to be assimilated," but in fact, living in the South left marks on many Jews' everyday practices and their deepest-held beliefs, about human difference, about the roles of men and women, and about God and the universe.[15] It also encouraged the development of a self-conscious identity as southern Jews, both distinct from and bound to their coreligionists elsewhere and the gentiles they lived among.

Readers will encounter a large but nonexhaustive collection of southern Jews in the pages of this book. In researching it, I often felt as though I was dipping a ladle into a vast lake of rich historical sources, made possible by the indefatigable commitment of southern Jews and their families to preserving their stories, as well as by forms of privilege. Despite their tiny numbers, Jews had the capacity to preserve the kind of first-person documentation from before the Civil War that is rare to find from nonwhite and nonelite southerners.[16] Additional sources within and beyond the usual tool kit of the Jewish historian, especially government and local press documents, also proved invaluable. I have tried to feature a diverse set of southern Jewish voices and experiences, including those well-known and more obscure, men and women, and Jews of different ethnic, racial, and class backgrounds; many more fascinating people, places, and stories still await the historian's attention.

This book proceeds chronologically, charting three different eras of southern Jewish history. Part I begins not in 1607 in Jamestown, Virginia, but in 1669 with the Fundamental Constitutions of Carolina, the document that first envisioned the possibility of European Jews settling—as Jews—in what would become the American South. While making brief forays into territories claimed by the French and Spanish, it focuses on the Eastern Seaboard in the era of conflicted English rule, and then on the early years of American governance as the nation expanded westward into the nineteenth century. In American Jewish history, these map onto a so-called "Sephardic" era and the beginnings, in the 1820s, of a new "German" one, reflecting different waves of migration. Among other topics, these early sections address the relationship between Jews and slavery, a crucial but often misunderstood topic. To be clear, Jews did not originate, innovate, or dominate chattel slavery in the Americas, but neither did they avoid or contest it. My discussion aims to highlight slavery's role in facilitating European Jews' whiteness and to humanize the people whose labor was central to Jewish homes and institutions in a slave society.

Part II follows a new population of central European Jews who arrived in a region mired in sectional tensions that would ultimately lead to a new nation and a bloody war. While enthusiastic "Confederate Jews" are certainly important to this story, I also highlight ambivalence among southern Jews, as well as the barriers they faced to Confederate belonging. I next consider the place of southern Jews in the fraught project of postwar Reconstruction and the institutionalization of a national, reconciliatory American Judaism. Part III begins by charting the coincidence of the rise of Jim Crow, the modernizing developments of "the New South," and the mass migration of Eastern European Jews. It pivots around the lynching of Leo Frank in 1913, a key moment in the histories of Jewish racialization and political activism, which would take unexpected turns across the World Wars and amid the ongoing struggle for Black civil rights. The book ranges from 1492 through 2017, although its main focus is on the three centuries from the 1660s through the 1960s. Throughout, familiar eras and events in southern history are seen from the perspective of people who could not always rely on being treated fairly, and who entertained a range of additional concerns, as small as getting the materials needed for their son to become a bar mitzvah (an adult male obligated to fulfill God's commandments), and as big as deciding whether to support the founding of a Jewish state in the Middle East. They inhabited a *Jewish* South, which of course could not exist apart from the South they shared with others; it was a South marked by networks, institutions, experiences, and concerns that linked them to one another, to people and places elsewhere, and to an ancient tradition.

It must be said that this history is a challenging and at times painful one. Given the extreme politicization of American and especially southern history, readers may be looking for uniform condemnation or celebration of southern Jews, but they will find neither. Southern Jews have been both privileged *and* vulnerable, political powerbrokers *and* targets of hate crimes, religious innovators *and* assimilationists. In the end, no source can fully or straightforwardly tell us what is in anyone's heart of hearts, and even if it could, these individual feelings do not exist apart from broader structures of power. My aim, then, is to trace the causes, rationales, and consequences of southern Jews' actions and to understand how they participated in southern, and by extension American, history—in ways both praiseworthy and shameful—as members of a minority community and as complex human individuals. I am convinced that anyone who truly wants to understand the history of the South, or the United States, needs to know their stories.

PART I
1669–1840

CHAPTER 1

Jews, Heathens, and Other Dissenters

Visiting Georgia in 1735, a colonial official wrote that "a Jew workman bred in the Brazil taught" the colonists to build houses "nimbly and in a neat manner." In 1741, as he navigated a growing population of "clamorous malcontents," another official wrote that "nothing had given me so much pleasure since my arrival" as the vineyard of "Mr. Lyon, a Portuguese Jew."[1] That these men took notice of these particular activities was no coincidence. The English understood the construction of homes to be a sign of land's possession, and they envisioned the "New World" as a garden that they should cause to "be fruitful and multiply," following God's command in Genesis. Founded in 1732, Georgia was a late outpost of the British Empire, cut out of the Carolina colony to create a charitable utopia.[2] At the southern edge of Britain's continental colonies, it was part of a large expanse of land that abutted the Atlantic Ocean south of the Chesapeake Bay and curved around the northern edge of the Gulf of Mexico. At various times, the British, the French, and the Spanish all exploited and relied on the peoples native to this hot, wet region. Ships took from its shores animal furs and skins, crops grown on seized land, and enslaved people; they returned with manufactured goods as well as laborers kidnapped from diverse African civilizations—although Georgia was free from slavery, at least at first.[3]

Amid a massive, ongoing, and violent exchange, Jews joined a fragile new colony. They hoped to find safety and prosperity, but it was far from guaranteed. Looking westward across the territory that would come to be known as the South, they knew that much of it was off limits to them. The places where they could and did live were governed by and for Christians. The early South—the South before "the South"—was a place where racial domination commingled with Christian power, even as diverse religious traditions found expression. Jewish men and women would carve out places for themselves in southern port cities. Indeed, Lyon—known in other sources as Abraham DeLyon—and his unnamed coreligionists were not only building shelter or growing crops but enacting British claims to land that they insisted was "empty," despite the active presence of Native peoples.[4] They also helped create a congregation, still in existence today, in which they continued to affirm their difference.

In Georgia, as in other colonial contexts, Jews were present in two ways: in the minds of colonial officials, who saw them as useful but persistently other, and as flesh and blood human beings, trying to build comfortable lives on the colonial frontier.[5] They were able to do so because of the presence of Native groups and enslaved Africans who, in the eyes of colonial elites, simply seemed more threatening. Jews troubled the ideals of English Protestant empire, and yet they were Europeans with a shared antipathy toward Catholic Spain.[6] Positioned on the right side of two out of three hierarchical dichotomies that defined England's empire, Jews would gain access to new political rights, as well as to the most valuable and violently acquired resources available: land and other human beings. Although part of a global and Atlantic community, the Jews of Charleston and Savannah, along with those soon living in other southern locales, would eventually come to see themselves as Americans. They would prove ready and willing to overthrow the political order in which they had gained these opportunities and to find their footing in an ambitious but violent new nation.[7]

In Virginia and in Barbados—colonized by the English in 1607 and 1627, respectively—freedom was defined by Christianity, but over the course of the seventeenth century, it was recast in terms of whiteness, sometimes quite literally on bureaucratic documents. This was a result of the growing number of Black and Indigenous Christians, but it occurred at the moment Jews were coming to reside in England and its colonies.[8] While no Jews appear to have settled in agricultural Virginia, Barbados was home to a Jewish congregation by 1654, made up of Jews fleeing the oncoming Portuguese in Brazil.[9] The next year, under the rule of Lord Protector Oliver Cromwell, the question of readmitting Jews to England itself was revived and, after a vigorous public debate, tacitly allowed. One reason that Englishmen were willing to entertain the presence of Jews in their midst was the hope that Jewish dispersion would facilitate the return of Christ.[10] Another was a growing culture of English "toleration," born of the realities of post-Reformation Protestant sectarianism and the alternating religious commitments of the country's monarchs. At the same time, philosophers were beginning to champion reason—over and above revelation—as a source of human knowledge, and to argue that humans possessed "natural rights."[11] This push toward freedom of expression, which historians associate with the "Enlightenment," was further encouraged by economic competition with the Dutch, who had granted Jews permission to settle in Amsterdam and the Dutch colonies in 1604.[12]

As non-Anglicans and as foreigners, Jews remained at a legal disadvantage, and they were occasionally targeted with specific restrictions. In Barbados, for instance, they were allowed to testify in court on the five books of Moses, but from 1688 to 1706 there were restrictions on Jewish slaveholding.[13] Gradually, the category of "white" worked to elevate the status of non-Anglican Europeans, including Jews.[14] By the end of the seventeenth century, significant numbers of Iberian Jewish refugees had settled in Port Royal, Jamaica; Newport, Rhode Island; and New York; as well as in the Dutch colonies of Curaçao and Suriname (which had been English before 1667). These communities included individuals whose distance from the Inquisition varied, but who understood themselves to be members of an expansive *nação*, or "nation," of Spanish and Portuguese Jews.[15] Through their participation in transatlantic trade and their ongoing connections with coreligionists on both sides of the Atlantic, some of these "Port Jews" acquired considerable wealth, which they used to establish synagogues, Jewish cemeteries, and *mikva'ot* (ritual baths).[16]

As they worked within the dynamic system that historians call "the Atlantic World," some Jewish traders likely ventured northward from Caribbean centers to the southeastern parts of North America.[17] It is perhaps not surprising, then, that Jews were imagined as part of the Carolina colony before they arrived there. On March 1, 1669, the Fundamental Constitutions of Carolina (FCC) was adopted by the province's eight founding proprietors. Overseen by Anthony Ashley Cooper and a young John Locke, this document laid out in punctilious detail their utopian plan for a new colony. It was frequently revised and never fully implemented, but it was widely circulated as an advertisement for emigration and it helped shape the contours of Carolinian society and politics. It envisioned an orderly, balanced, and hierarchical society run by a hereditary nobility under the authority of the king and the Church of England. It also granted explicit permission to "Jews, heathens, and other dissenters from the purity of Christian religion" to create "a church or profession."[18]

The relevant section begins by dividing those outside of the Church of England into two categories: "the natives of that place . . . [who are] utterly strangers to Christianity" and "those who remove from other parts to plant there [who] will unavoidably be of different opinions concerning matters of religion." The former, "whose idolatry, ignorance, or mistake gives us no right to expel or use them ill," are granted a negative form of toleration, while the latter will positively "expect to have [liberty] allowed them." Jews are clearly not "natives of the place," but their explicit mention later in the paragraph makes it unclear whether they are included as those "of different opinions." The language of "Jews, heathens, and other dissenters" suggests that Jews constituted a third category alongside Native Americans and dissenting Protestants. Indeed, in earlier writings Locke had distinguished Jews and other non-Christians from Christian dissenters.[19] Undergirding the acceptance of all these groups was the assumption that they "may be won over to embrace and unfeignedly receive the truth," of the Church of England. Jews were to be tolerated, then, but the nature and degree of their difference was left unclear, and the goal was to eliminate it altogether.[20]

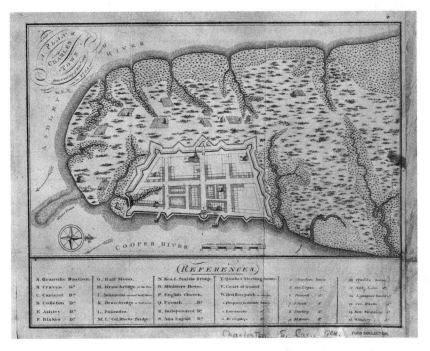

FIGURE 1.1. "A Plan of Charles Town" by Edward Crisp, 1704. From the
New York Public Library.

The city of Charles Town (figure 1.1; renamed Charleston in 1783) was
founded in 1670 and soon attracted a steady stream of European settlers,
among them a large number from Barbados, which was plagued by over-
crowded lands and declining fortunes. Ultimately centered on a peninsula
between the Ashley and Cooper Rivers and surrounded by dangerous
swamps, the new city, and its colony, was shaped by the pursuit of profit
and the conflict with Catholic Spain in nearby Florida.[21] For Jews en-
meshed in international trade networks, whose ancestors or coreligionists had been expelled or persecuted by the Spanish, Carolina would
have held considerable risk but also a clear appeal. The evidence from
this period is scarce, but it shows Jews seeking their place within a multireligious colonial project. The first concrete documentation of a Jew
in Carolina is from 1695, when Governor John Archdale, a Quaker, used
a Spanish-speaking "Jew for an interpreter" with the Yamasee.[22]

This was one among a number of Mississippian groups in the region, including the Westo, the Savannah, and the more proximate Natives who came to be known as "Settlement Indians." They shared a culture of agriculture and hunting, living in dispersed towns linked by kinship networks.[23] The encounter between the unnamed Jew and Yamasee was part of a complex system of intersecting economic and diplomatic ties. Carolinians relied on trade with Native Americans, primarily in deerskins and in enslaved people, and competed with the Spanish for alliances to ensure their security. These relationships provided the Yamasee and other groups with access to global markets and military support, but they also instigated conflict within and among Native groups, as well as between Natives and their so-called allies. In 1714, the frustrated Yamasee killed two colonial officials, triggering a bloody war that sharpened divisions and deepened distrust between Natives and the European settlers with whom Jews had cast their lot.[24]

The colony's Barbadian residents, among whom were likely its first Jews, brought with them a penchant for both slavery and single-crop agriculture. Relying on the knowledge and skill of enslaved Africans, they soon fixed upon rice as the colony's main crop for export, and by 1708 there were more enslaved people than free ones in Carolina, even as the colony continued to export large numbers of enslaved Natives.[25] Slavery enriched the colony but also inspired fear of rebellion, especially after 1693, when the Spanish offered freedom to any who escaped to Florida.[26] Although few Jews seem to have engaged in agriculture, from which they had been legally excluded in Christian Europe, they profited from slavery early on.[27] Jewish religious authorities understood slavery to be legally permitted, and shared with Christians the tradition that Africans were descendants of the biblical Noah's cursed son Ham.[28] In Barbados in 1679, all but five of fifty-four Jewish families had owned enslaved people, and Charleston records show that in 1696 Simon Valentine, a Jewish merchant who had previously lived in New York and Jamaica, purchased an enslaved man named Dick from Samuel Mincks, a fellow Jew.[29] Ashley Cooper and Locke had planned for slavery, firmly yoking it to race. The FCC declared that "every freeman of Carolina shall have absolute power and authority over his negro slaves, of what opinion or religion soever" and reiterated that religious affiliation would not affect "any man's civil estate or right."[30] In 1712 a law was passed stating yet again that baptism would not bring manumission.[31]

The FCC described the Church of England as "the only true and Orthodox, and the National Religion of all the King's Dominions, so also of Carolina."[32] In reality, however, the Church was slow to start in the colony. After 1701, the newly founded Society for the Propagation of the Gospel in Foreign Parts sent Anglican ministers from London, although there was often a shortage because many died or abandoned the disease-ridden colony.[33] Those who stayed fought uphill battles to convert Natives and enslaved Africans, among whom were practitioners of Indigenous religious traditions, Catholicism, and Islam.[34] Nor did the Church of England have a monopoly among European settlers. The FCC had required only that colonists believe in God and attend some kind of public worship, further dictating that "no person whatsoever shall disturb, molest, or persecute another for his speculative opinions in religion, or his way of worship."[35] Already by 1700, Anglicans accounted for less than half of the European settlers in the colony.[36]

Among the dissenting groups attracted to Carolina were Huguenots—Protestant refugees from Catholic France who were closely allied with the Anglicans—as well as Scottish Presbyterians, Quakers, Lutherans, and Baptists.[37] In 1697 Simon Valentine and a small group of fellow Jewish men joined with the Huguenots in requesting naturalization, which the colonial legislature granted them as part of an "Act for Making Aliens Free of this Part of this Province, and Granting Liberty of Conscience to all Protestants." Although associated here with Protestant dissenters, in other documents Jews were described as "of the Jewish nation," indicating that Jewish difference still went beyond a matter of "speculative opinions in religion" alone.[38] There is little evidence about Jewish practice in this period, but it is likely that Jews resembled the colonists described by minister Brian Hunt in 1728: "Not a few Parishioners worship God in their own way, that is at home in a way they do not apprize the world."[39]

In the face of Carolina's tremendous diversity, there were ongoing debates about the extent of toleration, especially in political life. In 1704 the Anglican Church was formally established, which meant, among other things, that non-Anglicans could not serve in public office. Dissenting Protestants responded by raising questions about the legitimacy of the governing assembly. They complained to the House of Lords that "all sorts of people, even aliens, Jews, servants, common sailors and negroes were admitted to vote at elections."[40] In trying to recover their own rights, Protestant dissenters carved out a conception of political belonging that excluded Jews and classed them with a range of communal outsiders. Ultimately, the establishment was upheld, but dissenters' political rights restored. The colony was divided into ten parishes, which acted as both religious and political districts; they were run by vestrymen elected by Anglican parishioners. After 1722, Charleston's skyline was dominated by Saint Philip's Church, a monumental structure with three large porticos, a cupola, and a dome. Its steeple was topped by a cock, invoking the anticipation of Christ's return and asserting Anglican power over the city.[41] Jews paid taxes that contributed to its maintenance and they lived almost literally in its shadow, looking up at its soaring steeple as they walked through the city. Catholics, never openly welcomed, were officially excluded from the colony in 1716.[42]

England's Catholic enemies configured race and religion very differently and in ways that explicitly excluded Jews. Inquisitorial documents from New Spain record in considerable detail accusations and punishments for "Guarding and Observing the Dead Laws of Moses," although not nearly as many as in Spain itself.[43] As historian David Graizbord argues, "Jews and *judeoconversos* constituted a 'race' or a consanguineous 'caste' that was culturally unassimilable, indeed toxic to the Old Christian community of faith—and blood."[44] In French Louisiana the very first article of the 1724 Code Noire required the colony's directors and officers "to drive out of the said country all Jews who may have established their residence there. These, as declared enemies of the Christian name, We command to leave in three months."[45] Adapted from codes used to govern French holdings in the Caribbean, the Code Noir forbade religions other than Catholicism and, among other regulations, required that enslaved people be baptized. While in practice some privileged Jews were allowed to operate within French territories, it is

unlikely that any Jews settled in New Orleans in the initial decades following its 1718 founding.[46] In Louisiana, as in Carolina, Jews were
imagined before they had arrived there, although in the French Catholic
context their settlement was pointedly forbidden.

By contrast, Jewish settlers arrived somewhat unexpectedly in the
new colony of Georgia, which was designed by its trustees as a charitable sanctuary for impoverished Englishmen and persecuted European
Protestants.[47] Among those collecting funds for the enterprise were a
group of Spanish and Portuguese Jews in London, who interpreted the
colony's promise of religious sanctuary as maximally inclusive and used
their funds to send a group of their coreligionists.[48] On paper, the colony's charter offered "liberty of conscience . . . in the worship of God to
all persons . . . except papists," which would seem to include Jews.[49] In
practice, however, the trustees complained that "certain Jews have been
sent to Georgia contrary to the intentions of the Trustees, and which
may be of ill consequences to the Colony."[50] They tried to persuade
resident trustee James Oglethorpe to make the Jews leave, but they had
already arrived, and to a community in the midst of a vicious epidemic.
According to Oglethorpe, Samuel Nunes Ribeiro, a Portuguese Jewish
physician, "immediately undertook our people and refused to take any
pay for it."[51] Jews were implicitly excluded from the vision of the colony
of Georgia, but the precarity of the colonial endeavor nevertheless enabled them to claim a place within it.

The group that arrived from London on July 11, 1733, included forty-
one Jews, who made up as much as a quarter of the colony's total
European population at the time.[52] Thirty-three were of Spanish or Portuguese descent, and eight were from German lands. They brought with
them a Torah scroll and a circumcision box, signaling their intention to
establish sacred space and perpetuate religious identity in the new city,
located on a bluff overlooking the Savannah River.[53] Shaped by its charitable mission, Georgia's population included an eclectic mix of "German
Pietists, Highland warriors, Lowland gentry, and English servants."[54] It
was settled less than twenty years after the traumatic Yamasee War, and
its survival was secured through careful diplomacy between James
Oglethorpe and Native groups. Especially important were the Creeks,

a powerful confederation with a decentralized and consensus-oriented political organization.[55] The trustees initially restricted land ownership and prohibited slavery in the colony, although there were other forms of unfreedom present, including indenture.[56] Among the early Jewish settlers there were a number of servants, including Shem Noah, possibly a man of African descent, who arrived as a servant to Zippora Nunes Ribeiro. In the following months, Abraham DeLyon's wife, two daughters, and "servant David" joined them, as did a Mr. Deas and his servant Abram.[57]

There is much more robust documentation of Jews in early Georgia than in Carolina, because they arrived later and in greater numbers. There were also several enthusiastic diarists in the colony who recorded their impressions, taking special interest in the Jews' internal divisions. An Anglican minister reported that compared with the German Jews, the Portuguese "are more lax in their way, and dispense with a great many of their Jewish Rites."[58] Whereas the former came from open Jewish communities, some of the Iberian Jews had lived portions of their lives as public Christians and suffered under the Inquisition. These differences apparently fueled discord between the two groups; Lutheran minister Johann Boltzius reported, "There is hate and persecution among themselves."[59] Evidence from elsewhere in the Jewish Atlantic shows that Portuguese Jews in particular were protective of their status as members of an exclusive *nação*.[60]

While ministers and state officials highlighted the novelty of Jewish conflict, the two groups were part of a shared community. Benjamin Sheftall, one of the so-called German Jews, kept records of births, deaths, marriages, arrivals, and departures of Jews in Savannah, regardless of origin.[61] Sheftall was a devout man who would live the rest of his days in Georgia. Within his first year there, he had recorded the community's first birth and its first marriage. In 1735 he noted the founding of a congregation. According to a Christian minister, "A boy speaking several languages, and especially good in Hebrew is their reader and is paid for his services."[62]

The congregation was called Mickve Israel—"hope of Israel"— gesturing toward the fervent messianic expectations that were shared by Jewish communities throughout the Atlantic world. A book of that name, published in 1650 by the Amsterdam rabbi Menasseh ben Israel, had argued that the readmission of the Jews to England would pave the way for the end of history and the advent of a new era of perfection. While Christian messianism centered on Christ's return and rule, Jews imagined the resurrection of the dead, a return to the land of Israel, and the rebuilding of the holy Temple. In 1651, Curaçao's congregation, the leader in the Americas at that point, had chosen the name Mikveh Israel; Barbados's congregation, founded in 1654, called itself Nidhe Israel, or "dispersed of Israel," pointing to the eventual ingathering of the exiles in the world to come. Messianic expectations flourished during these years of upheaval and transformation, reaching an apex with the appearance in the Ottoman Empire of a suspected messiah named Shabbatei Zevi. His 1666 conversion to Islam had disappointed most Jews, and yet they continued to express messianic longings. New York's congregation, in operation since the early 1700s, chose the name Shearith Israel, or the "remnant of Israel" who would be saved at the end of days.

Sheftall eventually purchased a burial ground and received a shipment of a Torah scroll, a Hanukkah menorah, and a parcel of Jewish books from London.[63] The new Torah scroll may have replaced a damaged original or been used to facilitate multiple worship services. The menorah would allow for observance of the minor postbiblical festival celebrating Jewish persistence under foreign rule. The books may have facilitated Torah study among adult men or the education of the growing number of Jewish children in the colony. Although not all children survived to adulthood—in 1734 the Sheftalls lost a son after his nurse fed him poisonous acorns—in the first seven years of the community's existence, Sheftall recorded eighteen Jewish births in the city.[64]

For Jewish women, the births—and deaths—of children must have been significant moments of religious reflection, as they considered the fragility of their bodies and the future of their community.[65] Among the initial Jewish settlers there were eight married women and seven girls, including Judith Olivera, married to Jacob, and their daughter Leah.[66] Sex and procreation were reliant on women's immersion in what

Jewish texts describe as "living water," in concert with their menstrual cycles. Purifying their bodies was one of just three commandments designated for women, and also seen as a vehicle of Jewish messianism, a means by which women could help prepare the world for its redemption.[67] A designated *mikvah* opened in Savannah in April of 1738.

A little over a month later, Anglican minister George Whitefield arrived in the colony. On his way to Georgia, Whitefield had visited a synagogue on the island of Gibraltar:

> I continued with them their whole Service and spent most of my Time there in secret Prayer to God. *That the Veil might be taken from their Hearts, and that blessed Time might come when his chosen people should again be engrafted into their own Olive-Tree and all Israel be saved.*[68]

For Whitefield and other Protestant ministers, Jews remained a theological problem and a target of evangelism. While there is no record of Whitefield's interactions with Savannah's Jews, both the Lutheran Boltzius and Methodist John Wesley made unsuccessful attempts to evangelize them.[69] Notions of Christian supremacy continued to exert an influence in other ways as well. In 1738, "the Jews applied for Liberty to sign" a petition of "settlers, freeholders, and inhabitants," but the organizers "did not think it proper to join them in any of our measures." The petitioners requested more liberal land policies as well as "the use of negroes," which they argued would "occasion great numbers of white people to come here." The organizers operated within a clear hierarchy of race and of class; servants were prohibited from signing to avoid the appearance of duress, as were widows and orphans, because some might claim "that they were not proper judges." No reason was given for the exclusion of Jews, although the organizers sought out the participation of Boltzius and the Lutherans.[70]

In this moment Jews were excluded as non-Protestants from the social and political life of the colony, and yet their application demonstrates their own feelings of belonging and their commitment to being counted among white "settlers, freeholders, and inhabitants." They worked in a number of capacities in support of the colony—for instance,

Abraham Minis supplied the colonial military fort at Frederica in addition to operating a popular tavern—and several joined the local ma-
sonic lodge.[71] Boltzius wrote in 1739, "The German Jews have in Savannah the same liberties as any Englishman. They drill with a rifle, as all
the soldiers do," a rather remarkable sight given the enthusiastic debates
that would soon be unleashed in Europe about the question of Jewish
military service.[72] The next year he elaborated,

> The Englishmen, nobility and common folks alike, treat the Jews as
> their equal. They drink, gamble, and walk together with them; in fact,
> let them take part in all their fun. Yes, they desecrate Sunday with
> them, a thing that no Jew would do on their Sabbath just to please a
> Christian.[73]

Jews were contrasted here with Englishmen and with Christians, who
treated these national and religious others equally, to their own moral
detriment. As in Carolina three decades earlier, Jews served as a point
of contention between dominant Anglicans and dissenting Protestants.
Anglicans might occasionally include Jews as part of a white society, but
dissenters were quick to recast the community in Christian terms. In
Boltzius's view, Jews were deniers of Christ who led good Christians
astray. And yet, by 1741 one of the trustees who had been against Jewish
settlement was arguing that Jews "behaved so well as to their morals,
peaceableness, and charity, that they were a reproach to the Christian
inhabitants."[74] These writers agreed that Jews were a distinct and identifiable group, although they came to different conclusions about their
character and influence.

In 1740, Parliament passed the Act for Naturalizing such Foreign
Protestants, and Others therein Mentioned, as are Settled or Shall
Settle, in any of his Majesty's Colonies in America. Thus classified, Jews
in the British colonies, along with Quakers, were now eligible to obtain
a form of naturalization that would transcend any one colony, and they
could do so without making an oath "upon the true Faith of a Christian."
Jewish naturalization would remain restricted in England proper, but
the colonies operated by different rules. As one British official put it in
1753, "The discouraging of [Jews] to go and settle in our American

colonies, would be a great loss, if not the ruin, of every one of them."[75] Few among those understood to be "professing the Jewish religion" took advantage of the new form of naturalization—between 1740 and 1753, only one Carolina Jew did so.[76] And yet this new law was a sign of increasing centralization across the British colonies and of the utility of Jews to the imperial project.

By 1740, however, most of Georgia's Jews had departed. The year before, the War of Jenkins' Ear had begun, a conflict between England and Spain apocryphally instigated by the severed appendage of an English ship's captain. Fear of the approaching Spanish—who might subject Jews to the Inquisition—led most of Savannah's Jews to flee over the course of the next two years; a number of families, including the Nuneses and the Oliveras, moved to nearby Charleston. The German Sheftall and Minis families would remain, but the congregation—their "hope of Israel"—disbanded.[77] Historian Alan Gallay has argued of the colonial South, "Monarchy, colonial proprietors, the church, merchants, colonists, *and* indigenous peoples all contributed to the construction of ideologies of imperialism through their thoughts and actions."[78] As merchants and colonists, and through interactions with other groups, so too did Jews. They brought their knowledge, their networks, and their God to the Americas and to the corner of it that would one day come to be known as "the South." Although they contributed enthusiastically to the project of British colonization, Jews still retained an ambiguous position. Seven decades after the Fundamental Constitutions of Carolina, it was still unclear whether they were equivalent to "dissenters," or if their difference would be interpreted as something more troubling.

CHAPTER 2

House of God

On July 27, 1751, Jacob Olivera dictated his last will and testament in Charleston.[1] Eighteen years after arriving in the Americas, and over a decade after fleeing Savannah in the wake of war with Spain, he channeled the tradition of the Jewish ethical will, which offers guidance to those left behind: "I recommend to my son to walk in the fear of God and in the path of virtue which is the last and best legacy I can leave him."[2] Olivera also left him a more concrete legacy—namely, household furniture, one half of his financial assets, and "my negro boy named Jones." Olivera's other major beneficiaries were his daughter Leah's four children. His wife Judith—and their son Isaac—had apparently already been buried in the Lowcountry soil's mix of sand, mud, and clay.[3] His will expressed familial ties and communal ones; Olivera left ten pounds to the "Portuguese synagogue of London" in exchange for the recitation of memorial prayers in his honor, and an additional ten pounds to "each male Jew that should have a hand in washing or burying my body," "according to the Jewish rite + customs." In making his final wishes known, Olivera expressed anxiety about the fate of his body and his soul, which he understood to be at the mercy of a providential God. He identified himself as a committed Jew as well as a comfortable colonizer.[4]

Two years before Olivera wrote his will, in 1749, a Jewish congregation was founded in Charleston. Presumably its members were the ones who took care of Olivera's burial, although when he died in May 1752 they did not yet have their own burial ground.[5] The congregation's first history, written in 1843, does not mention Olivera as a founder, but it does mention both of the executors of his will—his son David and his "good friend" Isaac DaCosta—as well as his son-in-law. Benjamin Sheftall's sons, Mordecai and Levi, also appear on the list, although they were children at the time.[6] Their father likely brought them from Savannah to receive religious instruction and access a *minyan*, or prayer quorum, in the process fostering Lowcountry ties. In 1748, Sheftall had written to a friend in London expressing his "grief" that thirteen-year-old Mordecai had no *tefillin* (phylacteries) or appropriate books to help him become a bar mitzvah.[7]

Sheftall wanted to initiate his son into gendered forms of Jewish practice; worship would have been led by men, with women praying in a separate section or remaining at home to oversee domestic ritual. This included preparing kosher food, lighting candles on the Sabbath, and cleaning in preparation for Passover. Unlike in Savannah, there is no record of a communal *mikvah* in Charleston, so if women did immerse, it would have been in private baths or in open water.[8] In that case, the Ashley River, the Cooper River, Charleston Harbor, and the Atlantic Ocean—bodies of water that absorbed the blood of enslaved people, the sweat of avaricious strivers, and the sins of newly baptized Christians—would have also soaked up Jewish women's impurities.

Charleston was a port city on the rise, soon to become the wealthiest city in British North America. One historian has described it as "an Anglican bastion filled with drunken revelers, games of chance, young debutantes, high fashion, slave patrols, and brutal beatings."[9] It also was home to a wide array of dissenting Protestant groups and a growing community of Jewish migrants.[10] At least ten Jews received local naturalization in the city between 1715 and 1743, most of them from London, where, in the absence of colonial imperatives, Jewish naturalization was much more difficult to acquire; between 1749 and 1775 there were also Jewish residents who arrived from Georgia, New York, Sint Eustatius, Gibraltar, The Hague, and German lands, possibly attracted by the new congregation as well as by commercial opportunities.[11] Following the lead of other Atlantic congregations, Charleston's Jews chose to follow the Spanish and Portuguese rite "as observed by the congregations of London and Amsterdam."[12]

Olivera's religious life was shaped by Atlantic Jewish traditions and by Christian religious currents. In and beyond Charleston, the 1740s were a time of vigorous debate about the nature of God and religious authority. The Church of England—which was formally established in Carolina in 1706 and in Georgia in 1758—was a staid and reasonable Church that relied on state power and reinforced social hierarchies.[13] It faced competition from dissenting groups; from "Irreligion, Deism, and a licentious Ridiculing [of] the Holy Scriptures and Matters of a Sacred Nature";[14] and from a movement described by many historians as the "Great Awakening." This dramatic series of revivals was led by George Whitefield, who had close ties to Georgia. Although he was an Anglican minister, Whitefield criticized his colleagues, insisting on a present, personal God who determined individual salvation and required experiences of conversion.[15] He and his allies also detached religious authority from Anglicanism's formal educational requirements, making it a matter of personal calling.[16]

Whitefield's theological vision and approach to religious authority empowered the uneducated, women, and even enslaved people, which was unnerving for many white Carolinians. In 1739, a group of enslaved Africans, likely on their way to Spanish Florida, had revolted near the Stono River, killing twenty-one European settlers and terrifying the rest. Some locals responded positively to Whitefield's message because they saw the Stono Rebellion, as well as recent epidemics and a devastating 1740 fire, as signs of God's disfavor. Others saw Whitefield, who criticized the treatment of enslaved people, as offering an invitation to disorder and even chaos; Anglican officials in Charleston tried to bring him before an ecclesiastical court, and a grand jury indicted one of his most prominent local converts.[17] Whitefield wrote of the city in 1741: "They seemed to me, at my first coming, to be a People wholly devoted to Pleasure."[18] Nevertheless, and although not as successfully as in other colonies, he did win souls both there and in Savannah, especially among dissenters.[19]

Jews in these cities could hardly have avoided Whitefield or the dramatic debates that he instigated. Whether or not they attended his revivals, they would have read about them in newspapers and heard about them from neighbors.[20] They may have rung in the ears of Jacob Olivera as he sat down to write his will, which included several invocations of the divine. Olivera and Sheftall—whose will was authored fourteen years later—both included in their wills the central *shema* prayer, "Hear O Israel the Lord our God the Lord is One," and a selection from Psalm 31; as Olivera translated it, "In thy hands I will enlist my spirit. Thou hast rescued me o Lord God of Truth."[21] The men insisted on God's unity—a counter to Christian trinitarianism—but their concern with salvation and the nature of the divine also echoes that of their neighbors. These wills suggest that the controversies of the Great Awakening may have influenced or at least encouraged the articulation of popular Jewish theology.[22] What's more, the congregation was founded less than a year and a half after George Whitefield's second, several-months-long stint in the city, when he had written, "Congregations in Charleston have been greater than ever."[23] That a Jewish congregation joined them may have been not only the natural outcome of a growing Jewish population, but also a result of this religious fervor.[24]

That the congregation was named Kahal Kadosh Beth Elohim (KKBE), or "Holy Community House of God," provides another indication that a distinctive religious culture was emerging in the Lowcountry. No records remain to explain the choice, but it deviated noticeably from the messianic names of earlier Atlantic Jewish communities. Whereas congregational names in Savannah, New York, Bridgetown, and elsewhere revolved around the people of Israel and their hopes of messianic redemption—drawing on prophetic texts, they were the "hope of Israel," "remnant of Israel," or "scattered of Israel"—Charleston's Jews described theirs as an edifice for the divine, suggesting a more ecumenical orientation and a feeling of attachment to the city.[25] The name "house of God" comes from Genesis 28:17, where it describes the site of Jacob's ladder, in Beer Sheva, which the medieval French commentator Rashi noted was located in "the South."[26] The second half of the verse refers to "Shaarey Shamayim," or "the gates of heaven," which echoed the names of Jamaica's newest congregation and of Bevis Marks, the Spanish and Portuguese congregation in London, founded in 1701.[27] Charleston's Jews thus linked their city—in the South of Britain's North

American colonies—to London and the Iberian Peninsula, as did other Atlantic Jews, but also to Jerusalem and to heaven itself.

KKBE's congregants soon elected a *hazan* (a service leader), a *parnass* (beadle), and a *mohel* (ritual circumcisor), as well as what is described in the 1843 history as a "sage and head of a rabbinical court."[28] Moses Cohen, the man elected to that position, did not receive a salary from the congregation and also worked as a storekeeper; it was unlikely that he was an ordained rabbi.[29] Even so, Cohen appears to have been much beloved. After he died in 1762, a large gravestone was erected in his honor, which included a poem—addressed to him—that describes the reaction to his death: "Alas! all that knew thee at thy departure, / Flowing Tears have fill'd their Eyes."[30] The stone features an engraving of two disembodied hands placed in the position assumed during the priestly benediction and within an elaborate oval frame. This image signals Cohen's place within a transatlantic community of priestly Jews. It also borrows from a "portrait gravestone" fad that was emerging among Christian Charlestonians in the 1750s, which alleviated fears about the fate of the body after death and created a visible aesthetic community across the city's burial grounds.[31] Moses was inserted into this ecumenical community, although what was worth protecting and highlighting was not the individual's visage or bust, but his hands engaged in ritual benediction.[32]

Unlike many Caribbean Jewish gravestones, which included extensive images associated with mystical beliefs and Portuguese text pointing to Iberian roots, Cohen's is sparse in its decoration and written in Hebrew and English alone (figure 2.1). In Hebrew he is titled an "accomplished sage" (*haham*), and in English a "R[ight] R[everend]," and "D[octor of] D[ivinity]," titles associated with Anglican bishops. There were, controversially, no bishops in the Americas; Charleston, which had grown enough to warrant the construction of a second Anglican church, remained under the authority of the Bishop of London.[33] Charleston's Jews, then, described their beloved religious leader as the height of English religious authority, positioning themselves in relationship to what was—even with the rising evangelical challenge—the colony's elite, established Church.[34]

FIGURE 2.1. Detail of the gravestone of Moses Cohen in Kahal Kadosh Beth Elohim's Coming Street Cemetery. Photo by author.

Cohen was buried in land the DaCosta family had purchased in 1754, which they would sell to the congregation two years after his death.[35] This plot was located beyond the city limits, but Jews also began to claim space within them. KKBE worshipped in three different buildings in its first fifteen years, first in a house around the corner from Saint Philips and then in locations a bit further afield, on and near King Street.[36] In 1765 a visitor to the city would note, "The public buildings are, an Exchange, a State-House, an Armoury, two churches for Episcopalians, one for Presbyterians, two for French and Dutch Protestants; to which may be added, meeting-houses for Anabaptists, Independents, Quakers and Jews."[37] Jews, grouped with the more radical dissenting Protestant groups, were part of the urban religious firmament. Meanwhile in Savannah, the Jewish community limped along, much diminished. In 1756 the minister Johann Martin Boltzius described "two German

Jewish families . . . who hold their divine service on the Sabbath in a house."[38] Three years later he described Benjamin Sheftall as holding "rigid to the Jewish divine service, holidays and superstitions."[39] Also in Savannah were a number of people of Jewish descent who represented the ever-present possibility of Christian conversion. Joseph Ottelenghe was an Italian-born Christian convert who came to Georgia in 1751 as a missionary with the Society for the Propagation of the Gospel, and the Portuguese-born James Lucena, who moved to Savannah in the mid-1760s, was a cousin of the Lopezes, a prominent Jewish family in Newport, although also an avowed Anglican.[40]

These individuals were not included in the communal records that Sheftall continued to maintain, although he did note when his wife and Abigail Minis were "brot to bed" with children, when his two-year-old son "departed this life," and when Abraham Minis died.[41] When Sheftall himself followed suit, his son Levi took over the records, noting the event in relationship to sacred time: "It was Thursday morning, about half an hour after 2 o'clock, being the second day of Halamoade Succoth [the intermediate days of the festival of Booths]."[42] Levi and his brother Mordecai maintained religious commitments and both married Jewish women from other Atlantic outposts; Mordecai wed the Amsterdam-born Frances Hart of Charleston in 1761, and seven years later his brother married Sarah De La Motta in Saint Croix.[43] Soon before his marriage, which was "to be had and solemnized according to the Jewish custom, rites, and ceremonies," Mordecai set up a trust, overseen by Isaac DaCosta, for Frances and their future children. It included considerable land holdings and "all those three negroe slaves known by the names of Joe, Anthony, and Phillis, together with the future issue and increase of Phillis."[44] To the traditional *ketubah*, or marriage contract, Mordecai added an additional legal document designed to secure his wealth in enslaved people and pilfered land. Jewish ritual was thus bound to acts of power.

Indeed, even establishing a congregation—like entering the *shema* into probate records or declaring a *hazan* to be equivalent to the Bishop of London—was both an act of piety and a sign of confidence. Jews had forged a place for themselves as white settlers through the pursuit of profit in the market and on the wharves.[45] Some women even became sole traders, in control of their own property, when their husbands granted them permission.[46] Jewish merchants benefited from expansive networks across the Atlantic world. In 1760, Isaac DeLyon of Savannah, whose father's vineyard had impressed colonial officials decades earlier, requested that Barnard Gratz of Philadelphia send him luxuries like fruits (cranberries and apples) and fish (mackerel and herring), as well as chocolate, gingerbread, linseed oil, and calf skins. In exchange, De-Lyon sent "four bundles of [deer] skins" acquired from Creek traders and "four barrels [of] rice," cultivated by enslaved Africans.[47] According to one calculation, Charleston exported at least 150,000 pounds of deerskins per year between 1731 and 1765; Georgia exported 200,000 pounds per year over the eight years to follow.[48]

In their ongoing competition with France and Spain over territory and resources—which periodically erupted into war—the British had continued to rely on trade and alliances with Native peoples.[49] At least one Jew, Moses Nunes, son of the physician Samuel Nunes Ribeiro, lived among the Creeks, operating as a deerskin trader, translator, and ad hoc diplomat. This work made Nunes a "cultural broker," a crucial lynchpin in colonial operations.[50] Deerskins remained significant to the Lowcountry economy, but by the 1760s they had long been replaced by rice as South Carolina's most important export. Each year Charleston's wharves shipped off millions of pounds of the grain, which required large numbers of laborers for its cultivation; so too did indigo, which became an important cash crop in the 1740s.[51] While Charleston hosted a sizeable community of merchants and others of the "middling sort," it was dominated by elite Anglican planters, who maintained sumptuous homes in town and valuable plantations—in truth, enslaved labor camps—in the country.[52]

In the aftermath of the Stono Rebellion, dozens of the rebels had been executed and new, draconian regulations imposed on enslaved people throughout the colony. A temporary duty was placed on slave imports, and yet by 1750, 70 percent of the fifty thousand people in Carolina were enslaved Africans. Charleston became host to one of the largest slave markets in North America.[53] While the slaveholding of

Jacob Olivera was modest compared with the grand country planters, then, it was not anomalous among urban Jews. Just two years before writing his will he had witnessed the sale of a woman named Flora to his son-in-law.[54] Isaac DaCosta was one of a number of Jews who owned import-export businesses that dealt, among other commodities, in enslaved people.[55] Jews also consumed, sold, and otherwise profited from crops produced by enslaved laborers; for instance, in 1762 Moses Lindo was made surveyor and general inspector of indigo.[56] Jews readily acted as cogs in the colonial machine.

In Georgia, slavery was legalized—and restrictions on land ownership lifted—in the early 1750s, leading to dramatic growth in the wealth and size of the colony. It too soon hosted an enslaved African majority.[57] By the time of his death in 1757, Abraham Minis had accumulated seventeen enslaved people and one thousand acres of land, which he bequeathed to his wife Abigail; she continued to run his tavern and became a successful businesswoman in her own right.[58] In 1765, Benjamin Sheftall left his wife Hannah two hundred acres of land and a lot in town, plus three enslaved people, Betty and her sons Jack and Ben, "for and during the time of [Hannah's] natural life." After Hannah's death, the two brothers were to be divided between their son Levi and his two children, who would presumably split the profits of a sale. By the following year, Levi and his brother Mordecai were each in possession of nine enslaved people, lots in town, and upwards of 650 acres of land.[59] The first person Levi had enslaved was a man from the West Indies named London, who worked alongside him as a butcher; among the many other people he would enslave over the course of his life were Quash, who was trained as a tanner, and women named Amy and Lucy.[60] Even as, on one piece of paper, Levi carefully documented the births and deaths of local Jews, communicating their spiritual value, on another he added acres and people to his ledgers, carefully counting their economic value. By the 1770s, Jews' share of the city's enslaved people (2.6 percent) was slightly larger than their share of the population (2.2 percent).[61]

What did Jones, Joe, Anthony, Phillis, Flora, Betty, Jack, Ben, London, Quash, Amy, or Lucy learn about the people who enslaved them?

How were their lives shaped by their enslavers' Jewish identities?[62] Most Jews were city dwellers, which meant that they lived in tight quarters with those they enslaved, who would have lacked the opportunities for community and cultural expression available on some large plantations. They may have been able to walk around the city on their own, or even hire themselves out to work, but that did not mean that their lives were free from surveillance, restriction, or cruelty.[63] Although enslaved Africans almost certainly facilitated domestic religious practice, it is unlikely that any converted to Judaism, even if Cohen did have a rabbinical court in operation in the 1750s that might have overseen them. Atlantic Jews—with the notable exception of those in Dutch Suriname—had rejected biblical mandates requiring the circumcision of slaves.[64] Furthermore, Jews were a minority in a society dominated by Protestants, who were themselves deeply suspicious of slave conversions. Though missionaries might claim that Christianity would improve the behavior of enslaved people, many white Carolinians continued to associate Christianity with freedom and conversion with danger. And of course, even when they could, enslaved people themselves were rarely eager to embrace their enslavers' religion, whatever it might be.[65]

Trade was the lifeblood of Charleston and Savannah, and land and enslaved people their most valuable commodities.[66] That Jews acquired both was both a sign and a vehicle of their inclusion in colonial society, in particular its mercantile community.[67] In 1750, Benjamin Sheftall became a naturalized citizen, the same year that he helped found the ecumenical Union Club, which gave aid to Georgia's orphans.[68] Isaac DaCosta became the first Jewish mason in Charleston in 1753, and by the 1760s Jews were serving in public positions as inspectors, clerks, wardens, and military officials.[69] What historian Francesca Trivellato has written about Sephardic Jews in Europe is true here as well: "Trade was a major vehicle of their acculturation," linking Jews to global networks and markets, even as it rooted them in their communities.[70] This was the experience of Jews throughout the British Empire to varying degrees and with different contours. Jewish communities were growing in Newport, New York, and Philadelphia in these years; in the 1760s Moses Cohen's sons Abraham and Solomon moved sixty miles up the Carolina coast to the town of Georgetown,[71] and by 1769 Isaiah Isaacs had settled in Richmond, a town of less than six hundred inhabitants on the banks of the James River.[72] These men pursued economic opportunity in frontier communities, apparently unconcerned about the possibility of an unfriendly reception or the negative implications for religious practice.

Jews also began to arrive in New Orleans, at the mouth of the Mississippi River, but only because French officials looked the other way, ignoring the 1724 Code Noir.[73] According to a local official, by 1759 Jews were "forming establishments here the progress and the danger of which have been observed by the whole country." There were reportedly six local Jews, as well as others engaging in temporary commerce in the city.[74] The best documented of these individuals is Isaac Monsanto, who had been born in The Hague before moving to Curaçao. In 1758 he purchased a young girl named Quetelle in New Orleans, the first indication of his intention to settle there.[75] Joined by a number of his siblings and coreligionists, Monsanto became a prosperous merchant, enslaver, and long-distance trader.[76] While he was able to live under the radar, this changed after the Seven Years' War, when New Orleans passed into Spanish hands.[77] Eventually, commercial regulations increased, and all non-Spaniards and non-Catholics were pressured to leave.

Although other, less affluent Jews were left alone, Monsanto was expelled in 1769; he and two other Jews were described as "undesirable on account of the nature of their business and of the religion they profess."[78] In British colonies, trade could facilitate Jews' integration, but here it intensified their outsider status. Monsanto might have reentered Jewish community by returning to Curaçao, joining family in Saint-Domingue, or moving to Charleston, and yet he chose to stay closer to what he must have seen as home, relocating to the Gulf coast city of Pensacola, two hundred miles eastward. A number of other Jews had preceded him to that city and to Mobile, both part of the new British colony of West Florida.[79]

In dire economic straits, Monsanto repeatedly used enslaved people as collateral for loans; in this way, Prince, Princess, Ceasar, Dolly, Jen, and Fanchonet helped him scrape by.[80] He and his brothers operated a storefront in the Mississippi River settlement of Manchac through the 1770s, where they engaged in illegal trade with New Orleans. Monsanto died in 1778 in much reduced circumstances, albeit within Spanish Louisiana. He likely received a Catholic burial, as would his brother Benjamin, the only Monsanto sibling to marry a Jew. Although there is no evidence that he ever formally converted, Benjamin's will included Catholic formulas and a request for "three masses for the repose of my soul."[81] Settlement in Catholic territory required the erasure of public Jewish practice and identity, even if not especially in death. Even so, over the course of a century, what had been imagined, in the English case, as a space of Jewish possibility, and in the French case, a space of Jewish absence, had become home to actual Jews. Their religious horizons were shaped by transatlantic religious networks, by provincial economies centered on land and slavery, and by imperial policies. Those under British rule could, for the most part, attain respectability and inclusion, albeit within a system that was starting to fray at the seams.

CHAPTER 3

The Cause of His Country

In 1770 "several Persons professing the Jewish Religion" requested that the Georgia assembly incorporate their burial plot in town, where some of their "Relations and Friends now lie interred."[1] This move would guarantee possession and eliminate an onerous fee to the Church of England. Although the Jewish congregation in Savannah was still inactive, the city of almost two thousand was home to an estimated twenty-seven Jewish men, women, and children. Their petition to the assembly emphasized Jews' early arrival in the colony and the venerable James Oglethorpe's role in granting them the land. At least one group of fellow citizens supported the effort on those grounds, but others countered with appeals to current economic concerns, undergirded by a clear distaste for Jews.[2] According to one group, Jews were "a people who might be presumed, from prejudice of education to have imbedded principles entirely repugnant to those of our holy religion [Christianity]."[3]

The legislation passed the House of Assembly but was rejected by the upper house. According to local Anglican minister Samuel Frink, "The late Commons House of Assembly were so far intoxicated with liberty principles as to endeavor to put Jews and Dissenters of all Denominations upon a footing with the church there."[4] As Frink's remarks indicate, Lowcountry Jews were advocating for themselves in an environment marked by Christian domination, by persistent suspicion, and by growing political unrest that would culminate in the American Revolution.[5]

Records of the Sheftalls, their neighbors the Minises, and Isaac DaCosta of Charleston shed additional light on these tumultuous times; they would embrace the language and the cause of liberty—within and beyond their communities—despite the very real risks and exclusions.[6]

Tensions between Britain and its North American colonists dated at least to the end of the Seven Years' War in 1763. British officials working to strengthen their authority and pay their debts had instituted a ban on further westward settlement into Indian territory and a series of new taxes, which sparked organized protests throughout the colonies.[7] After the punitive 1774 "Intolerable Acts," representatives from all the continental colonies except Georgia gathered in Philadelphia. One articulation of their frustrations came from Virginian Thomas Jefferson in *A Summary View of the Rights of British America.* Drawing on Enlightenment thought, Jefferson, an enslaver, decried Britain's "many unwarrantable encroachments and usurpations . . . upon those rights which God and the laws have given equally and independently to all."[8] At the heart of Jefferson's thought, and the revolutionary movement more broadly, was a tension between the rhetoric of inclusion and the realities of violent exclusion that it left untouched. The Philadelphia meeting led to the creation of the Continental Association, which called for a ban on all British imports and exports—with the important exception of rice, South Carolina's main cash crop—and the creation of local congresses and committees to help implement it.[9]

The revolutionary fervor coincided with, and may have inspired, renewed religious activism among Lowcountry Jews. For Savannah's Jews, where public toleration failed, private property proved useful; Mordecai Sheftall donated part of his own burial ground for the use of the Jewish community.[10] By 1774, "having a sufficient number of Jews here," the congregation resumed meeting in Sheftall's home.[11] The next year, there were efforts to create a new congregation in Charleston. A group of men led by Isaac DaCosta, the founding *hazan* of Kahal Kadosh Beth Elohim (KKBE), and closely linked by family ties, procured temporary rooms for worship and purchased land to build a synagogue.[12] Rare surviving meeting minutes show them to be men of tradition, who marked the Hebrew date, invoked Hebrew prayers, and praised those who respected community and authority. They also complained about Emanuel Abrahams and Myer Moses, who had insulted one of the congregation's founders, demonstrating "improper behavior . . . contrary to the[ir] institution + laws."[13] And yet, for all their traditionalism, DaCosta and his allies declared congregational independence and embraced the political vocabulary at the heart of the intensifying revolution struggle.[14] Echoing Jefferson's language, they accused Abrahams and Moses of an "illegal act in depriving the person of his just rights" and argued for "cool reason & deliberation."[15]

Just two weeks before this meeting, South Carolina's first Provincial Congress had gathered in Charleston. Despite laws prohibiting non-Christians from holding office in South Carolina, its Provincial Congress included Francis Salvador, a descendent of Iberian Jews who had arrived in South Carolina in 1773. Leaving his wife and children behind in London, Salvador had purchased a portion of his uncle's large landholdings in the backcountry, and in August 1774 he placed an advertisement for "an indigo overseer . . . to look after about thirty slaves."[16] In the eyes of the white men who elected him, the fact that he was one of the principal property owners in the Ninety-Six district was apparently more important than his identity as a Jew or a newcomer. He was present as the Provincial Congress heard a "devout and pious performance of divine service" by the rector of Saint Matthew's parish and presumably did not oppose its call for a "day of fasting, humiliation, and prayer before Almighty God."[17] In July 1776, Salvador was killed in a battle with a group of Cherokees and their loyalist allies. Major Andrew Williamson cast his final moments in a heroic light in a letter to the president of South Carolina, John Rutledge: "He asked whether I had beat the enemy? I told him yes. He said he was glad of it, and shook me by the hand—and bade me farewell—and said, he would die in a few minutes."[18] Williamson referred to him only as "Mr. Salvador"; he too apparently did not know or did not care that Salvador was a Jew.

Georgia was slow to formally join the patriot cause, a result of local political machinations, but also a sign that residents of the colony—newly flush from transatlantic trade and more vulnerable to attack by Spain and its Native allies—felt a greater reluctance to break with Great

Britain.[19] In July 1775, just three months after the outbreak of hostilities at Lexington and Concord, Levi Sheftall was part of a group of residents who called for "healing the unhappy divisions now subsisting between Great Britain and her colonies."[20] Nevertheless, when his brother became chair of the local parochial committee, which enforced the ban on British trade, Levi joined. Mordecai was later appointed commissary general of purchases and issues to the Georgia militia, and his teenage son Sheftall Sheftall obtained a position in commissary for Continental troops in the state.[21] Mordecai would contribute significant personal funds to the patriot cause, as would Abigail Minis and her son Philip, also born in Savannah, who advanced over $10,000 to the Continental army in 1777.[22]

It was not inevitable or obvious that Jews would support the revolution. Men like Salvador and Sheftall had fared well under British rule, and Salvador in particular enjoyed kinship and trade ties across the British Empire. There were legitimate fears that revolution would bring social disorder and even chaos, especially among suspect groups like "the Negroes, Roman Catholics, and Indians."[23] In Newport and New York, there were significant numbers of loyalist Jews.[24] We can assume that the topic was discussed with urgency during Friday-night meals in Jewish homes and before, after, or even during Sabbath worship in KKBE's temporary quarters and at Mordecai Sheftall's house. The bans on imported goods in particular brought nonelites, including women and especially merchants, into the realm of politics, forcing them to take sides.[25]

While there were risks to embracing the patriot cause, there was also the possibility that a break with the old would offer greater political inclusion and economic flourishing. South Carolina's March 1776 constitution certainly augured toward a new relationship between political and religious life, reorganizing parishes into secular counties. Four months later, a new nation was declared with the stated principle that "all men are created equal." State constitutions followed suit, touting "the rights and privileges" of "freemen." Jews could imagine themselves as "freemen" and as part of a "common cause" opposed to Britain and its supporters, whom newspapers cast as "resistant slaves, hostile Indians, and rapacious foreign mercenaries."[26] What seemed to be an expansive vision of equality was in fact limited to white men and reliant on the exclusion and demonization of others.[27] South Carolina's constitution—and other patriot writings—argued that continued British rule would place colonists in "a state of the most abject slavery," ignoring the actually enslaved people who constituted the majority in South Carolina and in Georgia.[28]

Rhetoric of religious liberty flourished even as full inclusion remained limited to Protestants.[29] The southern colonies abandoned the Church of England's establishment, although, apart from Virginia—which still encouraged "all to practice Christian forbearance, love, and charity"—they restricted officeholding to Protestants. South Carolina maintained an establishment of "the Christian Protestant religion."[30] Many insisted that Protestantism was a basic prerequisite of morality and social cohesion.[31] The challenges this raised for Jews became clear in October 1776, when a Charleston grand jury condemned "the ill practice of Jews opening their shops and selling of goods on Sunday, to the profanation of the Lord's-Day." For Jews who rested on Saturdays, giving up business on Sunday was a major economic blow. The grand jury also singled out "Jews and others" for "allowing their negroes to sell goods in shops, as such practice may induce other negroes to steal and barter with them."[32] Jews were seen as troubling insofar as they punctured Christian temporality and facilitated Black autonomy, especially in a time of heightened political tensions.[33]

Some patriots raised broader concerns about Jewish loyalty. In December 1778, a Charleston newspaper accused Jews of fleeing Savannah after its recent attack by the British, "dastardly turning their backs upon the country when in danger." The author had seen a suspicious group of newcomers, and "upon inspection and enquiry I found them to be of the Tribe of Israel." This notice drew on old ideas about Jewish greed and duplicity, but now Jews too had access to the popular press. "A real American and True hearted Israelite" responded, insisting that the author must have encountered a group of women and children. "Georgia Israelites" were in Savannah, defending their city, and "the Charleston Israelites hitherto have behaved as staunch as any other citizens of this

State."[34] Three years later, Georgia's loyalist governor, James Wright, sought "to prevent the Jews who formerly reside here from returning, or others from coming to settle here. For these people, my Lord, were found to a man to have been violent rebels and persecutors of the King's loyal subjects."[35] Suspicion of Jewish loyalty crossed battle lines, although in practice most Jews in the southern colonies in fact supported the patriot cause.

When Savannah fell to the British, many Jews did leave for Charleston. Historians have estimated that twelve Savannah Jews and thirty-six out of fifty-six identifiable Jewish men in South Carolina served in patriot forces.[36] At least thirteen Charleston Jews served under Captain Richard Lushington, a Quaker, and Isaac DaCosta's brother and nephew served in Captain James Bentham's militia alongside Myer Moses, one of the men whose misbehavior in the congregation they had previously decried.[37] Presumably congregational conflict gave way to battlefield camaraderie. The war was "chaotic, disorienting, and brutal," and it caused tremendous upheaval for Jews in both cities.[38] Levi Sheftall reported that "many Jews [were] continually coming and going . . . there was nothing but warr talked of & Every body had there [sic] hands & herts [sic] full."[39] His brother and nephew had been captured during the city's occupation and were imprisoned in the Caribbean for two years, "confined among the drunken soldiers and Negroes," according to Mordecai.[40]

In May 1780 Charleston surrendered to the British, sending Isaac DaCosta and other patriot Jews fleeing to Philadelphia. In July, Frances Sheftall wrote to her imprisoned husband from the South Carolina countryside in a state of despondence: "We have been strangers to [pleasure] for some time." Women like Frances faced new pressures and responsibilities during wartime. She was "obliged to take in needle work to make a living for my family," and was charged with overseeing enslaved members of the household, all of whom, she reported, had "been at the point of death."[41] Six Jewish children in the city had already died. Frances spent time, among others, with Abigail Minis, who had "sent some victuals" to Mordecai when he was first imprisoned by the British.[42] Frances seems to have taken comfort in the closeness of Jewish community, the rhythms of Jewish life, and the promise of divine protection. She wrote, "I still trust it to Providence owing that the Almighty never sends trouble but he sends some relief."[43]

Of his wartime experiences, Levi Sheftall later remembered, "During that [time I] had Several guns Loaded & Cocked ready to fire [at] my breast—but my god was pleased at Every danger [to rescue] me."[44] Sheftall expressed gratitude to God, but he also took active steps to alleviate danger. In 1780, after he was listed—along with five other Jews—among the patriots in Savannah to be punished by the British, he chose to accept a general pardon. He was one of nine Jewish men who took an oath of loyalty to the Crown in Charleston.[45] By contrast, his brother and nephew were paroled in New York in 1780 and traveled to the patriot stronghold of Philadelphia, where they reunited with Frances and their family. In November, Mordecai requested from the Continental Congress "some consideration for a man who has sacrificed every thing in the cause of his country."[46] Several months later, Isaac DaCosta wrote his own appeal, confessing that he had "nothing to support himself and his family."[47] These fellow expatriate southerners spent their time in Philadelphia seeking remuneration and engaging in religious affairs. In March of 1782, they were among those who met to formally establish Philadelphia's congregation; it was named Mickve Israel, echoing the messianic name of Curaçao's congregation and that of the one shuttered in Savannah.[48]

That year, following their surrender at Yorktown, the British retreated from Savannah and Charleston. In October, the Sheftall family left Philadelphia with their "two Negro servants" and a handful of other Jews.[49] The following year, the Treaty of Paris was signed, ending the war; Mordecai wrote that "an intier new scene will open itself, and the world . . . begin againe."[50] His son Sheftall invoked Psalm 119: "We are delivered from a cursed, proud nation."[51] Residents of devastated cities now worked to rebuild their economies and deal with former enemies in their midst.[52] Levi, along with another Jewish merchant, had been labeled a loyalist by the new government of Georgia, which meant that he would be banished from the state.[53] Mordecai undertook to clear his brother's name, a process that was fully completed only in 1787. He also began a decades-long and ultimately unsuccessful campaign to receive backpay or reimbursement for the funds he had committed to the cause.[54]

Even as the loyalty of individual Jews was put under the microscope, so, again, was their collective loyalty. In 1783, an author in the *South-Carolina Gazette and General Advertiser* wrote,

> The Jews have had a considerable share in our late Revolution. They have behaved well throughout. Let our government invite the Jews to our State and promise them a settlement in it. It will be a wise and politic stroke—and give a place of rest at last to the tribe of Israel.[55]

Others took a different view. A pamphlet was published in Savannah entitled *Cursory Remarks on Men and Measures in Georgia*, which argued that Jews' citizenship rights were "held by the slender tenure of good will." Pointedly, the author, "A Citizen," argued that "the Jew stands upon a level with the African slave who deserts the employment of his master." Although he made exceptions for the women of the Minis family, on account of their "long residence, upright demeanour, and inoffensive conduct"—their familiarity, class, and gender—he argued that on the whole Jews were greedy, indecorous, and too eager to participate in public life. If Jewish men were given free reign, they would inevitably replace Christianity with Judaism as the established religion.[56] The triumph of the patriot cause that so many Jews had supported could not totally erase the sense that they were a people apart whose belonging must be specially considered.

Writing under the name "Real Citizen," Levi Sheftall rose to the defense, noting happily that the original pamphlet had been met with "little countenance . . . from the public."[57] Levi was in fact defending his brother, since "A Citizen" had been commenting on a lawsuit brought against Mordecai by Samuel Nunes—a son of trader Moses Nunes and a Creek woman—who claimed that Sheftall had confiscated from him an enslaved person named Trimmer.[58] Sheftall argued that as an Indian, Nunes had no right to sue him, and the court agreed. Nunes's Native mother was deemed more important than his white Jewish father or his status as an enslaver. Even with occasional objections from white

Christians, then, European Jews could rely on the privileges of white citizenship, which placed their legal status above that of anyone with Native American or African heritage. Although he never regained the financial footing he had before the war, Mordecai continued to command respect, and went on to serve in several positions of public trust in Savannah.[59]

During and after the war, large numbers of people had moved and resettled. By 1782, veteran Jacob Cohen had settled in Richmond, Virginia, joining Isaiah Isaacs in business, and by 1785 they were advertising publicly as "the Jews Store."[60] Philadelphia-born Abram Mordecai engaged in trade with Creeks near the Georgia-Alabama border, where he cohabited with a Creek woman.[61] At least ten Jewish men arrived in Charleston during the revolution, and after the war the city saw an influx of Jews from the West Indies, along with a steady rise of Jewish migrants from central Europe. Over half of KKBE's contributors now came from England or the West Indies, with contingents from an array of other European countries, ranging from Ireland to Poland. In 1781 the congregation purchased land on Hasell Street, which had previously been occupied by a cotton-gin manufactory, in the hopes of building a proper synagogue.[62] Five years later, the congregation in Savannah was reestablished yet again.[63] These two Lowcountry communities were becoming increasingly intertwined. Of nineteen marriages that were recorded among Savannah Jews between 1733 and 1783, fourteen occurred in one of those places, and the Sheftalls repeatedly traversed the waterways between the swampy port cities. And yet they remained distinct in terms of history as well as identity; as we have seen, during the revolution "Georgia Israelites" were distinguished from "Charleston Israelites," and in 1786 Levi Sheftall noted that his children born in Charleston technically "cannot be entered at there [sic] birth" in Savannah's communal records.[64]

There is evidence that the new congregation that DaCosta and his allies had planned did operate in Charleston for a period. In the 1780s both Moses Molina and Joseph Salvador left money in their wills to "the Portuguese Jew Congregation of Beth Elohim Unve Shalom" (House of God and Mansion of Peace). The name invoked their mother congregation—what Salvador called "the German Jewish Congregation"—as well as congregations in Jamaica and Suriname.[65] It may have been an expression of Caribbean ties, messianic expectations, or a desire to move on from recent conflicts.[66] The state constitution had recently declared, "No person shall, by law, be obliged to pay towards the maintenance and support of a religious worship that he does not freely join in, or has not voluntarily engaged to support."[67] Now some Jews chose to place their support somewhere other than KKBE.

The congregation procured its own burial ground, where Isaac DaCosta was buried in 1783, and its own place of worship, around the corner from Saint Philip's Church, near Meeting Street.[68] The details of its history are fuzzy—within a decade the two congregations were reunited—but it serves as evidence that even as Charleston's Jews grew in number and embraced an American identity, some among them continued to nurture a specifically *Portuguese* Jewish identity. The transition from the British Empire to the American nation would bring many more changes, in Charleston, in Savannah, and beyond. The Sheftall diaries had begun by describing "persons . . . of our nation" in a fragile new colony; by 1790 they described "the people of our profession," members of a transnational diaspora, but also residents of a nascent region and citizens of a dynamic if unequal democracy.[69] These men and women looked to the new nation with eager anticipation.

CHAPTER 4

Blessings and Privileges

In June of 1790, Levi Sheftall, now president of Savannah's Mickve Israel congregation, wrote to President George Washington, thanking him for having "enfranchised us with all the privileges and immunities of free citizens, and initiated us into the grand mass of legislative mechanism."[1] Sheftall had bounced back from the accusations of loyalism that had dogged him after the revolution; he was an active participant in civic affairs and in Jewish life, while continuing to maintain the communal records that he had inherited from his father. In their pages, the summer of 1790 was marked not by presidential correspondence but by the birth of Judith Nunez Carvalho, the arrival of Samuel Benedix, and the deaths of a Moses Cohen and Sarah De La Motta, Sheftall's mother-in-law.[2] Migrants continued to move in and out of southern cities, and the warp and woof of Atlantic Jewish life—and death—continued apace, even as European Jewish men became public citizens.

As he would in his more famous letter, sent three months later to the Jews of Newport, Rhode Island, Washington assured Sheftall that the United States would accept and embrace its Jewish citizens. He ended with a prayer that "the inhabitants of every denomination participate in the temporal and spiritual blessings of that people whose God is Jehovah."[3] Both Washington and Sheftall were imbued with the optimistic Enlightenment ideals that had informed the American Revolution.[4] These ideas were also percolating in Europe, where they sparked prolonged debates about the place of Jews in nascent nation-states.[5] The German writer Christian Wilhelm von Dohm suggested, "Certainly, the Jew will not be prevented by his religion from being a good citizen, if only the government will give him a citizen's rights."[6] The United States Constitution, however, did not mention Jews at all. Rather, the outcome of the Constitution, the Bill of Rights, and the Naturalization Act of 1790 was that European Jewish men, without much handwringing, were classified as individual citizens and "free white persons."[7]

The religious landscape of the southern states was eclectic, including Judaism alongside Anglicanism, Catholicism, Enlightenment Deism, individual heterodoxies, occult practices, Native American and African-derived cosmologies, and early flashes of Baptist and Methodist evangelicalism.[8] Some rejected religion altogether; according to Joseph Salvador, who lived in the South Carolina backcountry, his neighbors had "no belief in Christ, little in Judaism or a future state . . . Rum is their deity."[9] And yet, where Newport's Jews argued for an absence of "persecution," Savannah's described the negative effects of "superstition" and "enthusiasm," suggesting that improper religious sentiment had impeded Jewish rights. Now, southern states were quicker to remove state support for established churches—post-Puritan Massachusetts came last, in 1833—even as they created legal pathways for the incorporation of religious congregations. The First Amendment granted citizens free exercise of religion on a federal basis, but it was the individual states that were responsible for determining the contours of religious freedom.[10]

Larger Jewish communities, both new and old, drafted charters and elected officers, creating state-authorized legal entities: Richmond's Beth Shalome in 1789, Savannah's Mickve Israel in 1789, and Charleston's Kahal Kadosh Beth Elohim (KKBE) in 1791.[11] These congregations were important sites of personal meaning and communal regulation. On the one hand, when Mordecai Sheftall's daughter was "suddenly taken in fits," he reported that "we had prayers for her in [synagogue], and I do thinke she began to mend from the time the prayers were finished."[12] On the other hand, in 1795 leaders punished Samuel Benedix and a friend for absenting themselves from the synagogue—and the obligatory hearing of a ram's horn blast—on the second day of Rosh Hashanah. Instead, they had stayed home and blown the shell of a conch, a non-kosher animal associated with both slavery and revolt in the Caribbean, which certainly could not have recommended it to synagogue leaders.[13]

Congregations also served as vehicles for Jews' public respectability. In 1794, KKBE erected a new synagogue, in the Georgian style, with a seventy-five-foot spire that mimicked the much larger one at Saint Michael's Church.[14] Governor William Moultrie attended the consecration ceremony, and in 1802 General Christopher Gadsden cited his "particular regard" for the congregation in offering a gift of volumes of the Mishnah and Maimonides.[15] Religious leadership and education in the city both proved intermittent, but by 1810 Charleston supported a *mikvah*, an oven for baking *matzah*, a Hebrew Benevolent Society, and a Hebrew Orphan Society. Charity allowed Jews to fulfill religious obligations while also demonstrating that they were responsible citizens. When Mordecai Sheftall died in 1797, following a stroke, he was praised in a Charleston newspaper for being "polite without effectation [sic], charitable without ostentation."[16] South Carolina Episcopalians once evaluated their own generosity in comparison to that of their Jewish neighbors: "It ought not to be believed that *Christians*, in seasons of prosperity, will be surpassed in generosity to the Almighty by Jews."[17]

Despite this genteel appreciation and the legal disestablishment of Christianity, a nonsectarian Protestantism continued to dominate conceptions of public order, creating what historian David Sehat has termed a "moral establishment." Pious evangelicals passed Sunday closing laws to encourage observance of the Christian Sabbath, which also limited the public activity of enslaved people, for whom Sunday was the sole day for making purchases.[18] Elected officials were required to swear Christian oaths, and public schools used Protestant texts, including the King James Bible, to instruct children. While belief and worship were protected, public life was organized in ways that alienated Jews.[19] In 1809 a Jewish legislator in North Carolina, Jacob Henry, was prevented from reassuming his seat because he was not a Protestant. In response,

Henry wrote an eloquent defense of religious liberty, echoing similar appeals by Jews around the world, including in Maryland, which was in the midst of ongoing battles over its so-called "Jew Bill."[20] Invoking deep-rooted anti-Spanish and anti-Catholic sentiments, he insisted, "If a man fulfills the duties of that religion, which his education or his conscience has pointed to him as the true one, no person, I hold, in this our land of liberty, has a right to arraign him at the bar of any inquisition." Although he never mentioned Judaism by name, he described "the religion I profess" as "inculcat[ing] every duty which man owes to his fellow men." Henry was allowed to remain in office, and the law, which also prevented Catholics from holding office, went mostly unenforced, although it would remain on the books until after the Civil War.[21]

In 1812, Jews in Charleston protested a day of thanksgiving that the state's governor had called using Christian language. The law implicitly excluded Jews, and while the governor quickly apologized in this case, there were other individual southerners who explicitly denigrated them, in public and in private.[22] A Charleston newspaper printed the claim that Jews were "outlawed and detested by the world, even their very name is the brand of reproach, disgrace and dishonest," and a businessman in that city wrote in his diary, "The only thing worse than a Jew is a Yankee. A Yankee can Jew a Jew directly."[23] And yet, as Rebecca Samuel, a Yiddish-speaking Jewish migrant in Petersburg, Virginia, put it in 1791, "One can make a good living here, and all live at peace. . . . Jew and Gentile are as one. There is no *galut* here."[24] She referenced the theological concept of exile, typically extended to the entirety of Jewish existence outside of the land of Israel and after the destruction of the Jerusalem Temple in 70 CE. Samuel reinterpreted it to refer to forms of discrimination and parochialism that seemed to be absent from her new home. In fact, many Jews were living comfortably in urban centers, where they worked as peddlers, merchants, auctioneers, and even as professionals and officeholders. There were Jews who went to college and joined nonsectarian civic and fraternal groups.[25] To take just one example, Zalma Rehina, who owned a dry goods business in Richmond and belonged to Beth Shalome, was also a grand master of the Royal Arch of Masons and part of the Richmond Light Infantry Blues.[26]

For Jews like Rehina, white citizenship in the new nation also brought freedoms of movement, travel, and residence. Young men went north for education and families relocated somewhere more comfortable during the heat of the summer months.[27] In the early 1800s several Jewish men—including Judah Touro, son of the *hazan* in Newport, Rhode Island—made their way to New Orleans, which had been handed from the Spanish back to the French, and ultimately, in 1803, passed into American control.[28] Some Jews chose to settle in small towns that had little in the way of Jewish community. Philadelphia-born Jacob Mordecai and his family were the only Jews in Warrenton, North Carolina, where they moved in 1797 to open a store; he later operated a female academy that educated a mostly-Christian student body.[29] While Rebecca Samuel appreciated the fact that "there is no rabbi in all of America to excommunicate anyone," she also complained of Petersburg, "We are completely isolated. . . . It won't do for a Jew." There was no Jewish cemetery nearby in case of death, and even in nearby Richmond, where she and her husband would eventually settle, Jews seemed to be neglecting their religious obligations.[30]

Southern Jews' experiences were different in big cities and in small towns, in Louisiana and Virginia, but almost all of them lived in some proximity to enslaved African-descended people. The same Constitution that made Jews citizens included the "three-fifths clause," which pointed to the dehumanizing features of slavery, and it provided for the end of the slave trade, albeit not for another two decades. Northern states soon passed gradual emancipation laws, but industrialization ensured that they also became increasingly reliant on cotton picked by enslaved Africans elsewhere.[31] Slavery was the context in which Jews most clearly acted—and were accepted—as white southerners, their difference fading into near-insignificance. It was likely not an accident that in their letter to Washington, Savannah's Jews did not, like their Newport coreligionists, describe citizenship as "generously afford[ed] to All . . . of whatever Nation, tongue, or language."[32] These Jews knew viscerally that equality had limits, in part because they helped enforce them.

They continued to participate in every aspect of slavery; there were those who testified in criminal cases against enslaved people and, as public officials, meted out the disproportionate punishments that they received.[33] There were a few prominent Jewish slave traders, many Jewish auctioneers and brokers who speculated in enslaved people, and a large number of Jews who purchased chattel when they could afford it.[34] In Richmond in 1820, the average Jewish household included three enslaved people.[35] By 1830, 83 percent of Jewish households in Charleston included enslaved people, just below the overall average of 87 percent.[36] While most Jewish enslavers—like most Jews—were urban merchants who had only a few enslaved members of their households, there were exceptions. Barnet A. Cohen, a planter in South Carolina, enslaved thirty-five people on five hundred acres of land at the time of his 1839 death, and Chapman Levy of Camden enslaved thirty-one people.[37]

Some of the best evidence for Jewish slaveholding comes from wills, in which Jews arranged to sell or bequeath the human beings over whom they claimed ownership. When Levi Sheftall died in 1809, he distributed specific "negroes"—Carolina, Cork, and London, along with Sproucer, her children Rose, George, Venus, and Jane, and any more to come—to each of his sons "as his property forever."[38] While most enslavers, like Sheftall, presented this as a pro forma transaction, others evinced some recognition of Black humanity. "It is my direction, desire, and earnest request," Chapman's mother Sara Levy wrote in her will, "that old Kennedy shall be kept with his wife and each treated with kindness and reasonable indulgence."[39] Even as she expressed her concern, however, Levy reasserted her domination and authority over their lives.[40]

A tiny number of Jews arranged for the manumission of enslaved people whose labor had fueled their fortunes. For instance, in 1796, Philip Hart's will—which also designated funds for Charleston's synagogue, a Jewish charity in Hamburg, and a number of local causes—granted freedom to "my negro woman Flora."[41] In 1803, Isaiah Isaacs of Richmond provided for the manumission of Rachel, James, Polly, Henry, and Williams. In so doing, he deliberately echoed the language of the founding documents, declaring that "all men are by Nature equally free," and offering the people he had enslaved "all the privileges and immunities of freed people." And yet, the recognition of American freedom's central irony did not prevent Isaacs from postponing its redress. The manumission was to unfold over a thirty-year period, with an additional thirty-one years for any children born to the women.[42]

In several cases, it appears that manumission was linked to a familial relationship. Moses Nunes of Savannah acknowledged the four children of "Mulatto Rose" as his own; after his death in 1790 they were manumitted and left generous bequests, which included other enslaved people.[43] In 1809 Samuel Jones of Charleston manumitted and left a large bequest to "My Negro Woman Jenny, and her Son Emanuel," whom he had likely fathered.[44] The rape of enslaved women by white men was a ubiquitous feature of life in slave societies, as a means of dominating enslaved people and increasing wealth through reproduction; it seems that Jews did not abstain from this practice.[45] Interracial partnerships between whites and free people of color were more unusual, especially outside of New Orleans, where a greater tolerance of interracial relationships was one legacy of the French and Spanish past.[46] US law forbade marriages between people classified as white and Black, Jewish law forbade marriages between Jews and gentiles, and both agreed that status passed through the mother.[47] And yet, records remain of several Jewish men who maintained long-term relationships with free women of color.

The relatively liberal language of Isaiah Isaacs's will may have been influenced by the fact that his brother David maintained a relationship with Nancy West, a free woman of color, for over forty years; living in Charlottesville, Virginia, between 1796 and 1817 they had seven children together. Isaacs's status as an outsider may have made their relationship more palatable to local white Christians, although eventually they were subject to a spiteful lawsuit alleging both fornication and miscegenation. Their arrangement was too domestic to qualify as the former, however, and since they were not legally married, they could not be guilty of the latter. Ironically, perhaps, this relationship brought together the offspring of a humble Jewish merchant and that of a US president. David and Nancy's daughter Julia Ann married Eston Hemings, one of four children fathered by Thomas Jefferson and born to Sally Hemings, a woman enslaved on his estate at Monticello.[48] Isaacs maintained his membership in Beth Shalome throughout his life and was buried in its cemetery, but there is no evidence that he tried to perpetuate Judaism or Jewish identities among his children. In one case, the children of white Jewish men with free women of color married each other. Narcissa Wilson was born to Judah Touro and Ellen Wilson in New Orleans and raised by Touro's cousin in Boston. Her husband, Richard Gustavus Forrester, was the son of a prominent Richmond Jewish lawyer and city councilman, Gustavus Adolphus Myers, and Nelly Forrester.[49] Wilson and Forrester were linked by their parallel origins, but it is unclear whether they felt like—or were accepted as—Jews.

Although slavery was a ubiquitous feature of southern Jews' economic and social lives, they seem to have rarely spoken about it. A few might raise concerns in private, but they were not necessarily motivated by visions of interracial harmony and equality; when she was seven years old, Wilson's grandfather, Samuel Myers, wrote to his brother-in-law in Boston, "I believe too that an effort must sooner or later be made to throw off the yoke of servitude, and that when it is, extermination of one or the other part of our population must be the result."[50] Although his own family gave evidence to the contrary, Myers continued to see the South in stark Black and white, made up of two races that were mutually exclusive and inevitably in conflict. Only a few Jews with ties to southern states saw things differently. Isaac Sasportas, who spent time with his uncle Abraham in Charleston, later planned a failed slave revolt in Jamaica, and Floridian plantation owner Moses E. Levy published an abolitionist pamphlet in London in 1828.[51] These Jews are the exceptions that prove the rule.

Most southern Jews took pleasure in the tremendous privileges they now enjoyed, not only as citizens but as members of white ruling minorities. They established comfortable households, they participated in the system of chattel slavery, and they developed strong local loyalties. Mordecai Sheftall's 1797 gravestone proudly described him as a "native of Savannah GA."[52] Rebecca Samuel criticized northern cities where "there is more *galut*. . . . The German Gentiles cannot forsake their anti-Jewish prejudice; and the German Jews cannot forsake their disgraceful conduct."[53] Despite ample evidence to the contrary, most southern Jews loudly proclaimed that, at least in the places where they lived, prejudice was a thing of the past. In 1820, thirty-one-year-old Doctor Jacob De La

Motta spoke at the dedication of Mickve Israel's new synagogue in Savannah. De La Motta had returned to the city of his birth two years earlier, after stints in Charleston, Philadelphia, and New York. He asked the crowd, rhetorically, "On what spot in this habitable Globe does an Israelite enjoy more blessings, more privileges, or is more elevated in the sphere of preferment and more conspicuously dignified in respectable stations?" De La Motta believed that there was none. Trained as a physician under Doctor Benjamin Rush, a signer of the Declaration of Independence, De La Motta was also a veteran of the war of 1812, a decorated mason, a former candidate for city alderman, and an enslaver. He sent copies of his speech to former presidents James Madison and Thomas Jefferson, both of whom responded graciously. Men like De La Motta had every reason to embrace the comforts that the new social order provided them and to ignore or accept the exclusions and injustices that made them possible.[54]

CHAPTER 5

Faith of Our Fathers

In 1815 Rachel Mordecai wrote a letter to the Irish writer Maria Edgeworth, complaining about her most recent novel's Jewish characters. While persecuted Jews in Europe may possess some of the negative characteristics attributed to them, Mordecai argued, "in this happy country, where religious distinctions are scarcely known, where character + talents are all sufficient to attain advancement, we find the Jews to form a respectable part of the community." Living in Warrenton, North Carolina, she explained, "[my] father's the only family of Israelites, who reside in or near it; all [my] juvenile friendships and attachments have been formed with those of persuasions different from [my] own."[1] Indeed, Rachel would not set foot in a synagogue until 1821, when she was thirty-three years old and visiting Charleston with her new fiancé, a widowed Jewish merchant named Aaron Lazarus. Rachel's letter was in some ways the apotheosis of her parents' hopes, embodying an ethos of familial loyalty, intellectualism, and Jewish pride described by their biographer as "enlightened domesticity."[2] It also demonstrated the liveliness and ambition of young Jews of her generation, whose sense of belonging in a region marked by chattel slavery and evangelical Christianity fostered profound reconsiderations of Jewish practice and belief.

In the 1820s, Charleston was a bustling commercial center and home to the largest Jewish population in the United States—as many as eight hundred people, or 5 percent of the white population.[3] This primacy was short-lived, however, as born southerners and migrants alike increasingly sought their fortunes in New York or New Orleans.[4] When the synagogue that Jacob De La Motta helped erect in Savannah burned down just nine years later, it took the reduced Jewish community about as long to rebuild.[5] In New Orleans, where Judaism had been banned under the French and Spanish, a new wave of migration made it the fifth-largest city in the United States and led to the establishment of a Jewish congregation, Shangarai Chasset (Gates of mercy), in 1827.[6]

Even with changes underway, the center of southern society remained the white male "master," who claimed ultimate authority over property and household, including women, children, and enslaved people. Although developed in the plantation context, nonplanting yeoman and urban professionals, including Jews, also expected to discipline their slaves, defend their honor, and protect their virtuous wives.[7] The gravestone of David Lopez, the Charleston Hebrew Orphan Society's first president, eulogized him as "patriotic as a citizen, humane as a master and as a father truly affectionate, as a husband [he leaves] a disconsolate widow." While his gravestone, erected sometime after his death in 1811, is the only one in the Coming Street cemetery to explicitly mention the role of master, others made clear the distinct expectations of southern Jewish men and women. Men were lauded for public characteristics like "honesty, integrity, and ingeniousness, whereas women were praised for "sincere piety and social virtues."[8]

Marriage had long been central to the delineation of gender, race, and status, and as romantic love emerged as a key criterion in the selection of a spouse, Jewish patriarchs tried to assert control over their families.[9] According to Isaac Cohen's 1787 will, his daughter Sara would receive her inheritance only "if she intermarry with any Jews or persons of her own profession (excepting David Cordoza)."[10] Sarah and David did in fact marry; their son, also named Isaac, never did but would maintain a long-term relationship—and produce three children—with Lydia Weston, a free woman of color.[11] Jewish men increasingly married white Christian women, especially but not only in small towns and frontier communities. Five of Jacob Mordecai's thirteen children married Christians, and two others stopped just short of doing so. After early romantic entanglements with Christians, his son Alfred, who graduated at the top of his class at West Point, married a Jewish woman from Philadelphia. His daughter Emma never married.[12] Even though the children of Jewish women would be considered Jewish regardless of the father, men were granted much more agency in the selection of a spouse.

An estimated 50 percent of the Jewish men who settled in New Orleans before the 1840s married Christians, and the long-time congregational president and functionary was married to a Catholic. While in most places, children of such marriages were raised as Christians, the initial congregational constitution there stipulated that "no Israelite child shall be excluded, either from the schools, from the Temple, or the burial ground, on account of the religion of the mother."[13] Most congregations tried to enforce endogamy, punishing Jews who married Christians, but in other ways they embraced the norms of southern mastery. Leaders of Charleston's Kahal Kadosh Beth Elohim (KKBE) granted Jewish divorces only twice before the Civil War, in 1788 and in 1840; divorce was illegal in South Carolina because of its perceived threat to the household.[14]

Southern Jews were influenced by the norms of mastery *and* traditional Judaism, a combination that encouraged filial piety but also forms of empowerment and rebellion. Most famously, on November 21, 1824, a group of young men crafted a letter to the leaders of KKBE affirming "the faith of our fathers" but complaining about apathy, neglect, and "defects" within Jewish worship. Specifically, they were concerned about the length of the services and their lack of intelligibility to English-speaking Jews. Led by Isaac Harby, a journalist, playwright, and teacher, the men were overwhelmingly educated, American born, and civically engaged. Their average age was just thirty-three, three of them were married to Christian women, and although six of their fathers served on the congregational board that they were addressing, the majority had not been members previously.[15]

The petitioners pointed to the Jewish "reformation" already underway in Europe, referring to recent forms of modernization at the Hamburg Temple, but they were also reacting to developments closer to home.[16] For one thing, Enlightenment thought persisted as an intellectual force within southern cities, although its more radical edges were increasingly sanded down within newly founded Unitarian churches. Isaac Harby was friendly with Samuel Gilman, Charleston's Unitarian minister, and in New Orleans Judah Touro become an important bene-factor of the Unitarian church and its minister Theodore Clapp; he gave money to the city's new Jewish congregation in 1827 but actually de-clined to join as a member.[17] In his diary from the 1830s, Charleston-born Joseph Lyons, a recent college graduate living in Savannah, drew on Enlightenment ideals to critique his own tradition. He described Hebrew as a "guttural, harsh, barbarous tongue," the synagogue as fated "not to be found in the U.S. fifty years hence," and himself as "almost an atheist."[18] Followed to their logical conclusions, the Enlightenment ideas that had underwritten Jewish inclusion could also cast serious doubt on Judaism.

Baptist and Methodist preachers had been evangelizing in the back-country South for decades, but in the early nineteenth century a series of dramatic revivals—described as a Second Great Awakening—spurred new success, especially among young people. It helped that by the 1820s, evangelicals had come to affirm rather than challenge the southern social order, defending patriarchal authority, diminishing the spiritual autonomy of Black Christians, and arguing for the biblical basis of slavery. By 1835, almost two-thirds of the South's population would embrace evangelicalism.[19] Undergirding the entire enterprise was Arminian theology, focused on individual conversion as the path to salvation. When evangelical revivals came to Warrenton, North Caro-lina, in the 1810s, Jacob Mordecai had rededicated himself to Judaism. After moving near Richmond in 1818, he led the congregation there as *hazan* and became a staunch defender of Jewish orthodoxy, even pen-ning a lengthy rejoinder to the Charleston reformers. A number of his children, however, converted to Christianity, including Rachel, who had defended Jews' honor to Maria Edgeworth; evangelical friends nursed her through a difficult pregnancy and she came to embrace Christ. Although her husband and her father vehemently objected, she was baptized on her deathbed in 1838, neither the first nor the last south-ern Jew to make that choice.[20]

Evangelicalism and Unitarianism were in competition with Judaism, but they were also models of religious rebellion within the framework of white mastery.[21] The Charleston reformers insisted that they wanted "not to *destroy* but to *reform* and *revise*." They approvingly cited the missionary efforts of evangelicals and described their goal as a "more rational means of worshiping the true God . . . not as *slaves of bigotry and priestcraft* but as the enlightened descendants of that chosen race."[22] Although elsewhere in their letter they approvingly cited vernacular services within Catholic churches—Saint Mary's was, and remains, located just across Hasell Street—the reformers here invoked Catholicism as a negative foil of Enlightenment. And although the liberty of enslaved Black people appeared never to have crossed their minds, they argued for perfect liberty of thought. Enslaved men named Henry, Merchant, and Marshall in fact worked as servants within KKBE's Hasell Street synagogue.[23] And in a revised 1820 constitution, the congregation explicitly excluded "people of color"—indicating that this was at least a spectral concern and at most an active possibility.[24] Just two years later, Denmark Vesey's failed revolt, centered on Emanuel African Methodist Episcopal Church, had roiled the city of Charleston, making it clear that enslaved people might not passively accept their status. Jews were needed more than ever as part of the white ruling class, especially in a city where people of color constituted the majority of the population.[25]

In 1831 Nat Turner, an enslaved man in Virginia, instigated a bloody revolt inspired by prophetic visions. Rebels like Vesey and Turner forced increased scrutiny on the institution of slavery, as did a cadre of pious northern Protestants, and a tiny number of white southerners, most famously the South Carolina–born sisters Sarah and Angelina Grimké.[26] Their call for the immediate abolition of slavery inspired among white southerners passionate defenses of slavery, draconian laws to protect it, and a militant defense of states' rights. In 1833 Jacob Mordecai, who enslaved around twenty people on his farm outside of Richmond, joined a Society for the Prevention of the Absconding and Abduction of Slaves; two men enslaved by his son-in-law, Aaron Lazarus, had been executed for their involvement in Nat Turner's rebellion.[27] After the violence subsided, Rachel described the "condition of the southern states" as "unenviable," being "necessarily surrounded by those whom we cannot permit ourselves to feel confidence." Although her family helped to protect and maintain slavery, she hoped that at some point they would be able to move beyond its grasp.[28]

Whatever qualms—if any—they had about their region's reliance on chattel slavery, southern Jews continued to cultivate their status as white citizens. With relative ease they entered business relationships with white Christians, they joined them in the nonsectarian moral space of the fraternal lodge, and they occasionally faced them in duels, seeking to prove their masculine honor through the threat of violence.[29] Unspoken but palpable within the efforts of Charleston's reformers was the eagerness to present Judaism as a religious faith perfectly compatible with the genteel norms of the urban slaveholding South. The congregational leaders had ignored their requests, however, and the group, calling themselves the Reformed Society of Israelites, started meeting on their own. They created the first reform prayerbook in the world and talked about building their own synagogue, but in a few years Harby moved to New York, and by the 1830s the group was defunct.[30]

On an 1833 visit to KKBE, the great Methodist itinerant Lorenzo Dow reported that "great respect is shown to strangers—they gave books in English, what they read in Hebrew—turning to and keeping pace, which, with the explanation given as they went along, was very satisfactory to me."[31] Four years later, the congregation revised its constitution, now promising to uphold "Minhog Sephardim, as always practised in this city," and forbidding "any alteration in the mode of worship in the Synagogue, except such as may be specified in this Constitution."[32] By that time the majority of the congregation was of central European, or Ashkenazi, extraction, but the Reformed Society of Israelites may have inspired a conservative backlash; at the same time, Ashkenazi Jews in this period tended to associate Spanish and Portuguese customs with elevated dignity and status, embracing what one historian has described as a "Sephardic mystique."[33]

The next year, KKBE's synagogue burned to the ground, a devastating blow for the congregation and its members. Solomon Nunes Carvalho

(1815–97), a Charleston-born artist, who, like Harby, would live out his later years in New York City, painted the sanctuary from memory, depicting it empty and bathed in golden light (figure 5.1).[34] Penina Moïse, whose brother Abraham had been one of the 1824 reformers, wrote "A Poetic Homily on the Late Calamity." Using Psalm 39 as her inspiration, she lamented the devastation of the building's loss:

> And Israel's Nestor o'er the ruin bends.
> In youth his hallelujahs here resounded.
> His age's hope these sacred precincts bounded.
> As falls the altar where in faith he bowe
> The Patriarch lifts his voice and weeps aloud.[35]

Plans were made to build a new synagogue in the Greek Revival style, redolent of democratic ideals and popular among houses of worship around the country, both Jewish and Christian.[36] Reflecting a common practice of temporary hiring out, or renting, of slave labor, the synagogue's builders included two enslaved artisans, named Kit and George.[37]

As the Jews of Charleston rebuilt, controversy visited them yet again, this time over the question of installing an organ in the new sanctuary. Organs were a mainstay of Charleston houses of worship, and there were European Jewish precedents for the practice; echoing the Reformed Society of Israelites' concerns about straying Jewish youths, proponents described the organ as a "laudable and sacred mode by which the rising generation may be made to conform to and attend our holy worship." A vocal minority, including Jacob De La Motta, who had relocated from Savannah to Charleston, objected, arguing that the organ was a violation of the traditional prohibition on musical instrumentation on the Sabbath. These dissenters seceded to form their own congregation, Shearith Israel, with De La Motta serving as *hazan*, but they soon instigated a dramatic court battle against the mother congregation.[38] Those on both sides of the conflict welcomed the intervention of the courts, although they also recognized that the public reputation of Jews and Judaism would be on trial. One antiorgan dissenter, N. Levin, described the court as "a christian Tribunal" and worried about testimony that might "injure us in the eyes of the christian community."[39]

FIGURE 5.1. *K.K. Beth Elohim* by Solomon Nunes Carvalho, Collection of Kahal Kadosh Beth Elohim. Image courtesy of Special Collections, College of Charleston Libraries.

Its opponents argued that the organ would encourage the violation of Jewish law, but the Court of Common Pleas refused to hear evidence on that question and decided against them. On appeal to the South Carolina Supreme Court they raised two additional points: they argued that their investments in the burial ground and the synagogue building should grant them a say, and that the reformers were extremists seeking "to substitute a new faith and worship of their own." In so doing, they invoked property rights, which were central to southern codes of mastery, and religious sectarianism, which was rife among American Protestants. The court, unconvinced on both counts, decided in favor of the pro-organ majority.[40] Despite the best efforts of the antiorgan faction to make Jewish law—and its violation—legible to southern Protestant judges, they found that the courts were much friendlier to Jews when they presented not as practitioners of an ancient tradition but as enlightened citizens of faith.

Meanwhile, the sisters and daughters of the congregation enacted their own religious rebellion, albeit in a quieter register. The ideal southern white woman was supposed to be submissive and private, but she was also understood to be morally superior, which created a pathway for public activity in realms like literature, benevolence, and education, especially for women who were not married.[41] This was the case with Penina Moïse, who became a widely recognized poet and hymnodist. Her *Fancy Sketch Book* (1833) was the first published book by an American Jewish woman. Soon after the destruction of the synagogue, another Charleston woman, Sally Lopez, founded a Sunday school at KKBE. The first Jewish Sunday school had been created earlier that year in Philadelphia by Rebecca Gratz, and the idea was quickly embraced in southern communities, where there were unmarried Jewish women eager for activity and children with little in the way of religious education.[42] Jacob Mordecai's daughter Emma instigated the founding of the Jewish Sunday school in Richmond in 1839. She had withstood pressure to convert to Christianity from her sister Ellen and thrown herself into Jewish causes, convinced of "[her] duty to adhere to the religion of [her] forefathers." Another Sunday school was founded in Columbia, South Carolina, in 1843.[43] These schools added to Jewish congregations, rather than trying to change them, and they fit squarely within southern conceptions of femininity, but they were radical in their own way. They recast Judaism as a set of ideas that could be taught in ways parallel to Christianity and by women newly empowered as religious authorities.[44]

In and beyond Charleston, southern Jews reconfigured their relationship to traditional Judaism. To be sure, some abandoned or ignored Judaism, but others worked hard to establish congregations and means of ritual practice, and to explain them using the grammar of southern culture. Although their identities were never limited to belief or worship, white Jews found that operating comfortably as southerners required invisibility of identity, conformity to gendered codes of mastery, and public presentation as a Church like any other. In 1841, Gustavus Poznanski, the *hazan* at KKBE, announced at the consecration of the new synagogue, "This synagogue is our temple, this city our Jerusalem, this happy land our Palestine, and so . . . our sons [will] defend *this* temple, *this* city, and *this* land."[45] In transposing the sacred geography of the land of Israel onto the South Carolina Lowcountry, Poznanski was not only expressing delight at the integration that Jews in Charleston had achieved but rejecting—as had Rebecca Samuel—the traditional idea of Jewish exile. This happy land was the United States, but it was also South Carolina.[46] Even, and perhaps especially, at a time when Jews were leaving the city for greener pastures in the north and west, those who remained embraced their positions as masters and mistresses; if anything it was Judaism that had to be reconsidered.

By the time of Poznanski's address, there had been Jews in Charleston for nigh on 150 years. What had begun as a smattering of Spanish and Portuguese merchants had become a large, comfortable, and creative community consisting of those American-born and migrant, of Iberian and central European extraction, traditionalist and reforming. Other Jews, likewise embedded within a Jewish Atlantic world, had followed the earliest pioneers to various parts of what would become "the South": to Charleston, to Savannah, and then to cities and towns ranging northward to Richmond and westward to New Orleans, where under French and Spanish rule they had been formally banned. Over the course of the eighteenth century, the societies built on this hot and inhospitable Native land had become increasingly dependent on the labor of enslaved Africans. Jews there enjoyed tremendous privileges, especially after the founding of the United States, which they not only accepted but pursued. Christianity was no prerequisite for practices of white supremacy, and Judaism no guarantee of emancipatory thinking. At the same time, Jews maintained forms of difference from their white Christian neighbors, and they fought assumptions of Christianity's universal embrace. As would remain clear in the tumultuous decades to come, white citizenship sometimes obscured but never eliminated the age-old divide between Christians and Jews.

PART II
1840–1878

CHAPTER 6

Peculiar Institutions

On August 29, 1852, the Jews of Galveston, Texas, consecrated a burial ground. To oversee the proceedings, Rosanna Osterman, who had lived in the city for almost fifteen years, invited Moses N. Nathans from New Orleans. The English-born minister, newly arrived from the Caribbean, congratulated and flattered Galveston's Jews. He predicted "the spread and growth of our peculiar institutions" in Texas, and marveled that Hebrew prayers were being recited, "on this verdant prairie, which once resounded with the war-whoop of the Indian."[1] He thus analogized the distinctiveness of Judaism to that of southern slavery and elaborated his own version of manifest destiny, a political ideology that imagined US sovereignty from the Atlantic to the Pacific as inevitable and beneficent. By the 1850s, a federal policy of Indian removal had pushed most Cherokees, Creeks, and other Native groups out of the southeast and into the far west, even as a peace treaty with Mexico had completed the United States' continental expansion.[2] This violent transfer of land was deeply intertwined with the politics of slavery, as politicians debated whether or not enslaved labor should be allowed in the new territories.[3]

Nathans's optimistic embrace of American empire was tempered only by his concerns about local religious life. There might not be another minister in Galveston for a long while, so he took the opportunity to exhort local Jews to greater piety. Galveston's Jews should circumcise their sons, ensure that their children married fellow Jews, and cease attending church services, Nathans argued. Even in a place with few Jews, the basics of Judaism could and should be followed, not only because God commanded them but for the sake of "public opinion, which, in all right-thinking societies condemns and frowns on irreligion and infidelity."[4] Speaking to immigrant Jews in a heterogeneous southern port city, he insisted that loyalty to Judaism was not a hindrance but a help to their local standing.

Galveston's burial ground was only one of a flurry of Jewish institutions created across the United States in the antebellum period, amid a mass migration of Jews from German-speaking lands. These new arrivals were incredibly mobile, always keeping an eye on other regions and nations, but they also worked to assert their place in southern communities. As they did, they would find that, depending on the context, they could access whiteness fully, conditionally, or not at all. They rejected Christianity, they were immigrants, and they were conspicuous as peddlers and merchants. All of this troubled white Christians, who felt besieged and increasingly powerless as slavery, the basis of their economy and society, was challenged and finally, after a bloody civil war, abolished. The South, now understood as a distinct region, included a heady and unstable mixture of "jealous yeomen and arrogant planters . . . pretending slaves and wary masters, post-seventeenth-century South Carolinians and pre-twentieth-century Lousianians," according to one historian.[5] Among them were enterprising Jews, including a growing number of immigrants, whose presence belies the popular image of the "Old South" as hermetically sealed, centered on plantations, and united in Protestant worship.

Nathans argued for the unique glory of the Jewish people—"our brethren in lineage and faith"—but others were less sanguine about the meaning of Jewish difference.[6] As the geography and economy of the South changed, the Enlightenment rationalism that had facilitated Jews' civic inclusion declined in influence. Increasingly, evangelicalism encouraged the view that Jews were stubborn unbelievers in need of conversion, and romanticism fueled ambivalence about Jews' connection to an idealized southern land and folk.[7] In the established eastern states in particular, public Christianity became increasingly noticeable.

When James Joseph Sylvester was appointed to a teaching position at the University of Virginia in 1842, for instance, a Presbyterian newspaper loudly protested, classifying Judaism with Catholicism and Unitarianism as "errors subversive of Christianity."[8] In 1844, Charleston Jews complained about a Christian thanksgiving prayer, as they had in 1812, but this time the governor refused to apologize. Instead he declared South Carolina a Christian state and claimed, "It did not occur to me, that there might be Israelites, Deists, Atheists, or an other class of persons in the State who denied the divinity of Jesus Christ."[9] After three decades, Jews were still an afterthought, but they no longer seemed to merit conciliation.

While these exclusions proved irritating to Jewish citizens, none did more so than Sunday closing laws. In Charleston in 1840, Jacob Meyer was found guilty of selling suspenders to a Black man on a Sunday, and five years later Solomon A. Benjamin faced the same charges for selling gloves. Benjamin appealed, complaining that the law violated his religious freedom, but the judge claimed that it was merely a police ordinance and that, in any event, Christianity was both part of the common law and the basis of morality.[10] The opinion expressed a "deep respect for the ancient people of whom the defendant is one," but set up a sharp distinction from "us, who are called Christians," insisting, "We say to [the Jews] simply, *respect us*."[11] Even as some Jews challenged local political institutions, however, others worked to become part of them. When ardent pro-slavery senator John C. Calhoun died in 1850, Charleston's Hebrew Benevolent Society and Hebrew Orphan asylum marched in his funeral parade, presenting themselves as proud white South Carolinians.[12] More directly, Judah P. Benjamin, Henry M. Hyams, and Doctor Edwin Warren Moïse all served in high political offices in Louisiana: as US senator, lieutenant-governor, and speaker of the legislature, respectively. All three men, enslavers married to Christian women, had been born to Jewish families in Charleston.[13]

By the 1840s, multicultural New Orleans had replaced Charleston as the region's main economic hub and Jewish center.[14] When Joseph Lyons contemplated moving there in 1835, he described it as "that emporium of wine, women, and segars [*sic*], etc."[15] While Lyons never actually moved, other Jews from Charleston did, joining coreligionists from eastern states as well as from Europe, all eager to make their fortunes in the freewheeling city. Texas also attracted Jewish migrants, to Galveston and places further inland. One of its most enthusiastic boosters was Jacob De Cordova, a Jamaican-born Jewish state legislator. On a tour of northern cities in 1858, he described Texas as a biblically resonant "land flowing with milk and honey." He felt pride in the state but also some estrangement from his audience, noting that "churches are to be found in every portion of the State; and I regret that I cannot speak on the subject with the fulness which its importance demands."[16] De Cordova felt empowered to speak publicly on behalf of the territory, while never forgetting that in some ways he remained outside of its mainstream.

In Texas and elsewhere in the Southwest, cotton was planted on what was seen as "virgin land" and picked by enslaved workers forced to maximum productivity. The crop they picked made fortunes locally, nationally, and globally, and yet its ascendance was accompanied by an intensified critique of the slavery upon which it relied. Even after the compromise of 1850, which admitted California as a free state and passed stricter fugitive slave laws, conflicts over the question of slavery's expansion continued, and many southerners moved to defend it by any means necessary.[17] In 1858 De Cordova published his lectures, specifically to refute critics who accused him of advocating for a "free soil" Texas. He declared himself to "have always been proslavery," and "def[ied] the sharpest of them to put his finger on a single sentence which leans in the slightest degree toward abolitionism."[18] Indeed, the abolitionist cause remained unpopular among Jews both North and South, perhaps because of the enthusiastic Christian piety, and occasional anti-Jewish sentiment, expressed by its leaders.[19]

The development of the Southwest encouraged continued movement away from eastern cities—through new steamboat and railroad lines—on the part of white Americans, who brought with them the people they enslaved. Among those entering the region were also central European immigrants, including the first mass migration of Jews in US history.[20] In German-speaking lands, Jews were subject to far-reaching restrictions on occupation and settlement, and their citizenship was an ongoing matter of public debate. Those who migrated sought to escape this fraught political status and to pursue greater economic opportunity. The average Jewish migrant was an unmarried man in his late teens or early twenties who began as a peddler in the hinterland, relying on relatives and coreligionists in larger cities to get started, while hoping to eventually settle down as a merchant. If he went to the Southwest, he could easily find himself in the cotton business. Some Jews became cotton factors who helped planters sell their crops in a port city, or proprietors of small-town general stores who accepted payment in cotton and extended credit to local planters. Among the most successful of these men was Henry Lehman, an immigrant from Bavaria, who established a store in Montgomery, Alabama, in the 1840s and soon went into business with his brothers, creating a firm that would endure until the 2008 financial crisis.[21]

Jewish businesses were part of the fabric of the developing southern frontier, and yet in an environment of intensifying political pressure and economic strife, they were increasingly viewed with mistrust. After the Panic of 1837, an earlier moment of financial crisis, the governor of Mississippi had argued that the Rothschilds, the European Jewish banking family to whom the states of Alabama and Mississippi were indebted, were "the blood of Shylock and Judas," Jewish villains of Shakespeare and the New Testament, respectively.[22] Local Jews of much more modest means were also viewed through the lens of anti-Jewish stereotypes. Former peddler David Steinheimer recalled an exchange with a farmer and his family in rural Georgia in the 1850s: "When I told them I was a Jew, they were astonished—they thought a Jew had horns." Curiosity could evolve into demonization, especially as peddling came under increased scrutiny as a disrupter of local economies; Jews were visible as peddlers, and in many critiques the two were conflated.[23]

Antipathy towards Jews found a particularly potent vehicle in the credit report, a new technology that became central to success in the increasingly impersonal—and risky—antebellum economy. Reporters were tasked with determining the creditworthiness of local businesses, and they regularly noted Jewish identity, often, and increasingly, to disparage them. In the mid-1840s Benjamin Mordecai, a prominent Charleston slave trader and businessman, was described rather benignly as an "Old & Rich Jew [and] keen merch[ant]." Ten years later, he was found to be "possess[ing] of a large share of the qualities so generally attributed to Israelites." His firm was a "Jew Concern" and "JEWS from A to Z. . . . If paying is profitable + politic they will pay."[24] Around the same time, a credit reporter pointedly described the Lehman brothers as "Jews, but though Jews, are [considered] almost as good as 'white men.'"[25]

In the late 1850s, Edward Rosewater, a teenaged telegraph operator living in Stevenson, Alabama, was similarly othered. He noted in his diary that an acquaintance had told him, "If I was a White man he would whip me."[26] Jews' racial privilege might be qualified in certain situations, then, but it was never fully eliminated. Rosewater, who had immigrated from Bohemia to Cleveland as a child, successfully pressed charges against a "big Russian [who] accosted and beat" him.[27] He enthusiastically participated in many aspects of small-town southern life, including hunting, eating barbecue, attending a minstrel show, and going to church, although he described one Methodist meeting as "awfull screaming & yelling."[28] Immigrant Jews adjusted quickly to southern life, including slavery, and some amassed the resources necessary to become enslavers themselves. Julius Weis, who came to New Orleans in 1845, initially expressed shock at seeing an enslaved person whipped, but went on to purchase several human beings himself.[29] Jewish merchants also sold to enslaved customers—in 1857 it was reported that the firm of Cohen and Levy of Richmond County, Georgia, was a "Jew shop but trades with negroes and all sorts."[30]

While evidence about their Jewish ties is sparse, historian Lauren Winner has found that "some slaves who were owned by Jewish families considered themselves Jewish." Evidence of these individuals comes from the baptism records of Black Jews who participated in and eventually converted to Christianity. They refer to "brother George . . . long a practitioner of the Israelite faith, on account of being [owned] by a Jew," and of "Sarah[, who] has had familiarity with the teachings of the Lord, though she was a Jew." A man known as "Paul the Jew," who had been enslaved in South Carolina, was baptized after becoming convinced that "perpetuating his loyalty to the Jews was no more than perpetuating his loyalty to his owner."[31] There were almost certainly others like them, who encountered Judaism through their enslavers, or through other means, and found power in its beliefs or practices, although they almost certainly did not undergo formal *halakhic* conversion.

One example is known of a Jew of color who was accepted as a fellow worshipper in a southern congregation. In the 1850s an African American man named Billy Simons regularly attended services at Kahal Kadosh Beth Elohim in Charleston, despite its rules excluding people of color. In 1857, the congregation's leader, Maurice Mayer, wrote to the *Allgemeine Zeitung des Judenthums* that Simons, who claimed to have been converted by Jewish enslavers in Africa, sat among white Jewish men in the sanctuary and was "the most observant of those who go to the synagogue." While Protestants ministering to enslaved Africans carefully selected their biblical texts to encourage docility, the cyclical nature of Torah reading meant that Simons would have heard—at least once a year, in Hebrew—the story of the Israelite slaves' exodus from Egypt. He and other enslaved Jews likely saw Judaism as one source of spiritual power that they could combine with African traditions.[32] Mayer had promised to bury Simons in a Jewish cemetery, although there is no evidence that he followed through.[33]

If Black Jews were all but invisible within most Jewish communities, the opposite was true of the new immigrants. By the time Mayer was writing about Simons, an Ashkenazi congregation had been in operation in Charleston for two years. Richmond gained an Ashkenazi congregation in 1841, and a separate "Polish" one in 1856.[34] In New Orleans, Shangarai Chasset switched from the Sephardic to Ashkenazi rite sometime in the 1830s, and a new Sephardic congregation, Netzufot Yehudah (Dispersed of Judah), was founded in 1845. It was organized by Gershom Kursheedt, a Richmonder, but primarily funded by its namesake, Judah Touro, by then a wealthy philanthropist undertaking a late-in-life return to religious observance. By the late 1850s New Orleans was home to two additional congregations—one in neighboring Lafayette and one catering to "Polish" Jewish migrants—as well as a Hebrew Benevolent Society (1844) and an asylum for widows and orphans (1856).[35]

When Touro died in 1854, he bequeathed hundreds of thousands of dollars to Jewish causes in New Orleans, in his birthplace of Newport, and beyond, ranging from the Hebrew Congregation of Hartford, Connecticut, to the indigent Jews of Jerusalem.[36] Although few had Touro's resources, many southern Jews were engaged in transnational political and philanthropic activities. Meetings were held in cities across the region in 1840, after Jews in Damascus were accused of ritual murder. When a Jewish emissary from the Holy Land came to the United States in 1849 to raise funds, he garnered support from Jews in New Orleans, Charleston, Richmond, Mobile, and Montgomery.[37] Another round of public meetings and petitions met news of the 1859 Mortara Affair, which involved the kidnapping and secret baptism of a Jewish child in Italy; it must have struck particularly close to home in Catholic-inflected New Orleans.[38] Southern Jews offered aid to coreligionists abroad, and, on some occasions, sought their guidance. When a proposed memorial statue of Touro was decried by some Jews as a graven image that violated the second commandment, members of the Touro Monument Association solicited opinions on the matter from four rabbis, in London, Breslau, Frankfurt, and Prague.[39]

Many of the new migrants went to places with no Jewish infrastructure at all, however, and they worked to build it up. In places like Macon, Georgia, and Vicksburg, Mississippi, Jews created makeshift households in boardinghouses, often overseen by Jewish women, where they received a room and a daily meal in keeping—as best they could—with Jewish dietary laws.[40] When a critical mass emerged, local Jews would purchase a burial ground or found a Hebrew benevolent society. They might gather in rented quarters for High Holiday services one year, and then endeavor to organize a congregation. Next came efforts to purchase a synagogue building, marked by a celebratory consecration ceremony, attended by Christian neighbors and addressed by a Jewish minister visiting for the occasion, as in Galveston. If all went well, they would hire a *hazan*, a nonrabbinic religious functionary, to lead services, teach children, give sermons, and facilitate other necessities of Jewish life. Although they came from European places where Jewish institutions were government funded, migrants now paid out of pocket for religious life, and their leaders were employees of the congregation.[41] And although they were excluded from congregational governance and practice, Jewish women—like their Christian counterparts—were frequently among the most enthusiastic participants and supporters.[42]

Whereas in 1790 there had been only 6 congregations in all of the United States, half of them in the South, one 1856 estimate found 26 congregations in southern states—out of 110 nationwide—with at least a dozen other incipient Jewish communities in the region.[43] In Tennessee, for example, Memphis Jews purchased a burial ground in 1847 and established a congregation in 1853; Nashville Jews hit the same milestones in 1851 and 1854, respectively; and Jews could also be found in the towns of Knoxville and Bolivar.[44] One Memphis Jew wrote in 1855 of his congregation, "Its members are newly assembled here from distant quarters of the world and various sections of the Union. It is natural to infer that different forms have been taught, different habits acquired, different modes of opinion on minor points inculcated."[45] Even as, for many Jews, membership and attendance remained optional, disagreements flourished among congregants and with *hazanim* over matters of language, custom, and religious reforms like mixed seating.

Among other things, leaders expressed disapproval of the ongoing trend of Jewish men marrying Christian women. And yet, such men were increasingly insistent about passing Judaism on to their children. By 1859 C. Goldenberg of New Orleans was regularly performing circumcisions on sons born to Jewish fathers and Christian mothers.[46] Circumcision could be made part of a conversion process, but it is unclear how many children underwent the required immersion in a Jewish ritual bath; according to a later report, Christian mothers "[did] not want to have their children baptised as Jews."[47] These women likely understood circumcision as a family practice, perhaps strange, but on its own negating neither whiteness nor Christianity. Circumcision was a clear marker of Jewish identity, but it was invisible at first sight, and it was linked to paternalistic values that white southerners could understand.[48] Circumcision was in fact one of the most widely practiced Jewish rituals in the South, even in far-flung places without Jewish institutions or skilled circumcisers. Many sons were circumcised well past the eighth day of life, and in at least one case, in Galveston, a new father performed the rite himself. Congregations prioritized hiring functionaries who could perform circumcisions, and a number of skilled *mohalim* began traveling the region.

American Jews were increasingly knit together through the travel of religious functionaries and individuals, through family and correspondence, and through nascent institutions. In and beyond the South they established lodges of B'nai B'rith, a Jewish fraternal order founded in 1843 in New York City.[49] And they subscribed to American Jewish newspapers, beginning with the *Occident and American Jewish Advocate*, founded in 1843 by Isaac Leeser, a Philadelphia *hazan* who had lived in Richmond in the 1820s. The *Occident* had a wide readership in the region, as indicated by mentions of contact with "A Southern Jew," and "A gentleman residing in the interior of one of the Southern States."[50] Leeser regularly published reports of goings on in southern communities; one 1846 issue included notice of Jewish activities in Columbia, South Carolina; Augusta, Georgia; and Claiborne, Alabama.[51] Leeser had a soft spot for the South, writing of Virginia, "We love this old commonwealth." Pointing to the new synagogues constructed in Mobile and New Orleans, he insisted that "more contributions are raised [in the South], in proportion to numbers and means, than in this vicinity."[52]

Sectional tensions led to splits in several Christian denominations in the 1840s and 1850s, but Jewish leaders were just beginning efforts to create a national denominational body out of far-flung congregations.[53] Leeser first attempted to create such a body in 1840 and finally had some success in 1859, in the aftermath of the Mortara Affair. The new Board of Delegates of American Israelites sought to coordinate Jewish political advocacy and religious life; its first meeting included representatives from Richmond, Charleston, New Orleans, Donaldsonville, Norfolk, Jackson, Baton Rouge, Petersburg, and Mobile, along with those from a host of northern cities.[54] The rancor that marked the development of sectional identities among Christians was rare among American Jews, a tiny minority newly linked through the power of travel and the press.

In December 1860, Henry Loewenthal of Macon, Georgia, wrote a letter to the *Israelite*, a Cincinnati newspaper founded by Rabbi Isaac

Mayer Wise. He had recently visited the northern part of Florida, which had become a US state in 1845, in order to perform circumcisions. "In short our brethren here are healthy and wealthy, and are greatly respected by their neighbors for their uprightness and honesty," he wrote, naming the Jewish families in Tallahassee and Quincy. He listed off some of the many other towns in the area—"too many for me, at present to mention"—where Jews could be found. Although the names and places differed, Loewenthal's letter was nearly identical to numerous others that had appeared in the American Jewish press, documenting the spread of Jews throughout the region and the nation and their desire to place themselves on an emerging map of American Judaism. This version, however, was published on December 21, 1860, just one day after South Carolina seceded from the United States. Having spent several decades establishing themselves as members of local communities and as participants in broader Jewish networks, Jews like Loewenthal would soon find themselves divided from their northern coreligionists by a bloody civil war.[55]

CHAPTER 7

Unhappy Contest

On April 12, 1861, as the first shots of the Civil War rang out over Charleston Harbor, newlyweds William and Rosa Flegenheimer boarded a steamer headed to Richmond, Virginia. They met—and had married two days earlier—in Baltimore, but each had also spent time in towns and cities further south. Rosa, an immigrant from Prussia, lived with her family in Elizabeth City, North Carolina, while William, who was from Baden, in the southwest of the German lands, traversed the upper South and the Mississippi Delta as a peddler, a bookkeeper, and a specialist in "fancy writing."[1] A month after they moved to Richmond, he was commissioned to inscribe the Virginia Ordinance of Secession, which accused the federal government of having "perverted [its] powers, not only to the injury of the people of Virginia, but to the oppression of the Southern slaveholding States."[2] As the conflict over slavery transformed into a civil war, Jews like the Flegenheimers, both migrants and those who had been born in the region, made deliberate and sometimes difficult choices. In the process, they established a wide range of relationships with—and made distinctive demands upon—the new Confederate States of America.

Among American Jews and their historians, there has been a prevailing assumption—celebrated by some and bemoaned by others—that southern Jews uniformly embraced the Confederacy. There certainly were many who did, especially acculturated elites in rabidly pro-secession states like South Carolina. And yet, Jews in the South had diverse loyalties and motivations, which could and did shift over the course of the long and bloody conflict and its aftermath. More left the region or tried to evade military service than has typically been remembered. For his part, William Flegenheimer chose to begin his married life in a new nation, built on white supremacy and Protestant Christianity, that he helped literally write into being.

Flegenheimer had spent the previous winter in Washington, DC, and attended the inauguration of Abraham Lincoln; although he later remembered "my sympathies then were quite naturally with the Democrats," a presidential inauguration would have been a spectacle for the twenty-eight-year-old immigrant to behold.[3] The candidate of the seven-year-old Republican Party, Lincoln had won 40 percent of the popular vote but 59 percent of the electoral vote in a crowded field of four candidates.[4] Lincoln was no radical abolitionist, but he was an antislavery unionist, and his election—just over a year after abolitionist John Brown's failed raid at Harpers Ferry—terrified many elite white southerners, whose wealth and power were bound up in the preservation of slavery.[5] South Carolina was the first state to secede, on December 20, claiming that Lincoln was "hostile to slavery" and that nonslaveholding states "encouraged and assisted thousands of our slaves to leave their homes."[6] Two weeks later, Benjamin Mordecai, the Charleston Jewish merchant who was also a prominent slave trader and enslaver, donated $10,000 to the cause.[7]

Mississippi, the second state to secede, also highlighted the issue of slavery; its long list of grievances included the charge that the United States "has enlisted its press, its pulpit and its schools against us, until the whole popular mind of the North is excited and inflamed with prejudice."[8] Indeed, the debate over slavery was not only political and economic but religious, rooted in understandings of biblical history and divine providence. Southern Christians had developed a robust defense of slavery as an active good that enabled the Christianization of enslaved people and protected them within a divinely ordered household.[9] Abolitionists, Black and white, on the other hand, decried slavery as an obvious evil and a gross deviation from biblical principles.[10] Those who would serve in high public offices in the Confederacy, like Louisiana senator Judah Benjamin, publicly defended slavery, but most Jews kept quiet. Take Alfred Mordecai, a son of the late Jacob Mordecai, the North Carolina educator cum Richmond antireformer, who had attended West Point and married a Philadelphian. He wrote at the beginning of the war, "This is the first time that I have attempted to express my opinions on this subject at any length, in writing, & I scarcely even speak of them." A number of factors may have encouraged Jews to stop their pens—personal ambivalence, concern about offending northern coreligionists or Christian neighbors, occupation with mundane matters of daily life, the Christian tenor of the public debate, and for immigrants, the novelty of their political inclusion. Alfred had enslaved at least one person and argued in favor of states' rights, but now, considering the prospect of war, he described slavery as "the greatest misfortune and curse that could have befallen us."[11]

American Jews had very little religious guidance on the topic. The various disincentives to speak on slavery applied also to congregational leaders, who were occupied with problems of religious observance and reform and had to worry about the opinions of the laypeople who employed them. As tensions escalated in early 1861, however, several northern rabbis went on the record on the morality of slavery. At the request of local Christians, Rabbi Morris Raphall of New York gave a public address on January 4, a national day of fasting and prayer called by President James Buchanan. Raphall's address, widely circulated in the South and elsewhere, argued that the Bible did sanction slavery, although like many ministers at the time, he criticized its current practice. He urged "our Southern fellow-citizens [to] adopt the Bible view of slavery, and discard that heathen slave code."[12] Two Baltimore rabbis weighed in on either side of the issue. Rabbi Bernard Illowy delivered a pro-slavery sermon on January 4, asking rhetorically, "Who can blame our brethren of the South for seceding?"; soon after he was offered a post at congregation Gates of Mercy in New Orleans, where he arrived in September 1861.[13] Almost the lone voice of opposition came from Rabbi David Einhorn, who described slavery as "a grievous sin." Jews were, he pointed out, "the offspring of a race which daily praises God for deliverance from the bondage of Egypt." By June Einhorn had been driven out of town, settling first in Philadelphia and ultimately in New York. Like Illowy, he left the slaveholding border city for a place where he could live in greater harmony with his values.[14]

Jewish leaders in southern states avoided the debate over slavery, although they did signal their support for secession. In Richmond, religious functionary George Jacobs of Beth Shalome issued a call for unity, but also prayed:

> If it be Thy will, O Lord! who weighest the destinies of all nations, that we should exist no longer in Union . . . Interpose Thy omnipotent power, that brother shall not lift up hand against brother, but that an equitable and peaceful separation may take place.[15]

Jacobs had been born in Jamaica the same year that slavery was abolished on the island, although he had gone on to enslave people himself. In Memphis, the Hungarian-born leader Simon Tuska responded to a public attack on Jewish honesty by insisting, "The Jews are ready, in common with their Christian brethren, to sacrifice their property and their lives in the defense of southern rights." He invoked the examples of Raphall, Benjamin Mordecai, and Rabbi Isaac Mayer Wise, whose Cincinnati-based *Israelite* clearly reflected his Democratic commitments and southern sympathies.[16] In Richmond, Memphis, and elsewhere white residents debated what path they should follow, in public meetings, hushed conversations, and concerned letters.[17] As Jewish leaders and laypeople contemplated the question of secession, they surely felt the added pressure of public skepticism and the weight of personal experience with capricious Christian publics and modern governments.

From his perch in remote Stevenson, Alabama, Edward Rosewater picked up on the ominous local mood. He wrote in his diary on January 1, 1861, "A strange feeling creeps through my veins. . . . [T]he relations between the Union & States are now looking gloomy." A few days later Rosewater, who had spent time in the abolitionist hotbed of Oberlin, Ohio, hedged his bets. He wrote to a participant in Alabama's secession convention, "ask[ing] him to introduce [a] Bill . . . for exemption of Telegraphers from Military Service."[18] In the following weeks, states continued to secede: by February, Florida, Alabama, Georgia, Louisiana, and Texas. Although his county would ultimately vote against secession, Rosewater heard a steady drumbeat of news and rumors, and he watched Jefferson Davis give a half-hour speech he described as "pretty warlike," which "assured Ala[bam]ans They c[ou]ld whip the Yankees."[19] As the local telegrapher, he was the first in town to read the Confederate Constitution, ratified on March 11, 1861.[20] This document echoed much of the language of the United States Constitution, including that of the First Amendment, which it replicated verbatim. Among the differences were laws protecting and regulating slavery and an addition to the preamble of the phrase "invoking the favor and guidance of Almighty God."[21] Slavery and divine authority were together entrenched as Confederate principles.

On March 21 in Savannah, Confederate vice-president Alexander Stephens celebrated the new Constitution: "With us, all of the white race, however high or low, rich or poor, are equal in the eye of the law. Not so with the negro. Subordination is his place."[22] Other leaders likewise attempted to create a consensus around the new nation by asserting the absolute nature of the color line. James Ferguson Dowdell of Alabama stated, "Let there be but two classes of persons here—the white and the black. Let distinction of color only, be distinction of class."[23] State constitutions affirmed this approach, defining bearers of rights as white men.[24] Those looking could find clear signs that Jews were included among them. The *Charleston Courier* had described Benjamin Mordecai's generous donation as "proof [of] the ancient spirit of Hebrew patriotism which counted no sacrifice too great for the defence of the faith or the country." South Carolina was full of patriotic Jews, the *Courier* argued; after all, they were members of "the race who founded, under God, the first Commonwealth the world has seen."[25] Mississippi newspapers did not mention that Mordecai was a Jew, describing the donation simply as "a patriotic New Year's gift" from "a noble southern citizen."[26]

According to congressman William Porcher Miles, the Confederate Committee on Flag and Seal selected the Saint Andrew's cross instead of the Latin cross because "it avoided the religious objection about the cross (from the Jews & many Protestant sects)," and southern politicians with Jewish roots were among the architects of Confederate power.[27] Abraham Charles Myers would serve as quartermaster general, David de Leon as surgeon general, and most famously, Judah Benjamin would rise to the highest echelons of the Confederate government. Born on the island of Saint Croix but raised in Fayetteville, North Carolina, and Charleston, Benjamin would serve as attorney general, secretary of war, and secretary of state in the Confederacy, and his face appeared on the Confederate two-dollar bill.[28] In 1864 he would write of "our faith in the doctrine that the negro is an inferior race and unfitted for social or political equality with the white man."[29] Judaism was in his family history, but for Benjamin, who largely eschewed Jewish ties in adulthood, white supremacy—the source of his power—was the faith that mattered.

On April 12, as shots were fired at Fort Sumter in Charleston Harbor and the Flegenheimers traveled to Richmond, Edward Rosewater watched the secession flag go up above the Stevenson courthouse.[30] Resistance to secession had been particularly strong in the upper and border South, but in the weeks to come, Lincoln called up US troops, and Virginia, Arkansas, North Carolina, and Tennessee seceded in response.[31] Rosewater noted in his diary that all those "not acknowledging authority [of the] Confederate St[ates are] to leave within 40 Days or to be considered Alien Enemies."[32] His family in Cleveland told him to stay put until the war was over, not because of ideology but because of "hard times with them."[33] Many Jews seem to have been uncertain of the wisdom of secession but unwilling to abandon their economic concerns. Ash Levy, a Richmond slave trader originally from Prussian Poland, wrote immediately after the war that although he had opposed secession, "I felt it to be my duty to go with the State as otherwise, I would have had to abandon my property which was all in the South."[34] Rosanna Osterman, the wife of a wealthy Galveston enslaver, did not want to abandon her assets or the family members they supported, although her "hopes, prayers, and wishes" were for there to be "no disruption between the North + South."[35]

For Jews, perhaps even more so than for other white southerners, commitments to the lives they had built were troubled by close ties to the North and concerns about political upheaval. In April 1861, Lavinia Minis wrote, "I am sick at heart . . . at the news of war. . . . [O]ur beloved country with all its many blessings is to be destroyed."[36] Her Savannah-born husband Abraham, namesake and great-grandson of the early Georgia settler, later recalled of his mother Dina that the "non-intercourse and lack of communication [with her daughters in Philadelphia] made [the war] full of trial + sorrow."[37] Another pair of female relatives felt not only a logistical divide but a political one between Savannah and Philadelphia. In January, Miriam Moses Cohen had written to her northern aunt, Rebecca Gratz, offering her commentary on the secession crisis. She imagined that the epitaph of the United States would read, "Here lies a people who in seeking the liberty of the negro, lost their own."[38] The two women stayed in touch, although later in the war, Gratz, a staunch Unionist, reported that Cohen wrote "not a word of fear or indeed of any thing but personal condition & feelings."[39] Cohen avoided matters of conflict in order to maintain familial ties, but also perhaps as a strategic projection of Confederate strength; if men waged war on the battlefield, women could do so, among other places, on the page.[40]

Men also felt the drama and pain of familial division, however; over a year into the conflict, a New York–born Jew living in Melbourne, Australia, was surprised by the split among his relations, writing to a cousin:

> Your remarks respecting the family at New Orleans has indeed caused us much surprise, for with all the bitter feeling and animosity displayed by the southern people I was not prepared to, neither can I believe that sectional prejudices could have estranged the family at N.O. to the extent of acting as you describe, other causes must have operated or letter have miscarried and I hope to hear such is the case in your next.[41]

From across the world, the intensity of the conflict seemed incomprehensible. But up close in New Orleans—as in Charleston, Richmond, and elsewhere—passions flared. In June 1861, members of the Jewish congregation in Shreveport complained about the New York *Jewish Messenger*'s Unionist sentiments. They passed resolutions describing it as "a black republican paper, and not worthy for Southern patronage," and vowed to cease subscription to "all Northern papers opposed to our holy cause."[42] Henry S. Jacobs, brother of Richmond's George Jacobs and the religious leader in Augusta, Georgia, agreed, later recalling that he had "abandon[ed] the agency of the paper and even my continuance as a subscriber in a letter which was rather caustic."[43] In the face of new political realities, far-flung Jewish families and networks formed deep fissures.

The *Jewish Messenger* had predicted in December 1860, "We may see those who have hitherto looked upon each other as brothers, meet one another as foes," and by the spring of 1861, white southerners had begun to mobilize for war.[44] Alfred Mordecai, who was married to Rebecca Gratz's niece Sarah, was recruited to join the Confederate side and urged by his family to do so.[45] He declined the offer, but also resigned his post in the US military in order to "avoid engaging in this unhappy contest against my kindred"; his son served in the United States army, while several of his nephews served in the Confederate army.[46] The elderly Dina Minis reportedly "dreaded to see grand-sons on both sides."[47] By that summer, Gratz had heard from her niece that "there is not a young man *at home* in all their large connection—of course they have all gone to fight against us!"[48] The trustees of Congregation Beth Israel in Macon, Georgia, passed a resolution exempting all soldiers from paying dues.[49]

In truth, not all Jewish men were eager soldiers.[50] In Florida, half of all Jewish men of military age eventually served in the Confederate military in some capacity, but only 11 percent volunteered in 1861, compared with 39 percent of all eligible Floridians.[51] The service records of those Jews who did serve in the Confederate army have been zealously compiled in local Jewish histories and in Simon Wolf's 1895 apologia, *The Jew as Patriot, Citizen and Soldier*. The most commonly cited, if imperfect, statistic is that around two thousand Jews served in the Confederate military, about a third of the numbers of the United States army, which had over twice as many enlisted men and access to a larger share of the American Jewish population.[52] Of those who served, the full-throated "Jewish Confederates"—many of them born southerners—are among the best documented and most studied.

Take the oft-reproduced photograph of Joshua Lazarus, Perry, and Isaac Harby Moses, three of five South Carolina brothers who served. Joshua and Perry enlisted on May 9 at ages twenty-one and seventeen, respectively (figure 7.1).[53] In the photo, taken early in the conflict, Joshua stands protectively behind his younger brothers, his hand, along with Isaac's, resting on Perry's shoulder. The Civil War was the first American conflict in which photography was widespread, and men going off to war regularly had their portraits taken to document their bravery for posterity and in case of death.[54] The Moses boys joined in the practice, presenting themselves as valiant Confederate soldiers and affectionate brothers.[55] Both of their parents were Charleston Jews; their father, a man named Andrew Jackson Moses, enslaved over thirty men, women, and children and their mother, Octavia Harby Moses, was the daughter of famed Charleston religious reformer Isaac Harby.[56] These brothers surely understood volunteering to be the obvious choice for honorable South Carolina gentlemen.

Men with more recent—and much humbler—southern roots were also among the volunteers. In Florida, most of them were single young men with little to lose, and of the forty-five who would serve over the course of the war, only one was an enslaver, with just 16 percent coming from slaveholding households.[57] Lewis Leon, a twenty-year-old clerk who volunteered for the Confederate army eight days after Fort Sumter, fit this profile. Leon had been born in Mecklenburg and arrived in Charlotte, North Carolina, by way of New York City, only three years earlier.[58] Jewish immigrants like Leon were attracted by the usual inducements of war—improved prospects, adventure, and a sense of belonging—but they also came from places in Europe where Jewish military service was highly politicized, alternately forbidden and used as a means of Jewish modernization.[59]

Philip Whitlock, an immigrant from Poland, volunteered for service in the Richmond Grays, later claiming, "I was very patriotic and loved the country of my adoption ... and thought that if I am negligent in my duty

FIGURE 7.1. From top, clockwise, Joshua Lazarus, Perry, and Isaac Harby Moses, Collection of Anne F. Jennings. Image courtesy of Special Collections, College of Charleston Libraries.

as a citizen of this country it would unfavorably reflect on the whole Jewish race and religion."[60] Jews might understand Confederate military service as an expression or vehicle of citizenship in a nation, or as an idealistic rebellion against the authority of an overbearing state. Jews had been prominent as rebels in the failed liberal European revolutions of 1848; among them was William Flegenheimer, who had fought as a teenager in Baden and was imprisoned by the Prussian Army. He did not volunteer for the Confederate army, but then again, his wife was pregnant at the time.[61] Whatever their motives, once they enlisted, Jewish men clothed in gray Confederate uniforms, immersed in the intensity of camp life, and fighting in battle, became members of a community of men working to defend slavery and white supremacy.[62] In his wartime diary Leon wrote reverently of the bravery of "our Father [General Robert E.] Lee," and on his twenty-first birthday he boasted that he was "doing a man's duty."[63]

Military service was not the only option for Jews who wanted to do their duty. Jewish men sold supplies to the Confederate army and to individual soldiers.[64] Women were encouraged to use their domestic skills in support to the war effort, which expanded their participation in public life. Across the region new groups put women to work sewing, knitting, collecting donations, and organizing benefits.[65] In July 1861, a local North Carolina paper recorded "$150 received from 'Jewish ladies' of Charlotte" and praised "the Jews of the town for their general liberality and patriotism manifested in the cause of the South."[66] Emma Mordecai, Alfred's unmarried sister and a longtime resident of Richmond, took food to soldiers in local hospitals, describing them in her diary as "noble, uncomplaining, all enduring heroes."[67] Rosanna Osterman, despite her opposition to secession, made donations to the hospitals in Houston and Galveston.[68] Two Jewish sisters from Charleston became especially prominent supporters of the Confederacy. Eugenia Levy Phillips, who was married to a former Alabama congressman, was arrested in Washington, DC, and imprisoned on suspicion of spying for the Confederacy; her sister Phoebe Pember served as superintendent of Richmond's Chimborazo hospital.[69]

Like their Christian neighbors, Jews participated in regular days of fasting, humiliation, and prayer and they heard sermons that cast the

Confederacy as God's chosen people.[70] In New Orleans, Bernard Illowy prayed, "O Lord, plead and vindicate thou, O Father, our cause: shield and guard thou our beloved country under the shadow of thy paternal love, and save us, thy children, from the fratricidal hands of the threatening and advancing enemy."[71] Maximilian J. Michelbacher of Richmond further elaborated his hopes that God would protect "the sons of the sunny South, to face the foe, to drive him back, and to defend our natural rights." The collective he invoked was more explicitly Jewish; he asked for God to "Be unto the Army of this Confederacy as thou wert of old, unto us, thy chosen people!"[72] There was a long tradition of Jewish prayers for the government, most importantly the formulaic "Hanoten Teshua," an early modern Hebrew prayer.[73] Nevertheless, these leaders crafted their own prayers, in English, communicating Jewish loyalty and invoking God's favor with new martial urgency.

Michelbacher offered Jewish support for the Confederacy, but he also made demands on it. On August 23, 1861, he wrote the first in a series of letters to General Robert E. Lee on behalf of "a class of citizens being Israelites, who take the greatest interest in the welfare of this confederacy." Michelbacher explained that the autumnal High Holidays were approaching and requested a two-week furlough on behalf of soldiers "of the Jewish persuasion." Addressing Lee "as a commander and as a Christian," he made the request "in the name of God, whom all of us do worship, who is the Ruler of Nations and the God of Battle," and insisted that its fulfillment would invite God's blessings.[74] The Jewish holiday season, stretching over three weeks, included seven days during which Jewish law demanded the cessation of work as well as worship in the company of ten adult Jewish men and a Torah scroll. If serving in the military was one among several competing expressions of southern manhood—along with providing for one's family, for instance—for Jewish men, fulfilling religious obligations was another.[75] Michelbacher described a common ground of piety and patriotism, however, casting Jews as citizens of a particular faith who wanted merely to "participate in holy services." This language helped situate Jews as pious Confederates, even as the request itself highlighted their deviation from a de facto Protestantism.[76]

In the early part of the war, camps were raucous and impious spaces, and even Protestant worship was hard to come by.[77] Lee refused Michelbacher's request, but did so by affirming his framing of southern Jews as loyal Confederates: "I feel assured that neither you or any member of the Jewish congregation would wish to jeopardize a cause you have so much at heart."[78] Michelbacher made similar requests at least two other times during the war, and was repeatedly refused on the basis of military necessity and because "it is impossible to grant a general furlough to one class of our soldiers."[79] Similar exchanges occurred with lower-level military officials as well; toward the end of the war, Emma Mordecai made note of a soldier who "got leave of absence from his command, came up to keep the day [Yom Kippur, in Richmond], walking all the way from Chaffin's Bluff after performing much arduous duty."[80] Jewish sacred time was distinct in its calendar and in the contours of its observance—this is why the soldier walked instead of rode to services—requiring Jews to solicit and military officials to consider special accommodations.

The number of Jews who might need such accommodations expanded in April of 1862, when the Confederate government passed the first conscription act in American history, requiring all men aged eighteen to thirty-five to serve. Jewish immigrants were no strangers to conscription, although their experiences and attitudes varied. While Prussian Jews had advocated for conscription as a vehicle of Jewish emancipation, the Russian Empire was notorious for its conscription policies. It required long terms of service for Jews as young as twelve years old, and passed the duty of filling conscription quotas on to local Jewish communities.[81] Philip Whitlock had vivid memories of his cousin's forced conscription in Russia, which may have been one motive for his emigration, although he still enlisted. Over the course of the war, nine Jewish Floridians furnished substitutes to serve in their stead, at a hefty price; others served in local militias or civil service jobs rather than in the army; and some fled the Confederacy altogether.[82] Samuel Fleishman of Marianna, Florida, for instance, went to New York while his family stayed behind, and David Steinheimer, a Bavarian subject, started the war in Georgia before leaving for Pittsburgh.[83] He later remembered, "I got [a] spell of the blues for I did not believe in war."[84] He would have been eligible for an immigrant exemption, but he may have been suspicious, since these often relied on support from foreign consuls; Jews like Steinheimer had reason to doubt that they could fully rely on representatives from German lands, where their rights continued to be the subject of heated debate.[85]

The Conscription Act included various exemptions, for immigrants, the medically compromised, and for ministers, providing another site where Confederate officials were compelled to interact with Jews *as Jews*.[86] Initially, "ministers of religion" were exempted, but in the fall of 1862 an early draft of a new conscription act apparently included only "ministers of the gospel." The *Richmond Dispatch* editorialized, "Whilst this is a Christian country . . . the Jewish ministers are entitled to exemption on the principals of the Constitution."[87] It is unclear who raised this issue, although Richmond was home to two vocal pro-Confederate Jewish ministers, Jacobs and Michelbacher. Furthermore, over the summer there had been a similar, and more protracted, debate in the Union about the military chaplaincy, which had originally been limited to "regularly ordained minister[s] of a Christian denomination." After the controversy it was changed to "some religious denomination."[88] The Confederate law quickly returned to the language of "every minister of religion," stipulating that each be "authorized to preach according to the rules of his sect and in the regular discharge of ministerial duties."[89] As in the Union, explicit Christian privilege gave way to more subtle forms of Protestant dominance, albeit in the name of military exemption rather than service. Both laws assumed the universality of "ministers" as religious leaders; the United States further naturalized denominations, and the Confederate States preaching, as religious norms.

In fact, there were few ordained rabbis in southern communities at the time, no formal Jewish denominational body, and preaching was still a novelty. Jack-of-all-trades religious functionaries led services, slaughtered meat, and fulfilled other communal religious needs, usually adopting the title "Reverend." The ill fit between Protestant conceptions of religious leadership and contemporary American Judaism could cut both ways. On the one hand, Simon Gerstmann of Savannah gained a ministerial exemption, even though he was merely a volunteer service leader working under Jacob Rosenfeld at Benai Berith Jacob. On the other hand, this required a constant stream of letters to Joseph E. Brown, the governor of Georgia, to whom he eventually admitted, "according to the Hebrew Religion they have no minister as they are generally termed but they have readers which answer to the term minister or pastor in the Christian Church."[90] As the new Confederate States of America went to war, its white male residents had to decide first whether or not to enlist and then how to respond to conscription. Jews faced these questions with a particular set of concerns, rooted in communal history and religious practice. In their requests, Michelbacher and Gerstmann confidently and pointedly reminded officials of these issues. In so doing, they insisted that the Confederacy was not only a Protestant republic but a multireligious one, in fact if not in self-conception or policy.[91]

CHAPTER 8

Infernal Crusade

In September 1862, Isaac Hirsch of Fredericksburg, Virginia, surveyed the scene following the Confederate victory at the Second Battle of Bull Run. He wrote in his diary: "I left the field with a heavy heart, as I had never seen the Romance of War in this shape before." He was troubled by the scene of "dead Yankees [who] could not be buried as I don't like to see any human being lay on the top of the earth and rot." The horrors of this scene were clear to anyone present, but it would have had a particular resonance for Hirsch, as a Jew. A rapid and respectful burial was among the religious practices that American Jews took most seriously, and it was now clearly denied to these "dead Yankees," including any Jews among them. Nevertheless, Hirsch determined, echoing Ezekiel 37, "It is a fit emblem for the invader of our soil for his bones to bleach on the soil he invades, especially of a people that wish to be left alone and settle down to their peaceful pursuits."[1] His revulsion at mass death was conditioned by his experience with Jewish practice, even as biblical text undergirded his overriding commitment to the Confederate cause.

By the fall of 1862, United States forces had captured Nashville, New Orleans, and Memphis, and a blockade was causing acute shortages of food, supplies, and currency within the Confederacy.[2] In Natchez, a Jewish child named Rosalie Beekman became the sole casualty, injured when the USS *Essex* shelled the city.[3] Edward Rosewater enlisted in the US army in Nashville and went to work at the War Department in

Washington. On January 1, 1863, he would send Abraham Lincoln's Emancipation Proclamation over the telegraph lines. Echoing William Flegenheimer's transcription of Virginia's secession, Rosewater facilitated the order offering legal freedom to the enslaved population of the seceded states.[4] Emancipation was not only a top-down process, however; large numbers of enslaved people had already begun to flee toward United States troops.[5] Support for the war and eagerness to serve were never universal, and mounting military setbacks further wearied many within the Confederacy. African Americans seeking freedom, women stranded at home, nonslaveholding whites, and even enlisted men became increasingly dissatisfied with the conditions of war.[6] For Jews, the disappointment was intensified by the dawning realization that white Confederate citizenship was not as inclusive as it initially had seemed.[7]

Amid a general mood of waning optimism, Christian revivals began to spread, first in the Army of Northern Virginia. According to one observer, the camps were "nearly converted into churches," with regular sermons and prayer meetings offering succor and solidarity. There were Jews among the new converts, but others stood by as spectators, surely feeling their distance from the proceedings and their fellow soldiers. In some moments at least, Jewish soldiers would have felt themselves to be serving in a Christian army.[8] In addition to being confronted with Christian fervor and surrounded by Christian assumptions, Jewish soldiers were estranged from Jewish community and observance. Outside of Yorktown, for instance, Edwin Kursheedt reported that he had depleted his private food supply, leaving him with army rations of non-kosher "bacon + crackers." He confessed, "I enjoyed the latter, but have not made up my mind to partake of the former."[9] In September 1863, Lewis Leon wrote, "I went to see the fight. I saw the enemy very plainly, and thus I spent my New Year's Day."[10] Jewish understandings of right eating and the organization of time were challenged, but not eliminated, by war.

Letters and diary entries otherwise filled with news about weather and furloughs, safety and danger, show Jewish soldiers coping with these distinctive challenges. Isaac Levy misremembered the date of Passover, but was nevertheless able to "observe the festival in a truly

Orthodox style," since his brother had purchased *matzah* and kosher beef in Charleston.[11] Kursheedt noted, "Since I have been here I have met with many of my New Orleans friends who are in the army, making me feel almost at home."[12] The home front and the battlefield were overlapping spaces, on top of which these men layered a map of Jewish networks that could offer religious and social support. Phillip Whitlock remembered Jewish families in Norfolk who invited him for meals and entertainment and cared for him when he was sick.[13] Marcus Spiegel, a US soldier, echoed these experiences, writing to his wife, "I have had lots of fun since I am in the Service and Especially in Virginia with Yehudim [Jews]," who invited him to dinner and gave him free board.[14] John Mayer of Natchez offered his hospitality to US sutlers Henry Frank and Isaac Lowenburg, who eventually stayed in town and married two of Mayer's daughters.[15] In Nashville there were Jews who worked to ensure the proper burial of Jewish Union soldiers as well as Confederate ones.[16] In these cases, at least, Jewish religious ties proved more important than "enemy" status.

Jewish loyalty—like loyalty more generally—was varied and amorphous, but it was also a matter of special scrutiny and fear, in both the United States and the Confederacy. In December, Union general Ulysses S. Grant issued General Orders no. 11, which proclaimed, "The Jews, as a class violating every regulation of trade established by the Treasury Department and also department orders, are hereby expelled from the department [of Tennessee]," a sizeable section of the occupied South.[17] Its enforcement was quickly impeded, however, first by a surprise Confederate attack and then by President Abraham Lincoln, who had been flooded with letters of protest from outraged Jewish individuals and groups.[18] Wartime antisemitism was not isolated to Grant or to the Union, however. A few months earlier there had been a gathering at the courthouse In Thomasville, Georgia, regarding "a class of German Jews, located among us, engaged in extortions in trade . . . [who] have no feeling common with the Confederacy." Those gathered had unanimously voted to prohibit German Jewish peddlers from entering Thomas County and to give local Jews—amounting to three families— ten days to leave.[19]

Georgia Jews responded with three public statements that pointed to their collective patriotism and to the injustice of ascribing the misdeeds of a few to the many. A group of Jewish soldiers, led by the Prussian-born Charles Wessolowsky, invoked gendered notions of bravery and belonging in the Savannah *Republican*: "[We are] willing . . . to struggle for our adopted country, to sacrifice all that is dear to us, to abandon our second home, and leave our wives and children to the care of strangers." Another letter, written by Jews serving in the Tattnall Guards, claimed that the Thomasville resolutions would "inaugurate a system of proscription and ostracism, from which humanity shrinks back with horror, and which would speedily tend to undermine and overthrow all the foundations of society." They indicted the kind of racism undergirding slavery, with little self-awareness, and echoed the potent fears its potential abolition instigated. Yet another group invoked more lofty ideals; the Thomasville resolutions were "at war with the spirit of the age—the letter of the constitution—and the principles of religion." With slightly different emphases and strategies, all three groups sought to defend their honor and to reshape popular understandings of Confederate identity.[20]

The early strain of Confederate discourse emphasizing white unity was rapidly breaking down. One soldier explained the Confederacy's setbacks as the outcome of insufficient Christian piety: "Certainly, if all our people were Christians, the war would soon end, for then every man would do his duty, and that is all we need to whip the Yankees."[21] In speeches and other writings, Confederate leaders placed the blame for their nation's troubled state on Jews, drawing on centuries of Christian suspicion of Jewish foreignness, greed, and political malfeasance. Savannah lawyer and Confederate officer George Anderson Mercer classed "Jews of the lower order" with "Yankee shopkeepers," and argued that "the Jews, who nearly all claim foreign protection, and thus avoid service, are the worst people we have among us."[22] The *Richmond Enquirer* identified "the Jew, whose ample pockets were stuffed with confederate money," as among those "foreigners" rushing to flee the Confederacy.[23] Even Judah P. Benjamin, who had distanced himself from his Jewish background, was continually identified—and denigrated—as a Jew. South Carolina diarist Mary Chestnut called him "Mr. Davis' pet Jew," and politician Thomas R. R. Cobb wrote, "A grander rascal than this Jew Benjamin does not exist in the Confederacy, and I am not particular in concealing my opinion of him."[24] At a time when norms seemed to be dramatically breaking down, white Christian southerners placed responsibility at the feet of those who stood outside Christianity, and, it was assumed, by extension, civilized morality.

In particular, Jews were readily linked to the "sins" of extortion and disloyalty, which many understood to be the causes of the Confederacy's setbacks.[25] In Talbotton, Georgia, weeks after the Thomasville meeting, a grand jury issued a statement blaming local Jews for extortion and speculation: We "advise and admonish our people to have as little as possible to do with this class, of no advantage to us, in any respect whatsoever."[26] Others raised more general fears about Jewish economic domination. Confederate congressman Henry Foote proclaimed in an 1863 speech, "The end of the war would probably find nearly all the property of the Confederacy in the hands of Jewish Shylocks."[27] A Florida representative argued that Jews "swarmed here as the locusts of Egypt. They ate up the substance of the country, they exhausted its supplies, they monopolized its trade."[28] There were Jews, some of whom had experience dodging border police in Europe, who illicitly crossed borders to speculate, but they were far from alone in finding ways to profit, and the public imagination—drawing on sources both biblical and literary—greatly inflated their numbers.[29]

In July of 1863 the United States claimed a crucial victory at the Battle of Gettysburg in Pennsylvania and occupied the river town of Vicksburg, Mississippi.[30] Witnessing bloody battles and ongoing setbacks, some soldiers looked for a way out. Isaac Arnold, a young Jewish immigrant, had enlisted in May 1861 in the Eighth Alabama Regiment, which was the first in the Confederacy to enlist "for the War"—however long or short—rather than for a limited period. He likely expected a speedy resolution, and by 1863, he had decided to make a run for it. More than 25 percent of immigrant soldiers in the Army of Northern Virginia deserted, as did 14 percent of southerners, who served tantalizingly close to their homes and families.[31] By 1863 desertion had become a serious hindrance to the Confederate army, and so when Arnold was captured and found guilty of desertion, he was sentenced to death.[32]

Styling himself "the Senior Minister of the Hebrews of the State," Richmond's Maximilian J. Michelbacher wrote to Robert E. Lee again, this time on Arnold's behalf. He described Arnold as "quite a young man, and without a relative in our country . . . [whose] heart and soul have always been and are now with the armies of the Confederate States of America in truth and honor."[33] Arnold's sentence was suspended, probably owing to the acute need for soldiers as much as to Michelbacher's advocacy. Later that year, Isaac Mayer Wise of Cincinnati wrote to officials in Washington, DC, requesting the release of a group of Jewish prisoners of war. He reported that "they were forced into the service of the Confederacy and were desirous to return to civil life as loyal and peaceable citizens."[34] In both cases, Confederate Jewish soldiers sought an exit from military service and Jewish leaders served as their advocates, making the case for their loyalty, whether to the Confederacy or to the United States.

This advocacy was shaped by religious sentiment and reputational concern. In his defense of Arnold, Michelbacher had emphasized his pitiable situation and his sincere loyalty, but also added:

> We fear that the fact of being an Israelite and of foreign birth has had an injurious tendency toward the decision of his deplorable fate—we hope for the sake of the common humanity of our race, that this report may be untrue. You, we feel assured, would not hesitate were it necessary to testify to the courage and soldierlike abilities of the Israelites in those legions of our beloved Confederacy.[35]

A week and a half later, Michelbacher gave a fast-day sermon responding to accusations of Jewish disloyalty more publicly. He argued that Jews were "not speculators nor extortioners" but enthusiastic soldiers and citizens, emphasizing their manliness and piety. He described Jewish "patriotism and valor [which has] never been doubted by such men as the magnanimous souls of Lee, Johnston, Jackson, and others of like manhood" and explained that Jews understood "the duties of the citizen [as] intimately associated with the services [owed] to God." He invoked the biblical figure of Nehemiah as a model and explicitly prayed that "the man-servants and the maid-servants Thou hast given unto us, that we may be merciful to them in righteousness and bear rule over them."[36] Whereas in earlier addresses Michelbacher had sidestepped the question of slavery, now, placed on the defensive, he publicly prayed for its perpetuation.

Later historians shared Michelbacher's concern about the reputation of American Jews, which is why stories of Jewish doubt and desertion have largely been forgotten. And yet, they need not be read as proof that those who doubted all Jews' loyalty were right; rather, they should be read as proving the humanity and complexity of Jewish southerners, who had good reason to doubt the beneficence and future longevity of the Confederacy and who were far from alone in taking action on such doubts. Southern Jews—and indeed "the South"—did not speak in one voice. There were those who remained committed to the Confederate cause. Soon after the occupation of New Orleans, Eugenia Levy Philips was imprisoned (again) in New Orleans for insulting US soldiers, and teenager Clara Solomon lamented in her diary, "I am sick at heart. . . . We are conquered but not subdued." Nine days later, she attended synagogue, where Rabbi James K. Gutheim "prayed earnestly for the Confederacy."[37] Gutheim and most of his congregation left the city rather than remain under United States rule. There were also southern Jews who bought slaves and made large sales for Confederate currency late in the conflict, demonstrating their faith in the nation.[38] These Jews nursed their hopes for Confederate victory in public and in private, but for at least one this was not enough. In North Carolina, Elizabeth Parker explained, "Supporting my home means also supporting [my neighbors'] God"; she converted to Christianity, which she understood to offer her both salvation and acceptance.[39]

Parker's conversion indicates that even as Jews shared in the struggles of war, defended their honor, and positioned themselves as white southerners, the boundary between Jews and Christians continued to be a meaningful one. In highly local contexts, Jews negotiated what it meant to be both Jews and southern men and women. In April 1864, Nat Strauss, a thirty-year-old immigrant from Alsace, was working for the commandant of conscription in Tallahassee.[40] His feelings, experiences, and commitment to epistolary friendship in many ways marked him as a soldier like any other.[41] "Every eye now is turned toward Virginia as the Mecca of our independence," he wrote to Adolph Proskauer, adding a prayer that, "God grant that we may not be disappointed." When Proskauer began to fight William Tecumseh Sherman's army in Georgia in May 1864, Strauss wrote, "Involuntarily my imagination pictured to me among the scenes of horror that marked the spot of the conflict, the familiar form of the friend, that but a few short weeks I grasped by the hand."[42]

Strauss's thoughts were occupied with his friends elsewhere but also with the small corner of the Confederacy where he had been placed. He initially wrote of Tallahassee, "Sunday all the year round [there is] not a soul in the street."[43] Despite this piety, in July 1864 he witnessed the violent lynching of a Black youth in retaliation for speaking to a white woman, a scene that would be repeated hundreds of times across the region in the decades to come. A large crowd had assembled "to see a human life launched into eternity." From Strauss's perspective, "The worse of it was that it was a mere boy . . . the ends of justice demanded his death, + a morbid appetite of man had to be satisfied, by the delectable spectacle." Strauss was troubled by the violent racism he saw, and by the war itself, which he variously described as "a war . . . that for horrors, atrocities, + outrages, has no parallel in history," a "carnival of blood," and an "infernal crusade."[44]

The choice of the term "crusade" was not incidental. Strauss attended several local church services, and he offered a sharp analysis of the theological confusion brought on by the Civil War, which he described as "a simple method to refute all the vagaries of those blatant Christians." At once an insider and an outsider to the Confederacy, he was particularly troubled by northern and southern Christians' equally vociferous claims to God's favor, which led him to ask, "Which is the right Jesus?" and to argue, referencing the popular line from Ezekiel, "The thousands upon thousands who have fallen a sacrifice on the altar of their <u>Christian</u> country + whose bones now lie bleaching on the plains + mountains of nearly every state will be an ample refutation of that claimed for efficacy of holy + catholic Christianity."[45] His experiences of the war fostered a critical perspective on Christianity but also seemed to deepen Strauss's Jewish commitments; he mused, "I am now assured that another Messiah will have to appear before matters will change materially. What say you, to waiting for ours?"[46] His Judaism helped create distance from the pervasive racism and Christianity around him, even as he continued to serve a nation that celebrated both.

Around the same time, Emma Mordecai moved to her Christian sister-in-law's farm outside Richmond, where she kept close track of the war news. "The enemy seem to be making an attack on all sides," she wrote in her diary on May 10, 1864; on October 1, "The unfavorable news from the Valley filled me with uneasiness about our boys there."[47] She too found private succor through prayer, which allowed for a shared religious sentiment with Christians: "I still feel undismayed & pray God to enable us to endure whatever awaits us in the way of evil."[48] After Richmond was evacuated on May 2, 1865, she wrote, "We must submit ourselves to Him—that in thus doing we were not humble before our foes but before God."[49] Mordecai also read the Bible and attended church with her sister-in-law, where she "heard some excellent remarks by good Mr. Walker upon the present state of things & our duty under them."[50]

Nevertheless, she too earnestly expressed her Jewish commitments. She returned to Richmond for holidays and religious services—noting that at the synagogue "very few [worshippers were] there"—and she prayed Jewish liturgy on her own.[51] On the holiday of Shavuot, she "read the services and reminded myself of my peculiar duties as an Inheritor of law given to us by Him who said 'I, the Lord, change not.'"[52] She eulogized her friend Isaac Levy as:

a fine young soldier, killed in the trenches near Petersb[ur]g. He & his brother Ezekiel Levy have observed their religion faithfully, ever since they have been in the army, never even eating forbidden food. . . . Isaac was an example to all young men of any faith—to those of his own most especially. A true Israelite without guile—a soldier of the Lord & a soldier of the South.[53]

Mordecai's masculine ideal was telling. Whereas Strauss had ridiculed Christianity in letters to a friend, she avoided discussing it directly, even in her private diary. Instead she gingerly presented Judaism as one faith among unnamed others. Like Strauss, however, she made the case that Judaism was equally suitable—if not more so—to the enactment of gendered Confederate patriotism.

As Emma Mordecai found in Richmond, wartime conditions severely challenged established Jewish communities. In Macon, the sole candidate for religious leader in June 1864 was a Mr. L. Z. Sternheimer, a man who had previously served the congregation without satisfaction and who was now suspected of "having knowingly circulated spurious and counterfitted [sic]" Confederate currency.[54] In Natchez in October, the congregation began to regroup, "the disturbances of the times having scattered each member all over the country."[55] Charleston's Kahal Kadosh Beth Elohim (KKBE) synagogue sustained considerable damage, and much of the congregation's precious Judaica, sent to Columbia for safekeeping in the war's last days, burned with that city.[56] Meanwhile, in New Orleans, Bernard Illowy (possibly the man depicted in figure 8.1) was fighting a furious campaign to reimpose traditional Jewish law. A group of young newcomers, having failed to create their own congregation, was now trying to introduce reforms within his congregation. An ally argued that they aimed to "conquer and [cause] the old Southerners [to] be subjugated."[57] Illowy also chastised local *mohalim* for circumcising the sons of Jewish men and non-Jewish women, worrying that they "would pass as Jews," although violating the principle of matrilineal descent. In early 1865, he wrote a manifesto discouraging conversion to Judaism.[58] Even as individuals committed to the United States and the Confederate States commingled in the occupied city, and coreligionists in other southern communities struggled to keep basic features of Jewish life afloat, Illowy fretted over what he saw as the overly porous boundary between Jew and Christian.

On April 9, 1865, Confederate general Robert E. Lee surrendered to US general Ulysses S. Grant at Appomattox Court House in Virginia. Emma Mordecai had first heard about it from "negro news," and when Grant's army passed victoriously northward through Richmond, she

FIGURE 8.1. *Portrait of a Hazan or Rabbi* by Henry Mosler (1869). The painting is thought to depict Rabbi Bernard Illowy. Gift of the Skirball Foundation, Skirball Museum, Skirball Cultural Center, Los Angeles, CA.

was standing on the roof of a neighbor's home. She described it as a "living stream, in one compact mass pouring up the road, as far as the eye could reach in both directions." Still committed to the now-dead Confederacy, she wrote, "They have finished their work of destruction and subjugation." Of course, the presence of the United States army was far from over, and it had also helped accomplish the emancipation of the South's enslaved population. This was likely what Mordecai had in mind when she first heard confirmation of Confederate defeat: "I felt terrified as to what the consequences might be, and my fears absorbed my grief."[59]

The transition to peacetime was disorienting. Freed people were "all doing as they please, and no one asserting any authority over them." As she saw it, "They will now begin to find out how easy their life as <u>slaves</u> has been, + feel the slavery of their freedom."[60] Like other white southerners, she spewed the racist belief that freed people were unable to attend to their own needs. And yet, she also reported that she "felt stiff and sore with [her] unaccustomed labours." In the absence of enslaved laborers, she was reduced to performing domestic "drudgery" and selling gold trinkets, cakes, and strawberries to support herself.[61] Walking through the streets of Richmond, she described "a strange looking place, with its heap of ruins, its streets traversed by U.S. Army wagons—sidewalks thronged with Yankee soldiers and saucy Negro women."[62] Twenty-six year-old Charlestonian Eleanor H. Cohen echoed this reflection: she wrote, "Peace has come, but, oh, God, what a different peace to the one we prayed for. . . . How it makes my Southern blood boil to see [Yankees] in our streets!"[63] Women who had been removed from the battlefield now felt the drama of war in new ways as they witnessed its consequences within urban space. Leaders of KKBE had to petition US military officials to regain control of their synagogue.[64]

The end of the war looked different through the eyes of the men who had fought it. Flegenheimer, who had worked as a clerk in the quartermaster department, entered the army only at the end of the war, and he spent the early part of 1865 in a Richmond hospital. He later remembered, "The war with all its horrors went on and I was constantly in the service in camp and on guard duty until the evacuation of the city."[65] Others, like Charles Wessolowsky and Lewis Leon, had been captured by US forces and finished out the war as prisoners.[66] Leon begrudgingly "took the cursed oath" of the United States and stopped in New York to visit family on his way southward.[67] Of course, there were many others who died in what is still the bloodiest war in American history. Joshua Lazarus Moses was killed at Fort Blakely in the last days of the war, although the brothers with whom he had so optimistically posed at its outset both survived. Eleanor Cohen eulogized him as "poor Josh Moses, the flower of our circle ... a noble man, another martyr to our glorious cause."[68] Confederate mourning was produced by Jews as well as by Christians, in a shared English language and in an unfamiliar Hebrew one.

In Richmond, Reverend George Jacobs kept a list of the soldiers whose funerals he had performed; they came from Louisiana, Texas, and South Carolina, as well as Virginia.[69] Charleston's Jewish cemetery records the fates of Isaac D. Valentine, felled in June 1862 during the battle of Sessionville; of Isaac Barrett Cohen, killed in January 1865 at Fort Fisher; and of Marx E. Cohen Jr., killed on March 19, 1865, at age 26, "on the battlefield of Bentonsville, N.C. . . . by volunteering the performance of a service in which he lost his life."[70] In death these men were cast as heroic Jewish Confederates, although in life those two identities did not always prove so stable or harmonious, in personal experience or in the minds of their fellow white southerners. For them, the war was over, but for the families and communities that survived them it would last much longer, confronting them with important new choices about how to understand the recent past and what kind of future to build.

CHAPTER 9

Scattered Nation

Andrew Jackson Moses, whose son Joshua had been killed in battle, described himself as "a very heavy loser by the War." US troops had pillaged his store and burned his cotton, and he was no longer, as he had once been, "the owner of Thirty-two freedmen," an oxymoron that pointed to the disturbance he felt at Black emancipation.[1] His troubles were economic and psychological; he had been stripped not only of his property but of his place as the white male master of an inviolable household.[2] The emancipation of enslaved people and the transformation of southern communities had begun as early as the fall of 1861, when the US navy conquered the Sea Islands of South Carolina. It continued everywhere that the US military entered seceded territory, with growing force after the Emancipation Proclamation of 1863 and the Confederate surrender at Appomattox in April 1865.[3] As formerly enslaved people became free laborers and citizens, they contested the bounds of freedom and remade the social and economic fabric of their communities. As they did so, white southerners' attitudes ranged from sympathetic advocacy to murderous violence.[4] Jews would variably be counted among their number and their victims.

Emma Mordecai was particularly troubled by a man named Cyrus, formerly enslaved by her sister-in-law, who claimed "he had a right to stay here, to bring here whom he pleased, to keep his family here." Like many other freedmen, he argued that his years of unpaid forced labor should be rewarded with an ownership stake on the farm, and he insisted that the United States would soon affirm his claim.[5] In the aftermath of President Lincoln's assassination in April 1865, this decision lay with Andrew Johnson, a Tennessean who hated slave-owning elites more than he hated slavery per se.[6] While the federal government chose not to redistribute property en masse, as Cyrus had hoped, it did create the Bureau of Refugees, Freedmen, and Abandoned Lands, which facilitated access to marriage, education, employment, and other benefits.[7] Its agents varied widely in their commitments and practices, however, which meant that freed people faced limited choices at best and outright coercion at worst.[8] Nevertheless, the bureau was central to the landscape of early Reconstruction. Formerly enslaved people who identified as Jews would certainly have come into contact with the bureau, and white Jews appear within its records requesting— and receiving—the restoration of confiscated land, engaging in conflicts with freed people, receiving bureau contracts, and listed as "former owners" of individuals receiving rations.[9]

In May, Johnson passed an Amnesty Proclamation that excluded fourteen categories of southerner, including those who had served in the Confederate government or possessed over $20,000 in wealth. These documents are well known to southern historians but the presence of Jewish petitioners has previously gone unnoticed. A number of Jews, most of them advanced in age or working as merchants, who maintained large stocks, were among the fifteen thousand people compelled to petition Johnson directly for amnesty; he freely granted it, restoring to white southerners land that might have otherwise been distributed among freed people.[10] Writing in the immediate aftermath of the Confederacy's defeat, petitioners crafted fascinating narratives about their political histories and identities. In June 1865, Benjamin Mordecai, the early funder of the secessionist cause, explained that "the influence of education and example led him in common with the people of the South to adopt ... a position of antagonism to the Federal authority." He described himself as a "citizen of the State of South Carolina."[11]

Abraham Minis mirrored and inverted Mordecai's rationale: "I was educated with a strong attachment to the Union." He added, "I believed it better for my home and my people," leaving ambiguous whether "his people" referred to Georgians, Jews, or his own family.[12] Texas booster Jacob DeCordova offered a remarkable account of a Unionist past and present. He wrote,

> With penitence and regret that I did not at every sacrifice leave the Confederate States, at the breaking out of the Rebellion . . . from the day I took the Oath of Allegiance to the so-called Confederate States [I have] been anxious to return to my duty and once more become a true + Loyal Citizen of the United States. . . . [I] most sincerely rejoice at the restoration of the Union which shall henceforth have my entire support rejoicing that the vexed questions of slavery and secession have finally been set at rest.[13]

Whether grounding it in the distant past or the moment of secession, principles or emotions, individual or collective interests, Jewish men worked to fashion postwar selves, and while some of them confessed Confederate loyalties, others claimed pro-Union commitments. Like other southern Unionists, these Jews believed that national citizenship would best serve their political and economic interests; in the aftermath of wartime antisemitism, they may have been additionally eager to prove their loyalty to the reigning government.[14]

This desire to be seen as "a true + loyal citizen" persisted in the years to come, as Jews came before the Court of Claims and the Southern Claims Commission, bodies set up to provide reimbursement to loyal citizens for property confiscated by the US army. For instance, a cluster of Jews from Savannah filed claims for cotton losses suffered during William Tecumseh Sherman's occupation of the city at the end of the war. At least some of these tethered their claims of loyalty to their Jewish identity. One was Simon Gerstmann, who had been designated an honorary "secretary" at a meeting following Lincoln's assassination, which cast blame on "those inglorious authors of treason, secession and rebellion."[15] He told the Court of Claims that he had founded Congregation Benai Berith Jacob in order to stay out of Confederate military service, and that no member of the congregation had served, although he later admitted that many had simply been too old. The court was surprised, but ultimately convinced of his loyalty. The congregation had its own successful claim, which asserted that "it was incorporated for religious purposes entirely." The two accounts conflicted in their description of the congregation's origins, but they agreed that its members had been, at the very least, ambivalent about the Confederacy.[16]

Whether or not it was in fact a refuge for Unionist Jews during the Civil War, the congregation's immigrant members supported one another in securing government funds and elaborating a postwar Unionist identity. Wealthy Jewish women also professed Unionism; in her own amnesty petition, Abraham Minis's mother Dina looked to the far distant past: "I am eighty years of age, perhaps one of the few now living, who sat on the knees of Gen[eral] Washington."[17] Rosanna Osterman, now a widow, looked forward, expressing her "hope for a speedy restoration of harmony, public prosperity, + uninterrupted feelings of unity between all sections of our country."[18] When she died in a steamboat accident the next year, her will reflected this cosmopolitan spirit. She left money to a many Jewish individuals and institutions, in Philadelphia, New York, and Cincinnati, as well as in Jamaica, Frankfurt, and Amsterdam.[19] Osterman's posthumous generosity, like that of Judah Touro a half-generation earlier, pointed to southern Jews' ongoing connections to coreligionists elsewhere.

Jews seem to have mended cross-sectional ties at an accelerated pace when compared with their Christian neighbors. American Jews were connected to some extent by newspapers and B'nai B'rith lodges, but they did not have denominations, let alone sectionally divided ones in which they could nurse separate visions of the Civil War past. The place of freed people in postwar religious life was not the heated topic of debate it was in white churches.[20] When Isaac Leeser traveled from Philadelphia to Richmond in the fall of 1865, then, he did not go as one of the many zealous northern missionaries seeking to purify southern religious life or uplift freed people; rather, he traveled to his first home in the United States to reassure the city's Jews of their enduring friendship.[21] Leeser described Richmond's Jews with profound sympathy: "They and their neighbors had passed through scenes strongly calculated to try men's souls."[22] Part of the city still lay in ruins, burnt by receding Confederate soldiers as they evacuated the city.[23]

Three years later, an obituary would blame Leeser's death on the outcome of the Civil War: "His sympathies all went out so strongly to the weaker side that the struggle shortened his life."[24] Notably, his Philadelphia pulpit was filled by the pro-Confederate Richmond *hazan* George Jacobs.[25] Jews in the North were willing to forget the recent past, and so too were those in the South. In 1866 George Jacobs's brother Henry, a *hazan* in Augusta, Georgia, wrote to Leeser about Myer S. Isaacs of New York's *Jewish Messenger*, who at the outset of the war had "became so political and violent in his crusade against the South" that Jacobs had canceled his subscription. Now, he wrote, "in the fulness of my heart, and in deference to his years and long services I held out freely the olive branch."[26] The Jews of Vicksburg, Mississippi, hired as their religious leader Bernard Henry Gotthelf, who had served as a chaplain in the US army.[27]

And yet Jews in Houston, Texas, advertised in the *Israelite* for a *hazan*: "A Southern acclimated person preferred."[28] Others also fused regional and religious identities. The year after Leeser's visit to Richmond, a Hebrew Ladies Memorial Association for the Confederate Dead was founded, part of a broader effort spearheaded by women in the city.[29] Its members distributed a fundraising appeal "to the Israelites of the South," calling on them to express "the gratitude and admiration of the living for those who so nobly perished in what we deemed a just and righteous cause."[30] Extending their wartime benevolence efforts, Jewish women also worked to support the broader Confederate memorial movement. Some even named their children after Confederate leaders like Jefferson Davis, General Robert E. Lee, and Joseph Eggleston Johnston.[31]

Veneration of the Confederacy, which came to be known as "the Lost Cause," would prove far more prominent than the narratives of Union loyalty that emerged in state documents.[32] It was often intertwined with Christian ideas and institutions, but its rituals and myths were sufficiently flexible to allow Jews to participate, both as individuals and collectively.[33] The women of Richmond's Hebrew Ladies Memorial Association expressed heartfelt conviction in league with their neighbors, but they also added an argument from Jewish particularity: "In time to come . . . when the malicious tongue of slander, ever so ready to assail Israel, shall be raised against us, then with a feeling of mournful pride will we point to the monument."[34] The commitment of Jews to the Confederate cause, through military service and its subsequent commemoration, would secure their place as members of white communities dominated by Christianity.

This felt like an important project in part because who exactly constituted "the Israelites of the South" was shifting in the immediate postwar years. Some Jews left the region in pursuit of greater stability—like Lazarus Straus, who moved from Columbus, Georgia, to New York City, where he would become the owner of Macy's department store.[35] Others arrived as part of a larger migration of ambitious businessmen; by 1880, 40 percent of the Jews in Macon, Georgia, had lived in the North during the Civil War.[36] The Rich brothers, immigrants who had earlier settled in Cincinnati, moved to Atlanta, where they would establish one of its major department stores.[37] Atlanta was a rail hub in the midst of a robust recovery from its wartime destruction; between 1860 and 1870, its Jewish population increased as much as eightfold.[38] Jews also moved from place to place within the region, following newly laid railroad tracks to small towns in need of merchants.[39]

Jews were settled in southern communities, both established and emerging, whose futures were uncertain and highly contested. White southerners attempted to turn back the wheels of emancipation by violently attacking communities of freed people, passing restrictive Black Codes, and electing former Confederate officials to public office as Democrats. In response, congressional Republicans passed a flurry of laws and constitutional amendments that extended rights to Black Americans. They abolished slavery for all but convicted criminals, extended the life of the Freedmen's Bureau, and redefined citizenship to include "all persons born or naturalized in the United States." At the same time, they forbade the election to federal office of Confederates who had previously taken oaths to uphold the US Constitution.[40]

In 1867 Congress passed the Reconstruction Act, which facilitated military occupation of southern states and required them to pass new constitutions guaranteeing Black political rights in order to reenter the Union.[41] At state constitutional conventions, delegates debated the suffrage of Black and ex-Confederate men; women were pointedly excluded.[42] In North Carolina, where white Republicans dominated the proceedings—there were 14 Black delegates out of 122 total—some argued that the state should go further than the federal government, excluding Confederates who had "violated the rules of civilized warfare" or used "threat, violence, or bribery" to prevent the exercise of the franchise.[43] Others opposed Black suffrage and officeholding outright, on the grounds that the formerly enslaved were "unfitted by previous education and habits of thought and self-reliance." They suggested excluding anyone of African descent from serving in the executive branch.[44]

Ultimately, North Carolina elaborated a new vision of citizenship, granting universal male suffrage and extending officeholding to all voters, except for those who were deemed morally suspect: criminals, duelists, and atheists. The state also eliminated property requirements for officeholding and its longstanding Christian oath, which Jews had been protesting for over half a century.[45] Singling out North Carolina, the Board of Delegates of American Israelites happily reported, "The Constitutions of the Southern States, adopted during the year, make no discrimination as against Israelites."[46] A letter "to the People of North-Carolina" printed along with the constitution alluded to its inclusiveness: "While giving suffrage to the colored people, the Convention has not been so inconsistent with itself, and with the great principles of Republican government, as to deny it to *any portion of the whites*" (emphasis added). It insisted that the constitution would not inaugurate social equality or integration among the races, a sign of Republicans' timidity and eagerness to appease white conservatives.[47] As North Carolinians reimagined political belonging, maintaining a Christian leadership in the state no longer seemed of primary importance; indeed, while many whites criticized Black Christian ministers who served in office for improperly mixing religion and politics, Jews were elected to public office, usually without comment.[48]

Among the most popular politicians in North Carolina was Zebulon B. Vance, the state's wartime governor, who had since reentered

Democratic politics. Around this time, Vance wrote a speech entitled "The Scattered Nation," which he would update and deliver to rapturous crowds for the rest of his life. In it, he argued, "The Jews are our spiritual fathers, the authors of our morals, the founders of our civilization."[49] Jews offered Vance a model for cultural continuity in the face of defeat that ex-Confederates could learn from, and he described Jews in lauda- tory terms as well as in racialized language.[50] They demonstrated "great longevity, freedom from malarious diseases, and peculiarities of form." His descriptions of Jews as the "soberest, most industrious, and moral people on the globe" also implicitly—and favorably—compared them with Black Americans. At a time when freed people were widely con- demned for illiteracy, dependence, criminality, and political avarice, he presented Jews as a literate and self-sufficient people who never com- mitted crimes, required charity, or sought political power.[51]

Jews become explicit objects of public interest in the presidential campaign of 1868, which pitted the Democrat Horatio Seymour against Republican Ulysses S. Grant.[52] Democrats took every opportunity to describe Grant as "the great Jew-hater," pointing to his wartime order expelling them from the Department of Tennessee.[53] Newspapers breathlessly reported on Jewish opposition to Republicans and support for Democrats, including Seymour, whose campaign used the motto "This is a White Man's Country; Let White Men Rule." A Jewish cor- respondent in Sumter, South Carolina, argued in the *Charleston Courier* that over and above their personal distaste for Grant, Jews:

> [would] be the last to lend themselves to a party, the essence of whose being consists in destroying that moral, intellectual, and phys- ical superiority which has been proudly maintained by the Caucasian race, from the time of Abraham to that of Victoria. . . . No respectable Jew can therefore vote for General Grant.[54]

This writer linked Jews to whiteness and to Democratic politics, pre- senting all three as naturally and mutually reinforcing identities. In Vance's rhetoric and in the discussions around Grant's campaign, then, Jews were cast not only as white citizens but as exemplars who high- lighted the inferiority of Blacks, the nobility of Confederates, and the depravity of Republicans. Jews were neither irrelevant nor uniformly opposed to white supremacist politics. Rather, they were both useful symbols and eager participants. Nevertheless, Grant was elected, winning six of the eleven states of the former Confederacy, and the next year Congress passed the Fifteenth Amendment, guaranteeing Black men's suffrage.[55]

Most southern Jews continued to align themselves with Democratic politics as voters and as officeholders, despite the party's program of voter intimidation and fraud.[56] Confederate veteran Adolph Proskauer was elected to the Alabama House of Representatives as a Democrat in 1869, representing a district that was 80 percent Black. Soon after, an investigative committee found "the evidence in the case clearly shows that fraud and violence was resorted to" in his election, although Proskauer himself was found innocent of the scheme. Among other tricks, someone pretending to be a deputy marshal took a Black man's ticket for the Republican candidate, threw it away, and ordered him to submit a vote for Proskauer, "which he did through fear."[57] His young Black opponent, Allen Alexander, gave an impassioned plea for justice before the state legislature, to no avail.[58] The next year, a Selma newspaper described Proskauer as "a gallant soldier" and "a firm and fearless advocate of the rights of the Southern people."[59]

In Donaldsonville, Louisiana, however, located in a parish that was 63 percent Black, two Jewish men served as Republican mayors and yet another as a local judge.[60] One of them, Marx Schoenberg, was shot and killed in a local clash over the ballot box in 1870. The exact course of events was unclear, but divergent partisan accounts presented him as the victim of either a Black mob or a white Democrat.[61] The Republican Party was enjoying success across the region thanks to an alliance of Black voters with "carpetbaggers" and "scalawags"— recent arrivals and established southerners, respectively, who supported Reconstruction.[62] Republicans—Jews included—had diverse motivations for their support of federal Reconstruction. Some may have been committed to racial equality, while others favored the party's progressive economic vision for the region or simply followed the flow of power and money.

Freed people were now a considerable voting bloc—especially in South Carolina, Mississippi, and Louisiana—and the expansion of government services created opportunities for profit, which could lead to fraud and corruption.[63] By 1874, former Confederate William Flegenheimer was a Republican, and he helped draft a statement lamenting that the party's economic principles had "been prostituted by selfish, ambitious, and unpatriotic men."[64] The most prominent—and notorious—Republican of Jewish heritage was Franklin J. Moses Jr., a Christian whose father was Jewish. His service as governor of South Carolina between 1872 and 1874 was marred by accusations of corruption, which earned him the title of "Robber Governor."[65]

There were also Christians of South Carolina Jewish heritage among Black political elites: Francis L. Cardozo, a Christian son of Isaac N. Cardozo and Lydia Weston, a free woman of color, served as the South Carolina state treasurer, and his brother Thomas became superintendent of public education in Mississippi, although he ultimately resigned under threat of impeachment.[66] The Jewish heritage of the Cardozos was largely erased by their racial identity, but Moses was described by Ohio Democrat Philadelph van Moses as "a little Jew carpet-bagger."[67] That Grant's alleged hatred of Jews had been seen as disqualifying for public office did not stop Democrats from now citing Moses's supposed Jewish identity as evidence of his depravity. The alliance of a "Jew" with Black interests seemed to be particularly galling to white South Carolinians.

This kind of disdain for Republicans was part of a broader effort by enraged white southerners to restore "home rule" and return Blacks to what they understood to be their divinely ordained position under white control.[68] Southern Democrats engaged in voter intimidation, fraud, and in vigilantism through groups like the Ku Klux Klan; between 1868 and 1871 an estimated four hundred people were lynched in the South, most of them Black and/or Republican, many sadistically tortured.[69] Given the enthusiasm of Jews as voters and officeholders in the Democratic Party, it is not inconceivable that some might have been perpetrators of this violence, although the Klan's secrecy makes it almost impossible to find definitive proof. Writing in the 1950s, statesman

Bernard M. Baruch recalled opening his father's trunk at their home in small-town South Carolina in the 1870s and finding a Confederate uniform and Klan regalia, which "exalted him in our youthful eyes."[70]

And yet, the contours of southern society were such that Jews could also be found among the Klan's victims, even when they kept their distance from Republican politics. These included S. A. Bierfield of Franklin, Tennessee, who reportedly informed his murderers at gunpoint that he was a supporter of the Democratic presidential ticket;[71] Samuel Fleishman of Marianna, Florida, who was friendly with local Freedmen's Bureau agents but not explicitly political;[72] and W. M. Lucy of Newnansville, Florida, about whom it was recalled "I have heard it said that Lucy was a republican, but I have never heard him say anything about it."[73] All of their stories were recounted by eyewitnesses in congressional testimony about the Klan's destructive activities.

Their Republican ties were tangential at best, but in the eyes of white vigilantes, these men were outsiders who symbolized the ascendance of Black citizenship and northern rule. All three were murdered in the troubled aftermath of local racial violence. Racist newspapers, which assumed that Black men required instruction, described Bierfield as "the Leader of the Negro Assassins," and Fleishman as "an Israelite" in search of "an opportunity of stirring up strife and animosity between the two races."[74] Fleishman was heard saying, "If the colored people are to be murdered in this way, for every black man that is murdered there should be three white people killed"; local whites interpreted this not as a statement of hyperbolic indignation but as a direct threat.[75]

Although Fleishman had settled in Florida two decades earlier, Bierfield arrived in Franklin, Tennessee, only a year before his murder; both were immigrants, as likely was Lucy. Some speculated that a jealous business rival had instigated Bierfield's murder, but he was also described as having traded "with negroes, and he persistently avoided the society of white men."[76] He was killed along with Lawrence Bowman, his Black clerk. Fleishman had suffered harassment inside his store even before his murder, which was witnessed by a Black Marianna resident named Joseph Nelson. The white perpetrator instructed

Nelson to say "that the Jew had insulted him."[77] The sensationalistic press reported that Fleishman had offered local Black men free ammunition, which in fact white vigilantes would forcibly remove soon before his murder.[78]

The store was a fraught space in which resources—and debts—were accumulated and local Blacks might be treated with some modicum of dignity as workers or customers. Nelson reported, "I always went to [Fleischman's] store to get what I wanted on credit," and the immediate impetus for Lucy's murder was a dispute over accounts. A relative of his wife gave as the motive: "Lucy was a Jew, and I think he was in great favor with the negroes. He got a great deal of trade from the negroes." His proximity to Black people, his occupation as a merchant, and his Jewish identity were mutually reinforcing signs of difference. Of Jews identifiable in the 1870 census returns for Georgia and the Carolinas, 82 percent worked as merchants, and in both Florida and Macon, Georgia, only a quarter of the Jews present in 1870 had resided in the same place ten years earlier.[79] Many Jews used transregional ties to their benefit, obtaining capital and credit from coreligionists in other places. And yet both storekeeping and peddling also placed Jews in positions of vulnerability. A handful of Jewish peddlers were robbed and murdered on southern roads, including at least one man who had served in the Confederate army.[80]

Whether or not these incidents were directly motivated by animus toward Jews, the prevalence of Jews in mercantile occupations continued to draw attention. According to the chief justice of the Alabama Supreme Court, "Most of our merchants from abroad with us are foreigners—what are called Jews sometimes."[81] In 1867 a credit reporter in Winnsboro, South Carolina, wrote, "Those German Jews . . . confine themselves particularly to the single business of merchandize. They can change their place of business easily."[82] Credit reporters regularly identified Jews as a distinctive kind of foreign merchant, but they varied in their assessments, describing some as "reliable as Jews generally are" and others as "wandering Jews," suspicious and untrustworthy.[83] There was similar disagreement about selling to freed people, which could be described as doing a "good business principally with the colored laborers" or as "credit[ing] the negroes too much."⁸⁴ While the relationship of sharecropper to landowner has been seen as the paradigmatic one between southern Blacks and whites in this period, many Jews worked as merchants. They competed with landowners as creditors but also fostered a distinctive pattern of engagement with the newly emancipated Black workers who surrounded them and whose freedom still seemed to so many white southerners like a direct threat.⁸⁵

CHAPTER 10

Holy Cause

Leon Schwarz, who served multiple terms as the Democrat mayor of Mobile, Alabama, remembered his childhood in Reconstruction-era Alabama through rose-colored glasses: "I was not born within the narrow confines of some city but . . . right out in the country." Although his was the only Jewish family in town, he recalled "the best of neighborly feeling and friendship between Christian people and Jewish folks." His father reportedly told his white neighbors, "I have come here to live among you and be one of you. Your troubles will be mine. Our religious faith will differ, that's all."[1] His parents were both immigrants, but his mother Augusta cooked for church benefits and sick neighbors, while his father Reuben's store served as a community crossroads. His was a childhood surrounded by "fine Alabama country Christian people" and "negroes all about us." Schwarz's account is highly stylized, filtered through white nostalgia of the 1930s and not a little self-righteousness. And yet, however blurry the view, he does offer a window onto small-town Jewish life at the end of Reconstruction. As the Civil War faded into the background, so too did immigrant pasts and memories of anti-semitism; many Jews allied with the white Christian majority or simply ignored recent history, setting their sights on economic prosperity, social acceptance, and sectional reconciliation. Schwarz's father was a B'nai B'rith member and *Israelite* subscriber who joined the Jewish congregation in nearby Selma. He was also a Democratic Party activist who unabashedly worked, according to his son, for "white supremacy."[2]

In 1873, Congress returned the franchise to almost all previously ex-cluded ex-Confederates. White southerners would continue to suppress Black voting through violence and fraud, leading to a gradual, piecemeal return of Democratic political power to the region, which its propo-nents described using the religious language of "redemption."[3] Among the most dramatic of these incidents occurred in April 1873, when a mob of white Democrats in Colfax, Louisiana, murdered dozens of African Americans with impunity after an election produced competing claimants to office throughout the state.[4] Even as violence against Black men and women continued, northern politicians declined to enlist federal troops to enforce laws protecting their rights. Instead, they and their constituents softened their memories of the Civil War's causes and let southern whites govern without check in the hopes of fostering cross-sectional sympathy among whites, known as "reconciliation." For white Protestants, revivals, benevolence, and temperance all cultivated piety as well as national camaraderie.[5]

The growing reluctance to oversee southern states had been further encouraged by the Panic of 1873, a dramatic stock market crash that depressed the American economy for the remainder of the decade.[6] Some Jews struggled to eke by—Schwarz's father would go bankrupt later in the decade—but many others relied on Jewish credit networks extending beyond the region to keep them afloat.[7] The Lehman family, whose business had started in the antebellum South, now had a major office in New York and served as a lifeline to many Jewish merchants.[8] According to historian Michael R. Cohen, the cotton trade in fact helped create a "golden age" of Jewish prosperity.[9] Jewish peddlers flourished, becoming middle-class shopkeepers and wholesalers; mer-chants held powerful crop liens on Black sharecroppers and white plant-ers alike, which they parlayed into entrepreneurial endeavors.[10] Already in 1868, Jews represented 3.6 percent of Atlanta residents earning more than $1,000 annually, although they constituted only around 1 percent of the city's total population.[11]

In 1860 David Steinheimer had been a clerk living in a Macon boardinghouse with no assets to his name. He went north during the War, but by 1870 he was in Atlanta, a married dry-goods merchant with his own household and a personal estate worth $4,000. Ten years later, he would be a tobacco dealer with four young children and three Black workers in his household; nurse Mary Cody, cook Lucy Robinson, and her husband Thomas, a farmer.[12] The economic viability of Jewish businesses and households was due in part to this kind of Black labor.[13] By 1870, 50 percent of Jews in Atlanta lived in households that employed Black domestic workers.[14] Confederate veteran Charles Wessolowsky of Albany, Georgia, lived with his wife, three children, one white domestic servant, and four Black people, including the family of domestic servant Millie Lafair.[15] Leon Schwarz remembered Black musicians playing at country dances and "Uncle Henry" Didlake and his wife "Aunt Martha" working in the Schwarz home, along with "favorites" Lena Benjamin, Della Molette, and "Uncle Dorsey," a yardman and preacher. He recalled his mother hovering over and correcting their work, however, and despite his claims of affection, he never granted Black workers the honorifics "Mr." or "Mrs."[16] Despite the warm memories of Jews like Schwarz, these relationships with Black workers— which would remain a feature of southern Jewish life well into the twentieth century—were fundamentally asymmetrical and often fraught.[17]

Jews elaborated their relationship to the region's racial binary in private domestic spaces and in the public sphere. Fractious local politics embroiled the lives of many, including Mathias Abraham Cohn and Edouard Weil, whose experiences and convictions led them into opposing parties. In 1871, Cohn served as a Republican state legislator in Arkansas. During his short term, he introduced "An Act to Encourage Industry," and afterward remained active in Republican politics, working alongside Black colleagues.[18] In the election of 1874, which returned Democratic rule to Arkansas, he ran unsuccessfully for justice of the peace and was described by a Democratic paper as supporting "the mongrel ticket."[19] In Alexandria, Louisiana, 250 miles due south from Little Rock and just 25 miles southeast of Colfax on the banks of the Red River, Democrat Edouard Weil was elected to a number of public offices and served as mayor in 1875 and 1876. In the course of his political career he obtained the strategic support of local Democratic newspapers, like the white supremacist *Caucasian*, and he looked the other way when a Republican printing press in town was destroyed in a partisan attack.[20]

These men's political careers peaked at slightly different moments—Cohn before and Weil after the return of Democratic rule to their states—but their political trajectories also had deeper roots. Cohn had immigrated from Hanover to Cincinnati, where he spent the war years as a civilian before making his way to Arkansas by way of Memphis. Weil, a Bavarian, had moved to Alexandria more than a decade before the Civil War, and had served in the Confederate military, rising from the rank of private to sergeant.[21] Cohn, who would have been understood as a "carpetbagger," also lived in a very different community than did Weil. Arkansas was a newer state with a significant Unionist population; during the Civil War it had seen little military action.[22] Alexandria, by contrast, which had an enslaved majority before the war, suffered serious damage in the spring of 1864. Weil, by virtue of his personal background and location, was more tied to the prewar order that Democrats sought to restore than was Cohn. Many more southern Jews identified with Weil than with Cohn, who must have also possessed some amount of political conviction and even courage.

And yet, with all their differences, Cohn and Weil were both publicly identified as committed Jews. Cohn was described in a Democratic paper as "an unworthy Jew . . . who has, for a long time, *unlike all but few of his race in this country*, lent himself, body and soul, to the ignoble service of the wicked and corrupt [Republican] party" (emphasis added).[23] Weil's political opponents likewise condemned him but carefully distinguished him from other Jews, who were generally well respected. According to the Republican *Weekly Louisianan*, "The Israelites, who are a majority of the business men of the town, although Democrats in politics, abhor such lawlessness, and unhesitatingly condemn it."[24]

On top of their political pursuits, both men were leaders in their local Jewish institutions. A few congregations had been established in new places during the Civil War, but in the fifteen years that followed, they popped up in more than twenty new towns, more than in the forty years before the war.[25] And amid the region's postwar hustle and bustle, established congregations—including the congregations that Cohn and Weil each led—constructed new synagogue buildings.[26] Synagogue seating capacity doubled nationwide in the 1860s, and Black and white churches also underwent a flurry of organizational development.[27] Architecturally, the new southern synagogues ranged from the twin towers of the Romanesque Temple Sinai in New Orleans (figure 10.1) to the Greek revival building in Natchez to the new Gothic synagogue built for Mickve Israel in Savannah.[28]

These elegant synagogues were settings for divine worship that also symbolized affluence and a commitment to the cities and towns in which Jews lived. The dedication of the Temple in Atlanta featured a procession of congregational leaders, followed by "fifteen girls all dressed in white . . . carrying the key of the Temple on a velvet cushion." It was a dramatic performance of female purity for "a large assembly of a Gentile audience."[29] When Congregation Mishkan Israel dedicated a repurposed Episcopal church in 1879, a correspondent from the *Selma Times*, who "had never seen so many Jews together before," was notably impressed with the grandeur of the event. Seven-year-old Leon Schwarz was also in attendance and later remembered it as one of the most important events of his childhood.[30]

Many of the new buildings included mixed seating and beautiful organs, which allowed Jews to practice in ways that did not unduly divide them from white Christians. Reform Judaism proved appealing to many southern Jews, surrounded by pious Christians and invested in projects of modernization, sectional reconciliation, and white citizenship.[31] The sentiment was not universal, however. Already in 1865, a New Orleans traditionalist had ridiculed reformers for what he described as their "gay visions of a fashionable divine service [with] family pews, Ladies and Gentleman together, beautiful choirs, [and] operatic music."[32] In Macon, Georgia, a decade later, a man named Mark Isaacs refused to pay his promised contribution to a new synagogue because he had given with "the expressed understanding that the innovations of latter-day reformers should never enter the portals of the synagogue and thereby destroy the ancient faith of our fathers." Isaacs lamented what he deemed the "deception" on the part of "the so-called Synagogue," which

Temple Sinai, New Orleans, La.

FIGURE 10.1. Temple Sinai, New Orleans, LA, built 1872—
postcard from 1913, William A. Rosenthall Judaica Collection,
College of Charleston. Image courtesy of Special Collections,
College of Charleston Libraries.

filed suit against him in a local court.[33] His was an uphill battle, though. By the end of Reconstruction, Reform Judaism was ubiquitous throughout the South.

Concerned about the weakness and unevenness of religious life in and beyond these far-flung congregations, Jewish leaders had long harbored hopes of a unified form of American worship, a centralized rabbinical court, and, most of all, a seminary to train qualified rabbis on American soil.[34] Now, at a moment when the federal government was gaining in power and cross-regional sympathy becoming a national preoccupation, they attracted renewed attention.[35] In 1873 a group of lay leaders allied with Isaac Mayer Wise met in Cincinnati to found the Union of Congregations of the South and West. Representatives from Natchez, Vicksburg, Shreveport, Galveston, Memphis, and Pine Bluff, Arkansas, were in attendance, constituting about 20 percent of the congregations gathered. Much more important than the political divide between North and South was Wise's long-standing ideological rivalry with "eastern" rabbis in New York and Baltimore. The organizers hoped that the union, formally titled the Union of American Hebrew Congregations, would "remov[e] all such section or geographic distinction."[36]

The new union's secretary addressed letters to Jewish contacts across the country requesting support, and many in the South responded with enthusiasm, including both Cohn and Weil. Cohn, who attended the initial union gathering in Cincinnati, promised "$500 on the day when the first Theological College is opened."[37] Weil wrote, "We are with you with heart + soul + hope to see 'our Institute' in a flourishing condition ere long."[38] Weil supported the union despite its largely northern constituency, Cohn supported it despite its association with the vocal Democrat Isaac Mayer Wise, and each participated despite the fact that it included the other. Indeed, supporters of the union saw it as a project of religious glorification and geographic unification. Nathaniel Levin, the secretary-treasurer of Kahal Kadosh Beth Elohim in Charleston, wrote, "Our ancestors guarding our Sacred Temple with arms in their hands were not engaged in a more Holy Cause."[39]

Others prayed that "the Almighty will crown your work with success," and sent money "to preserve Israel's Honor + to maintain our blessed religion." They promised "to solicit [donations] from fellow citizens of this place and neighborhood" and expressed their "pleasure in joining hands with sister congregations of the West + South or the whole Union." Levin's *hazan*, Joseph H. M. Chumaceiro, hoped for "additional strength to our sacred work," although he initially worried that this new body would constitute a "<u>second</u> Union or Confederacy . . . in warfare with the <u>first</u> Union," the Board of Delegates of American Israelites, founded in 1859 in New York.[40] The Civil War served as both backdrop and metaphor for new developments in American Judaism. The language of warfare, like that of honor and citizenship, pointed to a sense of manly duty these Jews felt as they sat down to write, in venerable Charleston, but also in newly burgeoning cities and tiny towns across the region.

From Natchitoches, Louisiana, one man reported that he was unable to raise funds because of a quarantine.[41] That fall, a devastating yellow fever epidemic spread through swampy southern cities, hitting Memphis and Shreveport especially hard. In September, a telegraph from Shreveport reached Cincinnati "stating that the ravages of the yellow fever in that place were terrible, and that our co-religionists were in need of assistance." Cincinnati Jews quickly raised over $800 and convened a meeting of local B'nai B'rith lodges to support "our suffering Shreveport brethren."[42] In the weeks and months to come, letters regularly appeared in the *Israelite* describing the ravages of the disease, the responses of local Jews, and the need for donations.

The epidemic diminished Jewish communities through emigration and death, it fostered religious devotion, and it bonded those living in the region's distinctive climate through suffering and displacement. In November, Abraham Ephraim Frankland, a Memphis merchant, reported the deaths of ninety-four local Jews, ranging from a two-week-old baby girl to an eighty-nine-year-old man. Referencing the book of Jeremiah, he wrote, "Weeping! wailing! and lamentation [was] beside you on every side."[43] Members of Shreveport's Jewish community gathered in a dilapidated schoolhouse in Greenwood, Texas, for Yom Kippur services, tears rolling down many of their cheeks.[44] Describing the death of his brother, one Georgia man "beseeche[ed] all Israelites in small villages to be true and steadfast in our case, and Jehovah will be with them even to the end everlasting."[45] Southern Jews drew on their own tradition to cope with the devastation and took pride in their contributions to broader relief efforts. The *Israelite* reprinted an account from the *Memphis Appeal* praising Rabbi Max Samfield for having "daily given succor and consolation to all regardless of their creed."[46]

Yellow fever was not a new problem; no one yet knew that it was spread by mosquitoes, and it reappeared almost every summer, disrupting public life and causing many quick but painful deaths.[47] At least since the 1850s, American Jews had shared yellow fever news and relief funds, and yet they responded to the 1873 epidemic with new vigor. The *Israelite* encouraged its readers, "Come forward and do your duty. Send bread and raiment to the mourning survivors."[48] The women of the Ahavas Achus Society in New Haven, Connecticut, offered their first ever donation outside their own city, and B'nai B'rith lodges from across the country sent contributions.[49] According to the careful records that Frankland kept, the most generous state was New York, which sent almost $7,000.[50] After a fundraising tour through the Midwest, Wise wrote, "If there exists any prejudice down South to Northern men, it is unjust. We find none in the North. Peace and good-will prevail, and ought to govern all."[51] Like the union, these responses combined long-standing American Jewish interests with the national focus on sectional reconciliation. A few months after the epidemic, B'nai B'rith granted Frankland a special medal at its annual convention in Chicago; according to one onlooker, when the death of Frankland's own son in the epidemic was mentioned, "the father's feelings gave way to tears and sobs and there was not seen [an] eye dry in the whole room."[52] B'nai B'rith had recently organized Grand District Lodge Number 7, which reached from Alabama to Texas, encompassing most of the affected states. Soon after, at the institution of a new lodge in New Orleans, a poem was circulated—in English and in German—declaring "North or South! Let love our hearts enshroud!"[53]

Five years later, there would be yet another, even more terrifying epidemic. Beginning in New Orleans and ultimately spreading from Georgia to Louisiana, the disease again brought disruption, fear, and death. One observer wrote, "The country between Louisville, Kentucky and New Orleans is one entire scene of desolation and woe." Nine days after the disease's arrival in Memphis—where death tolls would reach over five thousand—sixteen local Jews had been struck down; with the summer of 1873 still fresh in their memories, most others fled.[54] In Vicksburg, among the dead was Reverend Bernard Gotthelf, who had been described earlier that year as "vigorous and strong."[55] Yellow fever relief furthered postwar reconciliation efforts and cast "the South" as an object of interest, although all parts of the region were not equally affected.[56] When Jewish newspapers and fraternal orders once again undertook large-scale efforts to help "the sufferers," they were, even more than in 1873, described as "our brethren in the South" and "our unfortunate fellow citizens of the South."[57] In Cincinnati, a "Hebrew Southern Relief Association" was created to help "these southern people" seeking refuge in the city.[58]

American Jews eagerly entered into cross-sectional alliances, and their national institutions focused on political issues that transcended region or partisan politics, like Sunday closing laws, prayer in schools, and a proposed Christian amendment to the Constitution.[59] For the centennial exposition in Philadelphia in 1876, B'nai B'rith commissioned Confederate veteran Moses Ezekiel—who would also create a number of Confederate memorial works—to sculpt a piece titled *Religious Liberty*, a dramatic symbol of both American patriotism and Jewish reconciliation.[60] This general rule, however, did not stifle the political expression of individual editors like Rabbi Isaac Mayer Wise, who in 1874 had added *American* to the title of the *Israelite*. In the presidential election year of 1876, he explicitly encouraged readers of the *Israelite* to vote for Democrats, describing Reconstruction as a failed plot to impose Republican rule.[61] Southern Jewish Democrats could rely, then, on the continued support of the most prominent Jewish leader in the nation.

That July, white militiamen led by a prominent Democratic politician had murdered six Black residents and massacred many more in the town of Hamburg, South Carolina. Democrats in the state engaged in a brutal campaign of voter intimidation and fraud that was extreme even by the troubling standards of the Reconstruction South.[62] The election results were contested, but ultimately Wade Hampton III was declared the victor and the state returned to Democratic rule. This result was facilitated by the South Carolina Supreme Court, headed by Franklin J. Moses Sr., the Jewish father of the "Robber Governor." Among the consequences was the resignation of state treasurer Francis L. Cardozo and, later, his imprisonment on charges of conspiracy.[63] Although Cardozo was a Black man over thirty years younger than the judge, both were sons of Charleston-born Jewish fathers, who were distant from Judaism but deeply committed—in different ways—to South Carolina.[64] The presidential election that year was also contested; ultimately Republican Rutherford B. Hayes was declared the winner, on the promise of removing federal troops from southern states. White sectional reconciliation had won out, and while African Americans continued to vote and serve in public office, federal protection for their rights effectively disappeared.[65]

As southern states careened out of and back into the United States, their Jewish residents, many of them German-speaking immigrants, navigated complex relationships to the changing governments under which they lived, to their neighbors, both Black and white, and to their coreligionists elsewhere. Christianity continued to shape the contours of southern life in ways that marginalized Jews, and in times of economic or racial strife, they inspired a feverish anxiety that occasionally curdled into acts of expulsion and outright violence. This was the case even though most Jews adapted to the norms of southern whiteness, which meant at least tolerating—and in some cases enthusiastically embracing—slavery, the Confederacy, and Democratic politics. More and more southern Jews also embraced a Reform Judaism that cast their difference primarily as a matter of faith and worship that Christians could tolerate.

None of these commitments were universal among southern Jews, however, and, at a time of fierce sectional animosity, they could strengthen ties to northern coreligionists as well as strain them. The debate over religious reform was a national one, and the primary advocates both for and against were northerners who were nonetheless sympathetic to the southern cause. Once the Civil War ended, American Jews of all political stripes channeled their newfound affluence and a

growing spirit of reconciliation into cooperative efforts. They confidently planned for Judaism's perpetuation and elevation, in the South
and elsewhere. They could not know that their numbers were about to
increase in dramatic—and largely unwanted—fashion. The arrival of
eastern European Jewish immigrants, alongside new forms of racial
thinking and white domination, would complicate the place of Jews
within southern communities even as it brought new forms of transnational Jewish life to the region.

PART III
1878–1967

CHAPTER 11

Subtle Ostracism

In June of 1878, Charles Wessolowsky of Albany, Georgia, stepped off the train in Vicksburg, Mississippi. There were one hundred Jewish families there, of whom he wrote, "As usual, they have the sway of business and are well off." He complimented their religious leader, Bernard Gotthelf, who served on the local school board, and he visited the nearby national cemetery, established in 1866 as a resting place for some seventeen thousand Union soldiers.[1] The energetic Wessolowsky, who sported a full mustache, was traveling at the behest of the *Jewish South*, an upstart newspaper based in Atlanta. Its editor promised that it would educate Christians about Judaism and advance "the interests of Southern Judaism and the dignity of the South."[2] The paper was short-lived, but by the end of the nineteenth century there would be at least four other southern Jewish newspapers in circulation: the *Jewish Spectator* of Memphis, *Jewish Ledger* of New Orleans, *Jewish Tribune* of Atlanta, and a new *Jewish South*, founded in Richmond in 1893.[3]

These publications were agents and symbols of a broader "Jewish South," a web of relationships and an idea of solidarity that together helped acculturated Jews navigate the modernizing "New South." The Jewish South included Savannah, Charleston, Richmond, and New Orleans, port cities with multiple Jewish congregations, as well as the western island city of Galveston; inland towns, linked by rivers and railroads, where Jews had first settled in the years before the Civil War, like Nashville and Vicksburg; an array of small towns created from scratch, like Meridian, Mississippi, and Anniston, Alabama; and newly booming cities like Atlanta. By 1881 Jews lived in some 522 southern towns and cities, through which they circulated as they conducted business and advanced through the lifecycle.[4] Young Jews moved to new communities when they married, and the bodies of deceased Jews were brought home to rest.[5] In between, they traveled to visit friends and family and moved for new opportunities; Wessolowsky met young women from Montgomery visiting in Selma and had long conversations with Natchez Jews about their relatives in Georgia.[6] Religious functionaries traversed these networks attending to ritual needs that ranged from the circumcision of an infant son to the consecration of a synagogue.[7] These ties would persist across the decades to come, even as the people—and the idea—of the Jewish South faced profound challenges that to Wessolowsky would have seemed unimaginable.

By the time he set off from Albany, most federal troops had departed southern states, Democratic control had returned, and the region's economy was beginning to modernize in fits and starts. In 1886 Andrew Jackson Moses's wife, the ardent Confederate booster Octavia Harby Moses (figure 11.1), would argue that "a new and happier epoch has at length dawned for us."[8] Harby was right to notice that there were changes afoot. In the final decades of the nineteenth century the expansion of railroads, the arrival of new technologies and goods, and the growth of southern cities began to bring the region more firmly into national and global marketplaces. Although white men were still in charge, businessmen replaced planters as the engines of the southern economy, a shift that Jewish men both encouraged, as merchants and civic leaders, and benefited from.[9] It was accompanied by efforts to hold on to the past. For nearly a century to come, white southerners would work to carve up public space into Black and white and all but assure Democratic politicians victory. Southern Jews like Wessolowsky—who had lived in the region for decades if not since birth, supported the Confederacy and its memory, and acquired middle-class status and political power—had reason to feel confident. They saw themselves as respectable white southerners who embraced a different faith. And yet,

FIGURE 11.1. Octavia Harby Moses, c.1890. Image courtesy of Special Collections, College of Charleston Libraries.

as they hurtled into the twentieth century, which would bring mass migration, two world wars, and the establishment of a Jewish state in Palestine, their status would become in some ways more, rather than less, precarious.

A number of Jews had transformed modest shops into successful wholesale operations or prestigious department stores—like Thalhimer Brothers in Richmond, Rich's in Atlanta, and Neiman Marcus in Dallas—and their children were attending college and entering the professions in rising numbers.[10] While there were certainly Jews for whom decades in the South had produced little to no wealth, the overall ethos of the region's Jewish communities was middle class and optimistic. They socialized in clubs like the Wilmington Concordia Society, where an 1889 Purim ball included a gourmet non-kosher meal of lobsters, beef tongue, and ice cream.[11] They dedicated themselves to charitable causes like the Jewish orphan's homes in New Orleans and Atlanta, each of which was supported by a district grand lodge of B'nai B'rith, and which complemented the work of similar institutions in Cleveland and New York.[12] As a speaker at the New Orleans home's 1883 anniversary celebration put it, "Offerings of benevolence ... [come here] from every place amid the varied beauty of our genial South where Jewish hearts do beat."[13] These homes enabled the "protection" of vulnerable women and children, specifically on the part of Jewish men, who cast charity as a manly duty.[14] At the same time, Wessolowsky had written of Waco, Texas, "Our Jewish ladies here have as yet no society and with your permission we desire to say to you, that upon you depends the success of this undertaking of building the synagogue."[15] Jewish women carved out roles as active organizers and fundraisers, cementing their middle-class status while also ensuring the viability of Jewish institutions.[16]

The region was home to a growing number of ordained rabbis, many of whom enjoyed remarkably long tenures in their pulpits. They included Max Samfield of Memphis (1871–1915; figure 11.2), Max Heller of New Orleans (1886–1926), Edward N. Calisch of Richmond (1891–1946), Henry Cohen of Galveston (1888–1952), Isaac Marcusson of Macon (1894–1903, 1920–52), and David Marx of Atlanta (1895–1946).[17] Half of these men were born in the United States—just one, Marx, in the South—and all but one were alumni of the Hebrew Union College, the rabbinical seminary founded in Cincinnati in 1875 with reformer Isaac Mayer Wise at its head. Their primary responsibility was to act as "mixers," respectable representatives to white Christians.[18] Modern men, sporting dapper spectacles and mustaches, these rabbis collaborated with white ministers, contributed to the public good, and were beloved by their constituencies.[19] After Rabbi Max Heller visited Summit, Mississippi, one local Jew wrote, "Now I am asked: when will Mr. Heller be here again?" He praised Heller for "stimulat[ing] an interest in the young ones of our creed and show[ing] to the outside world that we have a religion which is worthy of respect."[20]

Rabbis like Heller helped usher their congregations further into the Reform camp.[21] Atlanta's Temple, for instance, adopted the Union Prayer Book, banned head coverings during worship, and held worship

FIGURE 11.2. Max Samfield, c.1895. Image courtesy of the
Jacob Rader Marcus Center of the American Jewish Archives,
Cincinnati, Ohio, at americanjewisharchives.org.

services on Sunday; when Isaac Mayer Wise died in 1900, the congregation held a special service to mourn "our sainted prince, teacher and
leader."[22] All three southern congregations with colonial roots came to
affiliate with Reform Judaism, even as their northern counterparts remained committed to traditionalism, and southern congregations were
noticeably overrepresented in the Union of American Hebrew Congregations (UAHC), which gradually became a Reform institution.[23]
While Jewish congregations in the South made up just 14 percent of
the nationwide total, they would come to constitute 41 percent of the

UAHC's members.[24] Reform Judaism encouraged its followers to center biblical texts, while acknowledging their human authorship; to conceive of the world in universalist terms, while maintaining Jewish identity; and to cultivate individual forms of religious thought and practice, in the process mediating relationships between Jews and Christians and between women and men. By 1904, the board of Charleston's Kahal Kadosh Beth Elohim would insist, "We pray on every occasion of worship that mankind shall become of one faith and adore the only true and living God." This reflection accompanied a decision to accept as members "brethren who marry out of the faith," specifically white Christians, since interracial marriage was illegal in South Carolina.[25]

In 1885 a rabbinical conference had met in Pittsburgh to produce an official platform for Reform Judaism, which attendees described as "adapted to the views and habits of modern civilization." This meant a rejection of the ritual and legal dimensions of Jewish practice in favor of ethical monotheism. The rabbis in Pittsburgh presented Judaism as a progressive religion perfectly at home in the United States.[26] No southern rabbis attended the Pittsburgh conference, but six wrote to express their regrets, and the following month a group called the Conference of Rabbis of Southern Congregations met in New Orleans to discuss the Platform. The Conference had been founded earlier that year with the goals of fostering rabbinic discussion, Jewish literature, religious education, and "fraternal feelings." It was modeled on an earlier Eastern Conference, but whereas that body was bitterly divided over the Pittsburgh Platform, the southern rabbis voted to endorse it.[27]

The Conference of Southern Rabbis also discussed preserving the "history of Jews in the southern states," and although it disbanded in 1893, individual southern rabbis took up the charge.[28] Rabbis Henry Cohen and Alfred G. Moses published articles about Jews in Texas and Alabama, respectively, in the New York–based *Publications of the American Jewish Historical Society*, and Rabbi Barnett Elzas published two books, *The Old Jewish Cemeteries of Charleston, S.C.* (1903) and *The Jews of South Carolina, from the Earliest Times to the Present Day* (1905).[29] They offered dry accountings of the "first Jews" in southern places, providing assurances of long and faithful residence. These efforts were part of a broader flourishing of historical narration in this period, including among former Confederates and their families.[30] Southern Jews served as participants and leaders in survivors' meetings, monument associations, the United Confederate Veterans, and the United Daughters of the Confederacy, and a number arranged their wartime diaries or memoirs for posterity.[31] When North Carolina's Confederate governor Zebulon Vance died in 1894, the B'nai B'rith lodge in Asheville cosponsored a wreath-laying ceremony with the United Daughters of the Confederacy.[32] Into the twentieth century, rabbis showered praise upon individual Jewish veterans and upon Judah Benjamin as a means of writing Jews into the heart of white southern memory and identity.[33]

Public office served as another expression of, and pathway toward, respectability. Wessolowsky had served as a Democratic state official in Georgia and took notice of Jews in public office in almost every town he visited, ranging from Ernestine Sterne, postmistress of Jefferson, Texas, to Mordecai Moses, mayor of Montgomery.[34] There were Jews— including religious leaders like Bernard Gotthelf and Max Samfield— who served on school boards, shaping the future of southern communities. Both Atlanta and Columbus, Georgia, even maintained de facto "Jewish" seats.[35] In Richmond there were two Jews on the school board in 1879, when a resolution was passed allowing Jewish children to miss school on the Day of Atonement and—in keeping with Reform practice—the first day of the New Year and the three pilgrimage holidays, Sukkot, Passover, and Shavuot.[36] Just four years later, the mere suggestion of Black men serving on the Richmond school board would lead to widespread panic about the threat of interracial sex and to the downfall of the Readjuster Party, an alliance of Black and white Virginians that had coalesced around concerns over the state debt.[37] Despite their differences from the majority, Jews were granted access to power that was pointedly denied to African Americans.

Many white southerners looked backward to the antebellum South, seeking to restore white patriarchal power, and they undermined federal law by restricting Black access to the ballot box and to public spaces through new policies, state constitutions, and the threat of violence. As one Black newspaper in Tennessee put it in 1888, "Daily the papers contain the record of lynchings." In stark contrast to the optimism of many southern Jews about their future in the region, this author declared baldly, "The condition of the Negroes of the south is almost hopeless."[38] When a mob of white agitators killed dozens of Black citizens and overturned an elected government in Wilmington in 1898, Jews were among their number. Former mayor Solomon Fishblate—actually a US army veteran—told a gathered crowd, "The choice in this election is between white rule and Negro rule. And I am with the white man, every time!"[39] After a Philadelphia newspaper drew a sympathetic comparison between Jews and African Americans, Herbert Ezekiel vehemently objected: "The Jew, as a rule, is a good citizen; the negro a bad, or, at the best an indifferent one. . . . Our people, though persecuted and driven from pillar to post, do not possess the criminal instincts of the colored race."[40] In New Bern, ninety-five miles up the coast from Wilmington, however, another Jew took a very different tack. Joseph Hahn, who had been elected sheriff on a fusionist ticket, used his power to appoint Black deputies before being removed from office by disgruntled white residents.[41]

White supremacy held a powerful appeal for some Jews, but its sway was not inviolable, and its manifestations were complex. A number of Jewish politicians advocated for improved health care and schooling for Black constituents, although none openly questioned the wisdom of segregation, and many echoed the paternalism of other southern whites.[42] In 1890, for instance, William Levy, who had served as alderman and mayor in Sherman, Texas, encouraged an audience at a Black college "to follow the example of my race, to inspire you to work intelligently, patiently and tirelessly." He presented himself as a sympathetic "friend" who could understand the plight of southern Blacks, and yet he chastised his audience for imprudent behavior and pointedly recommended that they avoid political activism altogether.[43] A few rabbis tiptoed into matters of racial justice. In Port Gibson, Rabbi Raisin noted in his diary, "They think me stubborn because I still decry the negroes' oppression. But what unprejudiced man could think otherwise?"[44] In New Orleans, Max Heller insisted on the "benevolence of separation" between the races and accepted an invitation to offer a prayer at Louisiana's 1898 disfranchisement convention.[45] And yet he also gave sermons calling on congregants to offer African Americans "our active sympathy, our energetic aid" and condemning "the drunken mob that kindles a pyre around a chained negro."[46] Even as he tolerated separation and hierarchy, Heller clearly understood that his Black neighbors suffered from disadvantage and injustice.

European Jews sometimes expressed solidarity or sympathy with African Americans, and, much more rarely, recognized the possibility for overlap between the two communities. In the late 1890s, the *Jewish South* reported on the appearance in New York of a Hebrew-speaking African, although the article insisted that he was "the only negro in the United States who is a Jew and one of the very few in the world."[47] In 1900 a "Black Jew" named Samuel Volskovitz, almost certainly the same man, attracted notice in the Nashville press. According to the paper, "The Jews are taking quite an interest in him, and contributing to his support as he is in a needy condition."[48] The existence of a "Black Jew" pointed to the religious rather than racial underpinnings of Jewish identity, but press coverage emphasizing his foreignness and novelty also made it clear that US Jews were reliably white. Into the twentieth century, Black southerners would claim Jewish identities of various kinds, seeing in Jewishness an alternative to American racial ideology. At the same time, Jews in the North and South alike participated in the popular pastime of blackface performance, which simultaneously expressed anti-Black racism and racial ambivalence.[49]

Even as the black-white racial binary hardened, Americans were increasingly dividing the world into many different racial categorizations, like "Teutons" and "Anglo-Saxons." These were "scientific" determinants of human behavior, linked to proper gender roles and stages of "civilization," which were used to explain and legitimize discrimination.[50] The question of how to place Jews within these schemes was raised in the late nineteenth century by a number of infamous cases of what was now routinely described as "anti-Semitism."[51] For instance, Joseph Seligman—who had peddled through rural Alabama before the Civil War—was turned away from the Grand Union Hotel in Saratoga Springs because he was a Jew.[52] Southern papers expressed outrage when they heard the news. The *New Orleans Daily Democrat* complained that northerners like Hilton had imposed on Louisiana a law that "sub-jects the keepers of public saloons to a heavy fine if they refuse to enter-tain" lower class Black people. And yet now they "justif[ied] the outrage of excluding from admission to a hotel a free white citizen, because of his religion or trade."[53]

A reporter who interviewed leading Atlanta Jews about the "Selig-man Affair" found that "they thought that it was useless to discuss the matter, and felt perfectly safe in assuming that neither Atlanta or Geor-gia would ever tolerate such a course."[54] There was a similar response in the 1890s, when Alfred Dreyfus, a Jewish officer in the French military who had been convicted of treason, became a cause célèbre; Rabbi Isaac Marcusson responded to a press inquiry, "I say it is not a matter for the Jews to discuss as a people. We try as much as we can to discourage the habit of separating the Jews from other people in matters outside of religion."[55] The open question was whether European-style antisemi-tism might find expression in their own backyard. Herbert Ezekiel of the *Jewish South* darkly warned, "The American is no more liberal-minded than his European brother."[56]

Antisemitic ideas trickled in from Europe and the North, but they also had local roots. Amid the promise of New South prosperity, many south-erners remained impoverished and shackled to plots of land that, growing the fickle cotton crop, never seemed to earn enough profit. As the Black writer W.E.B. Du Bois put it in his *The Souls of Black Folk*, "A pall of debt hangs over the beautiful land."[57] In Louisiana and southwest Mississippi in the early 1890s, a group known as the "Whitecaps" protested Black farming on Jewish-owned land through intimidation and violence.[58] Ac-cording to one Black resident, the group had "ordered our citizens to leave the Jews land."[59] Even Du Bois occasionally blamed this suffering on Jew-ish immigrants, describing, for instance, a case where "in the face of law and decency [an] enterprising Russian Jew . . . left the black man land-less."[60] Jews became a symbol of troubling outside forces, whether they were understood to enable or impoverish Black southerners.

The region's most enthusiastic Protestants saw Jews as damned Christ killers, and in 1905 an Atlanta Hebrew Christian Association was founded, part of a broader national movement to evangelize the Jews in preparation for Christ's return.[61] Religious concerns overlapped with economic ones in diatribes against greed and immorality. Members of the new Populist movement, which centered the policy concerns of farmers, blamed Jews for predatory banking practices. Those agitating for the prohibition of alcohol blamed them for rampant alcoholism— one advocate described their cause as a Christian battle against "the brewers, the anarchists, and the Sabbath-breakers," all categories that included a visible Jewish presence.[62] Newspapers began to label petty criminals as Jews, denying them a default whiteness.[63] "An American Jew" objected to this practice in the *Macon Telegraph*, insisting that Jews were only a religious sect, that "America is no soil for 'anti-Semitism.'" Macon's newspapers, he argued, should "stop treating the Jewish people of this community as though they were different from their neighbors."[64] Even Israel H. Peres of Memphis, a respected lawyer who had earned multiple degrees from Yale University and would go on to serve on the Memphis school board, felt that American Jews faced a "subtle ostracism."[65]

It did not help matters that Jews from eastern Europe had begun to arrive in the United States en masse. Most were lured by hopes of economic stability, but they were further encouraged by a wave of devastating antisemitic attacks and policies after the 1881, when Tsar Alexander II was assassinated.[66] The new arrivals attracted considerable attention: they spoke Yiddish instead of German or English, they were committed to orthodox Jewish practice or radical political ideologies, and many were impoverished.[67] According to one American Jew, ostensibly trying to garner sympathy for them, "Their garb [is] outlandish, their speech unintelligible, and their ways and manners wholly foreign to this country."[68] Some white Christians insisted that these inferior "Hebrews" or "Semites" should be excluded from entry into the United States altogether.[69] Already in 1886, New South prophet Henry Grady had written, "One northern immigrant is worth fifty foreigners."[70] Black leader Booker T. Washington encouraged white southerners to hire Black workers rather than "those of foreign birth and strange tongue and habits."[71] Although some white southerners wanted to restrict all immigration, others understood Jewish immigrants as potential white citizens.

Referencing the very promise that had been so cruelly denied to Black southerners after the Civil War, an Atlanta paper wrote: "It seems to be the correct thing to offer to Russian Jews, who are daily arriving here, if not 'forty acres and a mule,' at least the land part thereof."[72]

Southern Jews echoed this ambivalence about the arrival of Russian Jewish immigrants. Not only did they seem to have little in common with the new arrivals but there was always the specter of their violent rejection by white Christians unable or unwilling to distinguish among different kinds of Jews.[73] Established Jews made "sneers and unkind remarks" about the immigrants in private, and some argued in public venues that they were "a disturbing element" who should remain where they were.[74] Others pointed to their region as an ideal location for Jewish safety and flourishing. Wessolowsky was far from the first or last to muse, "How well it would be for some of our Jewish brethren living in those barbarous countries of Russia and Rumania to immigrate here to Texas, form Jewish colonies, on this fertile soil pursue the avocation of our forefathers, become shepherds like Moses and David."[75] Toward this end, southern Jews spearheaded a number of settlement schemes, part of a transnational effort to turn Jews into "productive" laborers worthy of citizenship.[76] Many more raised money to help the refugees, who slowly but surely had begun to arrive in the region. For instance, Macon's Jews welcomed a group of thirty Jewish immigrants in December 1881, initially housing them in their synagogue.[77]

Southern Jewish cemeteries bear silent but eloquent witness to these Russian Jews and their histories of migration. In Macon, Georgia, for example, we find a gravestone inscribed with the following: "Lena Sack. Beloved Wife of A. Roobin. Born in Bialystok Russia 1875. Died in Cordele, GA on Sept. 19, 1896."[78] She had begun her life in an industrializing city with a Jewish majority but died in an obscure crossroads town over sixty miles south of her final resting place. Although you can't tell from the gravestone alone, eastern European Jews like Roobin came to southern communities increasingly dominated by Jim Crow and a range of economic concerns. Their arrival would create new challenges and anxieties, not only for themselves but for their new neighbors, Jewish and Christian alike.

CHAPTER 12

The Alien Hebrew

Less than ten years after arriving in America, the family of the Polish-born Isaac David and Sarah Rubin posed for a photo to commemorate the Jewish New Year (figure 12.1). Included in the image is a recently arrived patriarch, J. L. Banon, who sports a substantial beard and covers his head in the manner of a pious Jewish man. A roughly contemporaneous photo shows a Passover seder in the home of Hyman and Esther Pearlstine, who had been born in Georgia and South Carolina, respectively (figure 12.2). Here, the men are clean-shaven or sport fashionable mustaches and are seated in an elegant dining room; one of the boys wears a uniform from the Citadel military academy, and three Black employees stand around the perimeter of the table, one of the two women holding a baby. These families were both headed by eastern European Jews and were members of Brith Shalom synagogue, an antebellum "Polish" congregation, where services were conducted in Hebrew, with gender-segregated seating and heads covered.[1] Both observed and documented Jewish holidays. Despite their similarities, however, these families were forged by different immigration histories and compelled to different forms of self-representation in the early twentieth century. The Rubins pose outside in the lush Charleston foliage, expressing visible signs of Jewishness, an image they sent to their friends through the mail. The Pearlstines, on the other hand, practice

FIGURE 12.1. I. David Rubin and family postcard. Image courtesy of Special Collections, College of Charleston Libraries.

FIGURE 12.2. Photo of the Pearlstine family's seder dinner. Image courtesy of Special Collections, College of Charleston Libraries.

indoors for a more private audience and clearly display their acculturation, including through the presence of Black laborers.

Jewish immigration intensified in the first years of the twentieth
century as targeted attacks on Jews in the Russian Empire—known as
"pogroms"—became more frequent. Most infamously, on Easter Sunday in 1903 drunken rioters in the Bessarabian town of Kishinev went
on a rampage of violence, including rape and property destruction.
They killed forty-nine Jews as state officials watched on.[2] This far-off
event inspired protest meetings across the United States, like one in
Richmond, where the governor of Virginia spoke, delicately casting it
as a violation of religious freedom.[3] In Savannah, Russian Jewish immigrant D. Epstein called for donations to facilitate "the colonization of
the Russian Jew" in the United States. Instead, those gathered passed a
milder motion encouraging attendees to "show their sympathy by joining one of the lodges of the Independent Order B'nai B'rith."[4] These
messages reflected competing impulses felt by southern Jews: to help
their coreligionists, wherever they might originate, and to prove their
rootedness in the places they lived.

By 1899 estimates indicated that the states of the former Confederacy
were home to just 9 percent of American Jews, and the foreign-born
proportion of the South's population would in fact halve between 1880
and 1910.[5] Nevertheless, the experience of these immigrants was distinctive and their presence striking. They arrived as southern states were
becoming increasingly fanatical in their commitment to racial segregation and Black disfranchisement, now with the approval of the federal
government. In 1896 the Supreme Court affirmed the principle of "separate but equal" accommodations for Blacks and whites, and in 1898 the
United States entered into war against Spain in the name of the "white
man's burden," which easily justified the subjugation of African Americans at home alongside so-called "barbarians" abroad.[6] The stakes of
racial categorization were clearer than ever.

While Jews like the Pearlstines might not enthusiastically endorse
the immigration of those like the Rubins, they did undertake a wide
array of projects to assist and Americanize them once they had arrived. In Atlanta, for instance, by 1896 acculturated Jewish women had

established a bath and a Sunday school in the Decatur Street immigrant district, with the goal of introducing new arrivals to proper
bodily comportment, biblical texts, and patriotic ideals.[7] Their work,
part of a broader expansion of women's activism, was conducted
under the auspices of the Ladies Hebrew Benevolent Society and the
local branch of the National Council of Jewish Women, founded in
1893. They saw themselves—and were seen by admiring men—as
"kind-hearted ladies [who] want to do this unfortunate people good."[8]
Like other reformist southern women, they believed in the power of
elites—including if not especially women—to improve "uncivilized"
groups through rationally administered educational and social programs.[9] Men were more likely to provide direct funds, through groups
like New Orleans' United Hebrew Benevolent Society and as individuals. For instance, in 1907, Max Ginsburger of Grenada, Mississippi, sent a personal check to Rabbi Max Heller "for the benefit of
the Russian Jews."[10] He clearly felt distinct from the new arrivals, but
also somehow responsible for them.

This work took place on a local level and in collaboration with northern coreligionists. Most significantly, starting in 1900, committees were
established across the region to coordinate with the New York–based
Industrial Removal Office (IRO). Its goal was to disperse Jewish immigrants to western and southern states in the hopes of alleviating the
suffering—and embarrassment—of Jewish poverty in New York City.
Local committees requested "removals" with particular occupational and
demographic characteristics. Macon's committee noted that their city
was "no place for common labor" because of the competition for low
wages with Black workers. By 1910 they had become particularly blunt:
"<u>Send good people</u>. Do not send common labor and if you have to—
send a fellow that will make a peddler but not one to work like a n[----]
because he never will—negro help dirt cheap."[11] Writing to their coreligionists in the North, Macon Jews spelled out some of the harsh realities
of southern economic life—the exploitation of African Americans and
their own eagerness to maintain distance from them. In their view, to
peddle was to be counted among "good people," in contrast to other
forms of unskilled "common labor" performed by African Americans.

Over the course of fifteen years, the IRO would send almost eighty thousand immigrants to fifteen hundred hinterland communities, a little under 10 percent of them to the states of the former Confederacy.[12] Among them were those like Philip Fireman, who wrote a letter describing his satisfaction with Macon: "The town is a very attractive one. Mr. Kaplan has found work for me as a shoemaker and I am getting $12 a week."[13] Others, including the majority of the families settled in Fort Worth, Texas, used IRO networks to move to places where they already had relatives. Between 1907 and 1914, Rabbi Henry Cohen of Galveston worked with the Jewish Immigrants' Information Bureau, which sought to divert immigrants from the dangers and attractions of New York City. He met thousands of Jews arriving directly from Europe, on the theory that "they can be more readily absorbed and assimilated [than in New York]."[14] The bureau's organizers in Europe discouraged religiously observant Jews from immigrating, and tried to send new arrivals to places in the North and West, where they imagined racial issues to be less fraught. Nevertheless, Galveston immigrants settled in thirty-three towns in former Confederate states, and about three thousand of them remained in Texas.[15]

The charitable relationships that were created between local Jews and the new arrivals were complicated. For instance, when the *Jewish Sentiment* of Atlanta praised clubwomen's success in ameliorating immigrants' filth and ignorance, the immigrants' leaders protested. "Let us work our way to prosperity and American citizenship in our own humble way," wrote Russian Jewish leader Leon Eplan, who had already been in the city for over a decade. "Be charitable to our needy, if you wish, but do not publish us as barbarians, constantly inviting the contempt of our fellow citizens."[16] Despite the IRO's successes, local committees often complained to New York that immigrants were ill-suited to their jobs or insufficiently grateful.[17] Some up and left town, with or without notice, leading one Macon organizer to insist, citing the availability of work and the presence of Reform and Orthodox congregations, "I can only say that there is no reason why the men who are here should not be satisfied."[18] Immigrants irritated their sponsors when they proved ungrateful and when they defied norms around money, language, and gendered behavior associated with the white middle class. For instance, an arrival to Lake Charles, Louisiana, racked up debts, and in Vicksburg, Mississippi, another "can not and seems unwilling to speak English."[19] In Paris, Texas, a migrant "misrepresented and made false statements. . . . He is not married to the woman he came here with, she being his sister. . . . He and his sister quarreled, thereby creating a disturbance and scandal in public to our great sorrow and mortification."[20]

The immigrants were, after all, complex human actors, whose happiness might require more than steady employment and a choice between two synagogues in a remote Georgia river city. Southern towns contrasted dramatically with New York and with the European places they came from, where Jewish life permeated the streets and everyday life. Macon was, according to its IRO committee, a "cotton + cotton seed center" with tens of thousands of residents, "chiefly farmers," and just a few hundred Jews; many immigrants had never lived in places where their demographic marginality as Jews was so obvious. Their neighbors were no longer peasants of varying ethnic backgrounds, dominated by an official Russian Orthodox Church, or a raucous mixture of migrants from around the world, but Black and white Christians of varying stripes, the majority of them evangelical Methodists and Baptists who met in racially segregated churches.[21] David L. Cohn, the son of Russian Jewish immigrants and a keen observer of his home region, wrote that in Greenville, Mississippi, race relations were governed "by unwritable codes, an intricate ritual of manners, and a constant adjustment among members of both races."[22] This would have been a lot to handle, even for the best-prepared immigrants.

And yet, as Jewish immigrants continued to arrive in New York, after Kishinev and after the failed 1905 Russian revolution, there were always some among them who headed southward. They arrived not only through the IRO, the Galveston Plan, or the smattering of short-lived colonization schemes in the region, but in order to join family or friends, pursue work opportunities, or seek a warmer climate. Menachem Mendel Frieden had brothers settled in Norfolk, Virginia; after arriving at Ellis Island, he immediately boarded a southbound train.[23] Others started in New York, most of them working in factories, especially in the booming garment industry. Once they came southward, there were, according to Freidan, three means of "doing business"—namely, religious work, peddling, and storekeeping.[24] Alexander Gurwitz followed the first path, working as a Judaica teacher and kosher meat slaughterer in San Antonio. He later remembered, "I labored hard at such work as I never had done in Russia." In addition to the basic challenges of slaughtering meat, delivering it, and teaching children, Gurwitz had to deal with competition and conflict among the city's Jewish communal workers, and was rarely paid enough to support his family. His wife Fannie supplemented their income by selling milk from their cows.[25]

Gurwitz felt that his idealized dreams "sank in the mud of San Antonio."[26] Not only was daily life taxing, but he lamented the absence of a daily *minyan* and the eagerness of Jewish merchants to make money instead of rest on the Sabbath. Nevertheless, Jewish immigrants from across eastern Europe did form vibrant enclaves. Gurwitz, who continued to wear a beard and skullcap, never really learned English and was able to make a living teaching in Yiddish throughout his career. Frieden remembered of Norfolk, "Everyone spoke Yiddish. . . . I had almost no association with non-Jews; all my business was with Jews."[27] Jewish immigrants were bound by the Yiddish language—they subscribed to New York's Yiddish *Daily Forward* and formed Yiddish cultural groups—and in larger cities, by physical proximity.[28] They congregated in Richmond's East End, Memphis's "the Pinch," and Atlanta's Decatur Street.[29]

By 1910, Atlanta was home to four kosher butchers, serving a population of 2,300 eastern European Jews, and a smaller number of immigrants from the Ottoman Empire, who by 1915 were worshipping in the Oriental Hebrew Association Or Ve Shalom (Light and peace), one of six congregations in the city.[30] In Richmond and Memphis—home to long-standing congregations with names like Beth Ahabah (House of love) and B'nai Israel (Children of Israel)—immigrant congregations chose names of famous Jewish philanthropists, Sir Moses Montefiore and Baron Hirsch, respectively. In Atlanta and San Antonio, they emphasized fellowship, choosing the names Ahavath Achim (Brotherly love) and Agudas Achim (Brotherly association), and in Knoxville they celebrated religious piety, choosing Heska Amuna—"Graspers of

faith."[31] These names tended to communicate a particularistic orientation and a longing for community and piety. Yiddish-speaking Jews in
Petersburg, Virginia, following in the footsteps of other Russian immigrant congregations and reflecting the close familial ties within the
community, named their congregation Brith Achim (Brotherly covenant).[32] Several new congregations called themselves "the people of" a
particular locale, embedding their identity within a transnational geography. In Memphis alone there was an Anshei Sphard (People of the
Sephardic rite) and an Anshei Galicia.[33] Congregations named Anshei
Sphard could also be found in New Orleans and in Atlanta.[34]

In 1912, immigrants in El Paso founded B'nai Zion, or "Children of
Zion," gesturing toward their sympathy with Zionism.[35] Launched in
earnest at the meeting of first World Zionist Congress in 1897, this nascent movement argued that Jews could escape European antisemitism
only through relocation and self-government. Its reception among established southern Jewish leaders had initially been tepid. The 1885 Pittsburgh Platform had rejected the idea of a "return to Palestine," and Rabbi
Max Heller's initial impulse was to predict that it would "fail from its
inherent opposition to the core of Judaism."[36] Herbert Ezekiel supported
it in theory but argued that the logistics were too far-fetched to make it
a worthwhile project. He suggested instead that Jews "devote their time
and energies to becoming good American citizens."[37] Zionism had
proved more convincing to Jews in eastern Europe, some of whom
brought it with them as they migrated. By 1903, Houston, Texas, was
home to a "Herzl Zion Society," which paid homage to Zionist leader
Theodore Herzl, and the next year a representative of the Federation of
American Zionists undertook a two-month tour of the region. Soon
there were Zionist groups in places like Austin and Tyler, Texas; the
Texas Zionist Organization boasted over one thousand members.[38]

While immigrants with Zionist proclivities raised funds to support
Jewish settlement in Palestine, those dedicated to Jewish socialism engaged in mutual aid, education, and political activism through the Arbeiter Ring, or Worker's Circle, which opened ten branches in the South
between 1907 and 1915.[39] In 1911, socialist writer Baruch Charney Vladek
went on a southern tour, writing an account that was published in the

Yiddish *Daily Forward*. While in New York and eastern Europe socialists usually rejected religious affiliation, he wrote that "in one place, I met a president of a congregation who had been one of the first active participants in the propagandist circles of New York at the beginning of the Jewish Socialist Movement in America."[40] He was likely referring to Bernhard Goldgar, president of Sherah Israel in Macon, who late in life still wrote movingly of his youthful conversion to socialism. A later retrospective about Macon's Arbeiter Ring branch almost certainly referenced him when it mentioned "the president of the shul [synagogue], who was an intelligent man and a radical Jew."[41] Jewish immigrant identity was complex, perhaps especially in the South, where houses of worship served as vital Jewish centers, subsuming but perhaps never fully extinguishing leftist political commitments.[42]

Goldgar, like so many of the Russian Jewish immigrants, was a storekeeper. Between 1900 and 1930, 63 percent of Russian Jewish immigrants in Atlanta worked as peddlers, merchants, or storekeepers; in 1909 Richmond's Jews included 15 wholesale merchants and 25 manufacturers, 111 humble tailors, and 287 middling retail merchants.[43] Many of these businesses relied on a Black clientele. Black educator Horace Mann Bond would remember of his childhood in the 1910s, "The Jew was the man who kept the pawnshop . . . where I sold papers on a Saturday; he was the man who operated the clothing store where my father took his five boys."[44] There is evidence—treasured by many contemporary Jews— that Jewish merchants treated Black customers with considerable respect, allowing them to try on clothing and hiring Black workers (figure 12.3).[45] The New York Yiddish *Daily Forward* even published a letter in its famous advice column purportedly written by a young man in a southern city who had fallen in love with a Black customer.[46]

And yet most of the recent immigrants seem to have been quickly initiated into the region's racial norms. Frieden remembered that when he first arrived, he "couldn't understand the attitude toward the blacks." Years later, living in Israel, he wrote that he feared his Black customers because he "had never before seen people of this color, their behavior brutish and lacking in manners."[47] Gurwitz tried and failed at peddling, in part because he felt it was degrading for "a Torah-learned Jew . . . to

FIGURE 12.3. M. H. Lazarus Hardware, with Black employees, early twentieth century. From the collection of the South Carolina Historical Society.

go knocking on Mexican doors and asking the poor customers to please buy my goods."[48] His conception of status, based on Jewish religious standards, now merged with local manifestations of the American racial hierarchy. Even the immigrant peddler who had fallen in love with his customer recognized that "[he] couldn't go around with her openly because [he is] white and she is colored" and reported that his friends had reacted with horror to his proposal of marriage.[49]

However positive individual encounters might have been, the relationship between storekeeper and customer could easily breed mistrust and resentment, as southern Jews had found throughout their history. Storekeeping was a familiar and reliable pathway to economic stability, and yet some feared, as Vladek put it, that Jews who served a Black clientele had "[given] up all the comforts of 'white' civilization"—in other words, "'blacken[ing]' themselves to make a living."[50] This anxiety about work and proximity to Blackness was echoed in the records of the Jewish Orphan Home in Atlanta. For instance, in the 1910s the home received a series of concerned letters about a family in Greensboro, North Carolina, who lived in a Black neighborhood—likely because of the father's business—and whose children had been "seen in company with negro children." The home employed Black workers as cooks and janitors, but anything less hierarchical or formal was suspicious.[51]

Immigrant Jews adapted to southern racial mores and were enlisted into them by established Jews and other white southerners. Miriam Glasser, who was born in Poland in 1888, was hired as a teacher at the Shaw School, one of two Black schools in Charleston, which exclusively hired white teachers, over the objections of local African American leaders. However honorable Glasser's own motives may have been, she became part of an effort to suppress the formation of a Black professional class.[52] When a Jewish immigrant merchant named Max Lubelsky was robbed and murdered in Charleston in 1910, a Black man named Daniel Duncan was speedily hanged for the crime, despite his claims of innocence. Although one newspaper noted, "The killing caused a sensation throughout the city, especially among the Jewish population in the upper part of town," Lubelsky was most often described as a "King street merchant" or "a white merchant."[53] If being a neighbor or salesman to African Americans might, in Vladek's words, "blacken" Jewish immigrants, being their teacher or alleged victim could "whiten" them, even if, as in the case of Lubelsky, he had served as a salesman and a neighbor as well.

Before his death, Lubelsky's life was captured in the 1910 census; he and his wife Rosa had immigrated to the United States in the early 1890s and become citizens; they had an eight-year-old son, who had been born in New York; and they lived in the rented building on King Street where they conducted business. While Lubelsky's race was clearly designated with a "W," his place of birth was described as "Russ. Yiddish," which made his religious identity visible to the state and to the historian.[54] Since 1899, "Hebrews" had been used as a racial classification within the US Bureau of Immigration, but organizations like the American Jewish Committee, an advocacy organization founded by New York elites in 1906, had successfully lobbied to keep it off the 1910 census; the language question was a compromise.[55] Unlike other immigrant groups, who were caught in the gap of statutes limiting citizenship to "white persons," and African-descended people, Jews' citizenship was not directly questioned. In fact, in district court in 1909, a Syrian immigrant in Atlanta named Costa George Najour pointed out, "If we are not 'white,' then the Jews should certainly be denied the rights of citizenship, as we are both of the Semitic family."[56]

And yet, these years were ripe with discussion of Jewish racial difference; popular periodicals and even elected officials described Jewish immigrants as inassimilable and as criminal. These associations were especially intense in New York City, where they were most visible, but they echoed across the country. At the port of Galveston, immigration officials deported more than four times as many Jewish women as did those in New York, claiming that they were "morally defective."[57] In 1910 the *Farmers Union News* published an article objecting to "the dumping of the foreign nations' refuse population into the South."[58] This general anti-immigrant sentiment coexisted and overlapped with a virulent anti-Catholicism and a persistent antisemitism. Despite the relatively minor scale of immigration to the South, the "Russian Jew" had become a familiar figure, especially visible in cities like Atlanta. At a time when 97 percent of Atlantans were American born, Jews constituted a third of the city's—and 20 percent of the state of Georgia's—foreign-born population.[59]

In 1906, the vulnerability of this community and the volatility of life in the Jim Crow South were made abundantly clear after a group of armed—and drunken—white men marched through Atlanta's Decatur Street nightlife district. They vandalized saloons and pawnshops, including a number owned by Jewish immigrants. The white men's rage had been fueled by sensationalistic newspaper reports accusing Black men of lustful, liquor-fueled assaults on white women. Many white residents blamed the chaos not on the white perpetrators but on the purveyors of liquor and their Black customers, claiming, "The white man who sells or gives away liquor to a negro is an enemy of his own race, an enemy of society, an enemy of law and order." Atlanta's city council revoked all "colored only" liquor licenses, including those owned by Jews, and the following summer, prohibition was instituted statewide.[60]

Jews had long been at odds with prohibition, which were rapidly moving to the center of white southern politics. Prohibitionists were motivated by a Christian perfectionist desire to eliminate sin, whereas southern Jewish activists, including many rabbis, tended to take inspiration from the Pittsburgh Platform's condemnation of "the problems presented by the contrasts and evils of the present organization of society."[61] They saw collective issues like child labor, education, health, prison reform, and, far more sparingly, workers' rights as the means to creating a better society.[62] Furthermore, almost all Jews used wine for ritual purposes, and many ran saloons or produced liquor.[63] In 1892, half of the officers of the Temple were current or former participants in the alcohol trade; the editor of the *Jewish South* argued that "we Israelites need no temperance literature, as we are not intemperate."[64] Prohibitionists periodically complained about Jews' involvement in the liquor trade. In Columbus, Georgia, a local leader decried "Jews and whiskey men" and declared that the Jewish president of the Board of Trade was unqualified because he "was not representative of the Christian people." An itinerant minister named John Cawhern condemned the "flat heeled, flat nosed, coarse haired, cross eyed slew footed Russian Jew whiskey venders whom the old Georgia politicians have licensed to poison our boys."[65]

Cawhern was not the only southern minister to cast Jews as physically—indeed, racially—deficient. In 1910 North Carolina minister Arthur Abernethy published a book called *The Jew a Negro: Being a Study of the Jewish Ancestry from an Impartial Standpoint*. Drawing on a novel mix of biblical history, ethnology, art history, and linguistics, along with, Abernethy admitted, his own examination of the bodies of lynched Black men, he went further than most southern antisemites of the turn of the twentieth century. He claimed that "the Jew . . . is the kinsman and descendant of the Negro, holding the Negro's features and characteristics through the long years of racial transmutations."[66] Abernethy's idiosyncratic book, published on the heels of others like *The Negro, a Menace to American Civilization* (1907), was far from representative of white southern thought, but what limited attention it received served as something of a Rorschach test of contemporaneous racial and religious attitudes.[67]

An article in the *Fool-Killer* of Moravian Falls, North Carolina, described Abernethy's theory alongside a competing one, which claimed that African-descended peoples did not descend from the biblical Adam but from his brother. This author insisted on the absolute veracity of the biblical text, a strategy that was gaining ground as a counter to controversial new theories of evolution and the higher criticism of the Bible. Black people, he argued, could not be related to Jews, whom the Bible made clear were descended from Adam.[68] Others went beyond biblical history in assessing Abernethy's argument, turning to ideologies of civilization. A negative review in the *Charlotte Observer*, which was favorably reprinted in the *American Israelite*, pointed to Jews' supposedly high level of civilization relative to African-descended peoples, lamenting that Abernethy's knowledge was "wasted upon the discussion of so puerile a question."[69] Thomas Dixon, author of virulently racist the *Clansman*, had likewise described Jews as part of "our race" who "had achieved a noble civilization."[70] Like Zebulon Vance and others before him, these white Christians cast Jews as an idealized other. Ironically, the most positive review of Abernethy's book came from a Black newspaper, which praised the book for proving "the Negro's high standing in the Bible," ignoring the argument about Jews altogether.[71]

Abernethy's book of "scientific" theories was produced within a context of widespread and ongoing conversations about Jewishness, Blackness, and American belonging, within and beyond the South. Echoing other critics of Jewish immigrant behavior, Abernethy argued that Jewish men, while less violent than Black men, were also "abnormally full-blooded" and sexually perverse, although their methods were "blandishment, ingenuity, and gold" rather than "brute force and crime."[72] These revelations touched upon theology—Abernethy claimed that Jesus Christ was not in fact a Jew—and upon politics. Jews had "stirred all Europe with their racial antagonisms," and, he darkly prophesied, "When the Negro is eliminated from the citizenship of the United States . . . the American government will turn its attention to the alien Hebrew."[73]

CHAPTER 13

No Peace

In 1924, Florida housewife Helen Apte wrote in her diary that "anti-Semitism is growing in this country," although she insisted, "It cannot touch [me]. . . . [I]n me burns the ancient pride of race."[1] As a young wife and mother—she married in 1909 and gave birth in 1913—the Georgia-born Apte proudly watched her brothers go off to fight in World War I and volunteered to support the war effort. In the 1920s she gained access to the vote and moved with her family to the boomtown of Miami, where they flourished on the white side of Jim Crow's racial division. A photo from that time shows a round-faced woman who clearly enjoys contemporary fashions; she sports bobbed grey hair, a floral top, and a sparkly necklace. And yet Apte surveyed the world around her with concern.[2] She saw the antagonism toward Jews that was growing, fueled by Christian piety and opposition to modernity, and that would only intensify amid the global struggles of the 1930s. One week before Apte gave birth to her daughter, a trial began in Atlanta that showed southern Jews—and the nation—just how limited the protections offered by wealth, connections, and white skin could be.

Leo Max Frank had been born to German Jewish immigrants in Cuero, Texas, and was raised in Brooklyn, New York (figure 13.1). After studying engineering at Cornell University, he moved to Atlanta to manage the National Pencil Factory, which belonged to his uncle, Confederate veteran Moses Frank. There he met and married Lucille Selig, a second-generation Atlantan and Apte's first cousin.[3] Frank, a thin, nervous man, was representative of long-standing patterns of

FIGURE 13.1. Leo M. Frank, 1914. Image courtesy of the
Cuba Family Archives for Southern Jewish History at
the Breman Museum.

transregional mobility and intimately connected to Atlanta's half-
century-old Jewish community. The Franks joined the local Reform
congregation, the Temple, donated to Jewish causes, and helped
organize events in support of the Jewish Orphan's Home.[4] On April 26,
1913, Frank paid a thirteen-year-old girl named Mary Phagan her wages;
he was the last to admit to seeing her alive. The next morning her dis-
figured body was found in the factory basement.

The public soon learned that Mary had been a member of the First
Christian Bible School, on her way to a Confederate Memorial Day
parade. As pictures of her cherubic face circulated, many came to see

her as the perfect symbol of a white Christian girl destroyed by New South industrialization. Her death seemed to prove that its combination of exploitation and freedom, and its consequent threat to white patriarchal order, was not only troubling but dangerous. The police quickly settled on Frank as their main suspect. A Black worker, twenty-seven-year-old janitor Jim Conley, claimed that Frank had killed Phagan in the course of a failed seduction. Conley admitting to disposing of her body and writing the note found at the scene, all of which he claimed to have done at Frank's behest.[5] Much of the newspaper coverage and trial testimony centered on questions of Frank's sexuality, casting him as a "pervert" who used his position to violate pure Christian girls. Conley claimed that before asking him to remove Phagan's corpse, Frank had told him: "Of course you know I ain't built like other men."[6] Although it seemed unlikely that a Black man with a criminal record and a history of drinking would be seen as more credible than a well-off white man, many in Atlanta saw Conley as an "untutored Afro-American" incapable of telling a sophisticated lie.[7] Mary Phagan's minister later suggested that a Black perpetrator would have been an unsatisfying suspect, too obvious to account for an angelic victim like Mary: "A Yankee Jew . . . here would be victim worthy to pay for the crime."[8]

Frank's community rallied behind him, insisting that he was as an upstanding husband, a pious synagogue-goer, and a wronged man, even an "American Dreyfus."[9] After his conviction, B'nai B'rith leaders acted on previous plans to create an Anti-Defamation League, and prominent Jews from the North stepped in to mount a public defense.[10] They succeeded in drawing attention to the case, but in the process enraged white southerners like Tom Watson, a lawyer and Populist politician whose newspaper spewed anti-Frank vitriol. He accused northern newspapers of butting into Georgia's business at the behest of wealthy northern Jews and argued that Judaism was inherently perverse: "Every student of sociology knows that the black man's lust after the white woman is not much fiercer than the lust of the licentious Jew for the gentile."[11] After a series of failed appeals, Georgia governor John M. Slaton commuted Frank's death sentence to life in prison, leading to riots in Atlanta and plans for a boycott of Jewish businesses. A small card was distributed at the time: "American Gentiles it is up to you. . . . Why not BUY from White People?"[12] The ties between whiteness and Christianity, usually more muted, were now made explicit.

Finally, on the night of August 16 a group of the leading men of Marietta, Phagan's home town, stormed the prison farm in Milledgeville where Frank was incarcerated, calling themselves "The Knights of Mary Phagan."[13] They kidnapped Frank and drove him back to Marietta, where they slid a noose around his neck and hanged him from an oak tree. Lynching was a southern tradition that overwhelmingly targeted Black men, especially those accused of sexual contact with white women. Indeed, on the very same day that Frank was lynched, so too was John Riggins, a Black man in southwest Georgia who had been accused of rape; an additional twenty African Americans were lynched in Georgia that year alone.[14] Georgia's record was particularly bloody, but throughout the South some four thousand people—five times as many Blacks as whites—were killed by vigilante mobs between 1880 and 1930. When sixty-eight-year-old Allen Brooks was lynched in Dallas in 1910, Edgar Goldberg, editor of Houston's *Jewish Herald*, had described it as "a crime to be condemned in the most stringent manner," although he also repeated the rationalizations that were common among otherwise genteel whites: "The people make the laws and the people can suspend the laws."[15]

While every lynching was distinct, they all served as powerful ritualized acts, suffused with Christian conceptions of sacrificial violence and retributive justice. Those present at Frank's lynching described it as "like some religious rite" and noted its "curiously reverent manner."[16] Onto his slight body had been loaded the weight of a whole host of anxieties about Jews, sex, and the new social order that had put white women in the workplace, farmers in the city, and power in the hands of wealthy industrialists. A lynching could not actually change what ailed the people of Georgia, although in that moment it probably felt like it had; the authority of white Christian men had been secured. Members of the Knights of Mary Phagan would continue to pursue this goal, just a few months later contributing to the revival of the Ku Klux Klan at nearby Stone Mountain.[17]

Frank's lynching had some antecedents. Most other white lynching victims were also established adults from out of state, and there was a longer history of work-related violence against Jews dating at least to the Reconstruction era.[18] Nevertheless, it was shocking. Personally devastated by the lynching, Frank's rabbi, David Marx, groped for answers.[19] He wrote to a correspondent, "Confidentially, such feelings were simply fanned into expression." He compared Frank to Socrates, Jesus, and the "man of suffering" found in Isaiah 53.[20] In one moment—either uncharacteristic or revealing—he suggested that Russian Jews were to blame for the antisemitism that killed Frank.[21] In the decades to come, Atlanta Jews worked to avoid public reminders of what had happened. As late as 1940 one woman reported, "As a subject to be talked about or make inquiries about, it's absolutely taboo here."[22] And yet its effects clearly lingered. On August 17, 1923, Helen Apte wrote in her diary, "Today is the anniversary of Leo Frank's death. I thought of that when I looked up the date to enter."[23] Frank's fate was a potent reminder that white supremacist violence need not limit itself to African American targets.

Already as the Leo Frank trial played out, southern Jews had begun turning their attention to the outbreak of war in Europe, raising funds for Jewish "war sufferers." Few Jews had any love for Russia, and there were Jewish peace activists and radicals who opposed the war on principle, but once the United States entered on the side of England and Russia in the spring of 1917, most southern Jews proved eager to "manifest the patriotism of [their] Congregation," counting themselves among the approximately one million southerners who served.[24] This was made easier by the fact that American Jewish leaders secured an official place for Judaism within military operations. The newly founded Jewish Welfare Board (JWB) provided services for all Jewish soldiers, acting as a Jewish equivalent to the Protestant YMCA and the Catholic Knights of Columbus.[25] Because many US military bases were located in southern states, the JWB worked extensively in the region—deploying fieldworkers, camp rabbis, and military chaplains—and in cooperation with local communities.[26] One JWB correspondent noted, for instance, "the lovely spirit in which the Atlanta Jews are ministering to the needs of our soldiers in and about Atlanta."[27]

Overseas, the JWB could act as an extension of the Jewish South. Visiting the JWB office in Paris in 1918, soldier Leon Schwarz encountered several southern acquaintances. Soon afterward, he attended the opening of a JWB clubhouse in Le Mans overseen by Chaplain James Heller, son of Rabbi Max Heller of New Orleans.[28] The government had sanctioned Judaism as an American faith, and yet many Jews remained painfully aware of the gaze of Christian soldiers. Rabbi Abraham Benedict Rhine of Hot Springs, Arkansas, found that some men from assimilated families "didn't care to be reminded of their faith in the camp amidst a multitude of Gentiles."[29] Rabbi Max Heller complained during a military speaking tour that "Jewish audiences consist, to an appalling extent, virtually exclusively, of Ghetto Jews,"[30] and one JWB representative in the South insisted that his replacement be an "American, of college breeding."[31] Even at war, US-born Jews continued to worry about the consequences of their association with Russian Jewish immigrants.

Chaplains were overwhelmingly Reform rabbis, and they came into conflict with soldiers from traditional backgrounds, who were in the majority. One lieutenant serving at Camp McClellan in Alabama complained that Rabbi Morris Newfield was trying to push Reform Judaism on the men, while Chaplain David Goldberg, a Texan, argued that the JWB-issued prayerbook, which was meant to serve all soldiers, smacked of "goluth [exilic] sentiment."[32] Nevertheless, Rabbi Rhine insisted, "We have brought a number of our young men at the camp nearer to Judaism, and . . . we have kept others from forgetting that they were Jews and that they owe an allegiance to their people and their God."[33] After attending Yom Kippur services at the Synagogue of Paris in 1917, Rabbi Henry Cohen's son wrote movingly: "I feel nearer to Judaism tonight than I have ever felt in my life."[34] Far from home, face to face with the traumas of war and his European coreligionists, Cohen experienced a Jewish awakening.

Jews were present within the Great War as soldiers, as victims of its violence on the Eastern Front, and as political actors agitating for universal and Jewish rights.[35] In cities and towns across the South, then, Jews watched European affairs with great interest. Zionists like Alexander Gurwitz rejoiced after the British Arthur James Balfour, first Earl of Balfour, offered support for "a national home for the Jewish people" in Palestine on November 2, 1917, while socialists celebrated the Communist overthrow of the Russian tsar several days later.[36] The war moved Helen Apte to an expression of theological providentialism:

> The great God sits on high, listening to the prayers of the German and the French and the Russian and the Turk—and now the American—all, all praying for victory. He sits on high and listens. I know he listens, and I know it will work itself out for good, as all things do.[37]

One year after the war ended, Apte noted that a bronze memorial tablet had been placed in the Temple in Atlanta to commemorate three of "our heroic dead." The war had inspired a wave of patriotic memorialization, including "honor rolls" that quantified patriotic service by listing names of Jewish soldiers and memorials to the war dead, which emphasized the quality of individual sacrifice.[38] And yet she wondered, "What did we accomplish? . . . [W]e seem further than ever from universal peace."[39] The progressive optimism of wartime had already begun to fester into an isolationist backlash. By 1926 she would write, "Armistice Day—a glorification of peace! Alas, what a farce: There is no peace."[40]

As a wave of postwar antisemitic violence spread in Europe, Jews in the United States faced forms of prejudice that were less extreme but still disturbing.[41] Detroit industrialist Henry Ford circulated theories of Jewish world domination, and elite institutions like Harvard University instituted quotas to restrict the admission of Jewish students. Jews were variously charged with controlling the world—as argued in the infamous forgery *The Protocols of the Elders of Zion*—and seeking to destabilize it through radical leftist politics, often glossed as "Bolshevism."[42] Although the war had already suppressed immigration, support for its restriction intensified, starting with the 1921 Emergency Quota Act and followed three years later by the National Origins Act. Immigration quotas would now be determined by the demographics of the US population in 1890, greatly reducing the numbers of southern and eastern European immigrants. These restrictions were premised on the widespread assumption that these immigrants—the vast majority of them Jews and Catholics, who had been welcomed into the American military—could not become good Americans.[43]

Black Americans had also come home from the war filled with a patriotic optimism that quickly dissipated; a series of vicious anti-Black riots broke out in cities across the country, and there was a dramatic uptick in lynchings.[44] Across the region, Democratic rule and racial segregation continued uninterrupted and even intensified. For instance, the very same year of the National Origins Act, Virginia passed a Racial Integrity Act, which redefined white people as those with "no trace whatsoever of any blood other than Caucasian," forbidding their marriage with nonwhites and requiring new forms of registration with the state.[45] New statutes were constantly being put on the books in order to ensure that no public space was conducive to racial mixing.[46] Large numbers of Black southerners voted with their feet, abandoning the region altogether as part of the so-called "Great Migration" to northern cities, while those who remained fought an uphill battle against Jim Crow through public political activism and in quiet acts of everyday resistance.[47]

Antagonism toward African Americans, immigrants, Catholics, and Jews came together in the agenda of the Ku Klux Klan, which emerged from the Great War newly powerful and expansive; by 1924 it boasted four million members. Although most of them lived outside the South, it had strongholds across the region. In Birmingham alone there were eighteen thousand members, amounting to almost half of registered voters in the city.[48] Klan members marched through southern towns and cities in white robes and burned crosses, directly and indirectly intimidating those who deviated from whiteness or Protestantism.[49] They expressed admiration for Jews' alleged racial purity, and occasionally respect for individual Jews, but they also argued that as a group Jews were "absolutely unblendable. . . . [To them] patriotism, as the Anglo-Saxon feels it, is impossible."[50] Occasionally Jews became targets of Klan harassment; in Texas Klansmen tarred and feathered a young Jewish man for "despoiling a Gentile girl," and they beat another because he had been seen fraternizing with a Black man.[51]

The Klan did not have a monopoly on antisemitic violence or language, however. In 1925, an angry mob in Williamston, North Carolina, abducted and castrated a Jewish salesman accused of assaulting "an American" woman.[52] Russian Jewish immigrant S. Brill recalled an occasion in Elizabeth City, sixty miles northeast, where "a fresh young man strolled in one day and began to make funny faces and talk like a comic Jew on the stage. When I made no reply to him he used dirty and insulting language."[53] Jews were subject to mob violence, acts of harassment, and public denigration. Fiery preachers like Mordecai F. Ham—a fundamentalist Baptist best known for converting a young Billy Graham—travelled through the region preaching sermons critical of Jews.[54]

Rabbi Ferdinand Hirsh claimed that Ham's sermons in Sumter, South Carolina, "weakened friendships and even divided families, as there were many mixed marriages in the town."[55] Indeed, intensified antisemitism could not erase the fact of southern Jewish integration. Perhaps most evocative of this paradox is the apocryphal claim of various southern Jewish merchants to have sold Klansmen the bedsheets for their distinctive costumes.[56] Some Jews did collaborate with the Klan, especially in places where Klansmen were members of the respectable middle class or politically influential. For instance, in 1923 Jewish merchant Alex Sanger sat on stage at an event celebrating the philanthropy of the Texas Klan.[57] Leon Schwarz of Mobile was friendly with several Klansmen. He wrote in his memoir, "I refuse to hold to account to this day men who joined the Klan in its infancy. With many who had political ambition, the Klan was just one more thing to join to get some votes."[58] And yet southern rabbis spoke out against the Klan's "injection of religious fanaticism into the body politic," and worked behind the scenes to limit Klan influence in their communities.[59]

Brill had apparently responded to antisemitic insult by hitting the man with a shoe stretcher; he later threatened to kill him, a provocation that went unpunished because a prominent local citizen came to his defense, noting that "he has been here two years now, we all know him; he is a good citizen, minds his own business." Although this goodwill was clearly dependent on familiarity and conformity, the storekeeper concluded that "the people over here have always been kind and friendly to me."[60] Hirsch claimed that Ham's sermon had in fact been inspired by an act of respect to himself; they had both attended a Kiwanis meeting at which Hirsch was asked to give the invocation, to Ham's great offense. He recalled another occasion on which the mayor, a fellow Kiwanian who had a Jewish law partner, granted permission for a Klan march but "stipulated that Jack Brenan, a Catholic, and myself, must lead the parade. Of course this was just a bit of humor, but I think exemplified the spirit of the town or at least its leading citizens, and the parade did not create a ripple."[61] Most southern Jews lived relatively comfortable day-to-day lives, with occasional bouts of awkwardness and a latent fear of violence that underscored the fragility of their standing as white men and women.

Rabbi Hirsch was an Ohio-born dropout of Hebrew Union College who in 1907, at just twenty-one years old, was hired by the congregation in Bessemer, Alabama. He later moved on to Athens, Georgia, and in 1919 to Sumter, South Carolina, where he would remain for almost a decade before finishing out his career in Monroe, Louisiana.[62] His papers offer a fascinating window into the mindset of a small-town rabbi in this era. At some point, likely in the 1920s, he wrote a poem about a Jewish woman named Pauline, like himself a northern transplant with a Jewish last name. Because of this, "the DARs were closed to her, as was the UDC. . . . [W]hen she learned these sad facts, did she show them she did care? / She joined up with the Civil League, no grandpas needed there." Rather than sulk in response to social rejection, the fictional Pauline finds other social outlets.[63]

Excluded on the basis of ancestry from southern society's most elite bastions, Hirsch, like his character and many other southern Jewish men and women of the day, did enthusiastically join civic groups like the Kiwanis Club, the Masons, the American Red Cross, the Scouts, and the Rotarians.[64] Jewish leaders also engaged in a proliferating number of explicitly interreligious efforts, ranging from local community chests to national organizations like the National Conference of Jews and Christians, founded in 1927.[65] In 1935 Hirsch told his congregation that "the outstanding accomplishment of the last year has been in the realm of Better Understanding," pointing to various interfaith services and his pulpit exchanges with a Methodist minister.[66] Civic and interfaith endeavors provided Jews with one avenue by which to reaffirm their bona fides as middle-class southern whites, but there were others. For instance, Atlanta Jews publicized a Jewish woman named Caroline Haas as the "first white child" born in the city. Impoverished immigrant women insisted that they be allowed to use funds from the Hebrew Orphans Home to hire Black maids.[67]

Their embrace of whiteness did not mean that southern Jews totally ignored the ongoing plight of African Americans, however. Steeped in Reform Judaism's brand of social justice, they supported "racial uplift" organizations like the National Association for the Advancement of Colored People (NAACP) and the Urban League, as well as—with the wounds of the Leo Frank case still fresh—the Association of Southern Women for the Prevention of Lynching.[68] Hirsch appears to have remained silent on Black rights, but the bolder of his colleagues spoke out on behalf of Black workers and in opposition to specific forms of segregation; Rabbi Ira Sanders enrolled Black women in the Little Rock School of Social Work, which he founded, before being pressured to expel them, and Rabbi David Marx of Atlanta lobbied for the desegregation of city parks.[69]

In recent decades a coalition of southern liberals, northern bureaucrats, and philanthropists had come to understand the South as a "problem" in need of reform.[70] Among them was Chicago Jewish businessman Julius Rosenwald, who funded Black colleges and provided matching grants to build 5,300 Black schoolhouses in rural areas of the South between 1912 and 1932.[71] He was a philanthropist from outside of the region, however; the average southern Jew was happy to contribute to general reform efforts, but when it came to the issue of Black civil rights, one among them wrote in the NAACP publication the Crisis that he was "satisfied to accept the situation as he finds it. He must make money, he must be in the good graces of his gentile neighbors, and whatever personal inclination he may possess to combat Negro hatred must be suppressed in the more vital and immediate issue of earning a livelihood."[72] Eleven years later, Samuel Rosenberg of Hampton, Virginia, reported in the same publication that "southern Jews from Rabbis to merchants regard the Negro as a second or third class being."[73] When the Jewish owner of Hammel Department Store in Mobile, Alabama, rebuffed calls to install a bathroom for Black customers in 1938, the local head of the NAACP responded: "We are bewildered that a member of one oppressed group, because of favorable geographical and other conditions, would be unsympathetic and recalcitrant in regard to the rights of another persecuted minority."[74] Most southern Jews were simply unwilling to stick their necks out for an unpopular cause.

Living within southern communities day in and day out, Hirsch and other southern Jews regularly found friendship among white Kiwanis Club members and their well-heeled ministers; more occasionally they allied themselves with selected Black middle-class leaders. From the growing numbers of Christian fundamentalists in the region, they maintained a posture of curious distance.[75] Joseph Goode, son of the rabbi in Petersburg, Virginia, remembered of his childhood in the 1920s that there was "a next door church—peopled by 'Holy Rollers'—their chants and abandonment to religious ecstasy is still vivid in my memory."[76] In a 1918 sermon about the deadly influenza epidemic then spreading around the world, Hirsch had expressed some envy of these Christians: "We Jews don't have revivals, nor protracted meetings or times when we may enjoy to the full the joy of faith. . . . I am not a missionary preacher. I can't threaten you with Hell or fire for not believing, nor a Heaven of gems for profession of faith." Nevertheless, he earnestly insisted that God was worth seeking out: "Heaven or Hell is in the heart. . . . God is with you if you only deserve His presence and seek Him with your whole heart."[77] In 1925 Hirsch responded to the Scopes "Monkey" trial in Dayton, Tennessee, a highly publicized contest over scientific theories of evolution. It drew public attention to fundamentalist Christians, who insisted that the account of creation in the Book of Genesis was literally true.[78] Hirsch introduced his congregants to the basics of higher and lower criticism of the Bible, as well as comparative religions. "Did Moses write the Five Books attributed to him?" he asked, answering, "I doubt it. . . . Yet this manner of their inception does not alter their value to the world."[79] Impressed by but opposed to his fundamentalist neighbors, he insisted that faith in God and the Bible could coexist with science and reason.

This was in keeping with the ethos of Reform Judaism, which despite its widespread influence, seemed to be undergoing something of a malaise amid the increased pessimism of the interwar period. Rabbi Edward Calisch of Richmond called for "the resuscitation of the dry bones of Reform Jewry."[80] Indeed, this perhaps explains Hirsh's wistful invocation of Christian revivals. Most rabbis pointed to congregational apathy as the primary cause. As early as 1911, Rabbi George Solomon had complained to his congregation of "an utter lack of interest in all things pertaining to the synagogue," and the following year he elaborated, "The pace [of life] has become so fast and furious, and life of the average men and women is so empty, inane, and vacuous."[81] Offering the layperson's perspective, Helen Apte wrote in her diary, "I wish I could get some real joy and consolation in going to temple." She attributed her estrangement to her own transgressions—"perhaps that is one of the penalties we pay for sinning"—and to her exposure to new ideas—"I have lost my simple faith, but I have acquired a philosophy."[82] The attractions of modernity that had intensified after the war served as distractions from religious observance.

Reform Judaism also came under threat from other religious movements. While evangelical missionaries to the Jews—like the Jewish-born Jacob Gartenhaus of the Southern Baptist Home Mission Board—found few converts, quite a few southern Jews had dabbled in Christian Science, which posited the power of the mind to affect bodily health.[83] Clara Lowenburg Moses of New Orleans hired a Christian Science healer and read its core text, Mary Baker Eddy's 1875 Science and Health with Key to the Scripture.[84] In the opinion of Rabbi Max Heller, it was "a system of religious and medical teaching which is a menace to the civic welfare," and he lamented the "many misguided Jews who claim that adherence to Christian Science is completely reconcilable with loyalty to Judaism."[85] Rabbi Alfred Geiger Moses of Mobile took a different tack, publishing a book called Jewish Science: Divine Healing in Judaism. He sought to contest Christian Science by offering Jews a practical, spiritual alternative to Reform Judaism's distant rationalism.[86]

Moses was not the only Jewish leader to actively contest the novel challenges of postwar life. Many sought to combine aspects of Judaism and modern leisure culture—for instance, by building synagogues with spaces for social gatherings. In keeping with national trends pioneered in New York by the innovative Rabbi Mordecai Kaplan, the building committee in Durham insisted that "a synagogue, particularly in the South, is not only a House of Worship but equally as important a community center."[87] What was true for adults seemed even more important for young people growing up amid movies, jazz music, and automobiles. Rabbi George Solomon of Savannah opened a summer camp in North Carolina in 1926, "Where the Jewish boy can not only feel thoroughly at home with Jewish influences, but at the same time be developed in the manly sports and activities."[88] By 1939 the many youth clubs established within Reform congregations were united within the National Federation of Temple Youth.[89] Southern college campuses became home to branches of Hillel and various Jewish fraternities and sororities, filled with large numbers of northern Jews unable to gain admission to elite northern universities because of restrictive quotas.[90]

For many, more troubling even than modern culture and alternative religions was the internal threat from Zionism. The Reform movement—and with it most southern rabbis—remained officially non-Zionist, insisting that Jews were a religious group fully at home in America. And yet, Jews in towns like Chattanooga, San Antonio, Birmingham, and Newport News were joining Zionist organizations and donating to Zionist causes in significant numbers.[91] Rabbi Max Heller had declared himself a Zionist in 1901 and went on to serve as president of both the Federation of American Zionists and the Central Conference of American Rabbis.[92] While his was initially a lonely position, over time he gained company from the likes of Rabbi Bernard C. Ehrenreich, a Hungarian-born graduate of the Jewish Theological Seminary who served Congregation Beth-Or in Montgomery from 1906 to 1921, and Rabbi Jacob Raisin, a Polish-born graduate of Hebrew Union College, who arrived in Charleston to lead Kahal Kadosh Beth Elohim in 1915.[93] In 1937 the Central Conference of American Rabbis issued a new platform, which affirmed "the obligation of all Jewry to aid in [Palestine's] upbuilding as a Jewish homeland."[94] Zionism had gradually gained currency within Reform circles over the course of the 1920s and 1930s as global antisemitism intensified and as eastern European Jewish immigrants and their children, who tended to be more sympathetic to its message, entered the movement's institutions in earnest.

These developments took place within a context of radically reduced immigration. A small number of Jewish immigrants continued to arrive in contravention of the newly restrictive laws, sneaking over the Mexican border into Texas or taking a boat from Cuba to Florida, and yet the decline in numbers was palpable.[95] Alexander Gurwitz described a sudden absence of those who "came fresh from the Judaism-soaked villages and shtetlech of Russia and Poland, just yesterday from the Rebbe's table, from the yeshiva, [who had] revived, by their very presence, the heart of Judaism in their fellow Jews here."[96] Jewish migrants like Gurwitz had settled into racially divided, majority Christian southern communities, only to find them shaken by a war that reconfigured the relationship between church and state and between southerners and the wider world. It had also inspired a new religious militance and anxiety about change among a segment of their white Christian neighbors. In this context, southern Jews sought the comfort of white citizenship, but they were unable to ignore the traumas of the Leo Frank lynching, the rise of the Klan, and the new immigration laws. And, at least in some cases, they were unable to forget the warm Jewish sentiment of days gone by.

CHAPTER 14

Port and Dock

In 1932, Ferdinand Hirsch (figure 14.1) gave a sermon insisting that, in the face of economic depression, "we must establish new spiritual values or resurrect some of the old ones." He agreed with many southern clergy that the Great Depression posed religious problems, but whereas most southern Protestants believed that it could be solved through individual salvation or that it was an unalterable sign of the end times, Hirsch highlighted the virtues of civic responsibility: "From this hour let us show that we have this faith in our selves, our neighbors, our city, our state and our nation, in its institutions, its officers and its future."[1] Hirsch's sermon was written in direct response to the March 1933 bank holiday declared by newly elected president Franklin Delano Roosevelt, who promised to bring the resources of the federal government directly into southern states. They had long suffered from recurring natural disasters and the volatile cotton market, problems that had only been exacerbated by the advent of nationwide economic depression in 1929.[2] Southern Jews did their best to navigate these troubled economic times, which buoyed a rising global antisemitism that would very soon reach a devastating crescendo.

The economic profile of southern Jews—in 1938 only 0.2 percent of Jews in North Carolina were unskilled workers, compared with 25 percent of whites and over 60 percent of Black residents in the state— along with expansive Jewish social service networks, left many protected from the worst of the suffering.[3] There were Jews who were ruined, however, and no Jewish organization was left totally untouched

FIGURE 14.1. Ferdinand K. Hirsch, c.1945, New
Orleans. *Jewish Ledger*, Golden Jubilee Edition,
vol. 102, no. 5 (August 3, 1945):57. Image courtesy
of Special Collections and Area Studies, George
A. Smathers Libraries, University of Florida.

by the upheaval.[4] At the annual meeting of Brith Shalom, an Orthodox
congregation in Charleston, the president described "the humiliation
of having to face pay day with an empty treasury."[5] The newly organized
Temple Emanu-El in Dothan, Alabama, went defunct, although it was
revived in 1938.[6] Religious communities—especially Black Protestants,
Catholics, and Jews—had long assumed burdens of social welfare owing
to the near-total absence of public aid in southern states. They now

faced tremendous pressure as the numbers of poor and unemployed skyrocketed.[7]

Whereas many white evangelicals were suspicious of charity, understanding misfortune to be caused by sin, Jews understood their responsibility for the well-being of others—especially of other Jews—to be both a religious obligation and a vehicle of civic belonging.[8] Building upon long-established Hebrew benevolent societies and orphan homes, southern Jews in the early twentieth century had begun to establish Jewish hospitals, including a B'nai B'rith hospital "for indigent persons" in Hot Springs, Arkansas.[9] Now, as the Depression deepened, they joined local efforts to alleviate suffering; for instance, in Memphis, Jewish women's groups—long active in charitable work—ran a well-baby clinic and a summer school for poor children, both of which served Jews and non-Jews alike.[10] After the passage of the Federal Emergency Relief Act, funds flowed into southern towns and cities; in Goldsboro, North Carolina, Gertrude Weil, a stalwart of the local synagogue and a political activist in the state, helped distribute the monies as chair of the City Emergency Relief Committee.[11]

Rabbi Meyer Levitt of Jackson discussed the Social Security Act of 1935 in his Yom Kippur sermon that year; in a letter to Roosevelt he argued that it was "drawn up in the spirit of Israel's ancient prophets, those eloquent and fearless protagonists of social justice and righteousness."[12] The New Deal instituted a five-day work week, finally relieving Jews of the pressure to work on their Sabbath, which had dogged them for decades.[13] Roosevelt had a number of Jewish advisors—including Mobile-born Joseph Proskauer—and many Jews served in his administration—like the Memphis-born Abe Fortas, who worked in the Department of the Interior—even as he advanced a newly inclusive vision of national belonging.[14] These moves, combined with his social policies, made him tremendously popular among American Jews, including southerners, most of whom had long voted for the Democratic Party.[15]

In 1938 Roosevelt declared the South "the Nation's No. 1 economic problem."[16] New Deal programs would transform the region in many ways, although they faced criticism from several quarters. Black southerners protested that the New Deal had come under the influence of southern whites, who excluded them from its bounty. Many white Christians saw it as a dangerous competitor for moral authority.[17] Others, including Populists like Louisiana politician Huey Long, who had a number of close Jewish associates, as well as the region's small number of Communists, argued that it did not go far enough.[18] The latter group, most vocal in industrial sections of North Carolina and Alabama, contended that the New Deal's basic premise—that capitalism could be tamed—was faulty, pointing admiringly to the Soviet Union's equitable economic system and its repudiation of racism.[19]

Northern Jewish Communists and labor organizers like Amy Schechter—daughter of Jewish Theological Seminary chancellor Solomon Schechter—came South to agitate for radical change, but there were also a small number of local Jews who committed themselves to the Communist cause.[20] The socialist Jewish Arbeiter Ring had expanded and then undergone a dramatic split in the 1920s, with more-radical members leaving for the universalist Industrial Workers of the World.[21] And yet in the 1930s members like David Merlin still celebrated "the great, inevitable rebuilding of the current economic structure." Sam Borenstein of Chattanooga, a former Arbeiter Ring member, ran for governor of Tennessee in 1930 on the Communist ticket, alongside Black Senate candidate Sherman Bell. Most southerners deeply feared Communists, however. Borenstein, who reportedly used his store to provide food and meeting space for Black and white Communists, was arrested multiple times at multiracial political meetings.[22]

Another radical, Joseph Gelders, had grown up in a Jewish family in Birmingham and come to serve as the head of the southern office of a Communist-aligned civil liberties group. In 1936, after advocating on behalf of a Communist political prisoner in Bessemer, he was kidnapped and flogged with a sawed-off baseball bat by four white men, who called him a "damned red" and "n[----] lover." His case attracted widespread and largely sympathetic news coverage, but his attackers—two National Guardsmen with ties to the largest employer in town—were never indicted.[23] Both Borenstein and Gelders had organized on behalf of the Scottsboro Boys, a group of young Black men falsely accused of raping white women, whose defense was funded by the Communist Party.[24] Their lawyer, Samuel Leibowitz, was a Jew from New York, and one prosecutor—echoing Tom Watson during the Leo Frank case—told the jury to "show them that Alabama justice cannot be bought and sold with Jew money from New York."[25] At the same time, Mississippi senators Theodore Bilbo and John Rankin blamed "New York Jews" for New Deal policies they disagreed with.[26]

Most southern Jews ignored or sought to distance themselves from the radicals. When a Chattanooga newspaper identified Borenstein as a Russian Jew, a coreligionist named Morris Koblentz wrote a letter distancing "Chattanooga Jewish citizens"—among whom, he noted, were many of the newspaper's advertisers—from this "band of ignorant and unmitigated trouble-makers."[27] Rabbi Benjamin Goldstein of Montgomery had been part of a Marxist study group, and when he expressed public support for the Scottsboro Boys, his congregation dismissed him. They feared offering any fuel to what was by now a long-standing association of Jews with Communist agitation.[28] Arguments that Jews constituted a dangerous element in modern societies were also being made abroad, most notably in Germany by Adolf Hitler and his Nazi Party. Already in 1930 Helen Apte, recently returned from a trip to Europe, described Germany as "struggling, prostrate, and lately becoming inflamed with anti-Semitism and Hitlerism."[29] Southern Jews closely followed news of Hitler's rise, reading about it in the *Texas Jewish Herald* and other Jewish papers and hearing about it in sermons like Morris Newfield's 1933 "Hitler and the German Jew Situation."[30] They came together to raise funds and political support; in 1933, for instance, Jews in Mobile, Alabama, raised $1,000 in a matter of months in order to "relieve distress" among German Jews, and they lobbied the city commission to unanimously express "regret for examples of racial and religious intolerance in Germany."[31]

Most public discourse about Hitler's regime expressed opposition if not outright horror. Alabama newspapers castigated the Nazis' "reign of terror." At the same time, they ignored or excused parallels between Nazi racism and Jim Crow, even after the passage of the 1935 Nuremburg laws, which stripped German Jews of citizenship, the ability to marry non-Jews, and access to many public accommodations. One paper wrote that Jews now enjoyed "fewer privileges than the Alabama Negro," and yet insisted that the situation in the South was different, because "Southern Negroes are satisfied with their status."[32] In 1939 Gertrude Weil wrote to a friend, "I do nothing but waste time hovering around the radio lest I miss something of the world's happenings."[33] From Galveston, Rabbi Henry Cohen, then in his seventies, wrote, "The European situation has depressed us, and we cannot foresee the result."[34] In November of 1938, Jewish homes and businesses were looted across Germany, and in the fall of 1939 the Nazis invaded Poland; fear, anger, and desperation intensified among Jews around the world, including in the South.[35] S. Brill of Elizabeth City, North Carolina, told an interviewer in the late 1930s, "I would want only one more hour to live for the privilege of killing that dog Hitler."[36]

Brill had been interviewed under the auspices of the Federal Writers' Project, which documented the attitudes and experiences of a handful of Russian Jewish immigrants.[37] Although admittedly performing for a representative of the government, all showed signs of relaxing adherence to traditional Judaism after decades in the country. Brill reported that while his wife remained religiously observant, "I haven't much what you call religion; I have seen too much and read too much."[38] The wife of Nathan Wild of Savannah was also strictly observant, and although he still attended synagogue regularly, he periodically rode in a car, offering his own interpretation of Jewish law to justify it.[39] Elizabeth Rabinowitz of Beaufort, South Carolina, on the other hand, "makes no claim to any strong religious feeling," and rarely went to synagogue. She had no objection to her son's marriage to a Christian woman because "he doesn't go to church and neither does she, so they get along fine."[40]

These religious transformations coincided with the immigrants' embrace of southern racial norms and American economic and political ones. Rabinowitz ran a popular store where "you are likely to find yourself sandwiched in between your colored washer-woman and the town's society leader." Within the store, the norms of Jim Crow segregation were suspended, but its proprietor otherwise reinforced them. She pointedly informed her interviewer that she had hired a Black woman to do her laundry and admitted that she suspected Black customers of stealing. She also bragged about her children's college educations and professional achievements, highlighting her family's upward social mobility.[41] Brill explicitly denigrated religious Jews, "with their long curly beards and unwashed bodies," and he gave his guiding principles in terms of economic and political uprightness: "I am a Jew, yes, but I am a man first and an American citizen who believes in fair play, in honest industry, and good citizenship. . . . I pay my taxes, I pay my bills, I never take an unfair profit, I give to every appeal for charity."[42] These immigrant Jews wanted it made clear that they were good white citizens.

And yet, they retained the residue of Jewish difference in their language, identity, and, for some, religious practice. They are described as reading Yiddish newspapers, socializing with Jewish families, and maintaining ties to synagogues. Many clearly felt, as the *Southern Israelite* had put it in 1928, that "it seems a useless effort for Jews to deny their Jewishness."[43] Brill readily admitted that he was "a Russian Jew by birth and accident," and Rabinowitz still identified as an "Orthodox Jew."[44] She and her husband—whom the interviewer disparagingly described as her "little dark, chunky, greasy-faced, spectacled mate"—could be heard yelling at each other in Yiddish across the store until he up and moved to Palestine. The interviewer noted that their store "has long been an institution in our town—and its pair of short, plump, rapidly-speaking, Yiddish-accenting Jewish proprietors among our most interesting characters."[45] These accounts cast Jewish immigrants as familiar characters but also somehow different in ways that might, but need not, be seen as benign and even charming.

Persistent Jewish difference could also fuel darker interpretations and justify acts of discrimination. In a divorce case in Birmingham in 1940, the outspoken lawyer Horace Wilkinson argued that full custody of the child should be given to his client, whose ex-wife's marriage to a Jewish man rendered her an unfit mother: "I do not think it to the best interest of the child to be raised in an atmosphere where money is a God." The judge agreed, although the Alabama Supreme Court overturned the ruling the next year.[46] The president of the National Council of Jewish Women's section in New Orleans insisted in 1940, "Now more

FIGURE 14.2. Gertrude Weil. Image courtesy of the
State Archives of North Carolina.

than ever before must we show ourselves interested in the welfare of our
fellow men, regardless of race and creed."[47] Brill told his interviewer, on
the other hand, that America "would be a better country if everybody
who say they believe in God and Jesus would practice the things they
say they believe."[48] Confronted with Christian suspicion, Jews had a few
options: they could ignore it, work to redress it, or critique it.

In the early 1940s Gertrude Weil (figure 14.2), then six decades into
a life surrounded by Christians, began to reflect critically upon Christianity's idea of "a 'kingdom of Heaven' in some envious world to come,"
its "terrible emphasis on Sin," and the concept of being "'saved' from his

inherited state by the vicarious sacrifice of a person who lived two thousand years ago."[49] By then, the news had become even more bleak. Following the December 1941 attack on Pearl Harbor in Hawaii, the United States was at war against Japan, Italy, and Germany. Southern Jews were now under new stress as they contemplated the lives they had led to that point and the horrible new lessons it was inflicting upon them. For Weil, they fostered an appreciation of "the Jewish ideal of justice and righteousness in human society here on earth" and "belief in the unity of God." She concluded, "Men should look into their own lives" and "should be responsible for building a better, happier salvation."[50] Apte, who had family ties to Germany, wrote, "Now, I feel no kinship for that soil, only horror, repulsion, and I'm glad they bombed it. I hope it is in ruins."[51] Soldier David Macarov had grown up in Jim Crow Atlanta, where, he admitted: "I felt an instinctive prejudice against dark skins. Given the choice, I would invariably sit by or talk to a white person, rather than a colored person, even though I knew such an attitude was wrong."[52] Serving in the US military in Calcutta, India, where he formed relationships with dark-skinned local Jews, he began to reconsider.

Jewish men and women like Macarov enlisted in the fight and their communities carefully documented their service; Birmingham alone counted 516 Jewish soldiers, 14 of whom were killed in action.[53] The war effort led these Jews out of the region, and it ushered in many others, including rank-and-file soldiers headed to army bases and a small cadre of elite scientists who worked in Oak Ridge, Tennessee, for a secret government effort to build a nuclear weapon.[54] Despite the many hurdles to wartime travel from Europe, the ongoing force of restrictive immigration laws, and the greater draw of New York, a tiny number of Jewish refugees arrived at southern ports.[55] Already before the war, Gertrude Weil had worked tirelessly to bring European relatives and friends to the United States, signing affidavits promising financial support and sending letters and funds around the world.[56] Local and national Jewish organizations also became involved in resettlement efforts: the University of Alabama Hillel sponsored two refugee students, and between 1938 and 1940 the United Jewish Fund of Birmingham, run by a woman named Dora Roth, had resettled 125 German Jews in the city.[57] As in an earlier era of immigrant resettlement, communities requested those who would fit in; Selma requested "a young, single man, English speaking, non-Sabbath observer, non-foreign type."[58] Jewish refugees also found their way southward through other means; for instance, the Committee on Displaced German Scholars placed Jewish academics within historically Black colleges like the Hampton Institute and Talladega College.[59]

The National Council of Jewish Women was at the forefront of refugee resettlement efforts, which cost thousands of dollars and occupied untold hours of volunteer labor.[60] In New Orleans, section president Helene Godchaux wrote in 1940 that "these past four years that have shaken us out of our lethargy and made us realize that there is too much to be done and too much to learn to be content to merely know how to sew a fine seam."[61] In December of 1938, a committee of councilwomen oversaw twenty-two affidavit requests and helped with a monthly quota of three family units sent from New York. The next year, five children were brought to New Orleans, and a new immigrant adjustment committee had contacted fifty-five families and individuals in the city.[62] The "Craft Corner" project, which trained refugee women to sew items for sale, provided a social outlet as well as an opportunity to "contribute to the support of their own households without receiving charity and without taking jobs from American citizens."[63] The women's expertise in sewing, which Godchaux had earlier belittled, now came in handy. Their "Port and Dock" committee greeted refugees at the boat, and as years passed, more of them had "pitiful stories to relate," of harassment by the German state police and of internment in concentration camps.[64]

Americans looked at Nazi Germany—and its widely criticized treatment of European Jews—as the antithesis of their own country, which in the months leading up to war had been cast by President Roosevelt as a champion of the "four freedoms"—of speech and worship and from want and fear.[65] In truth, the country was riven by racial division and inequality. Although Roosevelt took steps to eliminate racial discrimination in federal contracts, Black soldiers were relegated to segregated units, and large numbers of Japanese Americans were interned in camps throughout the West, including as far southeast as Arkansas.[66] Jews again served in segregated military units, benefiting from the services of an expanded Jewish Welfare Board and corps of Jewish chaplains.[67] Despite these forms of inclusion, however, a vocal minority of Americans sympathized with Nazi hatred. Although mostly based in the North, their number included men like Alabama's Father Arthur W. Terminiello, the Boston-born "Father Coughlin of the South," who argued that Jews were self-interested agitators who had pressured the United States into an unnecessary war.[68] By March 1944, Birmingham Jewish leader Lee B. Weil would describe antisemitism as "a serious factor in the life of Birmingham."[69]

The war against Nazi Germany made southern Jews more sensitive to antisemitism and more determined to resist it. For many, it nurtured the conviction that a Jewish state in Palestine was the best safeguard of their interests. In 1942 the Central Conference of American Rabbis, which for some time had been inching away from its historical anti-Zionism, passed a resolution calling for the creation of a "Jewish army" to fight under Allied command in Palestine. A contingent of conference members, alarmed by what they saw as the implication that Jews formed a separate nationality, channeled their fury into a new organization, the American Council for Judaism. As the venerable Rabbi Henry Cohen of Galveston, then seventy-nine years old, told it, the children of Orthodox immigrants had introduced into Hebrew Union College "nationalistic tendencies to which I am utterly opposed" and which were irreconcilable with the "American Judaism" of Isaac Mayer Wise. Worried that Zionism would threaten the safety of Jews in the United States and elsewhere, men like Cohen insisted, "We are Jews by religion and Americans by nationality."[70]

Southern Jews constituted roughly 4 percent of the American Jewish population but 40 percent of the council's membership in 1943. Chapters were organized in Houston, Norfolk, Richmond, New Orleans, Shreveport, Birmingham, Little Rock, and Charleston, and in some communities the council's passionate anti-Zionism seeped into congregational politics.[71] Leading members of Houston's Congregation Beth Israel refused to replace Rabbi Henry Barnston, an anti-Zionist, with Assistant Rabbi Robert Kahn, a Zionist then serving overseas as a chaplain. They further authored a list of anti-Zionist "Basic Principles" that they proposed all members should affirm, which included: "Our religion is Judaism. Our nation is the United States of America. Our nationality is American. Our flag is the 'Stars and Stripes.' Our race is Caucasian." Drawing on decades of Reform thought and against the backdrop of wartime, they clearly felt that a white American religious identity was more compelling, or at least safer, than a Zionist one.[72]

Two years later, Jacob Raisin, a staunch Zionist, resigned from his position as the long-time rabbi at the Reform Kahal Kadosh Beth Elohim in Charleston. What followed was a few years of instability in the pulpit, coinciding with the war's dramatic end in an explosion of atomic bombs over Nagasaki and Hiroshima. In 1947, congregational leaders elected Rabbi Allan Tarshish, a member of the American Council for Judaism. A group of members tried to scuttle the appointment of an anti-Zionist, even after he wrote a lengthy letter explaining his estrangement from the organization. He had joined, he argued, only because of his opposition to the Zionist argument that, as he put it, "we are homeless everywhere, even in America."[73] Nevertheless, at least one family resigned its membership in the congregation in May of 1948, after Tarshish neglected to mention the news of the founding of the State of Israel from the pulpit.[74] After another incident several years later, he wrote, "Some Charleston Jews still equate the American Council for Judaism with the Ku Klux Klan, think of it as supremely evil."[75]

Tarshish understood himself to hold a moderate, patriotic view, but decades of Zionist leadership and organizing in his city had nurtured a deep yearning for a Jewish state, and conflicts like those in Houston had tarnished the American Council for Judaism's reputation. Charleston proved a kind of quiet mirror image of Houston, where the politics were flipped, and where congregational opponents of a prospective rabbi were side-stepped, if not silenced. Despite the criticism of Tarshish, most of his congregants shared his insistence that America was their home. In 1950 they staged a series of bicentennial celebrations, invoking their congregation's long and distinguished history in Charleston. The festivities included the staging of a play, which began in a displaced persons camp in Germany and ended at "a synagogue in Charleston,

Victory Sabbath Morning, August 18, 1945."[76] This play reflected the pride that Jews in Charleston and elsewhere took in the fact that the American government had triumphed over a Nazi regime that had murdered six million Jews.

Now the new enemy was the Soviet Union and its "Godless Communism." On the one hand, Jews' associations with Communism—both imagined and real—led to forms of suspicion and even persecution.[77] As a result, the socialist Arbeiter Ring began a steady decline in membership from which it would never recover, and those with suspected Communist ties were purged from Jewish communal institutions.[78] On the other hand, a new vision of America as a "Judeo-Christian" or "tri-faith" nation offered Jews a clear role as a coequal religious community with Protestants and Catholics.[79] Although in some places they were still excluded from elite social clubs, in this new atmosphere, and with the help of the GI Bill, many southern Jews ascended the socioeconomic ladder, attending college and purchasing homes in newly built suburban communities.[80] Even more so than during World War I or the Depression, government resources had been pumped into the South, reshaping its demography and topography yet again. As one historian has argued, before the war cities like Mobile and Norfolk "were dozing southern seaports, but the war shook them awake."[81] Their new residents included northern Jewish businessmen in search of promising opportunities, scholars employed by expanding universities, and Holocaust survivors fresh from European displaced persons camps.[82]

Yet again, the growing prosperity and optimism that Jews in the South enjoyed was out of reach for their Black neighbors, despite their military service during the war and the intensifying public celebrations of American freedom and democracy. Although Black activists had pushed for change during the war, the GI Bill proved racially discriminatory in practice, housing policies severely curtailed Black home ownership, and the worst of Jim Crow continued unabated in the form of both violent attacks and routine segregation.[83] Soon these hypocrisies became matters of embarrassment and concern on the international stage, as the United States sought to prove its superiority to the Soviet Union in an unfolding Cold War.[84] In 1946 President Harry S. Truman appointed a Civil Rights Committee, which the next year published a report acknowledging that "it is almost always true that while indeed separate, [segregated Black and white] facilities are far from equal." In 1948 Truman desegregated the US military.[85]

Enraged southern Democrats understood these as the first steps toward Black equality and attempted to nominate an alternative to Truman at the 1948 Democratic National Convention. Charles Bloch, a Jewish lawyer born in Baton Rouge, gave a nominating speech for Georgia senator Richard B. Russell, invoking the Christian language of his allies: "You shall not be crucified on the cross of civil rights."[86] When these efforts failed, Bloch and the so-called "Dixiecrats" walked out of the convention, ultimately nominating for president Strom Thurmond, who won four southern states: South Carolina, Louisiana, Alabama, and Mississippi.[87] That same year, Pittsburgh-born Jacob Rothschild, a former army chaplain just two years into serving as rabbi of the Temple in Atlanta, gave a Yom Kippur sermon decrying recent acts of anti-Black violence. He charged his congregants with the "sin of neglect," telling them, "We who take pride in our heritage as Jews, we who bask in the glory of Southern tradition have a greater responsibility for enlightened action. . . . [N]ow is the time to act."[88] Bloch and Rothschild were at the leading edge and the extreme poles of a nascent debate among southerners, including Jews, about how best to respond to the possibility of desegregation.

Local Jewish groups were also aware of the shifting tides, although they were more tentative in their responses. Like other white southerners, members of the National Council of Jewish Women—still hard at work on refugee resettlement and other community projects—showed an awareness of racial problems, if also an unwillingness to fundamentally challenge segregation.[89] The New Orleans chapter reported that its most popular event in 1947 was on the topic of "Domestic Help," featuring a Black leader from the Urban League, who responded to their questions about "the servant problem in New Orleans."[90] In Charleston, the National Council of Jewish Women's chapter expressed support for the hiring of Black police "for work in negro districts involving negro cases," a tentative step that nevertheless made little headway.[91] For

Americans of all stripes, World War II had raised important questions, about the nature of human existence, the place of the United States in the world, and the contours of American society. All would persist—and would have special meaning for southern Jews—well into the second half of the twentieth century.

CHAPTER 15

Trembling Tribes

In 1950, members of the New Orleans section of the National Council of Jewish Women initiated a "very informal discussion" to "formulate the thinking of this group into some conclusions; we want a policy toward civil rights." Although the contents of the discussion were not documented, prepared introductory remarks trod lightly: "Although anthropologists say that there is absolutely no evidence of inequality between the two races . . . still many of us believe, in some degree and to some extent, that the negro is inferior. . . . [I]f you resist the elimination of segregation you are certainly not alone."[1] These women felt compelled to consider the tremendous injustice Black Americans were facing in their own backyards and the possibility of dramatic changes to the status quo. In the years to follow, as Black citizens intensified their demands for equality, most southern Jews would prove neither heroes nor villains. Rather, they were concerned if flawed individuals, grappling at the very same time with the aftershocks of the decimation of European Jewry. While some stood bravely in support of Black civil rights, drawing especially on resources from Reform Jewish thought, most were willing to abide racial injustice in the hopes—however misguided—of protecting their hard-won status as white southerners.

Black civil rights were considered a legitimate if sensitive topic of debate among B'nai B'rith brothers in South Carolina, as among councilwomen in New Orleans. In anticipation of forced school integration, in 1951 the state—with the full support of Solomon Blatt, its Jewish Speaker of the House—put forth a constitutional amendment repealing compulsory school attendance. The next year B'nai B'rith members meeting in Columbia discussed police training in "minority group problems," the placement of prodemocracy ads on Charleston buses, and their opposition to the schools measure, which they associated with "vitriolic appeals to race prejudice."[2] They also raised another aspect of the schools issues, namely the NAACP-sponsored "School Segregation Suit" coming out of Clarendon, South Carolina, which would eventually be bundled with *Brown v. Board of Education of Topeka*. Jewish organizations had long pursued civil rights causes as a means of ensuring Jewish equality, and there were discussions about whether B'nai B'rith's Anti-Defamation League (ADL) should file an amicus brief in support of school desegregation.[3] In Columbia, David Baker proposed a motion opposing an ADL brief, which he deemed "inimical to the best interest of the community relations of this region." The motion carried, but only after the chair cast a tie-breaking vote.[4] The next year Henry Yaschik argued "that there will be no violence attendant upon the Supreme Court decision. . . . Persons of any faith will be respected more if they fight for decency and we can take only one side—the humanitarian side!"[5] On the cusp of desegregation, southern Jews were far from united, but at least some were sympathetic to their Black neighbors and optimistic about what was to come.

In the end the ADL and a spate of other American Jewish organizations did file briefs in *Brown v. Board*, which was decided in 1954.[6] The US Supreme Court overturned *Plessy v. Ferguson*'s "separate but equal" doctrine, ruling that public schools must be desegregated. Public schools had served as crucial vehicles of acculturation for immigrant Jews, even as they were sites of ongoing battles against public prayers and Bible reading. American Jews understood their importance as well as their inequalities.[7] Some rabbis used their moral authority and local influence to urge for peaceful school integration. Rabbi Julian Feibelman of New Orleans organized a petition to the local school board urging compliance because "all children, black and white, are the children of God."[8] In Little Rock, Rabbi Ira Sanders spoke to the state legislature

FIGURE 15.1. South Carolina B'nai B'rith Convention, 1950s, Neidich-Rudowitz Papers. Image courtesy of Special Collections, College of Charleston Libraries.

in support of desegregation; women in his congregation joined a local group that made the pragmatic case for the importance of "open schools" for their children rather than a moral one for racial integration, a popular strategy among white moderates.[9] There were also local chapters that supported the desegregationist stances of their national organizations; both southern district grand lodges of B'nai B'rith voted to support the ADL's position, and the New Orleans section of the National Council of Jewish Women "promised to work toward an effective implementation of the Supreme Court Decision on Segregation."[10]

Others felt strongly that national organizations were inappropriately projecting a uniform "Jewish" position. Mississippi B'nai B'rith members reported that they were "worried about their standing in their respective communities and wanted all talks on segregation stopped immediately."[11] Some southern members protested and even resigned national organizations that they had supported for decades, accusing them of intrusion at best and stoking antisemitism at worst.[12] For their part, white southern ministers and churchgoers almost uniformly resisted their national denominations' stands in support of desegregation, insisting that the cause of racial injustice was individual Black sin.[13] The federal government declined to robustly implement school desegregation, and in many communities white southerners fought tooth and nail to resist it. In Arkansas, Governor Orval Faubus resisted with particular vigor, leading to a standoff at Little Rock's Central High School between enraged local whites and federal troops sent to protect Black students.[14] "Respectable" middle-class whites—250,000 in number by the end of 1956—forged a network of "citizens councils," designed to resist integration and protect white rule.[15] One observer described them as "an organized network of groups consciously working to remove dissenters," any one of whom could expect threats to "his job and his family's happiness."[16]

In several places, these groups excluded those who did not "believe in the divinity of Jesus Christ," but others went to great lengths to prove that they were not antisemitic, accepting and even recruiting Jewish members.[17] In 1957 the Association of Citizens' Councils of Mississippi published *A Jewish View on Segregation*, the author of which insisted, "I, personally, am a 'Jewish Southerner,' not a Southern Jew." He excoriated the Anti-Defamation League and the American Jewish Congress, arguing that Black advancement could best be achieved through continued segregation.[18] Unsurprisingly, Dixiecrat Charles Bloch enthusiastically joined a white citizens council, and created several short-lived organizations dedicated to the segregationist cause; in 1958 he published a book entitled *States' Rights: The Law of the Land*, which insisted that the decision in *Brown* had been unconstitutional, and he initiated a number of lawsuits seeking to impinge upon the rights of Black Georgians.[19]

Years, decades, or even generations in the South were not without their effect. Rabbi Perry Nussbaum of Jackson, Mississippi, wrote to a colleague in 1955, "I have members—and of course the Delta is full of such—who firmly believe that the Negro must be kept as a second-class citizen."[20] What was for some a deep conviction in the rightness of the status quo was for others a reluctance to disturb their precarious position. Some Jews reported that they had joined white citizens' councils reluctantly, owing to fear or pressure. There was clearly some countervailing pressure against joining, as well; the author of *A Jewish View of Segregation* was anonymous, while the parallel *A Christian View of Segregation* proudly bore the name of Presbyterian pastor Dr. G. T. Gillespie.[21]

White segregationists not only disciplined whites who disagreed with them but targeted Black southerners with various forms of intimidation: Mississippi vigilantes brutally murdered a fourteen-year-old boy named Emmet Till, while Alabama lawmakers voted to outlaw the NAACP.[22] Nevertheless, Black southerners continued to assert their rights as American citizens. They sent their children to integrated schools and they demanded the desegregation of other public facilities. In 1955, Black activists in Montgomery organized a boycott of city buses after Rosa Parks, a local seamstress and activist, was arrested for refusing to leave her seat in the "white" section. Among the leaders of the boycott was minister Martin Luther King Jr., who would soon attain regional and national fame as president of the Southern Christian Leadership Conference and as a major theorist of nonviolent resistance to unjust Jim Crow laws.[23] At the outset of the boycott, King drew on the language of American democracy and Christian piety that would suffuse the movement for Black civil rights in the years to come: "If we are wrong, the Supreme Court of this nation is wrong. If we are wrong, the Constitution of the United States is wrong. If we are wrong, God Almighty is wrong."[24] When *Life* magazine covered the boycott, it included a photograph of an interracial "Brotherhood Week" radio broadcast, which included Rabbi Seymour Atlas. His congregants reacted with horror, with some insisting that he begin submitting his sermons for advance approval.[25]

As one Birmingham Jew put it in 1957, "We are not able to take a position contrary to the community at large," by which he meant the white community.[26] Jews did not craft a religious defense of segregation, as did many Protestants, but they defended inaction—to themselves and to audiences of northern Jews—through a careful delineation of the proper bounds of "Jewish" activity. Rabbi William S. Malev argued in the periodical *Conservative Judaism* that he was in favor of integration but against any overt action by Jews as Jews: "Desegregation is not a Jewish issue but an American issue."[27] During the Suez Crisis the Norfolk, Virginia, chapter of the American Council for Judaism brought a resolution before the Union of American Hebrew Congregations forbidding public comments on "political" matters, broadly construed.[28] They castigated national organizations for claiming to speak for them, ostensibly about Zionism but also, it was implied, about desegregation.

Southern Jews tried to enact this compartmentalization in their daily lives, focusing on the rhythms of religious life that would assert their bona fides as anti-Communist, middle-class, white southerners: the construction and maintenance of their synagogues, the education of their children, and the demonstration of communal pride. They constructed modernist suburban synagogues boasting large parking lots, an acknowledgment that affluent members were driving, in violation of traditional Sabbath prohibitions.[29] The new synagogue built by Congregation Shearith Israel of Dallas, one of a growing number affiliated with the Conservative movement, included a social hall, classroom wing, and "Memorial to the Six Million."[30] Upon entering the contemporary building, which could accommodate 2,200 people, worshippers would "realize and feel an imprint of soulful reverence for holy experiences to come." Youths were sent for the summer to Jewish institutions like Camp Blue Star, which had been founded in the immediate postwar years;[31] circuit-riding rabbis traveled throughout North Carolina to galvanize local practice;[32] and a Mississippi Jewish Religious Association was founded to facilitate camaraderie and teacher training. Tellingly, one congregational leader wrote to Perry Nussbaum that "it should be held to a Jewish Religious Association and political and social problems left out."[33]

Two years after participating in the three hundredth anniversary of Jewish settlement in what would become the United States, a group of Jews in Richmond formed a Southern (American) Jewish Historical Society, and synagogues across the region marked their seventy-fifth and hundredth anniversaries with elegant dinners and slick commemorative publications.[34] Try though they might to avoid discussing segregation, however—even the southern regional ADL director insisted

"that anti semitism is still the major purpose of ADL and that segregation issues were only a minor problem"—there were radical segregationists within the resurgent KKK and other extremist groups who insisted
that Black activists were being manipulated by Communists, by Jews,
or by Communist Jews. South Carolina's ADL chapter reported little
antisemitism in the state, although it also admitted that "the KKK was
still in operation and a threatening force."[35]

Antisemitic material in the South reportedly increased by 400 percent
between 1954 and 1959, owing to the efforts of groups like the Christian
Anti-Jewish Party, later folded into the National States' Rights Party.[36]
The most dramatic expression of this ascendant antisemitism was a series
of attempted bombings at Jewish institutions in seven southern cities; in
several cases a group called the Confederate Union claimed responsibility. The most prominent institution targeted was the Temple in Atlanta,
which was led by civil rights advocate Jacob Rothschild. Although no
one was convicted of the crime, the bombing of the Temple attracted
national outrage, leading to an FBI investigation and new hate crimes
legislation; many believed "to bomb a religious building was totally out
of order." Black southerners complained that similar outrage had been
absent in the far more widespread bombings of Black churches and
homes.[37] Indeed, even as they proved the very real danger to Jews from
those who defined southern identity in narrow terms, the bombings
also demonstrated the widespread support they enjoyed from the many
who saw them as an upstanding white religious group.

The bombings represented the Jewish community's worst nightmare
come true, and they inspired a range of responses. Rothschild continued his support for civil rights unabated, forging an alliance with Martin
Luther King Jr., who would soon move to Atlanta to lead the Ebenezer
Baptist Church.[38] In Nashville, a rabbi told reporters,

> with a profound sense of shame, that with the exceptions of my sermons
> during the High Holidays last September, and one Parent-Teacher As-
> sociation address . . . I have not made a single public utterance or state-
> ment on this subject of integration, and have not been as active in
> behalf of social justice as my faith demands.[39]

Indeed, the bombs seemed to have awakened some from their complacency. A social scientist visiting Montgomery in 1959 found community members who invoked the memories of Joseph Gelders and Rabbi Benjamin Goldstein, outspoken proponents of social justice in the early 1930s who had suffered for their activism. Their examples "still urge some men on to act and think for themselves." And yet, he reported, "Some Jewish leaders spoke to me of a 'paradise lost.' 'It used to be so quiet, the Jewish community used to be so respected, Jewish leaders used to be welcomed in the best society.'" He concluded that "very few Jews possess both desegregationist views and a readiness to express them in words and action."[40] An opinion poll found that Jews were more supportive of civil rights for Black Americans than were white non-Jews, although they kept their opinions private; most non-Jews admitted that they did not know how Jews felt about the issue.[41] Another study, based on interviews collected between 1959 and 1962, corroborated this finding, but also found that more than half of respondents thought integration was moving too fast.[42]

This timidity could extend into the realm of Jewish worship. Synagogues were intimate spaces of religious fellowship in which African Americans had most often appeared as employees, not as worshippers; they also clearly paralleled white Protestant churches, which were notoriously resistant to integration.[43] While John and Vickie Kilmanjaro, Black Jews living in Greensboro, North Carolina, were married in the synagogue there in 1956,[44] in other communities rabbis felt compelled to ask their congregations for permission when African Americans— including both Jews and aspiring converts—sought to join them for worship. One community refused to accept a Black member in the immediate aftermath of the Temple bombing, but reversed course six months later, when the feeling of immediate danger had passed.[45]

The fight for desegregation proceeded in different communities with varying levels of speed and drama, but by 1960, southern Jews had been pushed to consider the possibility of Black equality in a number of charged spaces: the school, the bus, and the synagogue. The space in which Jews most often interacted with African Americans, however, was the store, which now became the target of boycotts and sit-ins demanding integration. What began at a Woolworth lunch counter in Greensboro, North Carolina, soon made its way to stores in other cities, including those that bore Jewish names and public identities. The owners of these stores—which had been important vehicles of economic mobility for their families—were now confronted with the question of integration head on, in a way that felt especially threatening. Few wanted to take the lead, fearing the loss of white business, and they resented the confrontational tactics of Black activists. In Atlanta, Richard Rich, the Jewish owner of a nearly century-old department store with a reputation for racial liberalism, was deeply disturbed to find his store targeted. He initially resisted acceding to the protesters' demands, supposedly in order to see how school desegregation efforts were resolved. Ultimately, Rich desegregated the store after a five-month boycott.[46]

In Charleston, Jewish storekeepers kept a close eye on the picketing in nearby Savannah, worried that they could be next.[47] By this point, Kahal Kadosh Beth Elohim's rabbi was Burton Padoll, who had taken the pulpit because of his interest in civil rights advocacy. Initially he observed of his congregants, "I don't know what you think or feel. Our conversations, both in public and in private, are by-and-large conducted on a level of pseudo-politeness."[48] His attention to the complaints of Black Charlestonians soon evinced real anger, though: "It was as though I had written dirty words upon these sacred walls." He insisted that social action—"the establishment of God's kingdom of Earth"—could not be disentangled from the Bible, liturgy, or Judaism itself.[49] On several occasions "rabid segregationists" in the congregation, mostly scions of old Charleston Jewish families, walked out in the middle of his sermons.[50]

Padoll had allies across the region, but they faced an uphill battle. In 1963 Rabbi Jacob Rothschild argued, "The Southern Jew . . . squirms and rationalizes," insisting that segregation was not a Jewish problem, when in truth, he argued, to separate American and Jewish problems was both morally wrong and politically unwise.[51] Iconoclastic Charlotte journalist Harry Golden, who had relocated to the South from New York in 1941, regularly advocated for Black civil rights in his newspaper, the *Carolina Israelite*, describing most southern Jews as "Trembling

Tribes of Israel," too fearful to stand up for what was right.[52] Charleston, Atlanta, and Charlotte all avoided the worst conflict over desegregation, thanks in part to the efforts of white moderates, including well-positioned Jewish businessmen. They understood integration as necessary for economic development—Atlanta boosters famously insisted that theirs was "a city too busy to hate." Deeper forms of inequality expanded under the guises of consumer rights and meritocratic individualism, but in these and other places African Americans began attending schools and patronizing hotels and restaurants alongside whites.[53]

In November of 1963, German-born Rabbi Adolph Philipsborn reported on the improved conditions he found in moving from Vicksburg, Mississippi, to Harlingen, Texas. In addition to the lush environment, he noted that the schools were integrated and that he personally had shared a hotel and a restaurant meal with his Black driver. While there were disagreements about President John F. Kennedy, "You can speak out without being bodily or professionally or socially threatened." Phillipsborn added a note to the letter, which was sent on November 24, 1963, explaining that "this letter was dictated before the unbelievable, the horrible, the murder of President Kennedy in Texas happened."[54] Kennedy had lost many votes from southern Democrats because of his support for civil rights, although he was well liked by many Jews, including Philipsborn. The moment of his death was famously captured on video by a Jewish immigrant well-wisher named Abraham Zapruder; his alleged assassin, Lee Harvey Oswald, was himself killed on live television by a Chicago-born Jewish nightclub owner named Jack Ruby.[55]

In the months leading up to Kennedy's assassination, the conflict over Black civil rights had intensified, as scenes of white southerners attacking Black protesters were broadcast to a worldwide audience. Among the most violent cities was Birmingham, where Martin Luther King Jr. was imprisoned in the spring of 1963.[56] The famous letter that he wrote there, now considered a classic of American rhetoric, pointed to the complex positions of Jews within the civil rights movement. He praised Golden as one of those who "have written about our struggle in eloquent, prophetic, and understanding terms" and drew direct parallels to Nazi Germany, insisting, "Had I lived in Germany during that time, I would have aided and comforted my Jewish brothers even though it was illegal." His most forceful message was for "white ministers, priests, and rabbis of the South," along with the "white moderate," all of whom he charged with abdicating moral responsibility in the struggle for racial justice.[57]

Most rabbis and communal leaders were too fearful of angering or endangering their constituents to make a public stand. A report from Birmingham again delineated a depoliticized sphere of "Jewish" activity: "The Jewish community leadership generally believes that Jews, as such, ought to stay out of the desegregation fight on the ground that it is a 'Christian problem' between whites and Negroes and not simply a racial problem."[58] Local rabbi Milton Grafman, widely understood to be a direct target of King's letter, called it "a beautiful literary document. But a vicious one." Speaking extemporaneously on Rosh Hashanah in 1963, Grafman encouraged his congregants to "stop being liberals in your parlors and in your offices" and to enter the public fray. Just days before Grafman's sermon, four girls had been murdered in a bombing of the city's Sixteenth Street Baptist Church. Grafman told his audience, "I'm just as sick at heart as you are about what's happened in our city." He insisted, "I want justice and I want equality for the Negro but I also want fairness and equality and decency for the white man."[59]

Rabbis like Grafman, who served in southern hotspots, came under pressure from Black activists, white officials, and northern coreligionists who made their support for King and the Civil Rights movement known. Grafman complained about the patronizing communications he had received from northern colleagues, "indicat[ing] what my duty should be . . . [when they] know nothing about what I've been doing."[60] In May 1963, after local white police viciously attacked nonviolent Black protesters in Birmingham, a group of northern rabbis had traveled to the city for a last-minute visit; the local Jewish community council ensured that it was not reported in local newspapers.[61] That August, King headlined the March on Washington, where he gave his "I Have a Dream" speech immediately following the remarks of Rabbi Joachim Prinz, who drew parallels between the plight of Black southerners and his own experiences in Nazi Germany.[62] The Union of American Hebrew Congregations selected King as a speaker at its biennial banquet, prompting a group of Mississippi rabbis to object; even the progressive Rabbi Perry Nussbaum wrote, "I am convinced that the Union has no regard at all for the security of the Jewish community in this State."[63] If Jews were going to make change, these rabbis felt, it needed to be through the quiet work of locals, and in ways that did not make it harder to live and work among white Christians.

And yet, northern Jews continued to protest in the region. In 1964 sixteen rabbis were arrested in Saint Augustine, Florida, alongside King.[64] Young Jews, who had been a noticeable presence in the 1961 Freedom Ride, now joined the Freedom Summer of 1964. Whereas the first of these grassroots projects had challenged segregation on inter-state buses, now the focus was on expanding education and voter regis-tration among southern Blacks. The battle for Black equality had moved into the ballot box, striking at the heart of white political power.[65] One northern Jewish lawyer working for civil rights described a class of "Mississippi marranos" who supported his efforts in private, drawing a modern parallel to crypto-Jews in Spain after 1492.[66] Other southern Jews—who had objected to the distant statements of the ADL—were angered by the presence of Jewish outside agitators. One Jackson Jew complained about self-righteous northern coreligionists who published reports suggesting, in his words, "Their problem then is one of getting the frightened, lazy, ignorant or even hypocritical Mississippi Jew to implement the solution."[67] When Rabbi Nussbaum began visiting im-prisoned Jewish freedom riders, which he understood as a rabbinic duty, several colleagues in the state vehemently objected; in their view, these Jews' radical political activity placed them beyond the pale.[68]

The summer of 1964 proved to be one of "brutality and mayhem" in Mississippi, as hostile whites burned churches, intimidated civil rights workers, and worse. On June 21, 1964, a white posse in the town of Philadelphia murdered James Chaney, a Black activist, and his white companions, Jewish New Yorkers Michael Schwerner and Andrew Goodman.[69] Less than two weeks later, President Lyndon Johnson, Kennedy's successor, signed the Civil Rights Act of 1964, which prohib-ited discrimination in public accommodations and employment. The deep divisions among American Jews were again made clear in Selma,

Alabama, where a peaceful march in support of voting rights was met with shocking violence on the part of local vigilantes and police officers serving under Sheriff Jim Clark. Sixty-five protesters were hospitalized following what came to be known as "Bloody Sunday," and soon after, a white civil rights activist and minister from Boston was murdered in the city. Sol Tepper, a Selma Jew and a close ally of Clark, insisted that Black activists must have been the minister's true murderers.[70]

When the march across the bridge was finally completed, it included Rabbi Abraham Joshua Heschel, a German refugee and professor at the Jewish Theological Seminary in New York, who famously claimed to have been "praying with my feet."[71] Tepper described them as "professional agitators of King's million-dollar racket."[72] Six days before the final march, Johnson had signed the Voting Rights Act of 1965, forbidding restrictions on voting "on account of race or color." Despite the protestations of many southern whites, including a few vocal Jews like Tepper, segregation and disfranchisement—the two pillars of racial injustice in the South—had been toppled by the federal government. That year Rabbi Burton Padoll admitted that his efforts to make a Jewish case for desegregation had failed. While acknowledging his congregants' "overwhelming fear of the loss of security," he made yet another appeal, now on the basis of American democracy. Nevertheless, in his own backyard, South Carolina politician Sol Blatt continued to fight a failing battle against school integration.[73]

An era of struggle for Black civil rights was coming to a violent close, although it was clear that racism was far from defeated. Southerners of all stripes knew in their bones that legislation could not immediately change public sentiment, individual behavior, or the weight of centuries of injustice. In 1966 Rabbi Abraham Ruderman accepted a pulpit in Greenville, Mississippi, because he was convinced it was an integrated "oasis of liberalism" and that its "problems are on the road to solution." Once there, however, he found that the ministerial association was still limited to whites and that poverty in the Black community was rampant, even after legal rights had been ensured.[74] In Jackson, Nussbaum continued to participate in interracial activism, although several members of his congregation's building committee boycotted its integrated dedication ceremony.[75] Congregation B'nai Israel in Little Rock invited segregationist Arkansas governor Orval E. Faubus to speak at their centennial. "You Israelites sure do set a good table," he quipped, before launching into a peon to religious freedom that unironically described America as a place "where each can worship in freedom and without fear."[76]

The following year Rabbi Nussbaum's newly built synagogue and his home were bombed, around the same time as the homes of a white academic and a white businessman.[77] Nussbaum reported, "The KKK, the John Birchers, and a host of 'anti-everything that is not white, Protestant, native Mississippi' organizations" had become increasingly active in the preceding months.[78] The rabbi, who posed for a press photo wearing his prayer shawl and rabbinic robes in his damaged office, fielded many sympathetic letters and calls after the bombing. He later reported that he had told "the leading Southern Baptist minister in Jackson to go to hell when he came around with his condolences, telling him to preach the following Sunday to his front pews, where all the rightists regularly gathered."[79] But some colleagues were conspicuously silent, and he also received hate mail. One letter, written by a "Former Jackson Resident," argued that given "the actions taken by SNCC, CORE, the New Left, and other negro groups against your Jewish people, don't you think it time that you realized that you are accomplishing nothing and that you are hurting your own people?"[80]

Many Jews would move into their own corner in the years to come. The State of Israel's surprising victory in the Six-Day War in June of 1967 would galvanize communal interest, converting or further marginalizing the region's remaining anti-Zionists even as it inspired solidarity with Palestinians among Black activists. Many of the latter soured on the moderate integrationist approach to achieving civil rights, and it was they who would become the loudest public voices following King's assassination in April of 1968.[81] In the preceding decades, Jews who were middle class but vulnerable had been confronted with difficult decisions about whether and how to advocate for a different society. They made their choices on the basis of shifting and variable assessments of their specific situations and of the imperatives of Jewish history and tradition.

Some individuals had encouraged the cause of Black civil rights, but for most, fear of antisemitism—dramatically realized in the synagogue bombings—and the comforts of white privilege, threatened with new intensity amid the sit-ins at Jewish-owned stores, proved powerful incentives in favor of opposition or at least quietude.

The period from the end of Reconstruction to the end of legal segregation coincided with one of the most tumultuous periods in Jewish history. Mass migration, the rise of racial antisemitism that culminated in the Holocaust, and Zionism's triumph in the creation of the State of Israel dramatically reshaped the terrain of Jewish life around the globe, including in the US South. The region's Jews had become more diverse, and they entertained a range of new concerns, but one old one remained: how to live peaceably with their neighbors and authentically as Jews. Under the long shadow of Jim Crow, Jews occupied a position that was at once privileged and precarious. They usually acted, and were accepted, as white people, which helped them gain access to the treasured comforts of prosperity and stability. And yet, even when they had white skin, fluent English, and affiliations with respectable Reform congregations, to some they seemed like outsiders. After almost three centuries, their presence still provoked the question of whether whiteness, Christianity, and power could or should be disentangled.

Epilogue

In July of 2023 I sat in the Bernard B. Jacobs Theatre, half a block from Times Square in Manhattan, and watched the lynching of Leo Frank. The musical *Parade*, which debuted on Broadway in 1998, is the third play about Atlanta Jews written by Alfred Uhry. It followed *Driving Miss Daisy*, the source material for the Oscar-winning film, which dramatized the Temple bombing, and *The Last Night at Ballyhoo*, about intra-Jewish tensions on the eve of World War II.[1] It was jarring but deeply moving to see an event that loomed so large in my life and research staged and performed by talented—indeed Tony Award–winning—professionals.[2] Photographs of the characters and images of newspaper clippings were projected above the actors, and during intermission, star Ben Platt sat on stage, remaining in character as an imprisoned Leo Frank. The tickets were not cheap but the house was full. I couldn't help looking around to watch the other audience members watch the events onstage. As I waited in line for the restroom, I heard someone ask a friend if it was a fictional or true story—they weren't quite sure. Every night a small piece of a New York City stage became Marietta, Georgia, 2023 became 1915, and large crowds bore witness to a profound tragedy of American history.

The weight of memory lies heavy and contested in American culture, with the South at the center of much of the discussion and Jews playing a complicated—but clearly compelling—role. Mother Emanuel AME Church in Charleston still gathers for worship and Bible study, although the city around it has changed. Following the murder of George Floyd in Minneapolis, and the racial justice protests it inspired in the summer of 2020, the city removed the monument of proslavery agitator John C. Calhoun, which used to stand a block away, competing with Emanuel's steeple for height.[3] A half-mile south, a plaque has been erected outside of Kahal Kadosh Beth Elohim commemorating the enslaved laborers who built their antebellum synagogue.[4] Even as it demonstrated that racism exceeds the borders of the South and persists beyond the civil rights legislation of the 1960s, the Floyd murder had forced a reconsideration of the antebellum period and its representation in the heart of the former Confederacy.

Southern Jews have been narrating their own history almost since it began, and yet the period since the 1970s has been marked by particularly intense forms of memorialization. The first salvo in this new movement was Eli Evans's 1973 study *The Provincials*, which showed "how Jews made of the American South a home." Written after he moved from Durham, his hometown, to New York City, Evans's account was a story of synthesis and success. It was also hugely popular and influential.[5] Not only did it lead Evans to write two more books, but it inspired many others to document and publicize the Jewish past.[6] The Southern Jewish Historical Society was founded in 1976; a decade later Macy B. Hart, a native of Winona, Mississippi, established the Museum of the Southern Jewish Experience in Utica, at the Reform movement's Camp Jacobs, which he directed.[7] Hart's museum began as a repository for precious Judaica from small-town congregations forced to close their doors due to dwindling numbers. In 2000, it became part of the Institute of Southern Jewish Life, which provides direct support for small-town southern Jewish communities. In 2021 a spin-off museum opened in downtown New Orleans.[8]

These projects were motivated by the realization that the Jewish South that people like Evans and Hart grew up in was in the process of disappearing. This was, of course, the result of broader processes. The region at large was reshaped in the last third of the twentieth century by highways, a service-based economy, air conditioning, and immigration from Latin America, Asia, and around the world.[9] Southern Jews became less likely to own Main Street stores and more likely to work as professionals in sunbelt cities like Atlanta, which elected a Jewish mayor, Sam Massell, in 1970, and helped send the Jewish Atlantan Jon Ossoff to the Senate in 2021; in corporate centers like Bentonville, Arkansas, which has had a synagogue since 2004; and in college towns like Oxford, Mississippi, where a Jewish Federation was created in 2015. Jews have come to enjoy remarkable levels of integration, counting among their number some of the region's wealthiest businesspeople and most prominent philanthropists. Greater numbers of Orthodox Jews, Jews by choice, and Jews of color came to populate the region, and the southern born have been joined by waves of migrants from northern states, as well as from the Soviet Union, Cuba, South Africa, and Israel.[10] In Nashville, already in 1982 a study found that less than 36 percent of local Jews had been born in middle Tennessee.[11]

Amid these dramatic changes, Jews felt that they had something to remember, and they also felt authorized to do so by broader trends in American culture, especially the white ethnic revival movement, which rooted American identity in an immigration narrative that most southern Jews could readily inhabit.[12] Although synagogues continued to be seen in many cases as "Jewish churches," forms of Jewish difference that exceeded the frame of religion gained greater acceptance. For instance, politically engaged evangelicals enthusiastically supported Zionist causes and the state of Israel, motivated in part by a vision of the end times requiring a Jewish presence in the Holy Land.[13] Local and state officials authorized Holocaust commissions, museums, and memorials, including in places marked by a studied silence about the horrors of slavery. Charlestonians erected a Holocaust memorial in 1999, which for over two decades sat directly between John C. Calhoun's statue and Mother Emanuel Church. Jewish history could be used to condemn prejudice elsewhere without fully confronting its prevalence at home.[14]

And yet forms of antisemitism have persisted alongside other forms of bigotry. Evangelicals intensified their efforts to enshrine Christian norms in public life in ways that marginalized Jews and other minorities, and radical far-right groups maintained that the Holocaust had not been real or bad. In the late 1980s and early 1990s David Duke—the former Ku Klux Klan leader and founder of the National Association for the

Advancement of White People—ran several campaigns for public office in Louisiana, which were unsuccessful but alarming.[15] Duke was among those gathered in Charlottesville, Virginia, in August 2017 to "Unite the Right" behind a defense of Confederate monuments that had been slated for removal. White men marched with tiki torches, shouting slogans that included "Jews will not replace us." In a progressive city with a Jewish mayor and against the backdrop of the first year of Donald J. Trump's tumultuous presidency, the protests turned deadly.[16] Nazis marched by the local synagogue; after services its president reported, "My heart broke as I advised congregants that it would be safer to leave the temple through the back entrance rather than through the front."[17] Members of a congregation that had been present in Charlottesville for over 125 years were made to feel like outsiders, caught up in racist attempts to preserve the Confederate past that also gestured to European genocide. Southern Jews felt threatened, but it was not only about Jews or the South.

In July 2023, I walked out into the clatter of Times Square. I felt gratified at the obvious public interest in southern Jewish history and grateful to *Parade* for introducing so many to one of its most troubling incidents. But I also knew that there was more to learn and to teach about the long and complicated relationship between Jews and the South. In contemplating that history, I have found wisdom in the writing of the feminist critic Adrienne Rich, the daughter of a Jewish father and a Christian mother, both of whom were from Alabama, although they raised her in the border city of Baltimore. In a famous 1982 essay she wrote of the frustrations and challenges of being simultaneously "white, Jewish, anti-Semite, racist, anti-racist, once-married, lesbian, middle-class, feminist, exmatriate southerner, *split at the root.*" While she is uncertain if these identities could ever be made cohesive, and admits that "at different times in my life I have wanted to push away one or the other burden of inheritance," she commits to an ongoing struggle with the realities of both racism and antisemitism: "We can't wait to speak until we are perfectly clear and righteous. There is no purity and, in our lifetimes, no end to this process."[18]

Although typically not understood as a southern Jewish figure, Rich was heir to centuries of complex and unstable dynamics that played out on the swath of land that we know of as "the South," although they were hardly exclusive or contained to it. When viewed from the vantage point of its Jewish residents, we still see a region shaped in many ways by binary racial politics, by rural spaces, and by insistent forms of regional identity. But we also see a story of a shifting social hierarchy shaped by religion as well as race, with diverse groups laying claim to places of varying size and character, and with geographic boundaries that remain alluring but insistently porous. In writing this book I have tried to inhabit Rich's combination of self-awareness, humility, and determination; it is my hope that the result will be useful for those—southern Jews, southerners, Jews, and others—who are committed to better understanding our shared past. To my mind, that is a necessary step toward building a more equitable future.

ACKNOWLEDGMENTS

First and foremost, I want to express my gratitude to Fred Appel, who led me to believe that I could write this book—I would not have had the chutzpah on my own! He shepherded this book with consummate professionalism, patience, and care.

The support of the National Endowment for the Humanities was critical, first in supporting a Summer Institute for College and University Faculty on southern Jewish history that I codirected in 2019, and later in granting me a yearlong fellowship to work exclusively on this book. Americans are incredibly lucky to have this kind of federal funding available to researchers, and I only wish more was available. A Council on Library and Information Resources grant to the College of Charleston Special Collections led me to write a related digital exhibit, focusing on nineteenth-century Charleston, called "Finding Judaism in the Holy City." I am grateful to Leah Worthington and Meaghan Cash for their support on that project. I am also grateful to Max Daniel and Alyssa Neely at the College of Charleston Special Collections, Mark Swick at Kahal Kadosh Beth Elohim, Anne F. Jennings, Dana Herman and Joe Weber at the American Jewish Archives, Amanda Kazden at the Skirball Cultural Center, William H. Brown at the North Carolina State Archives, Kayley Rapp at the Cuba Family Archives, and Caleb Del Rio of the University of Florida Libraries for their generosity in providing access to images.

This book would not exist if I had not lived for four years in Charleston, where I was first compelled to grapple seriously with southern Jewish history. Thank you to Dale Rosengarten and Harlan Greene, the students who took my courses in southern Jewish history, and the many gracious community members who shared with me their passion for

Charleston and its Jewish past, especially Anita Moïse Rosenberg and Randi Serrins. I codirected the NEH Summer Institute with Dale and with Michael R. Cohen; the long conversations we had about southern Jewish history before the institute profoundly shaped my thinking, as did the discussions I had with institute presenters and participants while it was taking place. Sylvester Johnson, Sally Promey, and my cohort in the Young Scholars in American Religion program—Joe Blankholm, Melissa Borja, Chris Cantwell, Matthew Cressler, Sarah Dees, Jamil Drake, Katharine Gerbner, Samira Mehta, and Alexis Wells-Oghoghomeh—offered crucial early encouragement.

Marcie Cohen Ferris has been an inspiring teacher and cheerleader. She is one of the many kind and dedicated people whom I came to know through the pursuit of southern Jewish history and who have helped me in ways small and large. Many of their names appear in the footnotes. Among my most valuable conversation partners have been Adam Domby, whom I was lucky to meet almost as soon as I moved to Charleston, and Joshua Parshall, whom I got to know through the Southern Jewish Historical Society. I am indebted to them both for answering stray text messages and phone calls as I waded out past my comfort zone as a historian.

Thank you to my colleagues in the Department of Religion and the Program in Jewish Studies at Oberlin College for their kindness and support. Oberlin—the college and the town—has been a wonderful place to do my work. Oberlin students Sarah Naiman and Ben Burton provided helpful research assistance, and Sasha Goldman offered crucial child care as I reached the finish line. Parts of the research from this book were presented at the Yale Modern Jewish History Colloquium, the McNeil Center for Early American Studies, the University of North Carolina at Chapel Hill, Duke University, the Southern Jewish Historical Society, the Indiana University–Purdue University Indianapolis Biennial Conference on Religion and American Culture, the University of Mississippi, and Rhodes College.

Adam Domby, along with Adam Jortner, Elijah Siegler, and Michael Cohen, read portions of this manuscript and offered feedback, as did Samira Mehta, Adrienne Krone, Jessica Cooperman, and the members of a Southern Historical Association second book workshop: David Ballantyne, Scott Huffard, and Zachary Lechner, and our convener Greg Downs. Tara Mendola gave feedback at a time when I needed an outside perspective the most. All of them pushed me in useful ways. Any remaining errors are mine alone.

Thank you to my extended family—Rabins, Schaers, Berkmans, and more—for their love and support, and to Susan Schaer and Norma Berkman for sharing their thoughts on several chapters. As I wrote, cats Hazel, Cardi, and the late Betty White enriched my daily life with companionship and silly antics. The many other cats I have helped care for through Community Action to Save Strays—and the people I worked with to do so—unexpectedly deepened my appreciation of the power of place and community in the years I worked on this book.

I am tremendously lucky to have a husband as brilliant and loving as Matthew Berkman. While I was writing this book, I gave birth to our daughter, Margalit Esther. I dedicate this book to our little family, with humble recognition of our small place in a much larger chain of history. As I write these words in February 2024, the world Maggie has inherited feels like a terrifying place, and the future uncertain. I pray for her sake—and for that of all our children—that we can find a way to make it kinder and more just.

NOTES

Prologue

1. Elizabeth Fenten, *Old Canaan in a New World: Native Americans and the Lost Tribes of Israel* (New York: New York University Press, 2022); Jonathan Boyarin, *The Unconverted Self: Jews, Indians, and the Identity of Christian Europe* (Chicago: University of Chicago Press, 2009); "The First Charter of Virginia, April 10, 1606," *The Federal and State Constitutions Colonial Charters, and Other Organic Laws of the States, Territories, and Colonies Now or Heretofore Forming the United States of America Compiled and Edited under the Act of Congress of June 30, 1906 by Francis Newton Thorpe* (Washington, DC: Government Printing Office, 1909), The Avalon Project, Yale Law School, Lillian Goldman Law Library, accessed July 23, 2020, https://avalon.law.yale.edu/17th_century/va01.asp; Tisa Wenger, *Religious Freedom: The Contested History of an American Ideal* (Chapel Hill: University of North Carolina Press, 2017), 6–7.

2. Eli Evans, *The Provincials: A Personal History of Jews in the South*, 3rd ed. (Chapel Hill: University of North Carolina Press, 2005); Clay Risen, "Eli N. Evans, Who Wrote about Jews in American South, Dies at 85," *New York Times*, August 2, 2022; Gary P. Zola, "Why Study Southern Jewish History?," *Southern Jewish History* (1998):1–22; Marni Davis, "In Memoriam: Eli N. Evans (1936–2022)," *Southern Jewish History* 26 (2023):1–8.

3. Isaac Mayer Wise, "A Sketch of Judaism in America," *American Jews' Annual* (1884–85), 37. The author most closely associated with this debate, and with the argument against southern regional distinctiveness, is Mark Bauman. See *A New Vision of Southern Jewish History: Studies in Institution Building, Leadership, Interaction, and Mobility* (Tuscaloosa: University of Alabama Press, 2019).

4. Two important readers collect some of this work: Marcie Cohen Ferris and Mark I. Greenberg, eds., *Jewish Roots in Southern Soil: A New History* (Waltham, MA: Brandeis University Press, 2006); Mark K. Bauman, ed., *Dixie Diaspora: An Anthology of Southern Jewish History* (Tuscaloosa: University of Alabama Press, 2006).

5. David Moltke-Hansen, "Mind and Place: Michael O'Brien and the American South," *U.S. Intellectual History Blog*, March 10, 2017, https://s-usih.org/2017/03/mind-and-place-michael-obrien-and-the-american-south-guest-post-by-david-moltke-hansen/. See Michael O'Brien, *Intellectual Life and the American South, 1810–1860* (Chapel Hill: University of North Carolina Press, 2010).

6. Michael A. Meyer, *Response to Modernity: A History of the Reform Movement in Judaism* (New York: Oxford University Press, 1988); Jonathan Sarna, *American Judaism: A History* (New Haven, CT: Yale University Press, 2004).

7. Thomas Tweed, *Crossing and Dwelling: A Theory of Religion* (Cambridge, MA: Harvard University Press, 2006), 54.

8. W. J. Cash, *The Mind of the South* (New York: Knopf, 1941), x, 54, 56.

9. In so doing this book complements the work of cutting-edge southern historians who have typically overlooked Jews. The excellent recent volume *A New History of the American South* includes no entries for Jews or Judaism in its index and acknowledges the presence of Jews only in passing. Studies of southern religion often deal exclusively with Christianity. W. Fitzhugh Brundage, ed., *A New History of the American South* (Chapel Hill, NC: University of North Carolina Press, 2023); Paul Harvey, *Christianity and Race*

in the American South (Chicago: University of Chicago Press, 2016); Daniel Stowell, *Rebuilding Zion: The Religious Reconstruction of the South, 1863–1877* (New York: Oxford University Press, 1998).

10. Flannery O'Connor, *Mystery and Manners: Occasional Writings* (New York: Farrar, Straus, and Giroux, 1969), 44.

11. Henry Goldschmidt and Elizabeth McAlister, eds., *Race, Nation, and Religion in the Americas* (Oxford: Oxford University Press, 2004), 7; see also Kathryn Gin Lum and Paul Harvey, *The Oxford Handbook of Race and Religion in American History* (Oxford: Oxford University Press, 2018).

12. Judith Weisenfeld, *New World a'Coming: Black Religion and Racial Identity during the Great Migration* (New York: New York University Press, 2018).

13. On a different group's relationship to southern whiteness, focused on the post–World War II era, see Cecilia Márquez's *Making the Latino South: A History of Racial Formation* (Chapel Hill: University of North Carolina Press, 2023).

14. Tony Michels, "Is America 'Different'?: A Critique of Jewish Exceptionalism," *American Jewish History* 96, no. 3 (2010):201–24; Rachel Gordan, "The Sin of American Jewish Exceptionalism," *AJS Review* 45, no. 2 (2021):282–301; Matthew D. Lassiter and Joseph Crespino, eds., *The Myth of Southern Exceptionalism* (Oxford: Oxford University Press, 2010); Natalie J. Ring, *The Problem South: Region, Empire, and the New Liberal State, 1880–1930* (Athens: University of Georgia Press, 2012); Derek Penslar, *Shylock's Children: Economics and Jewish Identity in Modern Europe* (Berkeley: University of California Press, 2001).

15. Cash, *Mind of the South*, 334.

16. In *Dispossessed Lives: Enslaved Women, Violence, and the Archive*, Marisa Fuentes has argued that archives of slavery "are partial, incomplete, and structured by privileges of class, race, and gender" (Philadelphia: University of Pennsylvania Press, 2016), 4.

Chapter 1

1. Edward J. Cashin, ed., *Setting Out to Begin a New World: Colonial Georgia: A Documentary History* (Savannah, GA: Beehive, 1995), 44, 61.

2. Thomas D. Wilson, *The Ashley Cooper Plan: The Founding of Carolina and the Origins of Southern Political Culture* (Chapel Hill: University of North Carolina Press, 2016).

3. Herbert S. Klein, *The Atlantic Slave Trade* (New York: Cambridge University Press, 2010); Alan Gallay, *The Indian Slave Trade: The Rise of the English Empire in the American South, 1670–1717* (New Haven, CT: Yale University Press, 2008); Noeleen McIlvenna, *The Short Life of Free Georgia: Class and Slavery in the Colonial South* (Chapel Hill: University of North Carolina Press, 2015).

4. Patricia Seed, *Ceremonies of Possession* (New York: Cambridge University Press, 1995), 18, 34; Cheryl I. Harris, "Whiteness as Property," *Harvard Law Review* 106, no. 8 (1993):1722; Claudio Saunt, *A New Order of Things: Property, Power, and the Transformation of the Creek Indians, 1733–1816* (New York: Cambridge University Press, 1999), 56–57.

5. Jonathan Sarna, "The 'Mythical Jew' and the 'Jew Next Door' in Nineteenth-Century America," in *Coming to Terms with America: Essays on Jewish History, Religion, and Culture*, 201–18 (Philadelphia: Jewish Publication Society, 2021).

6. On "imperial Protestantism" in this period, see Katherine Carté's *Religion and the American Revolution: An Imperial History* (Chapel Hill: University of North Carolina Press, 2021).

7. Jonathan Sarna, *American Judaism: A History* (New Haven, CT: Yale University Press, 2004); Charles Lippy, "Chastized by Scorpions: Christianity and Culture in Colonial South Carolina, 1669–1740," *Church History* 79, no. 2 (2010):253–70. There has been an impressive body of work on Jews, race, and religion in the Jewish Atlantic world, most of it focused on the Caribbean. Some works in this vein have dealt with Savannah, although there has been much less engagement with Charleston or New Orleans. Laura Leibman, *Messianism, Mysticism, and Secrecy: A New Interpretation of Early American Jewish Life* (Portland, OR: Vallentine Mitchell, 2012); Aviva Ben-Ur, "Jewish Savannah in Atlantic Perspective: A Reconsideration of North America's First Intentional Jewish Community," in *The Sephardic Atlantic*, edited by S. Rauschenbach and J. Schorsch, 183–214 (Cham, Switzerland: Springer International, 2017); Holly Snyder, "A Sense of Place:

Jews, Identity, and Social Status in Colonial British America, 1654–1831," PhD dissertation, Brandeis University, 2000.

8. Rebecca Goetz, *The Baptism of Early Virginia: How Christianity Created Race* (Baltimore, MD: Johns Hopkins University Press, 2012); Katharine Gerbner, *Christian Slavery: Conversion and Race in the Protestant Atlantic World* (Philadelphia: University of Pennsylvania Press, 2018).

9. Karl Watson, "Shifting Identities: Religion, Race, and Creolization among the Sephardi Jews of Barbados, 1654–1900," in *Jews in the Caribbean*, edited by Jane S. Gerber (New York: Littman Library of Jewish Civilization, 2014), 195.

10. Todd M. Endelman, *The Jews of Modern Britain, 1656–2000* (Berkeley: University of California Press, 2002), 15, 25; David Katz, *Philo-Semitism and the Readmission of the Jews to England, 1603–1655* (New York: Clarendon, 1982); Ismar Schorsch, "From Messianism to Realpolitik: Menasseh Ben Israel and the Readmission of the Jews to England," *Proceedings of the American Academy of Jewish Research* 45 (1978):196.

11. David Armitage, "John Locke, Carolina, and the Two Treatises of Government," *Political Theory* 32, no. 5 (2004):602–27; Jonathan Israel, *Radical Enlightenment: Philosophy and the Making of Modernity, 1650–1750* (New York: Oxford University Press, 2001).

12. "The religious upheavals of the sixteenth and seventeenth centuries meant that Englishmen enjoyed a freedom of religious expression which was matched nowhere in Europe, with the possible exception of the Netherlands" (Peter Harrison, *"Religion" and the Religions in the English Enlightenment* [New York: Cambridge University Press, 1990], 30). See also David Sorkin, *Emancipation: A History across Five Centuries* (Princeton, NJ: Princeton University Press, 2019), 32; Jonathan Sarna, "The Jews in British America," in *The Jews and the Expansion of Europe to the West, 1450–1800*, edited by Paolo Bernadini and Norman Fiering (New York: Berghahn Books, 2001), 519.

13. Richard S. Dunn, *Sugar and Slaves: The Rise of the Planter Class in the English West Indies, 1624–1713* (Chapel Hill: University of North Carolina Press, 2000), 108.

14. Watson, "Shifting Identities," 212; Jonathan Schorsch, *Jews and Blacks in the Early Modern World* (New York: Cambridge University Press, 2004).

15. David Graizbord, "Religion and Ethnicity among 'Men of the Nation': Toward a Realistic Interpretation," *Jewish Social Studies* 15, no. 1 (2008):32–65.

16. Leibman, *Messianism, Mysticism, and Secrecy.*

17. For one influential study using this framework, see Paul Gilroy's *The Black Atlantic: Modernity and Double Consciousness* (New York: Verso, 1993). See also Brian Ward, Martyn Bone, and William A. Link, eds., *The American South and the Atlantic World* (Gainesville: University of Florida Press, 2013).

18. Armitage, "John Locke," 608; Wilson, *Ashley Cooper Plan*. It applied to "any seven or more persons agreeing in any religion, shall constitute a church or profession," although formal Jewish worship required a quorum of ten adult men. "The Fundamental Constitutions of Carolina, March 1, 1669," *The Federal and State Constitutions Colonial Charters, and Other Organic Laws of the States, Territories, and Colonies Now or Heretofore Forming the United States of America Compiled and Edited under the Act of Congress of June 30, 1906 by Francis Newton Thorpe* (Washington, DC: Government Printing Office, 1909), The Avalon Project, Yale Law School, Lillian Goldman Law Library, accessed July 23, 2020, https://avalon.law.yale.edu/17th_century/va01.asp.

19. Nabil I. Matar, "John Locke and the Jews," *Journal of Ecclesiastical History* 44, no. 1 (1993):45–62.

20. "Fundamental Constitutions of Carolina."

21. Wilson, *Ashley Cooper Plan*; John J. McCusker and Russell R. Menard, *The Economy of British America, 1607–1789* (Chapel Hill: University of North Carolina Press, 1991), 170; Gallay, *Indian Slave Trade*, 4.

22. John Archdale, *A New Description of that Fertile and Pleasant Province of Carolina*, 22, quoted in James Hagy, *This Happy Land: The Jews of Colonial and Antebellum Charleston* (Tuscaloosa: University of Alabama Press, 1993), 6; Lippy, "Chastized by Scorpions," 262.

23. Gallay, *Indian Slave Trade*.

24. Gallay, 10; Gregory D. Smithers, *Native Southerners: Indigenous History from Origins to Removal* (Norman: University of Oklahoma Press, 2019); Steven J. Oatis, *A Colonial Complex: South Carolina's Frontiers in the Era of the Yamasee War* (Lincoln: University of Nebraska Press, 2004).

25. In Charles Town before 1715, more Natives were exported than Africans imported (Gallay, *Indian Slave Trade*, 7–8). Between 1700 and 1710 the number of Indian slaves in Carolina increased from 200 to 1,500 (Smithers, *Native Southerners*, 74). Jeffrey Robert Young, *Domesticating Slavery: The Master Class in Georgia and South Carolina, 1670–1837* (Chapel Hill: University of North Carolina Press, 1999); McCusker and Menard, *Economy of British America*, 175.

26. McIlvenna, *Short Life*, 57.

27. Derek Penslar, *Shylock's Children: Economics and Jewish Identity in Modern Europe* (Berkeley: University of California Press, 2001).

28. Schorsch, *Jews and Blacks*.

29. Watson, "Shifting Identities," 211; Ancestry.com, *South Carolina, Wills and Probate Records, 1670–1980* [database online] (Provo, UT: Ancestry.com Operations, 2015), vol. 54, *1694–1704*, p. 362, https://www .ancestry.com/discoveryui-content/view/1368108:9080?tid=&pid=&queryId=f726a182-e697-46b4 -b613-7c3f89e70976&_phsrc=FHZ220&_phstart=successSource, cited in Hagy, *This Happy Land*, 57; Dale Rosengarten, "Port Jews and Plantation Jews: Carolina-Caribbean Connections," in *The Jews in the Caribbean*, edited by Jane S. Gerber (New York: Littman Library of Jewish Civilization, 2014), 294–95.

30. "Fundamental Constitutions of Carolina."

31. Wilson, *Ashley Cooper Plan*, 80–81; Betty Wood, *Slavery in Colonial Georgia* (Athens: University of Georgia Press, 2007), 1; Paul Harvey, *Christianity and Race in the American South: A History* (Chicago: University of Chicago Press, 2016), 25.

32. "Fundamental Constitutions of Carolina."

33. Lippy, "Chastized by Scorpions," 253–70; S. Charles Bolton, *Southern Anglicanism: The Church of England in Colonial South Carolina* (Westport, CT: Greenwood, 1982), 18; Travis Glasson, *Mastering Christianity: Missionary Anglicanism and Slavery in the Atlantic World* (New York: Oxford University Press, 2012); Bradford J. Wood, "'A Constant Attendance on God's Alter': Death, Disease and the Anglican Church in Colonial South Carolina," *South Carolina Historical Magazine* 100, no. 3 (1999):204–20; H. Roy Merrens and George D. Terry, "Dying in Paradise: Malaria, Mortality, and the Perceptual Environment in Colonial South Carolina," *Journal of Southern History* 50, no. 4 (1984):533–50.

34. Goetz, *Baptism of Early Virginia*, 144; Annette Laing, "'Heathens and Infidels'? African Christianization and Anglicanism in the South Carolina Lowcountry, 1700–1750," *Religion and American Culture* 12, no. 2 (2002):197–228; Jon Sensbach, "Early Southern Religions in a Global Age," in Ward, Bone, and Link, *American South*, 45–60.

35. "Fundamental Constitutions of Carolina."

36. Bolton, *Southern Anglicanism*, 19.

37. Thomas J. Little, *The Origins of Southern Evangelicalism: Religious Revivalism in the South Carolina Lowcountry, 1670–1860* (Columbia: University of South Carolina Press, 2013). Katharine Carté writes of foreign Protestants that "most . . . were members of established churches in their home territories and were thus not considered schismatic (or guilty of dividing the church). They earned comparatively easy acceptance in Britain's Protestant world. Those persecuted for their Protestantism by Catholic authorities were also welcome" (*Religion*, 39).

38. "An Act for Making Aliens Free of this Part of this Province, and Granting Liberty of Conscience to all Protestants," in *The Statutes at Large of South Carolina*, vol. 2, edited by Thomas Cooper (Columbia, SC: A. S. Johnston, 1837), 131–32; Hagy, *This Happy Land*, 6; William Pencak, *Jews and Gentiles in Early America, 1654–1800* (Ann Arbor: University of Michigan Press, 2005), 120; *Grants, Sales, etc.*, book D, *1703–9, Colonial Records of South Carolina. Copied from the State Paper office, London* (Columbia, SC: Secretary of State's Office), cited in Barnett Elzas, *The Jews of South Carolina: From the Earliest Times to the Present Day* (Philadelphia: J.B. Lippincott, 1905), 20.

39. Quoted in Bradford Wood, "Constant Attendance," 218.

40. Frederick Dalcho, *An Historical Account of the Protestant Episcopal Church in South Carolina, from the First Settlement of the Province to the War of the Revolution* (Charleston, SC: E. Thayer, 1820), 65. See also Pencak, *Jews and Gentiles*, 121–22.

41. Louis P. Nelson, *The Beauty of Holiness: Anglicanism and Architecture in Colonial South Carolina* (Chapel Hill: University of North Carolina Press, 2009), 5, 35, 171.

42. Pencak, *Jews and Gentiles*, 122; "An Act to Encourage the Importation of White Servants into the Province," in Cooper, *Statutes at Large*, 647. Following the 1712 split between North and South Carolina, in 1729 South Carolina became a royal colony.

43. John F. Chuchiak, *The Inquisition in New Spain, 1536–1820: A Documentary History* (Baltimore, MD: Johns Hopkins University Press, 2012), 235.

44. David Graizbord, "Between Ethnicity, Commerce, Religion, and Race," in *Theorising the Ibero-American Atlantic*, edited by Harald Ernst Braun and Lisa Vollendorf (Boston: Brill, 2013), 35.

45. "The Code Noir of 1724, A Free Translation by Vernon Valentine Palmer," *Tulane European and Civil Law Forum* 34 (2019):105.

46. "Code Noir of 1724"; A. P. Nasatir and Leo Shpall, "The Texel Affair," *American Jewish Historical Quarterly* 53, no. 1 (1963):4; Bertram Korn, *The Early Jews of New Orleans* (Waltham, MA: American Jewish Historical Society, 1969), 2.

47. Betty Wood, *Slavery in Georgia*, 4–5.

48. Ben-Ur, "Jewish Savannah."

49. "Charter of Georgia: 1732," *The Federal and State Constitutions Colonial Charters, and Other Organic Laws of the States, Territories, and Colonies Now or Heretofore Forming the United States of America Compiled and Edited under the Act of Congress of June 30, 1906 by Francis Newton Thorpe* (Washington, DC: Government Printing Office, 1909), The Avalon Project, Yale Law School, Lillian Goldman Law Library, accessed July 23, 2020, https://avalon.law.yale.edu/18th_century/ga01.asp.

50. Mark I. Greenberg, "One Religion, Different Worlds: Sephardic and Ashkenazic Immigrants in Eighteenth-Century Savannah," in *Jewish Roots in Southern Soil*, edited by Marcie Cohen Ferris and Greenberg (Waltham, MA: Brandeis University Press, 2006), 28.

51. Cashin, *Setting Out*, 29–30. See also Pencak, *Jews and Gentiles*, 146–47.

52. Pencak, *Jews and Gentiles*, 144.

53. Sarna, "Jews in British America," 520; Malcolm Stern, ed., "The Sheftall Diaries: Vital Records of Savannah Jewry (1733–1808)," *American Jewish Historical Quarterly* 54, no. 3 (1965):243–77.

54. McIlvenna, *Short Life*, 1.

55. Gallay, *Indian Slave Trade*.

56. Paul M. Pressly, *On the Rim of the Caribbean: Colonial Georgia and the British Atlantic World* (Athens: University of Georgia Press, 2013), 28.

57. Stern, "Sheftall Diaries," 246–47; Ben-Ur, "Jewish Savannah."

58. The German-speaking Jewish minority warmly welcomed German-speaking Protestant arrivals to Georgia, offering them food and even attending their worship (Holly Snyder, "A Tree with Two Different Fruits: The Jewish Encounter with German Pietists in the Eighteenth-Century Atlantic World," *William and Mary Quarterly* 58, no. 4 [2001]:855–82). Greenberg, "One Religion, Different Worlds."

59. Pencak, *Jews and Gentiles*, 154.

60. Curaçao's Portuguese Jewish leaders had implored their New York brethren to limit the congregational influence of the "Germans [who they understood] are more in number than wee [*sic*]" (Eli Faber, "The Borders of Early American Jewish History," in Gerber, *Jews in the Caribbean*, 285).

61. What is described in the document as a "book" is labeled "diaries" by Malcolm Stern. J. H. Chajes warns against the enthusiasm for describing early modern egodocuments as "diaries" ("Accounting for the Self: Preliminary Generic-Historical Reflection on Early Modern Jewish Egodocuments," *Jewish Quarterly Review* 95, no. 1 [2005]:7–9).

62. Greenberg, "One Religion, Different Worlds," 34.

63. Stern, "Sheftall Diaries," 248.

64. Stern.

65. Alexis Wells-Oghoghomeh, *The Souls of Womenfolk: The Religious Cultures of Enslaved Women in the Lower South* (Chapel Hill: University of North Carolina Press, 2021).

66. Stern, "Sheftall Diaries."

67. Leibman, *Messianism, Mysticism, and Secrecy*.

68. Harry S. Stout, *The Divine Dramatist* (Grand Rapids, MI: Eerdmans, 1991), 58.

69. Greenberg, "One Religion, Different Worlds," 33.

70. Pat. Tailfer, Hugh Anderson, and D. A. Douglas, *A True and Historical Narrative of the Colony of Georgia in America* ... (Charleston: P. Timothy, 1741), in *Collections of the Georgia Historical Society*, vol. 2 (Savannah: Georgia Historical Society, 1842), 217–20.

71. Pencak, *Jews and Gentiles*, 152.

72. Derek Penslar, *Jews and the Military: A History* (Princeton, NJ: Princeton University Press, 2013), 39–41.

73. Malcolm H. Stern, "New Light on the Jewish Settlement of Savannah," *American Jewish Historical Quarterly* 52, no. 3 (1963):186.

74. Pencak, *Jews and Gentiles*, 147–48.

75. Sorkin, *Emancipation*, 74.

76. Jonathan Sarna and David Dalin, *Religion and State in the American Jewish Experience* (South Bend, IN: Notre Dame University Press, 1997), 56.

77. Greenberg, "One Religion, Different Worlds," 35.

78. Gallay, *Indian Slave Trade*, 1.

Chapter 2

1. His name is variously rendered Olivera, Oliveira, and D'Oliveira.

2. Ancestry.com, *South Carolina, Wills and Probate Records, 1670–1980* [database online] (Provo, UT: Ancestry.com Operations, 2015), *Will Book (1747–1752)*, p. 524, https://www.ancestry.com/imageviewer /collections/9080/images/007648975_00293?treeid=&personid=&usePUB=true&_phsrc=FHZ230& _phstart=successSource&pId=673990; Avriel Bar-Levav, "'When I was Alive': Jewish Ethical Wills as Egodocuments," in *Egodocuments and History: Autobiographical Writing in Its Social Context since the Middle Ages*, edited by R. Dekker (Hilversum, Netherlands: Verloren, 2002), 46; J. H. Chajes, "Accounting for the Self: Preliminary Generic-Historical Reflections on Early Modern Egodocuments," *Jewish Quarterly Review* 95, no. 1 (2005), 1–15. This is in contrast with Stanley Mirvis's finding that Jewish wills in Jamaica were highly formulaic, unlike ethical wills, with religious language limited to a "religious preamble" and "burial clauses" (*The Jews of Eighteenth-Century Jamaica: A Testamentary History of a Diaspora in Transition* [New Haven, CT: Yale University Press, 2020], 4).

3. Isaac was "shot by accident" in November 1734 (Malcolm H. Stern, "New Light on the Jewish Settlement of Savannah," *American Jewish Historical Quarterly* 52, no. 3 [1963]: 182).

4. Ancestry.com, *South Carolina, Wills and Probate Records, 1670–1980, Will Book (1747–1752)*, p. 522–24. F. E. Bonsteel and E. P. Carr, "Soil Survey of the Charleston Area, South Carolina" (USDA Natural Resources Conservation Service, 1904), 212, Internet Archive, accessed June 26, 2024, https://archive.org /details/charlestonSC1904.

5. James Hagy, *This Happy Land: The Jews of Colonial and Antebellum Charleston* (Tuscaloosa: University of Alabama Press, 1993), 63–64.

6. M. L., "The Jewish Congregation of Charleston," *Occident* 1 (1843–44):337.

7. Jacob Rader Marcus, *The Colonial American Jew*, vol. 2 (Detroit: Wayne State University Press, 1991), 989; Holly Snyder, "A Tree with Two Different Fruits: The Jewish Encounter with German Pietists in the Eighteenth-Century Atlantic World," *William and Mary Quarterly* 58, no. 4 (2001):855–82.

8. According to Hagy, the first *mikvah* was built in Charleston in 1809 (*This Happy Land*, 74). Laura Leibman, *Messianism, Mysticism, and Secrecy: A New Interpretation of Early American Jewish Life* (New York, 2012).

9. Benjamin L. Carp, "'Fix'd Almost among Strangers': Charleston's Quaker Merchants and the Limits of Cosmopolitanism," *William and Mary Quarterly* 74 (2017):83. See also Carp, *Rebels Rising: Cities and the American Revolution* (New York: Oxford University Press, 2007), 154.

10. Jennifer Van Horn, *The Power of Objects in Eighteenth-Century British America* (Chapel Hill, NC: University of North Carolina Press, 2017); Emma Hart, *Building Charleston: Town and Society in the Eighteenth-Century British Atlantic World* (Charlottesville: University of Virginia Press, 2010); John J. McCusker and Russell R. Menard, *The Economy of British America, 1607–1789* (Chapel Hill: University of North

Carolina Press, 1985). The colony as a whole had grown from 6,000 to 64,000 people (McCusker and Menard, *Economy of British America*, 172).

11. William Pencak, *Jews and Gentles in Early America, 1654–1800* (Ann Arbor: University of Michigan Press, 2005), 124; David Sorkin, *Emancipation: A History across Five Centuries* (Princeton, NJ: Princeton University Press, 2019), 73; Hagy, *This Happy Land*, 18–27.

12. M. L., "Jewish Congregation of Charleston," 338.

13. Louis P. Nelson, *The Beauty of Holiness: Anglicanism and Architecture in Colonial South Carolina* (Chapel Hill, NC: University of North Carolina Press, 2008); S. Charles Bolton, *Southern Anglicanism: The Church of England in Colonial South Carolina* (Westport, CT: Greenwood, 1982).

14. Jon Butler, *Awash in a Sea of Faith: Christianizing the American People* (Cambridge, MA: Harvard University Press, 1990), 148.

15. Thomas S. Kidd, *The Great Awakening: The Roots of Evangelical Christianity in Colonial America* (New Haven, CT: Yale University Press, 2007).

16. Donald G. Mathews, *Religion in the Old South* (Chicago: University of Chicago Press, 1977), 13; Travis Glasson, *Mastering Christianity: Missionary Anglicanism and Slavery in the Atlantic World* (New York: Oxford University Press, 2012); Timothy D. Hall, *Contested Boundaries: Itinerancy and the Reshaping of the Colonial American Religious World* (Durham, NC: Duke University Press, 1994).

17. Glasson, *Mastering Christianity*; Charles Lippy, "Chastized by Scorpions: Christianity and Culture in Colonial South Carolina, 1669–1740," *Church History* 79, no. 2 (2010): 253–70; David T. Morgan Jr., "George Whitefield and the Great Awakening in the Carolinas and Georgia, 1739–1840," *Georgia Historical Quarterly* 54, no. 4 (1970): 517–39.

18. George Whitefield, *A Continuation of the Reverend Mr. Whitefield's Journal . . .* (London: W. Strahan, 1744), 10.

19. Harry S. Stout, *The Divine Dramatist* (Grand Rapids, MI: Eerdmans, 1991); Morgan, "George Whitefield."

20. Frank Lambert, "'I Saw the Book Talk': Slave Readings of the First Great Awakening," *Journal of African American History* 87 (2002):12–25.

21. Olivera: Ancestry.com, *South Carolina, U.S., Wills and Probate Records, 1670–1980* [database online] (Provo, UT: Ancestry.com Operations, 2015), *Wills, etc.*, 1747–1756, 522, 524, https://www.ancestry.com/imageviewer/collections/9080/images/007648975_00293?treeid=&personid=&usePUB=true&_phsrc=FHZ230&_phstart=successSource&pId=673990. Sheftall: Ancestry.com, *Georgia, U.S., Wills and Probate Records, 1742–1992* [database online] (Lehi, UT: Ancestry.com Operations, 2015), *Wills vol. A, 1754–1772*, 248, https://www.ancestry.com/discoveryui-content/view/904846:8635?tid=&pid=&queryId=9e6f4013-0e16-4c89-b867-d4ae9d879a1b&_phsrc=FHZ235&_phstart=successSource.

22. Jonathan Sarna found no evidence of the Great Awakening's influence on American Jews (*American Judaism: A History* [New Haven, CT: Yale University Press, 2004], 30).

23. Luke Tyerman, *The Life of George Whitefield*, vol. 2 (New York: Anson D. F. Randolph, 1877), 180; Thomas Little has argued that the enthusiasm of the Great Awakening revivals "inspired new religious activities" (*The Origins of Southern Evangelicalism: Religious Revivalism in the South Carolina Lowcountry, 1670–1860* [Columbia: University of South Carolina Press, 2013], 145–46).

24. Hagy, *This Happy Land*, 11.

25. Mordehay Arbell, *The Portuguese Jews of Jamaica* (Kingston, Jamaica: Canoe, 2000), 29.

26. *Pentateuch with Rashi's Commentary*, translated by M. Rosenbaum and A. M. Silbermann (London: Shapiro, Valentine, 1929–34), Sefaria, accessed June 26, 2024, https://www.sefaria.org/Rashi_on_Genesis .28.17.

27. My gratitude goes to Jonathan Sarna for these points.

28. M. L., "Jewish Congregation of Charleston." Jonathan Sarna has argued, "Not any of the synagogues established prior to the Revolution ever hired a haham ('sage,' the title given to a rabbi in the Sephardic community)" (*American Judaism*, 15). Laura Leibman has argued that "Hakham" was a title for learned men and religious leaders who occupied a position akin to a rabbi (*Messianism, Mysticism, and Secrecy*, 320).

29. Hagy, *This Happy Land*, 60.

30. Moses Cohen Gravestone, Kahal Kadosh Beth Elohim collection, Mss 1047, Special Collections, College of Charleston Libraries, Charleston, SC.

31. Van Horn, *Power of Objects*. Portrait gravestones could also be found in New England, and often featured ministers: Allan I. Ludwig, *Graven Images: New England Stone-Carving and Its Symbols, 1650–1815* (Bridgeton, CT: Wesleyan University Press, 1966), 316.

32. Van Horn, *Power of Objects*; Leibman, *Messianism, Mysticism, and Secrecy*.

33. Bolton, *Southern Anglicanism* (Westport, CT: Bloomsbury Academic, 1982); Nelson, *Beauty of Holiness*; Jacob Kabakoff, "The Tombstone of the Reverend Moses Cohen," *American Jewish Archives* 17 (1965):77–79. On the "bishop controversy" of the late 1760s, see Katherine Carté's *Religion and the American Revolution: An Imperial History* (Chapel Hill: University of North Carolina Press, 2021), 104–14.

34. Abraham Da Costa served as religious leader for several years after Cohen's death and was followed in 1766 by Abraham Alexander, who had been sent from London; he also worked as a scrivener, clerk, and auditor in the city (Hagy, *This Happy Land*, 60).

35. The deed listed trustees in Charleston, London, Kingston, Bridgetown, New York, Newport, and Savannah: Barnett Elzas, *The Old Jewish Cemeteries at Charleston: A Transcription of the Inscriptions on Their Tombstones, 1762–1903*, S.C. (Charleston: Daggett Printing, 1903), 4.

36. Hagy, *This Happy Land*, 60.

37. Alexander Hewatt, *An Historical Account of the Rise and Progress of the Colonies of South Carolina and Georgia* (London: Alexander Donaldson, 1779), vol. 2, 290.

38. Pencak, *Jews and Gentiles*, 155.

39. Holly Snyder, "A Sense of *Place*: Jews, Identity, and Social Status in Colonial British America, 1654–1831," PhD dissertation, Brandeis University, 2000, 864.

40. Pencak, *Jews and Gentiles*, 158–59; Barratt Wilkins, "A View of Savannah on the Eve of the Revolution," *Georgia Historical Quarterly* 54, no. 4 (1970):577–84; Jacob Rader Marcus, *American Jewry, Documents, Eighteenth Century* (Cincinnati: Hebrew Union College, 1959), 208–9.

41. Malcolm Stern, ed., "The Sheftall Diaries: Vital Records of Savannah Jewry (1733–1808)," *American Jewish Historical Quarterly* 54, no. 3 (1965):249–50.

42. Stern, "Sheftall Diaries," 249.

43. David T. Morgan, "The Sheftalls of Savannah," *American Jewish Historical Quarterly* 62, no. 4 (1973):348–61.

44. Marcus, *American Jewry*, 352–53. Abraham Mendes Seixas did the same in 1777 when he married (Hagy, *This Happy Land*, 162). Jonathan Schorsch found that Phillis was one of the five most popular names for enslaved people in Barbados: Schorsch, *Blacks and Jews in the Early Modern World* (New York: Cambridge University Press, 2003), 241.

45. Navigating what historian Benjamin L. Carp has described as "the lived experience of cosmopolitanism," they sought to embody Atlantic world standards of refinement, according to the particularities of their locale ("'Fix'd Almost among Strangers,'" 78).

46. Hagy, *This Happy Land*, 219–24.

47. Marcus, *American Jewry*, 348–49; Philips later moved to New York and Philadelphia, becoming very wealthy during the war.

48. Albert E. Cowdrey, *This Land, This South: An Environmental History* (Lexington: University of Kentucky Press, 1996), 51; McCusker and Menard, *Economy of British America*; Gregory D. Smithers, *Native Southerners: Indigenous History from Origins to Removal* (Norman: University of Oklahoma Press, 2019), 66–67.

49. Smithers, *Native Southerners*.

50. Paul M. Pressly, *On the Rim of the Caribbean: Colonial Georgia and the British Atlantic World* (Athens: University of Georgia Press, 2013), 81, 175–76. Deerskin merchants were "cultural brokers between two worlds, an essential link between a hunting culture whose ceremonies and rituals remained opaque to most whites and a farming culture bent on improving all lands and bringing white 'civilization' beyond the frontier" (193). Jews regularly served as interpreters within their communities. Sheftall translated for Germans in Georgia; in Charleston, Isaac DaCosta and Joseph Tobias served as interpreters (Hagy, *This Happy Land*, 44, 186).

51. McCusker and Menard, *Economy of British America*.

52. Jeffrey Robert Young, *Domesticating Slavery: The Master Class in Georgia and South Carolina, 1670–1837* (Chapel Hill: University of North Carolina Press, 1999); Van Horn, *Power of Objects*.

53. J. Schorsch, *Jews and Blacks*, 60–61; Peter Wood, *Black Majority: Negroes in Colonial South Carolina from 1670 through the Stono Rebellion* (New York: Norton, 1975); Ira Berlin, *Many Thousands Gone: The First Two Centuries of Slavery in North America* (Cambridge, MA: Belknap Press of Harvard University Press, 1998).

54. Ancestry.com, *South Carolina, Wills and Probate Records, 1670–1980* [database online] (Provo, UT: Ancestry.com Operations, 2015), *Wills*, vol. *78a–78b, 1749–51*, June 16, 1749, https://www.ancestry.com/imageviewer/collections/9080/images/004753789_00075?ssrc=&backlabel=Return.

55. Hagy, *This Happy Land*, 186; letter of March 15, 1762, Aaron Lopez Papers, P-11, Box 14, AJHS, cited in Schorsch, *Jews and Blacks*, 266.

56. Hagy, *This Happy Land*, 187.

57. Noeleen McIlvenna, *The Short Life of Free Georgia: Class and Slavery in the Colonial South* (Chapel Hill: University of North Carolina Press, 2015), 95; Pressly, *Rim of the Caribbean*; Betty Wood, *Slavery in Colonial Georgia* (Athens: University of Georgia Press, 2007); Claudio Saunt, *A New Order of Things: Property, Power, and the Transformation of the Creek Indians* (New York: Cambridge University Press, 1999), 62, 66.

58. Pencak, *Jews and Gentiles*, 157; Pressly, *Rim of the Caribbean*. Their son Minis began importing goods like rum, sugar, candles, soap, and butter. The previous year a group of Creeks had complained that white settlers "spoil our hunting Ground and frightens away the Deers" (Saunt, *New Order of Things*, 62).

59. Morgan, "Sheftalls of Savannah," 350–51.

60. Kylie L. McCormick, "Father and Servant, Son and Slave: Judaism and Labor in Georgia, 1732–1809," MA thesis, University of Nebraska–Lincoln, 2016, 48.

61. Albert S. Britt Jr. and Lilla M. Hawes, eds., "The Mackenzie Papers: Collections of the Georgia Historical Society, Other Documents and Notes," pt. 2, *Georgia Historical Quarterly* 57, no. 1 (1973):140.

62. Focusing on the Caribbean, and especially the Dutch colonies of Suriname and Curaçao, Jonathan Schorsch found "only minimal exposure to Jewish concepts and practices . . . and the general non-integration of slaves into the religion of their master" (*Jews and Blacks*, 14).

63. Marisa Fuentes, *Dispossessed Lives: Enslaved Women, Violence, and the Archive* (Philadelphia: University of Pennsylvania Press, 2016); Berlin, *Many Thousands Gone*, 161. On Bridgetown Jews, Schorsch writes, "Their slaves, like those of their non-Jewish colleagues, worked in warehouses, shops, and taverns" (*Jews and Blacks*, 60). Michael Lawrence Dickinson, *Almost Dead: Slavery and Social Death in the Black Urban Atlantic* (Athens: University of Georgia Press, 2021).

64. Amsterdam's influential community had even imposed new regulations explicitly excluding people of color. Jonathan Schorsch argues that this may have been caused by the "sacramental and salvational status accorded to circumcision in some Converso circles" (*Jews and Blacks*, 179); see also Aviva Ben-Ur, *Jewish Autonomy in a Slave Society: Suriname in the Atlantic World, 1651–1825* (Philadelphia: University of Pennsylvania Press, 2021).

65. Bolton, *Southern Anglicanism*; Glasson, *Mastering Christianity*.

66. "It was solely through being white that property could be acquired and secured under law. Only whites possessed whiteness, a highly valued and exclusive form of property" (Cheryl I. Harris, "Whiteness as Property," *Harvard Law Review* 106, no. 8 [1993]:1724).

67. Hart, *Building Charleston*; Jennifer L. Goloboy, *Charleston and the Emergence of Middle-Class Culture* (Athens: University of Georgia Press, 2016). The elite class would have been out of reach: "Even for the most successful merchants, wealth never trumped birth" (10–11).

68. Snyder, "Sense of *Place*"; Morgan, "Sheftalls of Savannah."

69. Hagy, *This Happy Land*, 44.

70. Francesca Trivellato, *The Familiarity of Strangers: The Sephardic Diaspora, Livorno, and Cross-Cultural Trade in the Early Modern Period* (New Haven, CT: Yale University Press, 2009), 2.

71. Thanks to Dale Rosengarten for this tip. Barnett Elzas, *The Jews of South Carolina: From the Earliest Times to the Present Day* (Philadelphia: J. B. Lippincott, 1905), 241.

72. Sarna, *American Judaism*; Myron Berman, *Richmond's Jewry, 1769–1976: Shabbat in Shockoe* (Richmond, VA: Jewish Community Federation of Richmond, 1979), 3. Richmond was founded in 1742: Virginius Dabney, *Richmond: The Story of a City* (Charlottesville: University of Virginia Press, 2012), 16, 20.

73. France, "Edit du Roi, touchant l'état & la discipline des Esclaves Négres de la Louisiane, donné à Versailles, au mois de Mars 1724," *Recueils de reglemens, edits, declarations et arrets: concernant le commerce, l'administration de la justice et la police des colonies françaises de l'Amérique . . . ; [Avec le] Code noir . . .* (Paris: Hachette, 1794), facsimile on Gallica, accessed November 5, 2021, http://visualiseur.bnf.fr/CadresFenetre ?O=NUMM-84479&I=134&M=tdm.

74. A. P. Nasatir and Leo Shpall, "Texel Affair," *American Jewish Historical Quarterly* 53, no. 1 (1963):3–43.

75. Bertram Korn, *The Early Jews of New Orleans* (Waltham, MA: American Jewish Historical Society, 1969), 10.

76. Korn, *Early Jews*, 18.

77. Pressly, *Rim of the Caribbean*, 173.

78. Korn, *Early Jews*, 32.

79. Korn, 24–25.

80. Korn, 39.

81. Korn, 42–43.

Chapter 3

1. Allan D. Candler, ed., *The Colonial Records of the State of Georgia*, vol. 15 (Atlanta, GA: Franklin-Turner, 1907), 145–46. They had initially complained in 1762 because unclear marking made it impossible to create an enclosure, as required by Jewish law: Erik R. Seeman, *Death in the New World: Cross-Cultural Encounters, 1792–1800* (Philadelphia: University of Pennsylvania Press, 2011), 238.

2. Candler, *Colonial Records*, 15:154, 151.

3. Allan D. Candler, ed. *The Colonial Records of the State of Georgia*, vol. 17 (Atlanta, GA: Franklin-Turner, 1908), 573.

4. Albert S. Britt Jr. and Lilla M. Hawes, eds., "The Mackenzie Papers: Collections of the Georgia Historical Society, Other Documents and Notes," pt. 2, *Georgia Historical Quarterly* 57, no. 1 (1973):141.

5. Katherine Carté, *Religion and the American Revolution: An Imperial History* (Chapel Hill: University of North Carolina Press, 2021).

6. Candler, *Colonial Records*, 17:561. For a 1766 case of Presbyterian petitioning for building privileges associated with establishment, see Katherine Carté's *Religion and the American Revolution* (101–3).

7. Kathleen DuVal, *Independence Lost: Lives on the Edge of the American Revolution* (New York: Random House, 2015), xxiii; Benjamin L. Carp, *Rebels Rising: Cities and the American Revolution* (New York: Oxford University Press, 2007), 152.

8. Thomas Jefferson, *A Summary View of the Rights of British America*, Avalon Project, Jefferson Papers, Yale Law School, Lillian Goldman Law Library, accessed December 4, 2022, https://avalon.law.yale .edu/18th_century/jeffsumm.asp. Similar language is also found in the Continental Congress's Bill of Rights: South Carolina Provincial Congress, *Extracts from the Journal of the First Provincial Congress of South Carolina, 1775–6*, edited by William Edwin Hemphill (Columbia: South Carolina Archives Department, 1960).

9. Christopher Gould, "The South Carolina and Continental Associations: Prelude to Revolution," *South Carolina Historical Magazine* 87, no. 1 (1986):30–48.

10. Pencak, *Jews and Gentiles*, 161; Benjamin H. Levy, *Mordecai Sheftall: Jewish Revolutionary* (Savannah: Georgia Historical Society, 1999), 41–42.

11. Malcolm Stern, ed., "The Sheftall Diaries: Vital Records of Savannah Jewry (1733–1808)," *American Jewish Historical Quarterly* 54, no. 3 (1965):250.

12. James Hagy, *This Happy Land: The Jews of Colonial and Antebellum Charleston* (Tuscaloosa: University of Alabama Press, 1993), 60–61.

13. Fragments of Minutes of Congregation Beth Elohim, Charleston, South Carolina, January 27, 1775, American Jewish Historical Society, New York. On "the political utility of religion and the religious utility of politics," see Spencer W. McBride's *Pulpit and Nation: Clergymen and the Politics of Revolutionary America* (Charlottesville: University of Virginia Press, 2016), 7.

14. Robert A. Ferguson, *The American Enlightenment, 1750–1820* (Cambridge, MA: Harvard University Press, 1997); Lee Ward, *The Politics of Liberty in England and Revolutionary America* (New York: Oxford University Press, 2010).

15. Fragments of Minutes of Congregation Beth Elohim, Charleston, South Carolina.

16. *South-Carolina and American General Gazette*, August 26, 1774, 4; Hagy, *This Happy Land*, 34–36.

17. South Carolina Provincial Congress, *Extracts from the Journal*, 21, 30.

18. "Death of a Patriot, 1776: Letter from Major Andrew Williamson to the President of South Carolina, John Rutledge, August 4, 1776," in *A Documentary History of Jews in the United States, 1654–1875*, 3rd ed., edited by Morris U. Schappes, 45–47 (New York: Schocken, 1971).

19. Paul M. Pressly, *On the Rim of the Caribbean: Colonial Georgia and the British Atlantic World* (Athens: University of Georgia Press, 2013); Harvey H. Jackson, "Consensus and Conflict: Factional Politics in Revolutionary Georgia," *Georgia Historical Quarterly* 59, no. 4 (1975):388–401.

20. George White, *Historical Collections of Georgia* (New York: Pudney and Russell, 1854), 67.

21. David T. Morgan, "The Sheftalls of Savannah," *American Jewish Historical Quarterly* 62, no. 4 (1973): 354–55.

22. Pencak, *Jews and Gentiles*, 164.

23. Gould, "South Carolina and Continental," 38; Jennifer L. Goloboy, *Charleston and the Emergence of Middle-Class Culture* (Athens: University of Georgia Press, 2016), 32.

24. Holly Snyder, "A Sense of *Place*: Jews, Identity, and Social Status in Colonial British America, 1654–1831," PhD dissertation, Brandeis University, 2000, 417–22; Pencak, *Jews and Gentiles*, 163–65.

25. T. H. Breen, *The Marketplace of Revolution: How Consumer Politics Shaped American Independence* (New York: Oxford University Press, 2004), xvii.

26. "Constitution of South Carolina—March 26, 1776," Avalon Project, Yale Law School, Lillian Goldman Law Library, accessed December 4, 2022, https://avalon.law.yale.edu/18th_century/sc01.asp; Robert G. Parkinson, *The Common Cause: Creating Race and Nation in the American Revolution* (Chapel Hill: University of North Carolina Press, 2016), 20.

27. Peter Silver, *Our Savage Neighbors: How Indian Wars Transformed Early America* (New York: W. W. Norton, 2009).

28. Carp, *Rebels Rising*, 167.

29. Georgia's 1777 constitution stipulated, "All persons whatever shall have the free exercise of their religion," as long as "it be not repugnant to the peace and safety of the state": "Constitution of Georgia—February 5, 1777," The Avalon Project, Yale Law School, Lillian Goldman Law Library, accessed December 4, 2022, https://avalon.law.yale.edu/18th_century/ga02.asp. South Carolina's second constitution, passed the following year, offered "equal religious and civil privileges," but required "acknowledg[ing] that there is one God, and a future state of rewards and punishments, and that God is publicly to be worshipped": "Constitution of South Carolina—March 19, 1778," The Avalon Project, Yale Law School, Lillian Goldman Law Library, accessed December 4, 2022, https://avalon.law.yale.edu/18th_century/sc02.asp.

30. "Virginia Declaration of Rights," https://avalon.law.yale.edu/18th_century/virginia.asp; "Constitution of North Carolina: December 18, 1776," https://avalon.law.yale.edu/18th_century/nc07.asp; "Constitution of South Carolina, March 19, 1778," https://avalon.law.yale.edu/18th_century/sc02.asp; "Constitution of Georgia, February 5, 1777, https://avalon.law.yale.edu/18th_century/ga02.asp; all at The Avalon Project, Yale Law School, Lillian Goldman Law Library, accessed December 4, 2022. South Carolina also forbade disturbing or using "abusive language against any church," not only because it disturbed the peace but because it "hinder[ed] the conversion of any to the truth" ("Constitution of South Carolina, March 19, 1778").

31. David Sehat, *The Myth of American Religious Freedom* (New York: Oxford University Press, 2011).

32. John Almon and Thomas Pownall, eds., *The Remembrancer, or Impartial Repository of Public Events: For the Year 1778* (London: J. Almon, 1778), 342. See also Hagy, *This Happy Land*, 38.

33. Carp, *Rebels Rising*, 156.

34. "Slander and Reply: Letter in *The South-Carolina and American General Gazette*, Charleston, December 3, 1778," in Schappes, *Documentary History of Jews*, 92–93; Pencak, *Jews and Gentiles*, 128.

35. Jacob Rader Marcus, *American Jewry, Documents, Eighteenth Century* (Cincinnati: Hebrew Union College, 1959), 235.

36. Hagy, *This Happy Land*, 114; Pencak, *Jews and Gentiles*, 126.

37. Hagy, *This Happy Land*, 117; Benjamin L. Carp, "'Fix'd almost amongst strangers': Charleston's Quaker Merchants and the Limits of Cosmopolitanism," *William and Mary Quarterly* 74, no. 1 (2017):105; Robert Bentham Simons, "Regimental Book of James Bentham, 1778–1780 (continued)," *South Carolina Historical Magazine* 53, no. 1 (1952):13–18.

38. Goloboy, *Charleston*, 34.

39. Morgan, "Sheftalls of Savannah," 251.

40. "Patriot Captured: Capture of Mordecai Sheftall, Deputy Commissary-General of Issues to the Continental Troops for the State of Georgia, viz., 1778, December 29th," in Schappes, *Documentary History of Jews*, 57.

41. "Frances Sheftall, Wife of Mordecai Sheftall, Prisoner of War: 1780," in *The American Jewish Woman: A Documentary History*, edited by Jacob Rader Marcus (New York: Ktav, 1981), 30. On revolutionary Jewish letters: Michael Hoberman, "'How It Will End, the Blessed God Knows': A Reading of Jewish Correspondence during the Revolutionary War Era," *American Jewish History* 99, no. 4 (2015):281–313.

42. Pencak, *Jews and Gentiles*, 165.

43. She wrote in March, "Our Sabbath is coming on so fast," and "Mr. Jacobs is been a father to your children and a great friend to me" (Marcus, *American Jewry*, 262–65).

44. Kylie L. McCormick, "Father and Servant, Son and Slave: Judaism and Labor in Georgia, 1732–1809," MA thesis, University of Nebraska-Lincoln, 2016, 65.

45. Saul Jacob Rubin, *Third to None: The Saga of Savannah Jewry* (Savannah, GA: S. J. Rubin, 1983), 96–97; Hagy, *This Happy Land*, 113–20.

46. Marcus, *American Jewry*, 270.

47. Marcus, 273.

48. Marcus, 116.

49. Stern, "Sheftall Diaries," 252.

50. Snyder, "Sense of *Place*," 422.

51. Marcus, *American Jewry*, 40.

52. After the war, "the economic effects of British blockades, commercial collapse, military appropriation and corruption, uncollected rents, and deteriorated property had been devastating" (Carp, *Rebels Rising*, 218).

53. Rubin, *Third to None*, 35.

54. Levy, *Mordecai Sheftall*, 97.

55. Hagy, *This Happy Land*, 119.

56. Pencak, *Jews and Gentiles*, 166–68; A Citizen, "Cursory Remarks on Men and Measures in Georgia" (1784), in the digital collection *Evans Early American Imprint Collection*, University of Michigan Library Digital Collections, accessed June 26, 2024, https://name.umdl.umich.edu/N14539.0001.001.

57. *Georgia Gazette*, January 13, 1785, reprinted in Max J. Kohler, "Phases in the History of Religious Liberty in America with Particular Reference to the Jews," *Publications of the American Jewish Historical Society* 11 (1903):29–30.

58. Nunes-Ribeiro Papers P-468, American Jewish Historical Society, New York; Adam Jortner, "Sheftall's Shadow: Jeffersonians, Liberty, and Slavery in Savannah," paper presentation, Southern Jewish Historical Society Conference, Charlottesville, Virginia, October 2019.

59. Levy, *Mordecai Sheftall*, 98–99; Jortner, "Sheftall's Shadow."

60. Both men were thirty-five years old and German born. Isaacs would acquire real estate and enslaved people and would serve in public office. In the years before a congregation, he contributed to the Philadelphia congregation and he signed business documents in Hebrew. See Myron Berman, *Richmond's Jewry, 1769–1976: Shabbat in Shockoe* (Richmond, VA: Jewish Community Federation of Richmond, 1979).

61. Mark Bauman, "Jews and the Fur Trade along the Southern British Colonial Borderlands," *American Jewish History* 102, no. 2 (2018):219.

62. Hagy, *This Happy Land*, 119, 12.

63. Rubin, *Third to None*, 38; Stern, "Sheftall Diaries," 254.

64. Stern, "Sheftall Diaries," 253.

65. Moses Molina Will, December 6, 1785, https://www.ancestry.com/imageviewer/collections/9080/images/007648978_00641?treeid=&personid=&usePUB=true&_phsrc=FHZ246&_phstart=successSource&pId=901714, and Joseph Salvador Will, January 5, 1782, https://www.ancestry.com/imageviewer/collections/9080/images/0023463-00049?treeid=&personid=&usePUB=true&_phsrc=FHZ250&_phstart=successSource&pId=1113055, both at Ancestry.com, *South Carolina, U.S., Wills and Probate Records, 1670–1980* [database online] (Provo, UT: Ancestry.com Operations, 2015).

66. Laura Leibman, *Messianism, Mysticism, and Secrecy: A New Interpretation of Early American Jewish Life* (New York, 2012).

67. "Constitution of South Carolina—March 19, 1778," accessed January 18, 2024.

68. Hagy, *This Happy Land*, 64–66.

69. Stern, "Sheftall Diaries," 247, 265; Snyder, "Sense of *Place*," 417. Some newspaper notices of Jewish marriages in Charleston continued in the 1780s to refer to "the Jewish nation": Barnett Elzas, *Jewish Marriage Notices from the Newspaper Press of Charleston, S.C. (1775–1906)* (New York: Bloch, 1917).

Chapter 4

1. George Washington, "From George Washington to the Savannah, Ga., Hebrew Congregation, 14 June 1790," *Founders Online*, National Archives, accessed April 11, 2019, https://founders.archives.gov/documents/Washington/05-05-02-0279 (original source: *The Papers of George Washington*, Presidential Series, vol. 5, *16 January 1790–30 June 1790*, edited by Dorothy Twohig, Mark A. Mastromarino, and Jack D. Warren, 448–50 [Charlottesville: University Press of Virginia, 1996]).

2. David T. Morgan, "The Sheftalls of Savannah," *American Jewish Historical Quarterly* 62, no. 4 (1973):348–61; Malcolm Stern, ed., "The Sheftall Diaries: Vital Records of Savannah Jewry (1773–1808)," *American Jewish Historical Quarterly* 54, no. 3 (1965):243–77.

3. "George Washington to the Savannah, Ga., Hebrew Congregation."

4. Robert A. Ferguson, *The American Enlightenment, 1750–1820* (Cambridge, MA: Harvard University Press, 1994); Michael O'Brien, *Intellectual Life and the American South, 1810–1860* (Chapel Hill: University of North Carolina Press, 2010).

5. Pierre Birnbaum and Ira Katznelson, "Emancipation and the Liberal Offer," in *Paths of Emancipation: Jews, States, and Citizenship*, edited by Birnbaum and Katznelson, 3–36 (Princeton, NJ: Princeton University Press, 1995); David Sorkin, *Jewish Emancipation: A History across Five Centuries* (Princeton, NJ: Princeton University Press, 2019).

6. Christian Wilhelm von Dohm, "Concerning the Amelioration of the Civil Status of the Jews (1781)," in *The Jew in the Modern World: A Documentary History*, edited by Paul R. Mendes-Flohr and Jehuda Reinharz, 3rd ed. (New York: Oxford University Press, 2011), 29.

7. Shari Rabin, *Jews on the Frontier: Religion and Mobility in Nineteenth-Century America* (New York: New York University Press, 2017), 21. For instance, in 1800, Virginia tax documents listed Isaiah Isaacs as a "white male" (*Personal Property Tax Lists, 1799, Part 2 [Virginia State Library]*, call no. FHL Film 2024443, p. 18, family no. 9).

8. Jon Butler, *Awash in a Sea of Faith: Christianizing the American People* (Cambridge, MA: Harvard University Press, 1990); Christine Leigh Heyrman, *Southern Cross: The Beginning of the Bible Belt* (New York: Knopf, 1997).

9. "Joseph Salvador to His Cousin Emanuel Mendes Da Costa, Describing America, January 22, 1785," in *American Jewish History: A Primary Source Reader*, edited by Gary Phillip Zola and Marc Dollinger, sect. 2.01 (Waltham, MA: Brandeis University Press, 2014).

10. David Sehat, *The Myth of American Religious Freedom* (New York: Oxford University Press, 2011).

11. Sarah Barringer Gordon, "The African Supplement: Religion, Race, and Corporate Law in Early National America," *William and Mary Quarterly* 72, no. 3 (2015):385–422; Myron Berman, *Richmond's Jewry, 1769–1976: Shabbat in Shockoe* (Richmond, VA: Jewish Community Federation of Richmond, 1979); Saul Jacob Rubin, *Third to None: The Saga of Savannah Jewry* (Savannah, GA: S. J. Rubin, 1983), 39; James Hagy, *This Happy Land: The Jews of Colonial and Antebellum Charleston* (Tuscaloosa: University of Alabama Press, 1993), 73.

12. Jacob Rader Marcus, *American Jewry, Documents, Eighteenth Century* (Cincinnati: Hebrew Union College, 1959), 64.

13. Aviva Ben-Ur, "Jewish Savannah in Atlantic Perspective: A Reconsideration of North America's First Intentional Jewish Community," in *The Sephardic Atlantic*, edited by S. Rauschenbach and J. Schorsch (Berkeley, 2017), 210–11.

14. Daniel Kurt Ackermann, "The 1794 Synagogue of Kahal Kadosh Beth Elohim of Charleston," *American Jewish History* 93, no. 2 (2007):159–76.

15. Hagy, *This Happy Land*, 55.

16. Transcribed in Stern, "Sheftall Diaries," 268.

17. "Twenty-Eight Convention of the Pro. Epis. Church in So. Ca. held in Columbia on the 7th & 8th Feb. 1815," in Frederick Dalcho, *An Historical Account of the Protestant Episcopal Church in South Carolina, from the First Settlement of the Province to the War of the Revolution* (Charleston, SC, 1820), 553.

18. Alexis McCrossen, *Holy Day, Holiday: The American Sunday* (Ithaca, NY: Cornell University Press, 2000), 12.

19. Sehat, *Myth*; Berman, *Richmond's Jewry*.

20. David Sorkin, "Is American Jewry Exceptional? Comparing Jewish Emancipation in Europe and America," *American Jewish History* 96, no. 3 (2010):175–200.

21. Jonathan D. Sarna and David Dalin, *Religion and State in the American Jewish Experience* (South Bend, IN: Notre Dame University Press, 1997), 84. See also Seth Tillman, "What Oath (if Any) Did Jacob Henry Take in 1809? Deconstructing the Historical Myths," *American Journal of Legal History* 61, no. 4 (2021):35-1n7.

22. Hagy, *This Happy Land*, 40.

23. William Pencak, *Jews and Gentiles in Early America, 1654–1800* (Ann Arbor: University of Michigan Press, 2005), 133.

24. "Rebecca Samuel, January 12, 1791," in Zola and Dollinger, *American Jewish History*, 34–35; Berman, *Richmond's Jewry*.

25. Mark I. Greenberg, "Becoming Southern: The Jews of Savannah, Georgia, 1830–1870," *American Jewish History* 86, no. 1 (1998):55–75.

26. Berman, *Richmond's Jewry*.

27. Hagy, *This Happy Land*, 106.

28. Theodore Rosengarten and Dale Rosengarten, *A Portion of the People: Three Hundred Years of Southern Jewish Life* (Columbia: University of South Carolina Press, 2002); Bertram Korn, *The Early Jews of New Orleans* (Waltham, MA: American Jewish Historical Society, 1969).

29. Emily Bingham, *Mordecai: An American Family* (New York: Hill and Wang, 2003).

30. "Rebecca Samuel, January 12, 1791," in Zola and Dollinger, *American Jewish History*, 34–35; Berman, *Richmond's Jewry*.

31. Edward Baptist, *The Half That Has Never Been Told: Slavery and the Making of American Capitalism* (New York: Basic Books, 2014).

32. George Washington, "From George Washington to the Hebrew Congregation in Newport, Rhode Island, 18 August 1790," *Founders Online*, National Archives, https://founders.archives.gov/documents /Washington/05-06-02-0135 (original source: *The Papers of George Washington*, Presidential Series, vol. 6, *1 July 1790–30 November 1790*, edited by Mark A. Mastromarino, 284–86 [Charlottesville: University Press of Virginia, 1996]).

33. Bertram W. Korn, "Jews and Negro Slavery in the Old South, 1789–1865: Address of the President," *Publications of the American Jewish Historical Society* 50, no. 3 (1963):164; Mordecai Sheftall, for instance, issued warrants for local runaways in Savannah (Marcus, *American Jewry*, 63–64).

34. Korn, "Jews and Negro Slavery," 98–100.

35. Berman, *Richmond's Jewry*, 166.

36. Hagy, *This Happy Land*, 91.

37. Rosengarten and Rosengarten, *Portion of the People*, 101; Rosengarten, in *Jews across the Americas: A Sourcebook*, edited by Adriana M. Brodsky and Laura Arnold Leibman (New York: New York University Press, 2023), 142.

38. His daughters were not granted enslaved people but given equal shares to their brothers of the remaining estate (with the exception of a daughter who had received a large gift at her wedding): Ancestry.com, *Georgia, U.S., Wills and Probate Records, 1742–1992* [database online] (Lehi, UT: Ancestry.com Operations, 2015), vol. E–F, 1807–1827, 83–88, https://www.ancestry.com/discoveryui-content/view/160526:8635?tid=&pid=&queryId=9d719ae1-94d2-405b-b75d-d183522ea6c2&_phsrc=FHZ255&_phstart=successSource.

39. Korn, "Jews and Negro Slavery," 92. On white women's slaveholding: Stephanie E. Jones-Rogers, *They Were Her Property: White Women as Slave Owners in the American South* (New Haven, CT: Yale University Press, 2020); Saidiya Hartman, *Scenes of Subjection: Terror, Slavery, and Self-Making in Nineteenth-Century America* (New York: Oxford University Press, 1997).

40. Hartman, *Scenes of Subjection*.

41. Will of Philip Hart, February 3, 1796, Ancestry.com, *South Carolina, U.S., Wills and Probate Records, 1670–1980* [database online] (Provo, UT: Ancestry.com Operations, 2015), https://www.ancestry.com/discoveryui-content/view/1113761:9080?tid=&pid=&queryId=b75c40da-0cd6-49b4-a803-34bc4229b66c&_phsrc=FHZ262&_phstart=successSource.

42. Berman, *Richmond's Jewry*, 4; "Manumission of Slaves: The Will of Isaiah Isaacs of Virginia, August 30, 1803 and January 8, 1806," in *A Documentary History of Jews in the United States, 1654–1875*, 3rd ed., edited by Morris U. Schappes, 99–101 (New York: Schocken, 1971).

43. Korn, "Jews and Negro Slavery," 176–77; Jeffrey Robert Young, *Domesticating Slavery: The Master Class in Georgia and South Carolina, 1670–1837* (Chapel Hill: University of North Carolina Press, 1999), 66. According to Ira Berlin, "In the low country, planters often recognized and provided for their mixed-race offspring": *Many Thousands Gone: The First Two Centuries of Slavery in North America* (Cambridge, MA: Belknap Press of Harvard University Press, 1998), 161.

44. Hagy, *This Happy Land*, 100.

45. Marisa J. Fuentes, *Dispossessed Lives: Enslaved Women, Violence, and the Archive* (Philadelphia: University of Pennsylvania Press, 2016). On interracial relationships between Jewish men and women of color in the Caribbean context: Aviva Ben-Ur, "A Matriarchal Matter: Slavery, Conversion, and Upward Mobility in Suriname's Jewish Community," in *Atlantic Diasporas: Jews, Conversos, and Crypto-Jews in the Age of Mercantilism, 1500–1800*, edited by Richard L. Kagan and Philip D. Morgan, 152–69 (Baltimore, MD: Johns Hopkins University Press, 2009).

46. In 1795, Manuel Monsanto of New Orleans left funds to "the quadroon named Sofia" and her mother, "the mulattress Mamy," both of whom used the last name Monsanto, indicating they may have been his daughter and partner, respectively (Korn, *Early Jews*, 65). In Charleston, Sherry Sasportas was married to a free woman of color named Catherine by 1817: Amrita Myers, *Forging Freedom: Black Women and the Pursuit of Liberty in Antebellum Charleston* (Chapel Hill: University of North Carolina Press, 2011), 104. See also Philippe Girard, "Isaac Sasportas, the 1799 Slave Conspiracy in Jamaica, and Sephardic Ties to the Haitian Revolution," *Jewish History* 33 (2020):434.

47. Rabin, *Jews on the Frontier*, 60.

48. Joshua D. Rothman, *Notorious in the Neighborhood: Sex and Families across the Color Line in Virginia, 1787–1861* (Chapel Hill: University of North Carolina Press, 2003).

49. Berman, *Richmond's Jewry*.

50. Berman, 165.

51. Girard, "Isaac Sasportas"; Chris Monaco, "Moses E. Levy of Florida: A Jewish Abolitionist Abroad," *American Jewish History* 86, no. 4 (1998):377–96.

52. Benjamin H. Levy, *Mordecai Sheftall: Jewish Revolutionary* (Savannah: Georgia Historical Society, 1999), 48.

53. "Rebecca Samuel, January 12, 1791," in Zola and Dollinger, *American Jewish History*, 35.

54. Theodore Cohen, "Jacob De La Motta, M.D.: An Early American Jewish Medical Pioneer," *American Jewish Archives* 53, no. 1–2 (2001):175–86; Thomas J. Tobias, "The Many-Sided Dr. De La Motta," *American Jewish Historical Quarterly* 52, no. 3 (1963):209.

Chapter 5

1. Rachel Mordecai to Maria Edgeworth, August 7, 1815, Edgar E. MacDonald Papers, Mss1 M1453a, 1–6, Virginia Historical Society, Richmond, VA.

2. Emily Bingham, *Mordecai: An American Family* (New York: Hill and Wang, 2003), 5.

3. James Hagy, *This Happy Land: The Jews of Colonial and Antebellum Charleston* (Tuscaloosa: University of Alabama Press, 1993), 16.

4. In the 1820s, 56,000 white people left South Carolina, as would another 76,000 in the 1830s: William Freehling, *The Road to Disunion*, vol. 1, *Secessionists at Bay, 1776–1854* (New York: Oxford University Press, 1990), 255.

5. Gary P. Zola, "The Ascendancy of Reform Judaism in the American South during the Nineteenth Century," in *Jewish Roots in Southern Soil*, edited by Marcie Cohen Ferris and Mark I. Greenberg (Waltham, MA: Brandeis University Press, 2006), 172.

6. Bertram Korn, *The Early Jews of New Orleans* (Waltham, MA: American Jewish Historical Society, 1969).

7. Stephanie McCurry, *Masters of Small Worlds: Yeoman Households, Gender Relations, & the Political Culture of the Antebellum South Carolina Low Country* (New York: Oxford University Press, 1995).

8. Barnett Elzas, *The Old Jewish Cemeteries at Charleston: A Transcription of the Inscriptions on Their Tombstones, 1762–1903, S.C.* (Charleston: Daggett Printing, 1903), 29.

9. Karen Lystra, *Searching the Heart: Women, Men, and Romantic Love in Nineteenth Century America* (New York: Oxford University Press, 1992).

10. Isaac Cohen will, Ancestry.com, *South Carolina, U.S., Wills and Probate Records, 1670–1980* [database online] (Provo, UT: Ancestry.com Operations, 2015), https://www.ancestry.com/imageviewer/collections/9080/images/0023463-00056?treeid=&personid=&usePUB=true&_phsrc=FHZ342&_phstart=successSource&pId=1112541. Cardoza was a New York–born Jew who had been wounded in the revolution but took the loyalist oath in Charleston in 1780 (Hagy, *This Happy Land*, 23, 117).

11. On Lydia Weston, see Amrita Myers's *Forging Freedom: Black Women and the Pursuit of Liberty in Antebellum Charleston* (Chapel Hill: University of North Carolina Press, 2011, 67).

12. Bingham, *Mordecai*.

13. Korn, *Early Jews*, 196.

14. Hagy, *This Happy Land*, 177–79. In Georgia, according to the Sheftall records, in August 1799 "David Leion and his wife Hannah . . . parted as man and wife never to live together again, they disagreeing for a length of time before they parted": Malcolm Stern, ed., "The Sheftall Diaries: Vital Records of Savannah Jewry (1733–1808)," *American Jewish Historical Quarterly* 54, no. 3 (1965):269.

15. "Memorial to the President and Members of the Adjunta of Kahal Kadosh Beth Elohim of Charleston, South Carolina, Demanding Religious Reform, December 23, 1824," in *American Jewish History: A Primary Source Reader*, edited by Gary Phillip Zola and Marc Dollinger, 79–80 (Waltham, MA: Brandeis University Press, 2014); Robert Liberles, "Conflict over Reforms: The Case of Congregation Beth Elohim, Charleston, South Carolina," in *The American Synagogue: A Sanctuary Transformed*, edited by Jack Wertheimer, 274–92 (New York: Cambridge University Press, 1987); Gary P. Zola, *Isaac Harby of Charleston, 1788–1828: Jewish Reformer and Intellectual* (Tuscaloosa: University of Alabama Press, 1994); Hagy, *This Happy Land*, 128–60.

16. Michael A. Meyer, *Response to Modernity: A History of the Reform Movement in Judaism* (New York: Oxford University Press, 1988).

17. John Allen Macaulay, *Unitarianism in the Antebellum South: The Other Invisible Institution* (Tuscaloosa: University of Alabama Press, 2001); Korn, *Early Jews*.

18. Joseph Lyons, "Joseph Lyons: Random Thoughts of a Sick Soul," in *Memoirs of American Jews, 1775–1865*, vol. 1, edited by Jacob Rader Marcus (Philadelphia: Jewish Publication Society, 1955), 247, 252.

19. Christine Leigh Heyrman, *Southern Cross: The Beginning of the Bible Belt* (New York: Knopf, 1997).

20. Bingham, *Mordecai*.

21. To be sure, the reformers were more radical in their approach than their coreligionists in New York, who were requesting aesthetic changes at the same time. Jonathan Sarna, *American Judaism: A History* (New Haven, CT: Yale University Press, 2004), 56.

22. "Memorial to the President and Members of the Adjunta."

23. KKBE Meeting Minutes, 1846–52, p.118; 1846–52, pp.139–40; 1846-52, p.155; Lowcountry Digital Library, College of Charleston Libraries.

24. Barnett Elzas, *Constitution of the Hebrew Congregation Kaal Kodesh Beth Elohim, or House of God, Charleston* (Charleston, SC, 1904), 15–16.

25. Freehling, *Road to Disunion*; Bernard E. Powers, *Black Charlestonians: A Social History, 1822–1885* (Fayetteville: University of Arkansas Press, 1994), 3.

26. Gerda Lerner, *The Grimké Sisters from South Carolina* (New York: Houghton Mifflin, 1967).

27. Bingham, *Mordecai*. Mavidore, one of the enslaved fighters who was executed with Nat Turner in Charleston, belonged to Mordecai Cohen, a prominent local plantation owner and slave trader (Hagy, *This Happy Land*, 103).

28. Rachel Lazarus to George Mordecai, October 6, 1831, Edgar E. MacDonald Papers, Mss1 M1453a, 43–52, Virginia Historical Society, Richmond, VA.

29. For instance, in 1832 Dr. Philip Minis, a grandson of Abigail Minis, killed James Stark, a member of the Georgia legislature, as part of an affair of honor. Stark had called him a "damned Jew," but Minis was acquitted of any criminal wrongdoing: William Pencak, *Jews and Gentiles in Early America, 1654–1800* (Ann Arbor: University of Michigan Press, 2005). Jews also dueled each other—in 1812 Levi Sheftall's son Mordecai provoked a challenge from David Abendanon, a Jewish Charlestonian: Holly Snyder, "A Sense of *Place*: Jews, Identity, and Social Status in Colonial British America, 1654–1831," PhD dissertation, Brandeis University, 2000, 441.

30. Hagy, *This Happy Land*, 128–60; Korn, *Early Jews*.

31. Lorenzo Dow, *The Dealings of God, Man, and the Devil* (Norwich, CT: Wm. Faulkner, 1833).

32. J.S.G. Richardson, *Reports of Cases in Equity: Argued and Determined in the Court of Appeals and Court of Errors of South Carolina*, vol. 2 (Columbia: A. S. Johnston, 1846), 249.

33. Ismar Schorsch, "The Myth of Sephardic Supremacy," *Leo Baeck Institute Year Book* 34, no. 1 (1989):47–66.

34. Dale Rosengarten, "Portrait of Two Painters: The Work of Theodore Sidney Moise and Solomon Nunes Carvalho," in *By Dawn's Early Light*, by Princeton University Library, edited by Adam D. Mendelsohn, 139–187 (Princeton, NJ: Princeton University Library, 2016).

35. Penina Moïse, *Secular and Religious Works of Penina Moïse, with Brief Sketch of Her Life* (Charleston, SC: Nicholas G. Duffy, 1911), 248–49.

36. Gene Waddell, "An Architectural History of Kahal Kadosh Beth Elohim, Charleston," *South Carolina Historical Magazine* 98, no. 1 (1997):6–55.

37. "Our History," KKBE, accessed July 1, 2024, https://www.kkbe.org/ourhistory.

38. Allan Tarshish, "The Charleston Organ Case," *American Jewish Historical Quarterly* 4, no. 4 (1965):411–49, quote at 421.

39. Levin, N., to Isaac Leeser, June 12, 1842, Gershwind-Bennett Isaac Leeser Digital Repository, Penn Libraries, https://judaicadhpenn.org/legacyprojects/s/leeser/item/69480.

40. Shari Rabin, "Judges and Jews: Congregational Conflict and the Protestant Secular in 19th-Century America," *Religion* 48, no. 4 (2018):659–77.

41. McCurry, *Masters of Small Worlds*; Elizabeth Varon, *We Mean to Be Counted: White Women and Politics in Antebellum Virginia* (Chapel Hill: University of North Carolina Press, 1998).

42. Dianne Ashton, *Rebecca Gratz: Women and Judaism in Antebellum America* (Detroit: Wayne State University Press, 1997).

43. Bingham, *Mordecai*, 194.

44. Laura Yares, *Jewish Sunday Schools: Teaching Religion in Nineteenth-Century America* (New York: New York University Press, 2023).

45. Poznanski sermon, quoted in "The Rebuilding of the Temple," *Charleston Courier*, March 20, 1841, 2.

46. Abraham J. Peck, "That Other 'Peculiar Institution': Jews and Judaism in the Nineteenth Century South," *Modern Judaism* 7, no. 1 (1987):99–114.

Chapter 6

1. M. N. Nathans, "Ceremonial at Galveston," *Occident* 10 (1852):381.

2. Michael D. Green, *The Politics of Indian Removal: Creek Government and Society in Crisis* (Lincoln: University of Nebraska Press, 1982).

3. Edward E. Baptist, *The Half That Has Never Been Told: Slavery and the Making of American Capitalism* (New York: Basic Books, 2014).

4. Bryan Stone, *Chosen Folks: Jews on the Frontiers of Texas* (Austin: University of Texas Press, 2010), 56; M. N. Nathans, "Ceremonial at Galveston," *Occident* 10 (1852):379–84.

5. William Freehling, *The Road to Disunion*, vol. 1, *Secessionists at Bay, 1776–1854* (New York: Oxford University Press, 1990), 7.

6. Nathans, "Ceremonial at Galveston," 380.

7. Michael O'Brien, *Intellectual Life and the American South, 1810–1860* (Chapel Hill: University of North Carolina Press, 2010).

8. Melvin I. Urofsky, *Commonwealth and Community: The Jewish Experience in Virginia* (Richmond: Virginia Historical Society and Jewish Community Federation of Richmond, 1997), 31.

9. James Hagy, *This Happy Land: The Jews of Colonial and Antebellum Charleston* (Tuscaloosa: University of Alabama Press, 1993), 40.

10. Hagy, 38–39.

11. James A. Strobhart, *Reports of Cases Argued and Determined in the Court of Appeals and Court of Errors of South Carolina, on Appeals from the Courts of Law*, vol. 2 (Columbia, SC: A.S. Johnston, 1848), 521, 527.

12. Hagy, *This Happy Land*, 43.

13. Bertram Korn, *The Early Jews of New Orleans* (Waltham, MA: American Jewish Historical Society, 1969).

14. Lawrence N. Powell, *The Accidental City: Improvising New Orleans* (Cambridge, MA: Harvard University Press, 2012); Rashauna Johnson, *Slavery's Metropolis: Unfree Labor in New Orleans during the Age of Revolutions* (New York: Cambridge University Press, 2016).

15. Joseph Lyons, "Joseph Lyons: Random Thoughts of a Sick Soul," in *Memoirs of American Jews, 1775–1865*, vol. 1, edited by Jacob Rader Marcus (Philadelphia, 1955), 222.

16. Lecture on Texas, SC-2721, 5, American Jewish Archives, Cincinnati, OH.

17. Baptist, *Half That Has Never Been Told*.

18. Lecture on Texas, SC-2721, American Jewish Archives, 25, 2.

19. Jayme A. Sokolow, "Revolution and Reform: The Antebellum Jewish Abolitionists," in *Jews and the Civil War: A Reader*, edited by Jonathan D. Sarna and Adam Mendelsohn, 125–40 (New York: New York University Press, 2010); Louis Ruchames, "The Abolitionists and the Jews: Some Further Thoughts," in Sarna and Mendelsohn, *Jews and the Civil War*, 145–55; Jonathan Sarna, *American Judaism: A History* (New Haven, CT: Yale University Press, 2004); Ben Wright, *Bonds of Salvation: How Christianity Inspired and Limited American Abolitionism* (Baton Rouge: Louisiana State University Press, 2020). Writing from a diplomatic post in Egypt, Charleston-born Edwin De Leon, who would eventually join the Confederate cause, argued that abolitionism was "a mistaken philanthropy, which, in my judgment, has assumed to be wiser than Providence—stronger than God": "Propaganda for Slavery: Letter by Edwin De Leon from Alexandria, Egypt, June 30, 1860," in *A Documentary History of Jews in the United States, 1654–1875*, 3rd ed., edited by Morris U. Schappes (New York: Schocken, 1971), 400.

20. Baptist, *Half That Has Never Been Told*; Abraham Barkai, "German-Jewish Migrations in the Nineteenth Century, 1830–1910," *Leo Baeck Institute Yearbook* 30, no. 1 (1985):301–18.

21. Michael R. Cohen, *Cotton Capitalists: American Jewish Entrepreneurship in the Reconstruction Era* (New York: New York University Press, 2017); Hasia Diner, *Roads Taken: The Great Jewish Migrations to the New World and the Peddlers Who Forged the Way* (New Haven, CT: Yale University Press, 2015).

22. Baptist, *Half That Has Never Been Told*, 292.

23. "Sketch of David Steinheimer, Atlanta, Ga.," David Steinheimer Papers, Mss 26, Cuba Family Archives for Southern Jewish History, Breman Museum, Atlanta; Shari Rabin, *Jews on the Frontier: Religion and Mobility in Nineteenth-Century America* (New York: New York University Press, 2017), 26.

24. Shari Rabin, "'The Kingdom of Israel in This Town': Jewish Merchants in Antebellum Charleston," *Jewish Historical Society of South Carolina* 22, no. 1 (2017):8–10.

25. M. Cohen, *Cotton Capitalists*, 50.

26. Diary, August 16, 1859, box 4, folder 1, MS-503, Rosewater Family Papers, American Jewish Archives, Cincinnati, OH.

27. Diary, July 14, 1859, box 4, folder 1, MS-503, Rosewater Family Papers.

28. Diary, June 10, 1860, box 4, folder 2, MS-503, Rosewater Family Papers. See also September 19, 1859; February 7, 1864; June 10, 1860; box 4, folder 2, ibid.

29. Bertram W. Korn, "Jews and Negro Slavery in the Old South, 1789–1865: Address of the President," *Publications of the American Jewish Historical Society* 50, no. 3 (1963):195.

30. M. Cohen, *Cotton Capitalists*, 173.

31. Lauren Winner, "Taking Up the Cross: Conversion among Black and White Jews in the Civil War South," in *Southern Families at War: Loyalty and Conflict in the Civil War South*, edited by Catherine Clinton (New York: Oxford University Press, 2000), 199–200.

32. Alexis Wells-Oghoghomeh, *The Souls of Womenfolk: The Religious Cultures of Enslaved Women in the Lower South* (Chapel Hill: University of North Carolina Press, 2021).

33. Ralph Melnick, "Billy Simons: The Black Jew of Charleston," *American Jewish Archives* 32 (1980):3–8. Thanks to Adrienne Krone.

34. Hagy, *This Happy Land*, 269; Myron Berman, *Richmond's Jewry, 1769–1976: Shabbat in Shockoe* (Richmond, VA: Jewish Community Federation of Richmond, 1979), 154.

35. Korn, *Early Jews*; Mark Bauman, "Variations on the Mortara Case in Mid-Nineteenth-Century New Orleans," in *A New Vision of Southern Jewish History: Studies in Institution Building, Leadership, Interaction, and Mobility* (Tuscaloosa: University of Alabama Press, 2019), 18.

36. He also left money to non-Jewish charities and to both Jewish and non-Jewish individuals, including Moses Nathans: "Judah Touro's Will: Text of Will, dated New Orleans, January 6, 1854," in Schappes, *Documentary History of Jews*, 333–41.

37. Salo W. Baron and Jeannette M. Baron, "Palestinian Messengers in America, 1849–79: A Record of Four Journeys," *Jewish Social Studies* 5, no. 3 (1943):115–62.

38. Five months after the Mortara Affair, the New Orleans Association for the Relief of Jewish Widows and Orphans acted on behalf of Alice Levy, a French Jewish orphan who had been baptized by a well-meaning Catholic guardian. One month after that, Jacob Bernard of St. Louis went to New Orleans to circumcise his three sons, who had been placed in a Catholic asylum by their Catholic grandparents after their mother's death: Jonathan Frankel, *The Damascus Affair: "Ritual Murder," Politics and Jews in 1840* (New York: Cambridge University Press, 1997), 224–27; Berman, *Richmond's Jewry*; Bauman, "Variations on the Mortara Case"; Circumcision Deposition, 1859, United States, English, call no. RD-59, Courtesy of the American Jewish Archives, Cincinnati, OH.

39. Jonathan Sarna, "The Touro Monument Controversy: Aniconism vs. Anti-idolatry in a Mid-Nineteenth-Century American Jewish Religious Dispute," in *Between Jewish Tradition and Modernity: Rethinking an Old Opposition, Essays in Honor of David Ellenson*, edited by Michael A. Meyer and David N. Myers (Detroit: Wayne State University Press, 2014), 88.

40. Rabin, *Jews on the Frontier*, 37.

41. Rabin.

42. Ann Douglas, *The Feminization of American Culture* (New York: Knopf, 1977); Karla Goldman, *Beyond the Synagogue Gallery: Finding a Place for Women in American Judaism* (Cambridge, MA: Harvard University Press, 2001); Ann Braude, "Women's History Is American Religious History," in *Retelling U.S. Religious History*, edited by Thomas A. Tweed, 87–107 (Berkeley: University of California Press, 1997).

43. Rabin, *Jews on the Frontier*; "Congregations," *Occident and American Jewish Advocate*, December 14, 1856, 409.

44. "Congregations," *Occident and American Jewish Advocate*, December 14, 1856, 409; Selma S. Lewis, *A Biblical People in the Bible Belt: The Jewish Community of Memphis, Tennessee, 1840s–1960s* (Macon, GA: Mercer University Press, 1998).

45. "Memphis, Tennessee," *Occident* 13 (1855):306.

46. Circumcision Deposition, 1859; "A Circumcision Story in New Orleans," *Israelite*, January 28, 1859, 237; David Ellenson, "A Jewish Legal Decision by Rabbi Bernard Illowy of New Orleans and Its Discussion in Nineteenth Century Europe," *American Jewish History* 69, no. 2 (1979):174–95.

47. Bernard Illowy, "Louisiana," *Jewish Messenger*, February 3, 1865.

48. "In a period of multiple medical authorities, the *mohel* was an additional practitioner alongside female domestic healers, 'slave doctors,' professional doctors, and 'irregulars' advocating treatments like homeopathy and water cure." And at a time when family Bibles often stood in for birth certificates in the South, *mohel* records could serve that role for Jews: Shari Rabin, "Mohalim not Missionaries: Outsider and Insider Bodies in Southern Religious History," *Journal of Southern Religion* 18 (2016), jsreligion.org/vol18/rabin.

49. Joseph Buchler, "The Struggle for Unity: Attempts at Union in American Jewish Life: 1654–1868," *American Jewish Archives* 1 (1949):21–46; Rabin, *Jews on the Frontier*; Deborah Dash Moore, *B'nai B'rith and the Challenge of Ethnic Leadership* (Albany: State University of New York Press, 1981); David Henkin, *The Postal Age: The Emergence of Modern Communications in Nineteenth-Century America* (Chicago: University of Chicago Press, 2006).

50. A Southern Jew, "Jews in Savannah," *Occident* 1, no. 10 (1844):246–50; A gentleman residing in the interior of one of the Southern States, "A Child's Prayer," *Occident* 13 (1855):224–25.

51. "News Items," *Occident* 4 (1846):306–7.

52. "News Items," *Occident* 16 (1858):454–56.

53. Jon Butler, *Awash in a Sea of Faith: Christianizing the American People* (Cambridge, MA: Harvard University Press, 1990); C. C. Goen, *Broken Churches, Broken Nation: Denominational Schisms and the Coming of the American Civil War* (Memphis, TN: Mercer University Press, 1985).

54. First Annual Report, box 1, folder 1, 1859–77, Board of Delegates, American Jewish Historical Society, New York.

55. "Macon Ga.," *Israelite*, December 21, 1860, p. 198.

Chapter 7

1. Biography of William Flegenheimer, p. 12, Mss7:1 F6255:1, Virginia Historical Society, Richmond, VA.

2. Virginia Convention of 1861, "Virginia Ordinance of Secession (April 17, 1861)," *Encyclopedia Virginia*, last updated December 7, 2020, https://encyclopediavirginia.org/entries/virginia-ordinance-of-secession-april-17-1861.

3. Biography of William Flegenheimer, p. 15. On Jewish immigrant support for Democrats: Adam D. Mendelsohn, *Jewish Soldiers in the Civil War: The Union Army* (New York: New York University Press, 2022), 55.

4. Steven E. Woodworth and Kenneth J. Winkle, *Atlas of the Civil War* (New York: Oxford University Press, 2004), 65.

5. As historian William L. Barney has argued, "The liberty to own slaves, fears of those same slaves, defense of their homes, and a demand for the respect of an outside world that defamed them as sinners were all one and the same as a motive for secession and independence": *Rebels in the Making: The Secession Crisis and the Birth of the Confederacy* (New York: Oxford University Press, 2020).

6. "Confederate States of America—Declaration of the Immediate Causes Which Induce and Justify the Secession of South Carolina from the Federal Union," The Avalon Project, Yale Law School, Lillian Goldman Law Library, accessed May 19, 2021, https://avalon.law.yale.edu/19th_century/csa_scarsec.asp.

7. Theodore Rosengarten and Dale Rosengarten, *A Portion of the People: Three Hundred Years of Southern Jewish Life* (Columbia: University of South Carolina Press, 2002), 127.

8. "A Declaration of the Immediate Causes which Induce and Justify the Secession of the State of Mississippi from the Federal Union," The Avalon Project, Yale Law School, Lillian Goldman Law Library, accessed May 19, 2021, https://avalon.law.yale.edu/19th_century/csa_missec.asp.

9. John McKivigan and Mitchell Snay, eds., *Religion and the Antebellum Debate over Slavery* (Athens: University of Georgia Press, 1998); David Bailey, *Shadow on the Church: Southwestern Evangelical Religion and the Issue of Slavery, 1783–1860* (Ithaca, NY: Cornell University Press, 1985); John Daly, *When Slavery Was*

Called Freedom: Evangelicalism, Proslavery, and the Causes of the Civil War (Lexington: University Press of Kentucky, 2002); Edward Crowther, *Southern Evangelicals and the Coming of the Civil War* (Lewiston, NY: E. Mellen, 2000); Elizabeth Fox-Genovese and Eugene D. Genovese, *The Mind of the Master Class: History and Faith in the Southern Slaveholders' Worldview* (Cambridge: Cambridge University Press, 2005); Charles F. Irons, *The Origins of Proslavery Christianity: White and Black Evangelicals in Colonial and Antebellum Virginia* (Chapel Hill: University of North Carolina Press, 2008); Christine Leigh Heyrman, *Southern Cross: The Beginning of the Bible Belt* (New York: Knopf, 1997); Albert Raboteau, *Slave Religion: The "Invisible Institution" in the Antebellum South* (New York: Oxford University Press, 1978).

10. John R. McKivigan, *The War against Proslavery Religion: Abolitionism and the Northern Churches, 1830–1865* (Ithaca, NY: Cornell University Press, 1984); J. Brent Morris, *Oberlin, Hotbed of Abolitionism: College, Community, and the Fight for Freedom and Equality* (Chapel Hill: University of North Carolina Press, 2014).

11. "Isaac Mayer Wise, 'On to Richmond,' Describing Conditions in the Reconstruction South, the *Israelite*, June 28, 1867," in *American Jewish History: A Primary Source Reader*, edited by Gary Phillip Zola and Marc Dollinger (Waltham, MA: Brandeis University Press, 2014) 113.

12. Reported in the southern press—*Richmond Dispatch*, January 29, 1861, 1.

13. *Occident* 18 (January 24, 1861), cited in Irwin Lachoff, "Bernard Illowy: Counter Reformer," *Southern Jewish History* 5 (2002):53.

14. Zola and Dollinger, *American Jewish History*, 121. See also Eric Goldstein and Deborah Weiner, *On Middle Ground: A History of the Jews of Baltimore* (Baltimore, MD: Johns Hopkins University Press, 2018), 89–91.

15. Myron Berman, *Richmond's Jewry, 1769–1976: Shabbat in Shockoe* (Richmond, VA: Jewish Community Federation of Richmond, 1979), 177.

16. Simon Tuska, "Jews, Polish Jews, and 'Cold' Jews," *Memphis Daily Appeal*, January 23, 1861, 1. Mendelsohn, *Jewish Soldiers*, 29; S. D. Temkin, *Isaac Mayer Wise: Shaping American Judaism* (New York: Oxford University Press, 1992).

17. Gregg D. Kimball, *American City, Southern Place: A Cultural History of Antebellum Richmond* (Athens: University of Georgia Press, 2000), 223–27.

18. January 1 and 6, 1861, Edward Rosewater Diaries, series B, box 4, 3, Rosewater Family Papers, MS-503, American Jewish Archives, Cincinnati, OH. North Alabama had a small Unionist population; in Jackson county, in the Tennessee River valley, 18.6% of the population was enslaved: Margaret M. Storey, "Civil War Unionists and the Political Culture of Loyalty in Alabama, 1860–1861," *Journal of Southern History* 69, no. 1 (2003):77n16.

19. February 14, 1861, Edward Rosewater Diaries.

20. March 18, 1861, Edward Rosewater Diaries.

21. "Constitution for the Provisional Government," The Avalon Project, Yale Law School, Lillian Goldman Law Library, accessed May 19, 2021, https://avalon.law.yale.edu/19th_century/csa_csapro.asp. As historian Drew Gilpin Faust has argued, "The most fundamental source of legitimation for the Confederacy was Christianity": *The Creation of Confederate Nationalism: Ideology and Identity in the Civil War South* (Baton Rouge: Louisiana State University Press, 1988), 22.

22. Quoted in Stephanie McCurry, *Confederate Reckoning: Power and Politics in the Civil War South* (Cambridge, MA: Harvard University Press, 2010), 225.

23. Quoted in Faust, *Creation of Confederate Nationalism*, 36.

24. South Carolina's constitution twice specified that citizenship was limited to "free white person[s]"; it could be acquired from fathers, but not mothers, as well as through military service (McCurry, *Confederate Reckoning*, 79–80). Alabama even granted the vote to white men who were not citizens (McCurry, 81–82).

25. *Charleston Daily Courier*, January 3, 1861, 2.

26. *Weekly Mississippian*, January 16, 1861, 2; *Vicksburg Weekly Citizen*, January 21, 1861, 2.

27. William Porcher Miles to P.G.T. Beauregard, August 27, 1861, ESBL, MOC, cited in John M. Coski, *The Confederate Battle Flag* (Cambridge, MA: Belknap Press of Harvard University Press, 2009), 5. Robert N. Rosen, *The Jewish Confederates* (Columbia, SC: University of South Carolina Press, 2000); Anton

Hieke, *Jewish Identity in the Reconstruction South: Ambivalence and Adaptation* (Boston: DeGruyter, 2013), 113–14.

28. Rosengarten and Rosengarten, *Portion of the People*, 127. DeLeon's brother Edwin, the US consul in Egypt when the war broke out, eventually served as a Confederate diplomat: "Propaganda for Slavery," in *A Documentary History of Jews in the United States, 1654–1875*, 3rd ed., edited by Morris U. Schappes (New York: Schocken, 1971), 400–401.

29. McCurry, *Confederate Reckoning*, 340; see also James Traub, *Judah Benjamin: Counselor to the Confederacy* (New Haven, CT: Yale University Press, 2021).

30. April 12, 1861, Edward Rosewater Diaries.

31. Barney, *Rebels in the Making*.

32. August 22, 1861, Edward Rosewater Diaries.

33. August 23, 1861, Edward Rosewater Diaries.

34. Ash Levy to Andrew Johnson, July 18, 1865, Virginia, Amnesty Papers, compiled 1865–1867, record group 94, roll 0064, NARA, Fold3, accessed September 27, 2021, https://www.fold3.com/image/22951898/levy-ash-page-1-us-confederate-amnesty-papers-1865-1867; Berman, *Richmond's Jewry*, 167, 219; *First Annual Directory for the City of Richmond*, "Chapter IV, Volume 146—Ordnance Department—City Directory, Richmond, Virginia, 1859," p. 56, National Archives Catalog, accessed September 27, 2021, https://catalog.archives.gov/id/12499482.

35. Rosanna Osterman to Andrew Johnson, September 26, 1865, Texas, Amnesty Papers, compiled 1865–67, record group 94, roll 0054, NARA, Fold3, accessed September 27, 2021, https://www.fold3.com/image/24309813/osterman-rosanna-page-1-us-confederate-amnesty-papers-1865-1867; Bryan Stone, *Chosen Folks: Jews on the Frontiers of Texas* (Austin: University of Texas Press, 2010), 47.

36. April 14, 1861, box 2, folder 4, Minis Family MS-272, American Jewish Archives, Cincinnati, OH.

37. Abraham Minis to Andrew Johnson, February 7, 1867, Georgia, Amnesty Papers, compiled 1865–67, record group 94, roll 0021, NARA, Fold3, accessed September 27, 2021, https://www.fold3.com/image/20062381/minis-abraham-page-2-us-confederate-amnesty-papers-1865-1867.

38. Dianne Ashton, "Shifting Veils: Religion, Politics, and Womanhood in the Civil War Writings of American Jewish Women," in *Jews and the Civil War: A Reader*, edited by Jonathan D. Sarna and Adam Mendelsohn (New York: New York University Press, 2010), 298; Drew Gilpin Faust, *Mothers of Invention: Women of the Slaveholding South in the American Civil War* (Chapel Hill: University of North Carolina Press, 1996).

39. David Philipson, ed., *Letters of Rebecca Gratz* (Philadelphia: Jewish Publication Society, 1929), 438.

40. Stephanie McCurry, *Women's War: Fighting and Surviving the American Civil War* (Cambridge, MA: Belknap Press of Harvard University Press, 2019).

41. November 1862, David M. Klein Papers, MS-695, American Jewish Archives, Cincinnati, OH.

42. "Resolution of the Hebrew Congregation in Support of the Confederacy, Shreveport, Louisiana, May 1861," in Zola and Dollinger, *American Jewish History*, 109.

43. Henry S. Jacobs to Isaac Leeser, April 21, 1866, Gershwind-Bennett Isaac Leeser Digital Repository, Penn Libraries, accessed June 27, 2024, https://judaicadhpenn.org/legacyprojects/s/leeser/item/68586.

44. "Thanksgiving Address," *Jewish Messenger*, December 7, 1860, 172–73.

45. Emily Bingham, *Mordecai: An American Family* (New York: Hill and Wang, 2003), 113.

46. Bernhard Felsenthal, "The Jews and Slavery," *Sinai*, 1862, in Zola and Dollinger, *American Jewish History*, 97.

47. Abraham Minis to Andrew Johnson, February 7, 1867, Georgia, Amnesty Papers, compiled 1865–67, record group 94, roll 0021, NARA, Fold3, accessed September 27, 2021, https://www.fold3.com/image/20062381/minis-abraham-page-2-us-confederate-amnesty-papers-1865-1867.

48. Philipson, *Letters of Rebecca Gratz*, 423–24.

49. May 25, 1862, Mss 151, Temple Beth Israel, Macon, Georgia, Cuba Archives of the Breman Museum, Atlanta, GA.

50. Adam Mendelsohn has found that Jews enlisted in the Union army at relatively low rates compared with other ethnic groups (*Jewish Soldiers*, 26–27), with those originating in Bavaria, Hesse, and Bohemia

proving particularly reluctant. He also found a dozen Jews who enlisted in the Union army in Southern states: Louisiana, Mississippi, Tennessee, and Florida (241).

51. Daniel R. Weinfeld, "A Certain Ambivalence: Florida's Jews and the Civil War," *Southern Jewish History* 17 (2014):91–129.

52. Adam Mendelsohn, "Introduction: Before Korn; A Century of Jewish Historical Writing about the American Civil War," in *Jews and the Civil War: A Reader*, edited by Mendelsohn and Jonathan D. Sarna (New York: New York University Press, 2010), 1–26.

53. Rosen, *Jewish Confederates*, 168.

54. Jeff Rosenheim, *Photography and the American Civil War* (New York: Metropolitan Museum of Art, 2014); J. A. Brookes, "'The Last and Most Precious Memento': Photographic Portraiture and the Union Citizen-Soldier," *Civil War History* 65, no. 3 (2019):235–61.

55. Simon Wolf records other groups of brothers—the six Cohen brothers of North Carolina, the five Jonas brothers of Mississippi, the four Moses brothers of Georgia, and trios of brothers from Arkansas, Georgia, South Carolina, Virginia, Louisiana, and Alabama: *The American Jew as Patriot, Soldier, Citizen* (Philadelphia: Levytype, 1895), 109–10. See also Rosenheim, *Photography*.

56. Ancestry.com, *1850 U.S. Federal Census—Slave Schedules* [database online] (Lehi, UT: Ancestry.com Operations, 2004), The National Archive in Washington, DC, NARA Microform Publication M432, *Seventh Census of the United States, 1850*, Records of the Bureau of the Census no. 29, https://www.ancestry.com/discoveryui-content/view/92073030:8055?tid=&pid=&queryId=f1cc4fab-ceb7-4c03-b123-e3c5d41623e0&_phsrc=FHZ277&_phstart=successSource; Rosengarten and Rosengarten, *Portion of the People*.

57. Weinfeld, "Certain Ambivalence." "Peddlers and petty traders had particular reason to enlist in the early months of the war" (Mendelsohn, *Jewish Soldiers*, 65).

58. "Confederate Diary: Excerpts from the War Diary of Lewis Leon of North Carolina, April 1861 to April, 1865," in Schappes, *Documentary History of Jews*, 481–91; Leonard Rogoff, *Down Home: Jewish Life in North Carolina* (Chapel Hill: University of North Carolina Press, 2010).

59. Derek Penslar, *Jews and the Military: A History* (Princeton, NJ: Princeton University Press, 2013); Aaron Sheehan-Dean, *Why Confederates Fought: Family and Nation in Civil War Virginia* (Chapel Hill: University of North Carolina Press, 2007).

60. Philip Whitlock, Recollections (1908), 41–42, Mss5:1 W5905:1, Virginia Historical Society, Richmond, VA.

61. His son Henry was born on November 27, 1861: gravestone, Hebrew Cemetery, Richmond, Virginia, accessed via Find a Grave, https://www.findagrave.com/memorial/70516963/henry_flegenheimer; Penslar, *Jews and the Military*, 61, 54–56.

62. Joseph T. Glatthaar, *Soldiering in the Army of Northern Virginia: A Statistical Portrait of the Troops Who Served under Robert E. Lee* (Chapel Hill: University of North Carolina Press, 2011), 67. After his initial six-month term ended, Leon reenlisted, and incurred a minor wound at Gettysburg: James J. Broomall, *Private Confederacies: The Emotional Worlds of Southern Men as Citizens and Soldiers* (Chapel Hill: University of North Carolina Press, 2019).

63. "Confederate Diary," in Schappes, *Documentary History of Jews*, 483.

64. Adam H. Domby and Shari Rabin, "Simon Gerstmann's War: Religion, Loyalty, and Memory in the Post–Civil War Claims Courts," *Journal of Southern History* 87, no. 4 (2021):565–602; Julius Weis Autobiography, n.d., Ida Weiss Friend Collection, MSS 287 box 7, Louisiana Research Center, Tulane University Special Collections.

65. Faust, *Mothers of Invention*.

66. *Charlotte Democrat*, July 2, 1861, 3.

67. Ashton, "Shifting Veils," 286.

68. Rosanna Ostermann to Andrew Johnson, September 25, 1865, Case Files of Applications from Former Confederates for Presidential Pardons (Amnesty Papers) 1865–67, Microfilm Publication M1003, 73 rolls; NAID 656621, Records of the Adjutant General's Office, 1780's–1917, record group 94, NARA, Fold3, accessed September 27, 2021, https://www.fold3.com/image/24309813/osterman-rosanna-page-1-us-confederate-amnesty-papers-1865-1867.

69. Ashton, "Shifting Veils"; Rosengarten and Rosengarten, *Portion of the People.*

70. Pearl J. Young, "Secession as a Moral Imperative: White Southerners and Evangelical Theology," PhD dissertation, University of North Carolina, 2018; Paul Harvey, *Christianity and Race in the American South* (Chicago: University of Chicago Press, 2016), 94.

71. "A Curiosity," *Israelite*, February 14, 1862, 263.

72. "The Prayer of the C.S. Soldiers by Rev. M.J. Michelbacher. Minister of the Hebrew Congregation, 'House of Love', Richmond, Va," Maximilian J. Michelbacher Papers, Beth Ahabah Museum and Archives, Richmond, VA.

73. The prayer contains esoteric hints of resistance to gentile power within its pastiche of biblical quotations. Jonathan D. Sarna, "Jewish Prayers for the U.S. Government: A Study in the Liturgy of Politics and the Politics of Liturgy," *Moral Problems in American Life: New Perspectives on Cultural History*, edited by Karen Halttunen and Lewis Perry, 200–221 (Ithaca, NY: Cornell University Press, 1998), quotation at 204.

74. Maximilian J. Michelbacher to Robert E. Lee, August 23, 1861, Michelbacher Papers, Beth Ahabah Archives, Richmond, VA.

75. Paul Quigley, *Shifting Grounds: Nationalism and the American South* (New York: Oxford University Press, 2014).

76. Michelbacher to Lee, Beth Ahabah Museum and Archives, Richmond, VA.

77. Kent T. Dollar, "'Strangers in a Strange Land': Christian Soldiers in the Early Months of the Civil War," in *The View from the Ground: Experiences of Civil War Soldiers*, edited by Aaron Sheehan-Dean, 145–70 (Lexington: University Press of Kentucky, 2006).

78. Robert E. Lee to Maximilian J. Michelbacher, August 29, 1861, Maximilian J. Michelbacher Papers, Beth Ahabah Museum and Archives.

79. John William Jones, *Christ in the Camp; or, Religion in Lee's Army* (Richmond, VA: B. F. Johnson, 1887), 79–80. According to Lewis Leon, Lee did grant furlough for the High Holidays in 1863: "Confederate Diary," in Schappes, *Documentary History of Jews*, 488.

80. Emma Mordecai Diary, October 10, 1864, folder 103 in the Mordecai Family Papers #847, Southern Historical Collection, Wilson Special Collections Library, University of North Carolina at Chapel Hill.

81. Michael Stanislowski, *The Transformation of Jewish Society in Russia, 1825–1855* (Philadelphia, PA: Jewish Publication Society, 1983); Penslar, *Jews and the Military.*

82. Weinfeld, "Certain Ambivalence"; Domby and Rabin, "Simon Gerstmann's War."

83. Daniel R. Weinfeld, "Samuel Fleishman: Tragedy in Reconstruction-Era Florida," *Southern Jewish History* 8 (2005):31–76; "Sketch of David Steinheimer, Atlanta, Ga.," David Steinheimer Papers, Mss 26, Cuba Family Archives for Southern Jewish History, Breman Museum, Atlanta, GA.

84. "Sketch of David Steinheimer, Atlanta, Ga.," David Steinheimer Papers.

85. David Carlson, "Citizens of the County of Their Domicile: Conscription and Confederate Citizenship," *Civil War History* 62, no. 4 (2016):399–431; Paul Quigley, "Civil War Conscription and the International Boundaries of Citizenship," *Journal of the Civil War Era* 4, no. 3 (2014):373–97; Shari Rabin, *Jews on the Frontier: Religion and Mobility in Nineteenth-Century America* (New York: New York University Press, 2017).

86. Carlson, "Citizens of the County." The law encompassed not only citizens but "residents." Attorney General Thomas Bragg clarified that this category was limited to those who had established some intent to remain—"domicile"—although the exact parameters remained unclear and large numbers of immigrants continued to seek exemptions.

87. *Richmond Dispatch*, September 18, 1862, 2.

88. On the statute and efforts to have it changed: Jonathan D. Sarna and Benjamin Shapell, *Lincoln and the Jews: A History* (New York: St. Martin's, 2015), 100–110.

89. Bertram Korn, "Was There a Confederate Jewish Chaplain?," *American Jewish Historical Quarterly* 53, no. 1 (1963):64–65; Confederate States of America, "An Act to Further Provide for the Public Defence" (Richmond, 1862), p. 6, HathiTrust, accessed May 8, 2020, https://catalog.hathitrust.org/Record/010944952.

90. Domby and Rabin, "Simon Gerstmann's War"; Shari Rabin, "Working Jews: *Hazanim* and the Labor of Religion in Nineteenth-Century America," *Religion and American Culture* 25, no. 2 (2015):178–217.

91. On patronalism in relations between Confederate citizens and leaders: Gregory P. Downs, *Declarations of Dependence: The Long Reconstruction of Popular Politics in the South, 1861–1908* (Chapel Hill: University of North Carolina Press, 2011).

Chapter 8

1. Quote in Myron Berman, *Richmond's Jewry, 1769–1976: Shabbat in Shockoe* (Richmond, VA: Jewish Community Federation of Richmond, 1979), 194–95.

2. Steven E. Woodworth and Kenneth J. Winkle, *Atlas of the Civil War* (New York: Oxford University Press, 2004); Lisa Laskin, "'The Army Is Not Near So Much Demoralized as the Country Is': Soldiers in the Army of Northern Virginia and the Confederate Home Front," in *The View from the Ground: Experiences of Civil War Soldiers*, edited by Aaron Sheehan-Dean, 91–120 (Lexington: University Press of Kentucky, 2006); Thavolia Glymph, *The Women's Fight: The Civil War's Battles for Home, Freedom, and Nation* (Chapel Hill: University of North Carolina Press, 2020).

3. Jefferson Mansell, "'Now Occupied for Public Use': The Houses of Natchez behind Enemy Lines," *Southern Quarterly* 51, no. ½ (2013/2014):80.

4. Rosewater Diary, January 1, 1863, series B, box 4, 4, Rosewater Family Papers, MS-503, American Jewish Archives, Cincinnati, OH.

5. Initially held as "contraband" property, Black men were eventually enlisted in the US army: Stephanie McCurry, *Confederate Reckoning: Power and Politics in the Civil War South* (Cambridge, MA: Harvard University Press, 2010).

6. Keri Leigh Merritt, *Masterless Men: Poor Whites and Slavery in the Antebellum South* (New York: Cambridge University Press, 2017); McCurry, *Confederate Reckoning*; David Williams, *I Freed Myself: African American Self-Emancipation in the Civil War Era* (New York: Cambridge University Press, 2014).

7. Louis Schmier, "Notes and Documents on the 1862 Expulsion of Jews from Thomasville, Georgia," *American Jewish Archives* 32 (1980):9–22.

8. Drew Gilpin Faust, "Christian Soldiers: The Meaning of Revivalism in the Confederate Army," *Journal of Southern History* 53, no. 1 (1987):63; Lauren Winner, "Taking Up the Cross: Conversion among Black and White Jews in the Civil War South," in *Southern Families at War: Loyalty and Conflict in the Civil War South*, edited by Catherine Clinton (New York: Oxford University Press, 2000). Henry Beck, serving in the commissary late in the war, listened to a chaplain's sermon and, while in Charlotte, attended an Episcopal church: SC-788, Diary of Henry Beck, American Jewish Archives, Cincinnati, OH.

9. Edwin Kursheedt to Miss Sallie, n.d., Edwin I. Kursheedt Papers, Beth Ahabah Museum and Archives, Richmond, VA.

10. "Diary of Lewis Leon," in *A Documentary History of Jews in the United States, 1654–1875*, 3rd ed., edited by Morris U. Schappes (New York: Schocken, 1971), 488.

11. "Isaac Levy to his Sister, Leonora, Detailing the Celebration of Passover at a Confederate Encampment in Adam's Run, South Carolina, April 24, 1864," in *American Jewish History: A Primary Source Reader*, edited by Gary Phillip Zola and Marc Dollinger (Waltham, MA: Brandeis University Press, 2014), 112.

12. To Miss Sallie, c.1862, Edwin I. Kursheedt Papers, Beth Ahabah Museum and Archives, Richmond, VA.

13. Whitlock Reminiscences, Virginia Historical Society, Richmond, VA.

14. "[I] was invited down town by two of them for Dinner with all my Lieutenants. . . . Mr. Rosenbaum as well as Mr. Heller have invited me to come to town and board with them free of charge but I prefer my own boarding": entry for May 2, 1862, in Marcus M. Spiegel, *Your True Marcus: The Civil War Letters of a Jewish Colonel* (Kent, OH: Kent State University Press, 1985), 106. In Memphis he identified local Jews, wished them happy Sabbath, and joined them for lunch for Sabbath Hanukkah at a kosher boardinghouse, the proprietor of which knew Spiegel's father from Germany: entry for December 21, 1862, 196–202. In Baton Rouge he had Sabbath dinner at a local Jewish widow's home: entry for April 23, 1864, 331. On Passover with local Jews, see article in the *Israelite*, May 9, 1862 (359).

15. Aaron D. Anderson, *Builders of a New South: Merchants, Capital, and the Remaking of Natchez, 1865–1914* (Oxford, MS: University Press of Mississippi, 2013), 54.

16. Adam D. Mendelsohn, *Jewish Soldiers in the Civil War: The Union Army* (New York: New York University Press, 2022), 177, 182.

17. Jonathan D. Sarna, *When General Grant Expelled the Jews* (New York: Schocken, 2012), 7.

18. On wartime antisemitism in the North (although not described in regional terms): Gary L. Bunker and John Appel, "'Shoddy,' Anti-Semitism, and the Civil War," *American Jewish History* 82, no. 1 (1994):43–71. Sarna, *When General Grant Expelled*.

19. Anton Hieke, *Jewish Identity in the Reconstruction South: Ambivalence and Adaptation* (Boston: DeGruyter, 2013), 146. It appears none actually did leave.

20. Schmier, "Notes and Documents," 20, 18, 15.

21. Paul Quigley, *Shifting Grounds: Nationalism and the American South* (New York: Oxford University Press, 2014), 208.

22. David Carlson, "Citizens of the County of Their Domicile: Conscription and Confederate Citizenship," *Civil War History* 62, no. 4 (2016):416. Carlson documents many examples of antisemitism, but does not consider Jews as a category of special interest.

23. Andrea Mehrländer, "'With More Freedom and Independence than the Yankees': The Germans of Richmond, Charleston, and New Orleans during the American Civil War," in *Civil War Citizens: Race, Ethnicity, and Identity in America's Bloodiest Conflict*, edited by Susannah J. Ural (New York: New York University Press, 2010), 63.

24. Eli N. Evans, *Judah P. Benjamin: The Jewish Confederate* (New York: Free Press, 1988), 154; Adam D. Mendelsohn and Jonathan D. Sarna, eds., *Jews and the Civil War: A Reader* (New York: New York University Press, 2010), 38.

25. Yael Sternhell, *Routes of War: The World of Movement in the Confederate South* (Cambridge, MA: Harvard University Press, 2012); Drew Gilpin Faust, "'Sliding into the World': The Sin of Extortion and the Dynamic of Confederate Identity," in *The Creation of Confederate Nationalism: Ideology and Identity in the Civil War South*, 41–57 (Baton Rouge: Louisiana State University Press, 1988).

26. Hieke, *Jewish Identity*, 142

27. Winner, "Taking up the Cross," 196.

28. Carlson, "Citizens of the County," 417.

29. "Stern and Rosenberg were arrested under this grave charge [of counterfeiting]": Minutes, Temple Beth Israel, Macon, GA, Mss 151, Cuba Archives of the Breman Museum, Atlanta, GA; see also Whitlock Recollections, Virginia Historical Society, Richmond.

30. In March 1863 the Confederate States of America passed a much-reviled law authorizing the impressment of enslaved people into Confederate military service—soldiers were needed and 40% of the adult male population was enslaved—but it foundered upon white claims of personal property and Black resistance: William L. Barney, *Rebels in the Making: The Secession Crisis and the Birth of the Confederacy* (New York: Oxford University Press, 2020).

31. Joseph Glatthaar, *Soldiering in the Army of Northern Virginia: A Statistical Portrait of the Troops Who Served under Robert E. Lee* (Chapel Hill: University of North Carolina Press, 2011), 64.

32. Mark A. Weitz, *More Damning Than Slaughter: Desertion in the Confederate Army* (Lincoln: University of Nebraska Press, 2005).

33. Maximilian J. Michelbacher to Robert E. Lee, March 18, 1863, Beth Ahabah Museum and Archives, Richmond, VA.

34. "Must Wait," *Israelite*, October 16, 1863, 122. The prisoners of war were listed as Henry Mass, Julius Brannshweiger, Max Newgas, A. Wausserman, Louis Meyersburg, S. Cohen, and H. Brash.

35. Maximilian J. Michelbacher to Robert E. Lee, March 18, 1863, Beth Ahabah Museum and Archives, Richmond, VA. Jarret Ruminski, "'Tradyville': The Contraband Trade and the Problem of Loyalty in Civil War Mississippi," *Journal of the Civil War Era* 2, no. 4 (2012):511–37.

36. Maximilian J. Michelbacher, *A Sermon Delivered on the Day of Prayer, Recommended by the President of the C. S. of A., the 27th of March, 1863* (Richmond, VA: Macfarlane and Fergusson, 1863). Not everyone was convinced by the sermon. After reading it, Isaac Mayer Wise—protective of his own status but no

radical—complained that Michelbacher "never was and is not now a rabbi" and described his sermon as "political rigmarole dictated by some partisan stump speaker." He would concede only that Michelbacher "can sing and chant" (*Israelite*, June 19, 1863, 394).

37. Elliot Ashkenazi, ed., *The Civil War Diary of Clara Solomon: Growing up in New Orleans, 1861–1862* (Baton Rouge: Louisiana State University Press, 1995), 350–51.

38. Hieke, *Jewish Identity*,184; Mark I. Greenberg, "Savannah's Jewish Women and the Shaping of Ethnic and Gender Identity, 1830–1900," *Georgia Historical Quarterly* 82, no. 4 (1998):751–74; George Rable, "'Missing in Action': Women of the Confederacy," in *Divided Houses: Gender and the Civil War*, edited by Catherine Clinton and Nina Silber (New York: Oxford University Press, 1992), 134–46; *Israelite*, July 3, 1863, 2. After the war, Rachel Mayer of New York sued Benjamin Mordecai, who, acting as trustee, had invested her assets in now-worthless Confederate bonds: J.S.G. Richardson, *Reports of Cases Heard and Determined by the Supreme Court of South Carolina*, vol. 1 (Columbia, SC: R. L. Bryan, 1907), 384; Anton Hieke, "Rabbi Maurice Mayer: German Revolutionary, Charleston Reformer, and Anti-abolitionist," *Southern Jewish History* 17 (2014):77.

39. Historian Lauren Winner has argued that "the Civil War era saw more Jewish conversions to Christianity than any period prior to the war" because of new forms of intimacy with Christians ("Taking Up the Cross," 201).

40. *Donaldsonville Chief*, November 13, 1915, 1.

41. James J. Broomall, *Private Confederacies: The Emotional Worlds of Southern Men as Citizens and Soldiers* (Chapel Hill: University of North Carolina Press, 2019).

42. Nat Strauss to Adolph Proskauer, April 20 and May 29, 1864, Proskauer Family Papers, folder 2, MS-254, American Jewish Archives, Cincinnati, OH.

43. Nat Strauss to Adolph Proskauer, April 20, 1864.

44. Nat Strauss to Adolph Proskauer, July 3, 1864, Proskauer Family Papers, folder 2, MS-254.

45. Nat Strauss to Adolph Proskauer, July 3, 1864. Mark A. Noll, *The Civil War as a Theological Crisis* (Chapel Hill: University of North Carolina Press, 2006); Lincoln would also make this point in his second inaugural address.

46. Nat Strauss to Adolph Proskauer, July 3, 1864.

47. Emma Mordecai Diary, May 10 and October 1, 1864, folder 103 in the Mordecai Family Papers #847, Southern Historical Collection, Wilson Special Collections Library, University of North Carolina at Chapel Hill.

48. Emma Mordecai Diary, May 10, 1865.

49. Emma Mordecai Diary, May 2, 1865.

50. Emma Mordecai Diary, May 15, 1864.

51. Emma Mordecai Diary, May 29, 1864.

52. Emma Mordecai Diary, May 21, 1864.

53. Emma Mordecai Diary, June 15, 1864.

54. June 18, 1864, Mss 151, Temple Beth Israel, Macon, Georgia, Cuba Archives of the Breman Museum, Atlanta, GA.

55. Hebra Kaddisha Minute Book, 1864–75, October 9, 1864, folder 2, Natchez, MS, Congregation B'nai Israel Records, X-358, American Jewish Archives, Cincinnati, OH.

56. Theodore Rosengarten and Dale Rosengarten, *A Portion of the People: Three Hundred Years of Southern Jewish Life* (Columbia: University of South Carolina Press, 2002), 262; Kahal Kadosh Beth Elohim box 30, folder 1, College of Charleston Special Collections, Charleston, SC.

57. Joseph Jacobsohn to Isaac Leeser, June 28, 1865, Gershwind-Bennett Isaac Leeser Digital Repository, Penn Libraries, http://leeser.library.upenn.edu/documentDisplay.php?id=LSKAP0230. His replacement at Shaarey Chased, enthusiastic Confederate and religious reformer James K. Gutheim, would leave for New York in 1868, although he returned four years later: Emily Ford and Barry Stiefel, *The Jews of New Orleans and the Mississippi Delta* (Charleston, SC: History Press, 2012), 85.

58. "Louisiana," *Jewish Messenger*, February 3, 1865; see Shari Rabin, "Mohalim not Missionaries: Outsider and Insider Bodies in Southern Religious History," *Journal of Southern Religion* 18 (2016), jsreligion.org/vol18/rabin; Irwin Lachoff, "Bernard Illowy: Counter Reformer," *Southern Jewish History* 5 (2002):43–

67; David Ellenson, "A Jewish Legal Decision by Rabbi Bernard Illowy of New Orleans and Its Discussion in Nineteenth Century Europe," *American Jewish History* 69, no. 2 (1979):174.

59. Emma Mordecai Diary, April 13, 1865, folder 103 in the Mordecai Family Papers #847, Southern Historical Collection, Wilson Special Collections Library, University of North Carolina at Chapel Hill.

60. Emma Mordecai Diary, May 5, 1865.

61. Emma Mordecai Diary, May 4, 1865.

62. Emma Mordecai Diary, April 19, 1865.

63. "Eleanor H. Cohen, Journal Entries Detailing the Author's Love for both the North and the South, *Champion of the Lost Cause,* February 28, 1865," in Zola and Dollinger, *American Jewish History,* 100–101.

64. Kahal Kadosh Beth Elohim, box 40, folder 8, College of Charleston Special Collections, Charleston, SC.

65. Biography of William Flegenheimer, 20, Virginia Historical Society, Richmond, VA.

66. Louis Schmier, ed., *Reflections on Southern Jewry: The Letters of Charles Wessolowsky, 1878–1879* (Macon, GA: Mercer University Press, 1982), 11; "Confederate Diary," in Schappes, *Documentary History of Jews,* 491.

67. Glatthaar, *Soldiering in the Army,* 67; "Confederate Diary," in Schappes, *Documentary History of Jews,* 491.

68. "Eleanor H. Cohen, Journal Entries Detailing the Author's Love for both the North and South, *Champion of the Lost Cause,* February 28, 1865," in Zola and Dollinger, *American Jewish History,* 101.

69. "List of Soldiers of the Confederate Army Buried by George Jacobs—Richmond Va.," George Jacobs Papers, Beth Ahabah Museum and Archives, Richmond, VA.

70. Barnett Elzas, *The Old Jewish Cemeteries at Charleston: A Transcription of the Inscriptions on Their Tombstones, 1762–1903, S.C.* (Charleston: Daggett Printing, 1903), 88, 81, 30.

Chapter 9

1. "Andrew Jackson Moses," South Carolina, Case Files of Applications from Former Confederates for Presidential Pardons ("Amnesty Papers"), 1865–67, National Archives and Records Administration, Fold3, accessed September 14, 2021, https://www.fold3.com/image/22604750.

2. LeeAnn Whites, *The Civil War as a Crisis in Gender, 1860–1890* (Athens: University of Georgia Press, 2000); Craig Thompson Friend, ed., *Southern Masculinity: Perspectives on Manhood in the South Since Reconstruction* (Athens: University of Georgia Press, 2009).

3. Willie L. Rose, *Rehearsal for Reconstruction: The Port Royal Experiment* (Indianapolis: Bobbs-Merrill, 1964); Eric Foner, *Reconstruction: America's Unfinished Revolution, 1863–1877* (New York: Harper, 1988).

4. Stephanie McCurry has argued, "When slavery was ripped up, virtually everything was uprooted with it": *Women's War: Fighting and Surviving the Civil War* (Cambridge, MA: Belknap Press of Harvard University Press, 2019), 9; Gregory Downs, *After Appomattox: Military Occupation and the Ends of War* (Cambridge, MA: Harvard University Press, 2015), 2–3.

5. Emma Mordecai Diary, May 4, 1865, folder 103 in the Mordecai Family Papers #847, Southern Historical Collection, Wilson Special Collections Library, University of North Carolina at Chapel Hill.

6. Foner, *Reconstruction,* 176–84.

7. Nicole Turner, *Soul Liberty: The Evolution of Black Religious Politics in Postemancipation Virginia* (Chapel Hill: University of North Carolina Press, 2020).

8. Robert Harrison, "New Representations of a 'Misrepresented Bureau': Reflections on Recent Scholarship on the Freedmen's Bureau," *American Nineteenth Century History* 8, no. 2 (2007): 205–29.

9. Benjamin Mordecai, Petition, December 12, 1865, Assistant Commissioner, M869, roll 28, https://www.ancestry.com/discoveryui-content/view/3733059:62309?tid=&pid=&queryId=a5ad9d62-5403-4d46-8a5a-b04c240ce438&_phsrc=FHZ319&_phstart=successSource; "Report of Persons and Articles Employed and Hired at Alexandria, LA during the Month of September, 1867," https://www.ancestry.com/discoveryui-content/view/3174761:62309?tid=&pid=&queryId=51399179-e304-4c55-a819

-1a22b1955a35&_phsrc=FHZ328&_phstart=successSource; Charles Brown vs. M. Kowalski, Records of the Field Office, M1905, roll 62, https://www.ancestry.com/discoveryui-content/view/3245797:62309?tid=&pid=&queryId=48ae49f0-1f41-4346-a4de-f33d52a2329b&_phsrc=FHZ325&_phstart=success-Source; Rations of Meat, Records of the Field Office, M1909, roll 51, 19, https://www.ancestry.com/discoveryui-content/view/2305061:62309?tid=&pid=&queryId=1f450cc4-9f87-4669-8673-9395ae9a41bd&_phsrc=FHZ331&_phstart=successSource; all from National Archives and Records Administration, Ancestry.com, *U.S., Freedmen's Bureau Records, 1865–1878* [database online] (Lehi, UT: Ancestry.com Operations, 2021).

10. Bradley R. Clampitt, "'Not Intended to Dispossess Females': Southern Women and Civil War Amnesty," *Civil War History* 56, no. 4 (2010):325–49; Donald G. Nieman, introduction to *From Slavery to Sharecropping: White Land and Black Labor in the Rural South, 1865–1900* (New York: Garland, 1994), viii.

11. "Benjamin Mordecai," South Carolina, Amnesty Papers, National Archives and Records Administration, Fold3, accessed September 14, 2021, https://www.fold3.com/image/22604124.

12. "Abraham Minis," Georgia, Amnesty Papers, National Archives and Records Administration, Fold3, accessed September 14, 2021, https://www.fold3.com/image/20062381.

13. "Jacob DeCordova," Texas, Amnesty Papers, National Archives and Records Administration, Fold3, accessed September 14, 2021, https://www.fold3.com/image/22549398.

14. Susanna Michele Lee, *Claiming the Union: Citizenship in the Postwar South* (New York: Cambridge University Press, 2014).

15. "The Great Meeting Yesterday," *Savannah Daily Herald*, April 23, 1865, 1.

16. Adam H. Domby and Shari Rabin, "Simon Gerstmann's War: Religion, Loyalty, and Memory in the Post–Civil War Claims Courts," *Journal of Southern History* 87, no. 4 (2021):565–602.

17. "Mrs. D. Minis," Georgia, Amnesty Papers, National Archives and Records Administration, Fold3, accessed September 14, 2021, https://www.fold3.com/image/20062440.

18. "Rosanna Osterman," Texas, Amnesty Papers, National Archives and Records Administration, Fold3, accessed September 14, 2021, https://www.fold3.com/image/24309813.

19. Rosanna Osterman, Ancestry.com, *Texas, U.S., Wills and Probate Records, 1833–1974* [database online] (Provo, UT: Ancestry.com Operations, 2015), https://www.ancestry.com/imageviewer/collections/2115/images/007574032_00173?treeid=&personid=&usePUB=true&_phsrc=FHZ346&_phstart=successSource&pId=607866. Her will—reminiscent in its scope of Judah Touro's much-heralded 1854 will—had been written in 1862, indicating that in her mind, at least, the Civil War had never really severed her Jewish ties. See Bryan Stone, *Chosen Folks: Jews on the Frontiers of Texas* (Austin: University of Texas Press, 2010), 55–57; "The Loss of the Carter—125 Passengers Lost—Bodies Identified," *Spirit of Democracy* (Wooster, OH), February 14, 1866, 2.

20. Elizabeth L. Jemison, *Christian Citizens: Reading the Bible in Black and White in the Postemancipation South* (Chapel Hill: University of North Carolina Press, 2020).

21. Daniel Stowell, *Rebuilding Zion: The Religious Reconstruction of the South, 1863–1877* (New York: Oxford University Press, 1998). Isaac Mayer Wise visited Richmond in 1867 and spewed racist ideas about freed people and the future of the South: "On to Richmond," *Israelite*, June 21, 1867, 4; "On to Richmond II," *Israelite*, June 28, 1867, 4.

22. Isaac Leeser, "Richmond, Va.," *Occident and American Jewish Advocate*, November 1865, 376–79.

23. David Blight, *Race and Reunion: The Civil War in American Memory* (Cambridge, MA: Harvard University Press, 2001), 34; Megan Kate Nelson, *Ruin Nation: Destruction and the American Civil War* (Athens: University of Georgia Press, 2012).

24. Isaac Leeser Obituary, Gershwind-Bennett Isaac Leeser Digital Repository, Penn Libraries, accessed September 14, 2021, http://leeser.library.upenn.edu/documentDisplay.php?id=LSTCAT_item76. See also Adam D. Mendelsohn, *Jewish Soldiers in the Civil War: The Union Army* (New York: New York University Press, 2022), 196.

25. "The feature of the program was an interesting address by Rev. George Jacobs, late of Richmond, now of Philadelphia": "Richmond, Va.," *Israelite*, July 9, 1869, 7.

26. Henry S. Jacobs to Isaac Leeser, April 21, 5626 (1866), Gershwind-Bennett Isaac Leeser Digital Repository, Penn Libraries, http://leeser.library.upenn.edu/documentDisplay.php?id=LSDCBx3FF1_27.

27. "Vicksburg, Miss.," *Israelite*, March 18, 1870, 11; Bertram W. Korn, "Jewish Chaplains during the Civil War," in *Jews and the Civil War: A Reader*, edited by Adam Mendelsohn and Jonathan Sarna (New York: New York University Press, 2010), 347; Mendelsohn, *Jewish Soldiers*, 198–99.

28. "Notice," *Israelite*, August 10, 1866, 6. Thank you to Josh Furman for alerting me to this source.

29. Karen L. Cox, *Dixie's Daughters: The United Daughters of the Confederacy and the Preservation of Confederate Culture* (Gainesville: University Press of Florida, 2003).

30. "Hebrew Memorial Association," *Richmond Dispatch*, June 9, 1866, 1.

31. Anton Hieke, *Jewish Identity in the Reconstruction South: Ambivalence and Adaptation* (Boston: DeGruyter, 2013), 198–99; Clara L. Moses, "Clara L. Moses: War Days in Old Natchez," in *Memoirs of American Jews, 1775–1865*, vol. 1, edited by Jacob Rader Marcus (Philadelphia: Jewish Publication Society, 1955), 265. Octavia Harby Moses was involved in Confederate commemoration in Sumter, South Carolina: "Sumter Monumental Association," *Sumter Watchmen*, December 13, 1871, 3. In 1870, Benjamin Mordecai could be found raising funds for a Home for Mothers, Wives, and Daughters of Confederate Soldiers: *Charleston Daily News*, January 29, 1870, 3.

32. Charles Reagan Wilson, *Baptized in Blood: The Religion of the Lost Cause, 1865–1920* (Athens: University of Georgia Press, 2009).

33. Elizabeth Jemison notes that white Christians "transformed their proslavery theology into a postemancipation paternalism" (*Christian Citizens*, 7).

34. *Richmond Dispatch*, June 9, 1865, 1. See also Karen L. Cox, *Dixie's Daughters*.

35. Oscar Solomon Straus, *Under Four Administrations: From Cleveland to Taft* (New York: Houghton Mifflin, 1922), 20–21.

36. Hieke, *Jewish Identity*, 68.

37. Hieke, 73; Steven Hertzberg, *Strangers within the Gate City: The Jews of Atlanta, 1845–1915* (Philadelphia, Jewish Publication Society, 1978), 36.

38. Hertzberg, *Strangers*, 35–36.

39. Lee Shai Weissbach found that 76% of the communities he studies that had at least 100 Jews by the 1870s could be reached by rail directly: *Jewish Life in Small-Town America: A History* (New Haven, CT: Yale University Press, 2008), 39; see also R. Scott Huffard, *Engines of Redemption: Railroads and the Reconstruction of Capitalism in the New South* (Chapel Hill: University of North Carolina Press, 2019).

40. Martha S. Jones, *Birthright Citizens: A History of Race and Rights in Antebellum America* (New York: Cambridge University Press, 2018).

41. Foner, *Reconstruction*, 271–79.

42. Brian K. Fennessy, "'Works Meet for Repentance': Congressional Amnesty and Reconstructed Rebels," in *Freedoms Gained and Lost: Reconstruction and Its Meanings 150 Years Later*, edited by Adam H. Domby and Simon Lewis, 159–80 (New York: Fordham University Press, 2021).

43. Richard L. Hume and Jerry B. Gough, *Blacks, Carpetbaggers, and Scalawags: The Constitutional Conventions of Radical Reconstruction* (Baton Rouge: Louisiana State University Press, 2008), 141.

44. *Journal of the Constitutional Convention of the State of North-Carolina, at Its Session 1868* (Raleigh: Joseph W. Holden, 1868), electronic ed. (Chapel Hill: Academic Affairs Library, University of North Carolina at Chapel Hill, 2002), https://docsouth.unc.edu/nc/conv1868/conv1868.html.

45. Karin L. Zipf, "'The Whites Shall Rule the Land or Die': Gender, Race, and Class in North Carolina Reconstruction Politics," *Journal of Southern History* 65, no. 3 (1999):499–534; Hume and Gough, *Blacks, Carpetbaggers, and Scalawags*; Jonathan Sarna and David Dalin, *Religion and State in the American Jewish Experience* (South Bend, IN: Notre Dame University Press, 1997).

46. "The Board of Delegates," *Occident* 26, no. 4 (July 1868):152.

47. "Constitution of North Carolina of 1868," North Carolina General Assembly, accessed September 14, 2021, https://www.ncleg.gov/documentsites/legislativepublications/Constitutions/NCConstitution%20 (1868).pdf, now available at https://webservices.ncleg.gov/ViewDocSiteFile/56196.

48. Jemison, *Christian Citizens*; Leonard Rogoff, *Down Home: Jewish Life in North Carolina* (Chapel Hill, NC: University of North Carolina Press, 2010), 82.

49. "The Scattered Nation—Eloquent Lecture in Baltimore on the Children of Israel by Hon. Z.B. Vance," *Wilmington Morning Star*, February 17, 1874, 2; Hieke, *Jewish Identity*, 128; Rogoff, *Down Home*, 82–87. Rogoff argues that the speech "secured the Jews' racial and civic place as Americans" (99).

50. Gregory P. Downs, *Declarations of Dependence: The Long Reconstruction of Popular Politics in the South, 1861–1908* (Chapel Hill: University of North Carolina Press, 2011), 17–18.

51. "Scattered Nation," 2. "Internal evidence within the essay would indicate that it was written sometime between 1868 and 1873": Selig Adler, "Zebulon B. Vance and the 'Scattered Nation,'" *Journal of Southern History* 7, no. 3 (1941):370. See also Jemison, *Christian Citizens*.

52. Jonathan D. Sarna, *When General Grant Expelled the Jews* (New York: Schocken, 2012).

53. "The 'Republican' and the Jews," *Daily Arkansas Gazette*, June 10, 1871, 2. See also *Daily Arkansas Gazette*, June 7, 1871, 1.

54. "Judge F.J. Moses," *Charleston Daily Courier*, August 5, 1868, 2.

55. Gregory P. Downs, "The Southern Nation, 1860–1880," in *A New History of the American South*, edited by W. Fitzhugh Brundage (Chapel Hill: University of North Carolina Press, 2023), 293.

56. Rogoff, *Down Home*, 82; Downs, "Southern Nation, 1860–1880," 295.

57. "Proskauer-Alexander Case," *Alabama State Journal*, December 4, 1869, 2. In Florida, Morris Dzialynski was elected to the Jacksonville City Council as a Democrat in 1868: Daniel R. Weinfeld, "A Certain Ambivalence: Florida's Jews and the Civil War," *Southern Jewish History* 17 (2014):91–129. Nat Strauss was elected to the Alabama legislature in 1870 as a Democrat: *Montgomery Advertiser*, November 20, 1870, 3.

58. "Legislature of Alabama," *Selma Morning Times*, December 5, 1869, 1.

59. "Personal," *Selma Morning Times*, August 13, 1870, 3.

60. Stuart Rockoff, "Carpetbaggers, Jacklegs, and Bolting Republicans," *American Jewish History* 97, no. 1 (2013):39–64.

61. Rockoff, "Carpetbaggers."

62. · Foner, *Reconstruction*, 294.

63. Fennessy, "'Works Meet for Repentance,'" 162.

64. "The Two Conventions," *Richmond Dispatch*, October 8, 1874, 1. The previous year he appeared on the Freedmen's Bank "register of signatures of depositors": "William Flegenheimer," no. 5867, roll 7, Richmond, Virginia, June 21,1870–June 29, 1874, Register of Signatures of Depositors, Ancestry.com, *U.S., Freedman's Bank Records, 1865–1874* [database online] (Lehi, UT: Ancestry.com Operations, 2005), https://www.ancestry.com/discoveryui-content/view/252440:8755?tid=&pid=&queryId=20664e48-d6e7-4d85-b08d-38dda58a9e06&_phsrc=FHZ334&_phstart=successSource.

65. Theodore Rosengarten and Dale Rosengarten, *A Portion of the People: Three Hundred Years of Southern Jewish Life* (Columbia: University of South Carolina Press, 2002); Benjamin Ginsberg, *Moses of South Carolina: A Jewish Scalawag during Radical Reconstruction* (Baltimore, MD: Johns Hopkins University Press, 2010).

66. Rosengarten and Rosengarten, *Portion of the People*; Blight, *Race and Reunion*; E. W. Brock, "Thomas W. Cardozo: Fallible Black Reconstruction Leader," *Journal of Southern History* 47, no. 2 (1981):183–206.

67. *Report of the Joint Select Committee to Inquire into the Condition of Affairs in the Late Insurrectionary States, Made to the Two Houses of Congress February 19, 1872* (Washington, DC, 1872), 539.

68. Jemison, *Christian Citizens*, 79.

69. Blight, *Race and Reunion*, 114; Martha Hodes, "The Sexualization of Reconstruction Politics: White Women and Black Men in the South after the Civil War," *Journal of the History of Sexuality* 3, no. 3 (1993):402–17.

70. Bernard M. Baruch, *Baruch: My Own Story* (New York: Holt, Rinehart and Winston, 1957), 32.

71. The account here and below of Bierfield's death relies on the following: "The Avengers of Blood," *Memphis Daily Appeal*, August 20, 1868, 1; O. J. Kennedy, "Slanders Refuted," *Tennessean*, September 24, 1868, 3; *Testimony Taken by the Joint Select Committee to Inquire into the Condition of Affairs in the Late Insurrectionary States, Miscellaneous and Florida* (Washington, DC, 1872); Paul Berger, "The Untold Story of the First Jewish Lynching in America," *Forward*, December 8, 2014.

72. The account here and below of Fleischman's death relies on the following: *Testimony Taken by the Joint Select Committee*, 81–82, 90, 145; Daniel R. Weinfeld, "Samuel Fleishman: Tragedy in Reconstruction-Era Florida," *Southern Jewish History* 8 (2005):31–62. Weinfeld mentions all three murders in his article.

73. *Testimony Taken by the Joint Select Committee*, 197.

74. "The Avengers of Blood," *Memphis Daily Appeal*, August 20, 1868, 1; Weinfeld, "Samuel Fleishman," 51.

75. *Testimony Taken by the Joint Select Committee*, 190.

76. "Avengers of Blood."

77. *Testimony Taken by the Joint Select Committee*, 138.

78. Weinfeld, "Samuel Fleischman," 53.

79. Weinfeld, "Certain Ambivalence," 117–18; Hieke, *Jewish Identity*, 92

80. Patrick Q. Mason, "Sinners in the Hands of an Angry Mob: Violence against Religious Outsiders in the U.S. South, 1865–1910," PhD dissertation, University of Notre Dame, 2005; "A Commendable Act," *Times-Picayune*, July 11, 1876, 4; "Death of Henry Hyams," *American Israelite*, July 21, 1876, 6; "Let There Be Light," *American Israelite*, August 18, 1876, 6. Jacob Kriss was allegedly murdered by a group of Black men: Clive Webb, "Jewish Merchants and Black Customers," in *Fight against Fear: Southern Jews and Black Civil Rights* (Athens: University of Georgia Press, 2011), 60; Michael R. Cohen, *Cotton Capitalists: American Jewish Entrepreneurship in the Reconstruction Era* (New York: New York University Press, 2017).

81. *Index to the Reports of the Committees of the Senate of the United States, for the Second Session of the Forty-Second Congress* (Washington, 1872), 1858.

82. Hieke, *Jewish Identity*, 89.

83. Hieke, 157.

84. Cohen, *Cotton Capitalists*, 108, 110. In Natchez "the Jewish merchant community became the prime purveyors of plantation supplies and mercantile credit to the emerging black croppers": Aaron D. Anderson, *Builders of a New South: Merchants, Capital, and the Remaking of Natchez, 1865–1914* (Oxford, MS: University Press of Mississippi, 2013), 55.

85. Nieman, *From Slavery to Sharecropping*. Jewish merchants in Natchez owned plantations that they acquired as payments for planter debts (Anderson, *Builders of a New South*).

Chapter 10

1. Leon Schwarz Memoir, MS-570, p. 4, Leon Schwarz Papers, folder 1, American Jewish Archives, Cincinnati, OH.

2. Leon Schwarz Memoir, p. 4. Apparently, he "functioned a bit 'too well'" in one election, since Democrats won in their district, which contained over seven times as many Black as white voters.

3. Eric Foner, *Reconstruction: America's Unfinished Revolution, 1863–1877* (New York: Harper, 1988), 564–601; Brian K. Fennessy, "'Works Meet for Repentance': Congressional Amnesty and Reconstructed Rebels," in *Freedoms Gained and Lost: Reconstruction and Its Meanings 150 Years Later*, edited by Adam H. Domby and Simon Lewis (New York: Fordham University Press, 2021), 173; Elizabeth L. Jemison, *Christian Citizens: Reading the Bible in Black and White in the Postemancipation South* (Chapel Hill: University of North Carolina Press, 2020), 76–77.

4. Charles Lane, *The Day Freedom Died: The Colfax Massacre, the Supreme Court, and the Betrayal of Reconstruction* (New York: Henry Holt, 2008); David T. Ballantyne, "Remembering the Colfax Massacre: Race, Sex, and the Meaning of Reconstruction Violence," *Journal of Southern History* 87, no. 3 (2021):427–66.

5. Ed Blum, *Reforging the White Republic: Race, Religion, and American Nationalism, 1865–1898* (Baton Rouge: Louisiana State University Press, 2005); David Blight, *Race and Reunion: The Civil War in American Memory* (Cambridge, MA: Harvard University Press, 2001), 126.

6. Nicolas Barreye, "The Politics of Economic Crises: The Panic of 1873, the End of Reconstruction, and the Realignment of American Politics," *Journal of the Gilded Age and Progressive Era* 10, no. 4 (2011): 403–23.

7. "Assignee's Notice of Appointment," *Selma Dollar Times*, November 6, 1878, 4; "District Court of the United States," *Montgomery Advertiser*, October 2, 1878, 4; Richard L. Bushman, *The Refinement of America: Persons, Houses, Cities* (New York: Vintage Books, 1993); Linda Young, *Middle Class Culture in the Nineteenth Century: America, Australia, and Britain* (New York: Palgrave Macmillan, 2003); Burton J. Bledstein and Robert D. Johnston, eds., *The Middling Sorts: Explorations in the History of the American Middle Class* (New

York: Routledge, 2001); Stuart M. Blumin, *The Emergence of the Middle Class: Social Experience in the American City, 1760–1900* (New York: Cambridge University Press, 1989).

8. They served as a reliable customer for the cotton that functioned as currency in small southern towns: Elliot Ashkenazi, *The Business Jews of Louisiana, 1840–1875* (Tuscaloosa: University of Alabama Press, 1988).

9. Michael R. Cohen, *Cotton Capitalists: American Jewish Entrepreneurship in the Reconstruction Era* (New York: New York University Press, 2017). See also Adam D. Mendelsohn, *The Rag Race: How Jews Sewed Their Way to Success in America and the British Empire* (New York: New York University Press, 2015).

10. Cohen, *Cotton Capitalists*; Mendelsohn, *Rag Race*; Aaron D. Anderson, *Builders of a New South: Merchants, Capital, and the Remaking of Natchez, 1865–1914* (Oxford, MS: University Press of Mississippi, 2013).

11. Steven Hertzberg, *Strangers within the Gate City: The Jews of Atlanta, 1845–1915* (Philadelphia: Jewish Publication Society, 1978), 40.

12. "Autobiography of David Steinheimer," Mss 26, Cuba Archives of the Breman Museum, Atlanta, GA; Atlanta Ward 2, 1870, Fulton, GA, roll M593_151, p. 189A, Ancestry.com, *1870 United States Federal Census* [database online] (Lehi, UT: Ancestry.com Operations, 2009), https://www.ancestry.com/discoveryui -content/view/3239834:7163?tid=&pid=&queryId=fc6eb54e-b95d-4b6e-9cf6-01505ddf6457&_phsrc =FHZ285&_phstart=successSource; 1880 US Census, population schedules, Atlanta, GA, NARA micro- film publication roll 148, p. 218B (Washington, DC: National Archives and Records Administration), An- cestry.com and The Church of Jesus Christ of Latter-day Saints, *1880 United States Federal Census* [database online] (Lehi, UT: Ancestry.com Operations, 2010), https://www.ancestry.com/discoveryui-content/view /7746203:6742?tid=&pid=&queryId=042b1ee2-1cc7-465a-ac28-e543c3ab63fb&_phsrc=FHZ281& _phstart=successSource.

13. Anderson, *Builders of a New South*, 6.

14. Hertzberg, *Strangers*, 182.

15. 1870 US Census, population schedules, Albany, Dougherty, GA, NARA microfilm publication roll M593_147, p. 461B (Washington, DC: National Archives and Records Administration), Ancestry.com, *1870 United States Federal Census* [database online] (Lehi, UT: Ancestry.com Operations), https://www.ancestry .com/discoveryui-content/view/4558773:7163?tid=&pid=&queryId=1165c4fd-6eb4-476d-ae90 -f746216af40b&_phsrc=FHZ288&_phstart=successSource.

16. Leon Schwarz Memoir, p. 4. In Natchez as well, many Jewish mercantile families employed Black domestic workers by 1880: Anderson, *Builders of a New South*, 158.

17. Rebecca Sharpless, *Cooking in Other Women's Kitchens: Domestic Workers in the South, 1865–1960* (Chapel Hill: University of North Carolina Press, 2010).

18. He served as an election judge, attended a Republican convention that nominated a racially inte- grated slate, became a member of the state board of education, and was the secretary of Arkansas Industrial University's Board of Trustees under the leadership of a Black president: *Daily Arkansas Gazette*, January 14, 1873, 4; *Daily Arkansas Gazette*, November 7, 1873, 4; *Daily Arkansas Gazette*, October 26, 1873, 4; letterhead, August 15, 1873, MS-72, box A1-3, folder 2, Union for Reform Judaism Records, American Jewish Archives, Cincinnati, OH; *Israelite*, July 25, 1873, 5; Thomas Rothrock, "Joseph Carter Corbin and Negro Education in the University of Arkansas," *Arkansas Historical Quarterly* 30, no. 4 (1971):277–314.

19. *Daily Arkansas Gazette*, October 15, 1874, 4.

20. Jacob Morrow-Spitzer, "'Free from Proscription and Prejudice': Politics and Race in the Election of One Jewish Mayor in Late Reconstruction Louisiana," *Southern Jewish History* 22 (2019):5–41; *Louisiana Democrat*, October 15, 1879, 2.

21. Confederate military service and time spent in the North seem to have been more reliable determi- nants of political affiliation than timing of migration: Alabama Democratic legislator Adolph Proskauer and the murdered Republican mayor of Donaldsonville, Marx Schoenberg, had both arrived in the South before the Civil War, but whereas Proskauer was a Confederate veteran, Schoenberg was not, and like Cohn he had previously lived in Cincinnati. Morrow-Spitzer notes the conflicting example of Samuel Levy, who served as mayor of Shreveport for a few months in 1873 and was both a Confederate veteran and a radical Republican.

22. Nat Coulter, "The Impact of the Civil War upon Pulaski County, Arkansas," *Arkansas Historical Quarterly* 41, no. 1 (1982):67–82; Carl H. Moneyhon, *The Impact of the Civil War and Reconstruction on Arkansas: Persistence in the Midst of Ruin* (Fayetteville: University of Arkansas Press, 2002).

23. *Daily Arkansas Gazette*, June 10, 1871, 2. A. Kowalski was included on a list of men proposing a state Republican convention in 1872 and offering their support for liberal Republican Horace Greeley, who received Democratic support: "National and State Reform," *New Orleans Republican*, July 12, 1872, 5.

24. Morrow-Spitzer, "Free from Proscription," 32.

25. Hertzberg, *Strangers*, 33; Emily Ford and Barry Stiefel, *The Jews of New Orleans and the Mississippi Delta* (Charleston, SC: History Press, 2012); Louis Ginsberg, *History of the Jews of Petersburg, 1789–1950* (Petersburg, VA, 1954).

26. Saul Jacob Rubin, *Third to None: The Saga of Savannah Jewry* (Savannah, GA: S. J. Rubin, 1983), 180–85; Hieke, *Jewish Identity*, 245, 251.

27. Daniel Stowell, *Rebuilding Zion: The Religious Reconstruction of the South, 1863–1877* (New York: Oxford University Press, 1998), 81, 182; Nicole Turner, *Soul Liberty: The Evolution of Black Religious Politics in Postemancipation Virginia* (Chapel Hill: University of North Carolina Press, 2020); Jonathan Sarna, *American Judaism: A History* (New Haven, CT: Yale University Press, 2004), 124; Lauren Winner, "Taking Up the Cross: Conversion among Black and White Jews in the Civil War South," in *Southern Families at War: Loyalty and Conflict in the Civil War South*, edited by Catherine Clinton (New York: Oxford University Press, 2000).

28. Ford and Stiefel, *Jews of New Orleans*; Rubin, *Third to None*, 175, 184–85.

29. Temple Minutes, August 31, 1877, Mss 59, box 7, folder 10, Ida Pearle and Joseph Cuba Archives, Atlanta, GA.

30. Leon Schwarz Memoir, p. 10.

31. "Civilization" linked gender, race, and power: Gail Bederman, *Manliness and Civilization: A Cultural History of Gender and Race in the United States, 1880–1917* (Chicago: University of Chicago Press, 1995), 23.

32. Joseph Jacobsohn to Isaac Leeser, June 28, 1865, Gershwind-Bennett Isaac Leeser Digital Repository, Penn Libraries, accessed September 13, 2021, http://leeser.library.upenn.edu/documentDisplay.php?id=LSKAP0230. His replacement at Shaarey Chased, enthusiastic Confederate and religious reformer James K. Gutheim, would leave for New York in 1868, although he returned four years later: Ford and Stiefel, *Jews of New Orleans*, 85.

33. August 3, 1875, News Clipping, Mss 151, Congregation Beth Israel, Macon, Ida Pearle and Joseph Cuba Archives, Atlanta, GA; Steven H. Moffson, "Identity and Assimilation in Synagogue Architecture in Georgia, 1870–1920," *Perspectives in Vernacular Architecture* 9 (2003):157.

34. Shari Rabin, *Jews on the Frontier: Religion and Mobility in Nineteenth-Century America* (New York: New York University Press, 2017).

35. Joseph Buchler, "The Struggle for Unity: Attempts at Union in American Jewish Life, 1654–1868," *American Jewish Archives* 1 (1949):21–46; Shari Rabin, "The *American Israelite* and American Israelites in the Era of Citizenship," in *Yearning to Breathe Free: Jews in Gilded Age America*, edited by Adam Mendelsohn and Jonathan D. Sarna (Princeton, NJ: Princeton University Press, 2023), 273–305.

36. "The Congregational Conference," *Israelite*, August 1, 1873, 5.

37. M. A. Cohn, August 15, 1873, Union for Reform Judaism, MS-72, box A1-3, folder 2, American Jewish Archives, Cincinnati, OH.

38. Edouard Weil, October 14, 1873, MS-72, box A1-3, folder 1, Union for Reform Judaism Records.

39. Nathan Levin, November 3, 1873, MS-72, box A1-3, folder 1, Union for Reform Judaism Records.

40. Joseph H. M. Chumaceiro, August 31, 1873, MS-72, box A1-3, folder 1, Union for Reform Judaism Records.

41. Isaac Jacob, September 17, 1873, MS-72, box A1-3, folder 3, Union for Reform Judaism Records.

42. "A Call for Help," *Israelite*, September 19, 1873, 6.

43. DeathRoll, November 14, 1873, report of A. E. Frankland, B'nai B'rith MS-900 A2c-1, folder 3, American Jewish Archives, Cincinnati, OH.

44. Correspondence, *Israelite*, October 24, 1873, 5.

45. Valdosta, GA, Letter, *Israelite*, November 21, 1873.

46. Reprinted as "An Incident of the Yellow Fever Epidemic," *Israelite*, October 31, 1873, 2.

47. Margaret Humphreys, *Yellow Fever and the South* (Baltimore, MD: Johns Hopkins University Press, 1999).

48. "Memphis and Shreveport," *Israelite*, October, 17, 1873, 4.

49. Chronology of the Daughters of 1853, "May 29, 1853—Ahavas Achus Society, 'Love of Sisters', founded by Marianna Ullman for the purpose of standing watch over the sick and the dead," Daughters of '53, New Haven Museum Whitney Library, MSS 1, Charleston LHBS, October 15, 1878, Jewish Heritage Collection, College of Charleston, Charleston, SC.

50. Alan Kraut, "A.E. Frankland's History of the 1873 Yellow Fever Epidemic in Memphis, Tennessee," *American Jewish Archives* 59, no. 1–2 (2007):89–98; Writings, Abraham E. Frankland Papers, MS-464, American Jewish Archives, Cincinnati, OH.

51. *Israelite*, November 7, 1873, 4. Edward Blum points to the later 1878 yellow fever epidemic as a key site of reconciliation for white evangelicals (*Reforging the White Republic*).

52. Elias Eppstein Diaries, January 25, 1874, 1871–1903, MS-220, American Jewish Archives, Cincinnati, OH.

53. MS-900, B1h-9, folder 12, American Jewish Archives, Cincinnati, OH.

54. Edward Blum, "The Crucible of Disease: Trauma, Memory, and National Reconciliation during the Yellow Fever Epidemic of 1878," *Journal of Southern History* 69 (2003):797; *American Israelite*, August 23, 1878, 6.

55. Louis Schmier, ed., *Reflections on Southern Jewry: The Letters of Charles Wessolowsky, 1878–1879* (Macon, GA: Mercer University Press, 1982), 60.

56. Blum, "Crucible of Disease." Charleston's Ladies Hebrew Benevolent Society expressed gratitude to God for "a summer blessed with health for our city" and expressed "deep sympathy [for] their afflicted sister cities," sending $25 to B'nai B'rith leaders in New Orleans: Charleston Ladies Hebrew Benevolent Society, box 3, folder 1, October 15, 1878, Jewish Heritage Collection, College of Charleston Special Collections, Charleston, SC.

57. *American Israelite*, August 30, 1878, 6; *American Israelite*, September 6, 1878, 6.

58. *American Israelite*, December 6, 1878, 2; *American Israelite*, September 20, 1878, 6.

59. Rabin, "*American Israelite*."

60. Deborah Dash Moore, *B'nai B'rith and the Challenge of Ethnic Leadership* (Albany: State University of New York Press, 1981), 35. *Virginia Mourning Its Dead* would be erected at his alma mater, the Virginia Military Institute, in 1903: Samantha Baskind, "Moses Jacob Ezekiel's *Religious Liberty* (1876) and the Nineteenth-Century Jewish American Experience," in *A Companion to Nineteenth-Century Art*, edited by Michelle Focos, 1–16 (Hoboken, NJ: John Wiley, 2019).

61. *Israelite*, August 4, 1876, 4, cited in Morrow-Spitzer, "Free from Proscription."

62. Richard Zuczek, "The Last Campaign of the Civil War: South Carolina and the Revolution of 1876," *Civil War History* 42, no. 1 (1996):18–31; Richard Kilgo Ackerman, *Wade Hampton III* (Columbia: University of South Carolina Press, 2007), 188–92.

63. Ackerman, *Wade Hampton III*, 217.

64. Theodore Rosengarten and Dale Rosengarten, *A Portion of the People: Three Hundred Years of Southern Jewish Life* (Columbia: University of South Carolina Press, 2002).

65. Foner, *Reconstruction*, 564–86.

Chapter 11

1. Christopher Waldrep, *Vicksburg's Long Shadow: The Civil War Legacy of Race and Remembrance* (New York: Rowman and Littlefield), 72–79.

2. Wessolowsky served as associate editor under the colorful Atlanta religious functionary E.B.M. Browne, who founded the newspaper. Quote from Janice Rothschild Blumberg, "E.B.M. Browne: The Atlanta Years," *Southern Jewish History* 5 (2002):16. The number of Jewish publications in America tripled between the 1870s and 1890s: Jonathan Sarna, *American Judaism: A History* (New Haven, CT: Yale University Press, 2004), 138; Louis Schmier, ed., *Reflections on Southern Jewry: The Letters of Charles Wessolowsky, 1878–1879* (Macon, GA: Mercer University Press, 1982), 59–61.

3. Janet Rothschild Blumberg, *Prophet in a Time of Priests: Rabbi "Alphabet" Browne; a Biography* (Baltimore, MD: Apprentice House, 2012), 28. In 1888 Max Samfield, editor of the *Spectator*, complained about "the indifference of the Southern rabbis who seem not to care whether the South has its own organ or not": Samfield to Max Heller, Memphis, February 22, 1888, Heller Papers, box 5, folder 3, American Jewish Archives, Cincinnati, OH. See also Selma Lewis, *A Biblical People in the Bible Belt: The Jewish Community of Memphis, Tennessee, 1840s–1960s* (Macon, GA: Mercer University Press, 1998); Steven Hertzberg, *Strangers within the Gate City: The Jews of Atlanta, 1845–1915* (Philadelphia: Jewish Publication Society, 1978); Myron Berman, *Richmond's Jewry, 1769–1976: Shabbat in Shockoe* (Richmond, VA: Jewish Community Federation of Richmond, 1979).

4. Statistics, MS-72, box D-3, folder 1, Union for Reform Judaism records, American Jewish Archives, Cincinnati, OH. Increasing numbers of those buried in Charleston's Coming Street cemetery had died in other cities, like St. Augustine, Chattanooga, and Atlanta: Barnett A. Elzas, *The Old Jewish Cemeteries at Charleston, S.C.* (Charleston: Daggett Printing, 1903), 41.

5. Elzas, 41.

6. Schmier, *Reflections on Southern Jewry*. In Mobile he met Adolph Proskauer and Nat Strauss, who more than a decade earlier had exchanged wartime letters, and in Selma, Louis Gerstmann, whose brother Simon had continued his quest to gain payment for wartime confiscations from the federal government. In Alexandria, Louisiana, he met Edouard Weil. In Austin, Texas, "we enjoyed a ride through the city offered to us by the courtesy of Mr. DeCordova" (Schmier, 100).

7. "Dedication Services of the Synagogue," *Selma Times*, June 8, 1879, 3; Schmier, *Reflections on Southern Jewry*, 91–92. See letter from Giddings, Texas, demanding that Max Heller perform the writer's wedding ceremony, despite a conflict: July 24, 1889, Max Heller Papers, box 1, folder 4, American Jewish Archives, Cincinnati, OH.

8. "To the Survivors' Associations of Sumter County," *Watchman and Southron*, June 8, 1886, 2.

9. Aaron D. Anderson, *Builders of a New South: Merchants, Capital, and the Remaking of Natchez, 1865–1914* (Oxford, MS: University Press of Mississippi, 2013), 219.

10. Michael R. Cohen, *Cotton Capitalists: American Jewish Entrepreneurship in the Reconstruction Era* (New York: New York University Press, 2017); Berman, *Richmond's Jewry*; Hertzberg, *Strangers*; Clive Webb, "Jewish Merchants and Black Customers in the Age of Jim Crow," *Southern Jewish History* 2 (1999):55–80; Bryan Stone, *Chosen Folks: Jews on the Frontiers of Texas* (Austin: University of Texas Press, 2010).

11. Leonard Rogoff, *Down Home: Jewish Life in North Carolina* (Chapel Hill, NC: University of North Carolina Press, 2010), 149.

12. Schmier, *Reflections on Southern Jewry*; "Independent Order of B'nai B'rith," *American Jewish Year Book*, 1900–1901, 104; *New Orleans Times-Picayune*, January 17, 1875, 1; "Grand Convention of the B'nai B'rith Association," *Times-Picayune*, May 6, 1878, 1. B'nai B'rith leaders offered lofty peons to brotherhood, but also enacted discipline on wayward members and lodges.

13. Caroline Light, *The Pride of Race and Character: The Roots of Jewish Benevolence in the Jim Crow South* (New York: New York University Press, 2014), 44.

14. Light; Idana Goldberg, "Gender, Religion and the Jewish Public Sphere in Mid-Nineteenth Century America," PhD dissertation, University of Pennsylvania, 2004.

15. Schmier, *Reflections on Southern Jewry*, 111.

16. Evelyn Brooks Higginbotham, *Righteous Discontent: The Women's Movement in the Black Baptist Church, 1880–1920* (Cambridge, MA: Harvard University Press, 1994); Karla Goldman, *Beyond the Synagogue Gallery: Finding a Place for Women in American Judaism* (Cambridge, MA: Harvard University Press, 2001).

17. A number of these men have been subjects of biographies and articles: Henry Cohen II, *Kindler of Souls: Rabbi Henry Cohen of Texas* (Austin: University of Texas Press, 2007); Barbara Malone, *Rabbi Max Heller: Reformer, Zionist, Southerner, 1860–1929* (Tuscaloosa: University of Alabama Press, 1997); Myron Berman, "Rabbi Edward Nathan Calisch and the Debate over Zionism in Richmond, Virginia," *American Jewish Historical Quarterly* 62, no. 3 (1973):295–305; G. Wilkes, "Rabbi Dr. David Marx and the Unity Club," *Southern Jewish History* 9 (2006):35–68.

18. Hollace A. Weiner, "The Mixers: The Role of Rabbis Deep in the Heart of Texas," *American Jewish History* 85, no. 3 (1997):289–332.

19. December 2, 1899; May 11, 1897; Max Heller Papers, box 5, folder 1, American Jewish Archives, Cincinnati, OH.

20. March 6, 1895, Max Heller Papers, box 2, folder 8.

21. September 23, 1899, Max Heller Papers, box 1, folder 4.

22. Temple Minutes, April 3, 1900, The Temple, Cuba Archives of the Breman Museum, Atlanta, GA; Hertzberg, *Strangers*, 69–72.

23. Saul Jacob Rubin, *Third to None: The Saga of Savannah Jewry* (Savannah, GA: S. J. Rubin, 1983), 182; Gary P. Zola, "The Ascendancy of Reform Judaism in the American South during the Nineteenth Century," in *Jewish Roots in Southern Soil: A New History*, edited by Marcie Cohen Ferris and Mark I. Greenberg, 156–91 (Waltham, MA: Brandeis University Press, 2006).

24. Lee Shai Weissbach, "East European Immigrants and the Image of Jews in the Small-Town South," in *Dixie Diaspora: An Anthology of Southern Jewish History*, edited by Mark Bauman (Tuscaloosa: University of Alabama Press, 2006), 110; Rogoff, *Down Home*, 169.

25. Kahal Kadosh Beth Elohim records, 1904, Jewish Heritage Collection, College of Charleston Special Collections, Charleston, SC.

26. "Declaration of Principles" (1885), Central Conference of American Rabbis, accessed February 23, 2024, https://www.ccarnet.org/rabbinic-voice/platforms/article-declaration-principles/.

27. Gary P. Zola, "Southern Rabbis and the Founding of the First National Association of Rabbis," *American Jewish History* 85, no. 4 (1997):353–72.

28. Zola. They also encouraged the acquisition of historical documents. Conference of Rabbis of Southern Congregations, SC-2435, SC-2436, American Jewish Archives, Cincinnati, OH.

29. In 1903 a layman named William E. Myers published a text called *The Israelites of Louisiana*, because, he argued, "every class and element in the heterogenous population of our Pelican State has had its encomiast and memorialist . . . except the Jew": Adam D. Mendelsohn, *Jewish Soldiers in the Civil War: The Union Army* (New York: New York University Press, 2022), 218.

30. Beth Wenger, *History Lessons: The Creation of American Jewish Heritage* (Princeton, NJ: Princeton University Press, 2010); Laurie Maffly-Kipp, *Setting Down the Sacred Past: African-American Race Histories* (Cambridge, MA: Harvard University Press, 2010); Adam Domby, *The False Cause: Fraud, Fabrication, and White Supremacy in Confederate Memory* (Charlottesville, University of Virginia Press, 2022).

31. *Charlotte Democrat*, March 2, 1894, 3; Karen L. Cox, *Dixie's Daughters: The United Daughters of the Confederacy and the Preservation of Confederate Culture* (Gainesville: University of Florida Press, 2003). "By 1896, three-quarters of the counties in the former Confederate states could claim 'camps' of the United Confederate Veterans; somewhere between a fourth and a third of all living veterans joined": Edward L. Ayers, *The Promise of the New South: Life after Reconstruction* (New York: Oxford University Press, 1992), 334.

32. Berman, *Richmond's Jewry*, 227; Rogoff, *Down Home*.

33. Adam Mendelsohn, "Introduction: Before Korn: A Century of Jewish Historical Writing about the American Civil War," in *Jews and the Civil War: A Reader*, edited by Mendelsohn and Jonathan D. Sarna, 1–26 (New York: New York University Press, 2010); David Weinfeld, "Two Commemorations: Richmond Jews and the Lost Cause during the Civil Rights Era," *Southern Jewish History* 20, no. 3 (2020):77–123.

34. David Blight, *Race and Reunion: The Civil War in American Memory* (Cambridge, MA: Harvard University Press, 2001), 135. William Flegenheimer was first vice-president of a "Hayes and Wheeler Campaign Club" in Richmond: *Richmond Dispatch*, June 20, 1876, 1. Jewish mayors also served in this period in Wilmington, North Carolina, and in Marianna, Florida, where Samuel Fleishman had been murdered a decade earlier. In Wilmington in 1878, S. H. Fishblate was elected mayor (Rogoff, *Down Home*, 162).

35. Hertzberg, *Strangers*; Scott M. Langston, "Being Jewish in Columbus, Georgia: The Business, Politics, and Religion of Jacob and Isaac Moses, 1828–1890," *Southern Jewish History* 18 (2015):42.

36. *Richmond Dispatch*, May 27, 1879, 1; Berman, *Richmond's Jewry*, 236.

37. Jane Dailey, "The Limits of Liberalism in the New South: The Politics of Race, Sex, and Patronage in Virginia, 1879–1883," in *Jumpin' Jim Crow: Southern Politics from Civil War to Civil Rights*, edited by Dailey, Glenda Elizabeth Gilmore, and Bryant Simon (Princeton, NJ: Princeton University Press, 2000), 103.

38. Elizabeth L. Jemison, *Christian Citizens: Reading the Bible in Black and White in the Postemancipation South* (Chapel Hill: University of North Carolina Press, 2020), 125–26.

39. *American Israelite*, July 6, 1883, 5.

40. Eric Goldstein, *Price of Whiteness: Jews, Race, and American Identity* (Princeton, NJ: Princeton University Press, 2006), 55.

41. Leonard Rogoff, "A Tale of Two Cities: Race, Riots, and Religion in New Bern and Wilmington, North Carolina, 1898," *Southern Jewish History* 14 (2011):37–75.

42. Goldstein, *Price of Whiteness.*

43. William Levy, "A Jew Views Black Education: Texas—1890," *Western States Jewish Historical Quarterly* 8, no. 4 (1978):354.

44. Jacob S. Raisin, "My Life's Tragi-comedy," Rabbi Jacob S. Raisin Diary, 1892–1905, May 25, 1903, Lowcountry Digital Library, College of Charleston Libraries.

45. Bobbi Malone, "Rabbi Max Heller, Zionism, and the 'Negro Question': New Orleans, 1891–1911," in *The Quiet Voices: Southern Rabbis and Black Civil Rights, 1880s to 1990s*, edited by Mark K. Bauman (Tuscaloosa: University of Alabama Press, 2007), 26.

46. Malone, "Rabbi Max Heller," 32; Goldstein, *Price of Whiteness*, 61.

47. *Jewish South*, October 14, 1898, 3.

48. "Black Jew," *Nashville Banner*, August 16, 1900, 5. Isaac Mayer Wise responded in the *Israelite*, claiming that he was probably not really Black: "That Colored Jew," *American Israelite*, July 19, 1900, 7.

49. Judith Wiesenfeld, *New World a' Coming: Black Religion and Racial Identity during the Great Migration* (New York: New York University Press, 2018). Members of the Temple in Atlanta participated in minstrel shows, and the prizewinners in Richmond's Purim costume contest included a man dressed as a "negro dude" and a woman dressed as a "colored nurse": Goldstein, *Price of Whiteness*, 58; *Jewish South*, March 11, 1898, 3. See also Michael Alexander, *Jazz Age Jews* (Princeton, NJ: Princeton University Press, 2001); Michael Rogin, *Blackface, White Noise: Jewish Immigrants in the Hollywood Melting Pot* (Berkeley: University of California Press, 1996).

50. Matthew Frye Jacobson, *Whiteness of a Different Color: European Immigrants and the Alchemy of Race* (Cambridge, MA: Harvard University Press, 1998); Goldstein, *Price of Whiteness*; Britt P. Tevis, "'Jews Not Admitted': Anti-Semitism, Civil Rights, and Public Accommodation Laws," *Journal of American History* 107, no. 4 (2021):847–70; Gail Bederman, *Manliness and Civilization: A Cultural History of Gender and Race in the United States, 1880–1917* (Chicago: University of Chicago Press, 1995); Tisa Wenger, *Religious Freedom: The Contested History of an American Ideal* (Chapel Hill: University of North Carolina Press, 2017).

51. News of anti-Jewish acts and sentiments in Europe, along with suspicion of newly arriving Jewish immigrants, circulated in American and southern newspapers: *Weekly Times-Democrat*, May 15, 1886, 5; *The Times*, January 20, 1887, 1; *Livingston Journal* (Alabama), February 17, 1887, 3; "A Scathing Rebuke," *Austin American-Statesman*, October 16, 1887, 2; *Montgomery Advertiser*, August 26, 1888, 1. See Leonard Dinnerstein, *Antisemitism in America* (New York: Oxford University Press, 1994).

52. "Jew and Gentile," *New York Herald*, June 20, 1877, 3.

53. *New Orleans Daily Democrat*, June 21, 1877, 4. This was ironic because it was actually Seligman who was an associate of U.S. Grant: Tevis, "'Jews Not Admitted,'" 852

54. *Atlanta Constitution*, June 26, 1877, 1.

55. *Macon Telegraph*, September 18, 1899, 2. The *Macon Telegraph* was just one southern newspaper that offered regular coverage in the late 1890s. For instance, November 19, 1897, 1; January 5, 1899, 2; November 21, 1897, 4; see also Paula Hyman, *The Jews of Modern France* (Berkeley: University of California Press, 1998); Maurice Samuels, *Alfred Dreyfus: The Man at the Center of the Affair* (New Haven, CT: Yale University Press, 2024).

56. *Jewish South*, January 21, 1898, 6.

57. W.E.B. Du Bois, *The Souls of Black Folks*, 8th ed. (Chicago: A. C. McClurg, 1909), 126. On revisions to this material in subsequent editions: George Bornstein, "W.E.B. Du Bois and the Jews: Ethics, Editing, and the Souls of Black Folks," *Textual Cultures* 1, no. 1 (2006):64–74.

58. M. Cohen, *Cotton Capitalists*, 194.

59. William F. Holmes, "Whitecapping: Anti-Semitism in the Populist Era," *American Jewish Historical Quarterly* 63, no. 3 (1974):244–61. In 1893 an "itinerant peddler of the Russian Jew type" was robbed and

murdered in Atlanta, as were a number of Syrian peddlers: Marni Davis, *Jews and Booze: Becoming American in the Age of Prohibition* (New York: New York University Press, 2014).

60. Du Bois, *Souls of Black Folks*, 170.

61. Howard N. Rabinowitz, "Nativism, Bigotry, and Anti-Semitism in the South," in Bauman, *Dixie Diaspora*, 277. In 1890, the president of the University of Virginia told a northern Jewish publication, "All intelligent Christians deplore the fact that the historical evidences of Christianity have so little weight with your people" (Hertzberg, *Strangers*, 175). See also Yaakov Ariel, *Evangelizing the Chosen People: Missions to the Jews in America, 1880–2000* (Chapel Hill: University of North Carolina Press, 2000).

62. William A. Link, *Paradox of Southern Progressivism, 1880–1930* (Chapel Hill: University of North Carolina Press, 1992), 57. See also Ayers, *Promise*; Joe Creech, *Righteous Indignation: Religion and the Populist Revolution* (Urbana: University of Illinois Press, 2006); Joe L. Coker, *Liquor in the Land of the Lost Cause: Southern White Evangelicals and the Prohibition Movement* (Lexington: University of Kentucky Press, 2007); Davis, *Jews and Booze*; Dinnerstein, *Antisemitism in America*; John Paul Giggie, *After Redemption: Jim Crow and the Transformation of African American Religion in the Delta, 1875–1915* (New York: Oxford University Press, 2008).

63. *Macon Telegraph*, September 29, 1892, 6; Goldstein, *Price of Whiteness*, 53.

64. *Macon Telegraph*, September 29, 1892, 6.

65. "The Literary Side," *Times-Picayune*, May 27, 1896, 1; Roger W. Tuttle, ed., *Biographies of Graduates of the Yale Law School 1824–1899* (New Haven, CT: Tuttle, Morehouse and Taylor, 1911), 650; "Penalty of a Race," *Commercial Appeal* (Memphis), February 20, 1898, 11; Deborah Dash Moore, *B'nai B'rith and the Challenge of Ethnic Leadership* (Albany: State University of New York Press, 1981), 77.

66. Hasia Diner, *Jews of the United States, 1654–2000* (Berkeley: University of California Press, 2004).

67. Eli Lederhendler, *Jewish Immigrants and American Capitalism, 1880–1920: From Cast to Class* (New York: Cambridge University Press, 2009); Tony Michels, *A Fire in Their Hearts: Yiddish Socialists in New York* (Cambridge, MA: Harvard University Press, 2005).

68. Hertzberg, *Strangers*, 126.

69. Goldstein, *Price of Whiteness*; Dinnerstein, *Antisemitism in America*; John Higham, *Strangers in the Land: Patterns of American Nativism, 1860–1925* (New Brunswick, NJ: Rutgers University Press, 1955).

70. Cited in Marni Davis, "Toward an 'Immigrant Turn' in Jewish Entrepreneurial History: A View from the New South," *American Jewish History* 103, no. 4 (2019):446.

71. Booker T. Washington, "The Atlanta Compromise Speech" (1895), Black Past, accessed February 15, 2024, https://www.blackpast.org/african-american-history/1895-booker-t-washington-atlanta-compromise-speech/.

72. *Atlanta Constitution*, March 1, 1882, 4.

73. Rabbi Morris Newfield of Birmingham warned his congregation, perhaps with Jewish political radicals in mind, "A faithless Jew is a faithless man; such men create prejudice and ill-will": Mark Cowett, "Rabbi Morris Newfield and the Social Gospel: Theology and the Societal Reform in the South," *American Jewish Archives* 34 (1982):58.

74. Hertzberg, *Strangers*, 126.

75. Schmier, *Reflections on Southern Jewry*, 86.

76. Derek Penslar, *Shylock's Children: Economics and Jewish Identity in Modern Europe* (Berkeley: University of California Press, 2001).

77. *Macon Telegraph and Messenger*, December 2, 1881, 1.

78. *The Jewish Burials of Macon, Georgia in these Rose Hill Cemeteries*, folder 19, Mss 135, Gus B. Kaufman Family Papers, the Breman Museum, Atlanta, GA. On Bialystok: Rebecca Kobrin, *Jewish Bialystok and Its Diaspora* (Bloomington: Indiana University Press, 2010).

Chapter 12

1. Jeffrey Gurock, *Orthodoxy in Charleston: Brith Sholom Beth Israel and American Jewish History* (Charleston, SC: College of Charleston Library, 2004).

2. Steven Zipperstein, *Pogrom: Kishinev and the Tilt of History* (New York: Liveright, 2018). Tobias Geffen claimed to have been motivated to leave Lithuania "as a result of the Kishinev pogrom": autobiography of Rabbi Geffen, SC-3884, American Jewish Archives, Cincinnati, OH.

3. Tisa Wenger, *Religious Freedom: The Contested History of an American Ideal* (Chapel Hill: University of North Carolina Press, 2017), 151.

4. "Will Move Slowly," *Savannah Morning News*, December 31, 1903, 12.

5. *American Jewish Year Book*, 1899; Don H. Doyle, *New Men, New Cities, New South: Atlanta, Nashville, Charlotte, Mobile, 1860–1910* (Chapel Hill: University of North Carolina Press, 1990), 12.

6. Matthew Frye Jacobson, *Barbarian Virtues: The United States Encounters Foreign Peoples at Home and Abroad, 1876–1917* (New York: Hill and Wang, 2000).

7. Beth Wenger, "Jewish Women and Voluntarism: Beyond the Myth of Enablers," *American Jewish History* 79, no. 1 (1989):13–36.

8. "Cheap Baths Lead to Sad Division," *Atlanta Constitution*, May 11, 1896, 7. See also Faith Rogow, *Gone to Another Meeting: The National Council of Jewish Women, 1893–1993* (Tuscaloosa: University of Alabama Press, 1993); Idana Goldberg, "Gender, Religion and the Jewish Public Sphere in Mid-Nineteenth Century America," PhD dissertation, University of Pennsylvania, 2004.

9. Robert H. Wiebe, *The Search for Order, 1877–1920* (New York: Farrar, Straus, and Giroux, 1967); Susan Curtis, *A Consuming Faith: The Social Gospel and Modern American Culture* (Columbia: University of Missouri Press, 2001).

10. February 8, 1907, Heller Papers, box 2, folder 16, American Jewish Archives, Cincinnati, OH.

11. Stanley Bero to Mr. Bressler, February 22, 1910, Mss 135, folder 10, Gus Kaufman family papers, Ida Pearle and Joseph Cuba Archives, Atlanta, GA. In Fort Worth a correspondent initially explained that there were "nine white schools, one high school": Hollace A. Weiner, "Removal Approval: The Industrial Removal Office Experience in Fort Worth, Texas," *Southern Jewish History* 4 (2001):10.

12. Jack Glazier, *Dispersing the Ghetto: The Relocation of Jewish Immigrants across America* (Ithaca, NY: Cornell University Press, 1998), 196.

13. Philip Fireman to Jaffe, March 23, 1910, Kaufman Papers, folder 10, Cuba Archives of the Breman Museum, Atlanta, GA.

14. Letter to Henry Cohen, April 16, 1914, MSS-263, box 1, folder 4, American Jewish Archives, Cincinnati, OH.

15. Bryan Edward Stone, "The Galveston Diaspora: A Statistical View of Jewish Immigration through Texas, 1907–1913," *Southern Jewish History* 21 (2018):121–77; Sarah Imhoff, *Masculinity and the Making of American Judaism* (Bloomington: Indiana University Press, 2017), 97–127.

16. "Cheap Baths Lead to Sad Division," *Atlanta Constitution*, May 11, 1896, 7; Mark Bauman, "The Ethnic Broker," in *Dixie Diaspora: An Anthology of Southern Jewish History*, edited by Bauman (Tuscaloosa: University of Alabama Press, 2006), 250; Steven Hertzberg, *Strangers within the Gate City: The Jews of Atlanta, 1845–1915* (Philadelphia: Jewish Publication Society, 1978) 129.

17. One man was found to be "incompetent" in his work as a paper hanger, and was sent to Atlanta "where we were told he secured a job as a maker or mixer of paint": To Louis Witt, June 16, 1905, Kaufman Papers, Cuba Archives of the Breman Museum, Atlanta, GA.

18. To Louis Witt, February 1, 1905, Kaufman Papers.

19. Lee Shai Weissbach, "East European Immigrants and the Image of Jews in the Small-Town South," in Bauman, *Dixie Diaspora*, 118.

20. Weiner, "Removal Approval," 24.

21. Department of Commerce and Labor, Bureau of the Census, *Religious Bodies: 1906*, bulletin 103, 2nd ed. (Washington, DC: Government Printing Office, 1910), https://www2.census.gov/library/publications/decennial/1900/bulletins/demographic/103-religious-bodies.pdf.

22. David Lewis Cohn, *God Shakes Creation* (New York: Harper and Brother, 1935), 6.

23. Lee Shai Weissbach, ed., *A Jewish Life on Three Continents: The Memoir of Menachem Mendel Frieden* (Stanford, CA: Stanford University Press, 2013).

24. Chlotilde R. Martin, "The Levines in the Melting Pot," in the Federal Writers' Project papers #3709, folder 877, Southern Historical Collection, Wilson Library, University of North Carolina at Chapel Hill; Weissbach, *Jewish Life on Three Continents*, 227 (quote).

25. Alexander Z. Gurwitz, *Memories of Two Generations: A Yiddish Life in Russia and Texas*, edited by Bryan Stone (Tuscaloosa: University of Alabama Press, 2016), 304.

26. Gurwitz, *Memories of Two Generations*, 305; Joshua Parshall, "Yiddish Politics in Southern States: The Southern District of the Arbeter Ring, 1908–1949," PhD dissertation, University of North Carolina at Chapel Hill, 2017.

27. Weissbach, *Jewish Life on Three Continents*, 243.

28. Autobiography of Rabbi Geffen, p. 14, SC-3884, American Jewish Archives, Cincinnati, OH; Joshua Parshall, "Yiddish Politics in Southern States."

29. Myron Berman, *Richmond's Jewry, 1769–1976: Shabbat in Shockoe* (Richmond, VA: Jewish Community Federation of Richmond, 1979); Selma S. Lewis, *A Biblical People in the Bible Belt: The Jewish Community of Memphis, Tennessee, 1840s–1960s* (Macon, GA: Mercer University Press, 1998); Hertzberg, *Strangers*.

30. Hertzberg, *Strangers*, 77; Marni Davis, "Toward an 'Immigrant Turn' in Jewish Entrepreneurial History: A View from the New South," *American Jewish History* 103, no. 4 (2019):429–56; Yitzchak Kerem, "The Settlement of Rhodian and Other Sephardic Jews in Montgomery and Atlanta in the Twentieth Century," *American Jewish History* 85, no. 4 (1997):373–91; letter to Max Heller, October 31, 1916, box 1, folder 1, American Jewish Archives, Cincinnati, OH; M.J.B. Wooten, "From the Eastern Mediterranean to the Deep South: Ottoman Jewish Emigres in 20th-Century Montgomery and Atlanta," MA thesis, Vanderbilt University, 2021. Sephardic migrants from Rhodes founded the congregation Ahavat Shalom in 1910, followed by Or Hahayim, dominated by Jews from the Turkish mainland. In 1914 they combined to create the Oriental Hebrew Association Or Ve Shalom (Hertzberg, *Strangers*).

31. Berman, *Richmond's Jewry*; Hertzberg, *Strangers*; Lewis, *Biblical People*, 76–77; Wendy Lowe Besmann, *A Separate Circle: Jewish Life in Knoxville, Tennessee* (Knoxville: University of Tennessee Press, 2001), 41.

32. Louis Ginsberg, *History of the Jews of Petersburg, 1789–1950* (Petersburg, VA, 1954). New congregations sprouted up across the region. In Petersburg, a group began meeting in the 1890s and formally incorporated in 1908. Congregational minutes and sermons were in Yiddish and just three families supplied sixteen of the thirty-seven members

33. Lewis, *Biblical People*, 77–82.

34. Hertzberg, *Strangers*, 94

35. Hollace A. Weiner, "The Mixers: The Role of Rabbis Deep in the Heart of Texas," *American Jewish History* 85, no. 3 (1997):289–332.

36. "Penalty of a Race," *Commercial Appeal* (Memphis), February 20, 1898, 11; "Rabbi Max Heller Discusses Zionism," *Times-Picayune*, November 18, 1899, 12; Myron Berman, "Rabbi Edward Nathan Calisch and the Debate over Zionism in Richmond, Virginia," *American Jewish Historical Quarterly* 62, no. 3 (1973):295–305. Zionism was contested in Jewish communities throughout the world, including by diaspora nationalists and socialists. Acculturated American Jews worried that it would raise questions about Jewish loyalty in a period of intense patriotism, and may have been uncomfortable with parallels to Black efforts to emigrate to Africa. The parallel was noted in a letter reprinted in the *American Israelite* (January 19, 1899, 5).

37. *Jewish South*, February 4, 1898, 6.

38. Jonathan D. Sarna, "Converts to Zionism in the American Reform Movement," in *Zionism and Religion*, edited by Shmuel Almog, Jehuda Reinharz, and Anita Shapira (Hanover, NH: Brandeis University Press, 1998), 188–203; Judah Bernstein, "American Zionism on the Jewish Frontier, 1898–1948," paper presented at the Southern Jewish Historical Society Conference, November 4, 2017, Cincinnati, OH; Bryan Stone, *Chosen Folks: Jews on the Frontiers of Texas* (Austin: University of Texas Press, 2010), 95.

39. Parshall, "Yiddish Politics."

40. Baruch Charney Vladek, "How Do the Jews Live in the South?," *Jewish Daily Forward*, March 22, 1911, 5.

41. "Narrative of Bernhard Goldgar," Kaufman Papers, Mss 135, folder 10, Cuba Archives of the Breman Museum, Atlanta, GA; "Anarchist Parsons—A Letter from a North Carolina Communist Found among His Papers—Mrs. Parsons Interviewed," *Weekly Star*, May 21, 1886, 1; Vladek, "How Do the Jews Live."

42. Annie Polland, "'May a Freethinker Help a Pious Man?': The Shared World of the 'Religious' and the 'Secular' among Eastern European Jewish Immigrants to America," *American Jewish History* 93, no. 4 (2007):375–407.

43. Marni Davis, *Jews and Booze: Becoming American in the Age of Prohibition* (New York: New York University Press, 2014); Berman, *Richmond's Jewry*, 268.

44. Horace Mann Bond, "Negro Attitudes toward Jews," *Jewish Social Studies* 27, no. 1 (1965):4; see also Clive Webb, "Jewish Merchants and Black Customers in the Age of Jim Crow," *Southern Jewish History* 2 (1999):62n19.

45. Lynn Robertson, "A Good Living Can Be Made in Trade," *Jewish Historical Society of South Carolina Magazine* 24, no. 1 (2019):5.

46. Isaac Metzker, ed., *A Bintel Brief: Sixty Years of Letters from the Lower East Side to the Jewish "Daily Forward"* (New York: Schocken Books, 1971), 96.

47. Weissbach, *Jewish Life on Three Continents*, 231, 241.

48. Gurwitz, *Memories of Two Generations*, 303.

49. Metzker, *Bintel Brief*, 96.

50. Vladek, "How Do the Jews Live," 5.

51. Caroline Light, *The Pride of Race and Character: The Roots of Jewish Benevolence in the Jim Crow South* (New York: New York University Press, 2014), 73.

52. Pearlstine/Lipov Center for Southern Jewish Culture and Jewish Heritage Collection, College of Charleston, "Jacob Glasser / Max & Rosie Goldstein," Mapping Jewish Charleston, accessed February 24, 2024, https://mappingjewishcharleston.cofc.edu/1910/jacob-glasser-max-rosie-goldstein/; *Charleston City Directory*, 1910, p. 116, Ancestry.com, *U.S., City Directories, 1822–1955* [database online] (Lehi, UT: Ancestry .com Operations, 2011), https://www.ancestry.com/discoveryui-content/view/852636976:2469?tid =&pid=&queryId=e7d3125e-79bd-4300-9b4d-b7a59cda9f57&_phsrc=FHZ290&_phstart=success Source; Michael Fultz, "Charleston, 1919–1920: The Final Battle in the Emergence of the South's Urban African American Teaching Corps," *Journal of Urban History* 27, no. 5 (2001):635–36.

53. "Tragic End," *Times and Democrat* (Orangeburg, SC), June 23, 1910, 1; "Evidence Strong," *Bamberg Herald*, August 18, 1910, 1; "Other Hangings," *Columbia Record*, December 1, 1910, 8.

54. Charleston Ward 11, Thirteenth Census of the United States, 1910 (NARA microfilm publication T624, 1,178 rolls), Records of the Bureau of the Census, Record Group 29, National Archives, Washington, DC, Ancestry.com, *1910 United States Federal Census* [database online] (Lehi, UT: Ancestry.com Operations, 2006), https://www.ancestry.com/discoveryui-content/view/26446805:7884?tid=&pid=&queryId =05d9a199-a3a7-4959-a0d6-96673999e278&_phsrc=FHZ293&_phstart=successSource.

55. Eric Goldstein, *Price of Whiteness: Jews, Race, and American Identity* (Princeton, NJ: Princeton University Press, 2006); Katharine Benton-Cohen, *Inventing the Immigration Problem: The Dillingham Commission and Its Legacy* (Cambridge, MA: Harvard University Press, 2018), 102.

56. Davis, "Toward an 'Immigrant Turn,'" 451. See also Goldstein, *Price of Whiteness*.

57. Stone, *Chosen Folks*, 93; Imhoff, *Masculinity*.

58. *Farmers Union News*, February 16, 1910, clipping found in Kaufman Papers, Mss 135, folder 10, Cuba Archives of the Breman Museum, Atlanta, GA.

59. Hertzberg, *Strangers*, 84; Arthur Remillard, *Southern Civil Religions: Imagining the Good Society in the Post-Reconstruction Era* (Athens: University of Georgia Press, 2011).

60. Davis, *Jews and Booze*, 126; Gregory Mixon, *The Atlanta Riot: Race, Class, and Violence in a New South City* (Gainesville: University Press of Florida, 2005).

61. "Declaration of Principles" (1885), Central Conference of American Rabbis, accessed February 23, 2024, https://www.ccarnet.org/rabbinic-voice/platforms/article-declaration-principles/.

62. Weibe, *Search for Order*; Curtis, *Consuming Faith*; William A. Link, *Paradox of Southern Progressivism, 1880–1930* (Chapel Hill: University of North Carolina Press, 1992).

63. Marni Davis, "'No Whisky Amazons in the Tents of Israel': American Jews and the Gilded Age Temperance Movement," *American Jewish History* 94, no. 3 (2008):143–73.

64. Davis, 168, 150.

65. Davis, *Jews and Booze*, 131.

66. Arthur Abernethy, *The Jew a Negro: Being a Study of the Jewish Ancestry from an Impartial Standpoint* (Moravian Falls, NC: Dixie, 1910), 103.

67. C. Vann Woodward, *The Strange Career of Jim Crow* (New York: Oxford University Press, 1955), 78.

68. "Sambo's Uncle Adam," *Fool-Killer*, February 1, 1910, 4; George Marsden, *Fundamentalism and American Culture* (New York: Oxford University Press, 2006).

69. *Charlotte Observer*, March 3, 1910, 4; *American Israelite*, March 10, 1910, 4.

70. Goldstein, *Price of Whiteness*, 46.

71. *Washington Bee*, February 19, 1910, 4.

72. Abernethy, *Jew a Negro*, 110.

73. Abernethy, 107.

Chapter 13

1. Helen Jacobus Apte, *Heart of a Wife: The Diary of a Southern Jewish Woman*, edited and with essays by her grandson Marcus D. Rosenbaum (Wilmington, DE: Scholarly Resources, 1998), 93.

2. Apte, *Heart of a Wife*.

3. Leonard Dinnerstein, *The Leo Frank Case* (New York: Columbia University Press, 1966).

4. "B'nai B'nai Picnic," *Atlanta Constitution*, June 26, 1910, 2; "Acknowledgement of Donations," *American Israelite*, July 20, 1911, 3; "Savannah Social News," *Atlanta Constitution*, February 18, 1912, 1; "Dance for Orphans Home," *Atlanta Constitution*, August 11, 1912, 2; "I.O.B.B. Dance a Success," *Atlanta Constitution*, August 18, 1912, 5.

5. Jeffrey Melnick, *Black-Jewish Relations on Trial: Leo Frank and Jim Conley in the New South* (Jackson: University Press of Mississippi, 2000); Dinnerstein, *Leo Frank Case*.

6. Sarah Imhoff, *Masculinity and the Making of American Judaism* (Bloomington: Indiana University Press, 2017), 225–43.

7. Leo M. Frank, MS-237, box 1, folder 6, American Jewish Archives, Cincinnati, OH.

8. Nancy MacLean, "The Leo Frank Case Reconsidered: Gender and Sexual Politics in the Making of Reactionary Populism," *Journal of American History* 78, no. 3 (1991):917.

9. Deborah Dash Moore, *B'nai B'rith and the Challenge of Ethnic Leadership* (Albany: State University of New York Press, 1981), 211.

10. Moore, 108.

11. Leonard Rogoff, "Is the Jew White? The Racial Place of the Southern Jew," *American Jewish History* 85, no. 3 (1997):212.

12. Leo Frank, SC-3585, American Jewish Archives, Cincinnati, OH.

13. August 17, 1915, Leo M. Frank, MS-237, box 1, folder 6, American Jewish Archives.

14. W. Fitzhugh Brundage, *Lynching in the New South: Georgia and Virginia, 1880–1930* (Urbana: University of Illinois Press, 1993), 277; Donald G. Mathews, "The Southern Rite of Human Sacrifice: Lynching in the American South," *Mississippi Quarterly* 61, no. 1/2 (2008):27–70; Amy Kate Bailey and Stewart E. Tolnay, *Lynched: The Victims of Southern Mob Violence* (Chapel Hill: University of North Carolina Press, 2015).

15. Bryan Stone, *Chosen Folks: Jews on the Frontiers of Texas* (Austin: University of Texas Press, 2010), 98–99.

16. Mathews, "Southern Rite," 30.

17. Dinnerstein, *Leo Frank Case*; Melnick, *Black-Jewish Relations*.

18. Bailey and Tolnay, *Lynched*, 197, 199.

19. May 7, 1914, Henry Cohen, MSS-263, box 1, folder 3, American Jewish Archives, Cincinnati, OH.

20. David Marx to Anna Carroll Moore, September 21, 1915, Leo M. Frank, MS-237, box 1, folder 6, American Jewish Archives.

21. Steven Hertzberg, *Strangers within the Gate City: The Jews of Atlanta, 1845–1915* (Philadelphia: Jewish Publication Society, 1978), 212.

22. Marjorie Liebman to Annie, n.d., Henry Cohen, MSS-263, box 1, folder 3, American Jewish Archives, Cincinnati, OH.

23. Apte, *Heart of a Wife*, 82.

24. Congregations purchased Liberty Loans: Saul Jacob Rubin, *Third to None: The Saga of Savannah Jewry* (Savannah, GA: S. J. Rubin, 1983), 237. Congregations partook of opportunities for patriotic collaboration,

as when New Orleans' Temple Sinai hosted a joint patriotic wartime event with local Unitarians (November 25, 1917, Max Heller, MS-33, box 5, folder 20, American Jewish Archives, Cincinnati, OH). Cohen was appointed by the governor to the Texas branch of the Committee of Mercy for the Women and Children Made Destitute by the World War: Jaclyn Granick, *International Jewish Humanitarianism in the Age of the Great War* (New York: Cambridge University Press, 2021); Kari Frederickson, "The South and the State in the Twentieth Century," in *A New History of the American South*, edited by W. Fitzhugh Brundage (Chapel Hill, NC: University of North Carolina Press, 2023), 399.

25. Jessica Cooperman, *Making Judaism Safe for America: World War I and the Origins of Religious Pluralism* (New York: New York University Press, 2018). On the First World War in the South: John Paul Giggie and Andrew J. Huebner, eds., *Dixie's Great War: World War I and the American South* (Tuscaloosa: University of Alabama Press, 2020).

26. Cooperman, *Making Judaism Safe*.

27. Harry Cutler to Eugene Oberdorfer, December 28, 1917, National Jewish Welfare Board, Army-Navy Division Records, I-180, series 19, box 335, American Jewish Historical Society, New York, Ancestry.com, *U.S., Jewish Welfare Board, War Correspondence, 1917–1954* [database online] (Provo, UT: Ancestry.com Operations, 2012), https://www.ancestry.com/discoveryui-content/view/1186212:1865?tid=&pid=&queryId=d786d72a-c7e9-4238-a4de-381a0fb9bf37&_phsrc=FHZ299&_phstart=successSource.

28. Leon Schwarz Memoir, MS-570, folder 1, American Jewish Archives, Cincinnati, OH.

29. Rabbi A. B. Rhine to Mr. Goldsmith, August 5, 1917, National Jewish Welfare Board, Army-Navy Division Records, I-180, series 19, box 337, American Jewish Historical Society, New York, Ancestry.com, *U.S., Jewish Welfare Board, War Correspondence, 1917–1954*, https://www.ancestry.com/discoveryui-content/view/1202466:1865?tid=&pid=&queryId=9d43f89a-9b3e-47eb-86cb-79bfec48d88f&_phsrc=FHZ316&_phstart=successSource.

30. Max Heller to Chester J. Teller, August 2, 1918, MS-33, box 5, folder 19, American Jewish Archives, Cincinnati, OH.

31. Cooperman, *Making Judaism Safe*, 102.

32. Cooperman, 113, 117.

33. Rabbi A. B. Rhine to Mr. Goldsmith, August 5, 1917.

34. Henry Cohen Jr. to Henry Kohen, Kol Nidrei 1917, Henry Cohn Papers, MSS-263, box 1, folder 2, American Jewish Archives, Cincinnati, OH.

35. Granick, *International Jewish Humanitarianism*.

36. Alexander Z. Gurwitz, *Memories of Two Generations: A Yiddish Life in Russia and Texas*, edited by Bryan Stone (Tuscaloosa: University of Alabama Press, 2016), 316; Josh Parshall, "Yiddish Politics in Southern States: The Southern District of the Arbeiter Ring, 1908–1949," PhD dissertation, University of North Carolina at Chapel Hill, 2017, 81.

37. Apte, *Heart of a Wife*, 74.

38. Rubin, *Third to None*, 239; March 3, 1918, Heller Papers, box 1, folder 20, American Jewish Archives, Cincinnati, OH; Hollace Ava Weiner and Lynna Kay Shuffield, "Monuments and Memory: Fort Worth's World War I 'Tribute to Our Boys,'" *Southern Jewish History* 20 (2017):69–95.

39. Apte, *Heart of a Wife*, 81-2.

40. Apte, 125. Helen was chair of the Peace and Arbitration committee of the National Council of Jewish Women's chapter in Miami.

41. Jeffrey Veidlinger, *In the Midst of Civilized Europe: The 1918–1921 Pogroms in Ukraine and the Onset of the Holocaust* (New York: Macmillan, 2021).

42. Leonard Dinnerstein, *Antisemitism in America* (New York: Oxford University Press, 1994); Paul Hanebrink, *A Specter Haunting Europe: The Myth of Judeo-Bolshevism* (Cambridge, MA: Belknap Press of Harvard University Press, 2018).

43. Katharine Benton-Cohen, *Inventing the Immigration Problem: The Dillingham Commission and Its Legacy* (Cambridge, MA: Harvard University Press, 2018); Libby Garland, *After the Gates Closed: Jewish Illegal Immigration to the United States, 1921–1965* (Chicago: University of Chicago Press, 2014).

44. C. Vann Woodward, *The Strange Career of Jim Crow* (New York: Oxford University Press, 1955), 115; Brundage, *Lynching in the New South*.

45. Lisa Lindquist Dorr, "Arm in Arm: Gender, Eugenics, and Virginia's Racial Integrity Acts of the 1920s," *Journal of Women's History* 11, no. 1 (1999):143–66.

46. Woodward, *Strange Career*, 116; Glenda Elizabeth Gilmore, *Gender and Jim Crow: Women and the Politics of White Supremacy in North Carolina, 1896–1920* (Chapel Hill: University of North Carolina Press, 1996).

47. Isabel Wilkerson, *The Warmth of Other Suns: The Epic Story of America's Great Migration* (New York: Vintage Books, 2010); Evelyn Brooks Higginbotham, *Righteous Discontent: The Women's Movement in the Black Baptist Church, 1880–1920* (Cambridge, MA: Harvard University Press, 1994); Edward L. Ayers, *The Promise of the New South: Life after Reconstruction* (New York: Oxford University Press, 1992).

48. Mark Cowett, "Morris Newfield, Alabama, and Blacks, 1895–1940," in *The Quiet Voices: Southern Rabbis and Black Civil Rights, 1880s to 1990s*, edited by Mark Bauman and Berkley Kalin (Tuscaloosa: University of Alabama Press, 1997), 39–49; Dan J. Puckett, *In the Shadow of Hitler: Alabama's Jews, the Second World War, and the Holocaust* (Tuscaloosa: University of Alabama Press, 2014).

49. Kelly Baker, *Gospel according to the Klan: The KKK's Appeal to Protestant America, 1915–1930* (Lawrence: University Press of Kansas, 2011), 8, 165, 174.

50. Stone, *Chosen Folks*, 123.

51. Stone, 128.

52. Leonard Rogoff, *Down Home: Jewish Life in North Carolina* (Chapel Hill, NC: University of North Carolina Press, 2010), 203.

53. W. O. Saunders interview with S. Brill, folder 737, Federal Writers' Project papers #3709, Southern Historical Collection, Wilson Library, University of North Carolina at Chapel Hill.

54. Jerry Hopkins, "No Guarantees: Mordecai F. Ham, Evangelism and Prohibition Meetings in Texas, 1903–1919," *East Texas Historical Journal* 44, no. 2 (2006):44.

55. Ferdinand K. Hirsch Life History, c.1955, Ferdinand Kilsheimer Hirsch Papers, MS-264, folder 10, American Jewish Archives, Cincinnati, OH.

56. Steven Whitfield, "Jews against the Ku Klux Klan," Southern Jewish Historical Society lecture, November 2016, Natchez, MS.

57. Stone, *Chosen Folks*, 121–22.

58. Puckett, *Shadow of Hitler*, 200.

59. Stone, *Chosen Folks*, 131n47.

60. W. O. Saunders interview with S. Brill, folder 737, Federal Writers' Project papers #3709, Southern Historical Collection, Wilson Library, University of North Carolina at Chapel Hill.

61. Ferdinand K. Hirsch Life History, c.1955, Ferdinand Kilsheimer Hirsch Papers, MS-264, folder 10, American Jewish Archives, Cincinnati, OH.

62. Confirmation Programs, Ferdinand Kilsheimer Hirsch Papers, folder 2.

63. Ferdinand Kilsheimer Hirsch Papers, folder 5.

64. Ferdinand K. Hirsch Life History, Ferdinand Kilsheimer Hirsch Papers, folder 5.

65. Alison Collis Greene, *No Depression in Heaven: The Great Depression, the New Deal, and the Transformation of Religion in the Delta* (New York: Oxford University Press, 2016); Kevin M. Schultz, *Tri-faith America: How Catholics and Jews Held Postwar America to Its Protestant Promise* (New York: Oxford University Press, 2013); Benny Kraut, "Towards the Establishment of the National Conference of Christians and Jews: The Tenuous Road to Religious Goodwill in the 1920s," *American Jewish History* 77, no. 3 (1988):388–412.

66. 1934–35 Report, Ferdinand Kilsheimer Hirsch Papers, folder 4, American Jewish Archives, Cincinnati, OH.

67. Eric Goldstein, *Price of Whiteness: Jews, Race, and American Identity* (Princeton, NJ: Princeton University Press, 2006), 58; newspaper clippings, Temple Records, Mss 59, container 15, folder 5, Cuba Archives of the Breman Museum, Atlanta, GA; Caroline Light, *The Pride of Race and Character: The Roots of Jewish Benevolence in the Jim Crow South* (New York: New York University Press, 2014), 150–82.

68. Goldstein, *Price of Whiteness*; James L. Moses, *Just and Righteous Causes: Rabbi Ira Sanders and the Fight for Racial and Social Justice in Arkansas, 1926–1963* (Fayetteville: University of Arkansas Press, 2018).

69. Moses, *Just and Righteous Causes*, 46; Berkeley Kalin, "A Plea for Tolerance: Fineschriber in Memphis," in *The Quiet Voices: Southern Rabbis and Black Civil Rights, 1880s to 1990s*, edited by Mark K. Bauman

and Berkley Kalin, 50–66 (Tuscaloosa: University of Alabama Press, 2007); Clive Webb, *Fight against Fear: Southern Jews and Black Civil Rights* (Athens: University of Georgia Press, 2011), 21. Rabbi Benjamin Goldstein offered support for Black sharecroppers: Cowett, "Rabbi Morris Newfield," 47. Rabbi Newfield in Birmingham befriended Booker T. Washington and wrote sermons in support of striking Black miners.

70. Natalie J. Ring, *The Problem South: Region, Empire, and the New Liberal State, 1880–1930* (Athens: University of Georgia Press, 2012).

71. Rogoff, *Down Home*, 225; Hasia Diner, *Julius Rosenwald: Repairing the World* (New Haven, CT: Yale University Press, 2017).

72. David H. Pierce, "Is the Jew a Friend of the Negro?," *Crisis* 30 (August 1925), cited in Clive Webb, "Jewish Merchants and Black Customers in the Age of Jim Crow," *Southern Jewish History* 2 (1999):72.

73. Samuel A. Rosenberg letter, *Crisis* 43 (April 1936), 122, cited in Webb, 72.

74. Puckett, *Shadow of Hitler*, 189.

75. George Marsden, *Fundamentalism and American Culture* (New York: Oxford University Press, 2006).

76. Louis Ginsberg, *History of the Jews of Petersburg, 1789–1950* (Petersburg, VA, 1954), 77.

77. Sermon, November 1, 1918, Ferdinand Kilsheimer Hirsch Papers, folder 7, American Jewish Archives, Cincinnati, OH.

78. Michael Lienesch, *In the Beginning: Fundamentalism, the Scopes Trial, and the Making of the Antievolution Movement* (Chapel Hill: University of North Carolina Press, 2007).

79. "Evolution and the Bible," n.d., Ferdinand Kilsheimer Hirsh Papers, folder 7, American Jewish Archives, Cincinnati, OH.

80. Myron Berman, *Richmond's Jewry, 1769–1976: Shabbat in Shockoe* (Richmond, VA: Jewish Community Federation of Richmond, 1979), 283.

81. Rubin, *Third to None*, 233–34.

82. Apte, *Heart of a Wife*, 155.

83. Walker Robins, "Jacob Gartenhaus: The Southern Baptists' Jew," *Journal of Southern Religion* 19 (2017), http://jsreligion.org/vol19/robins; Yaakov Ariel, *Evangelizing the Chosen People: Missions to the Jews in America, 1880–2000* (Chapel Hill: University of North Carolina Press, 2000).

84. Wendy Machlovitz, *Clara Lowenburg Moses: Memoir of a Southern Jewish Woman* (Natchez, MS: Museum of the Southern Jewish Experience, 2000); Ellen Umansky, *From Christian Science to Jewish Science: Spiritual Healing and American Jews* (New York: Oxford University Press, 2005), 10.

85. February 25, 1913, Heller Papers, box 5, folder 20, American Jewish Archives, Cincinnati, OH.

86. Umansky, *From Christian Science*.

87. Rogoff, *Down Home*, 209; David Kaufman, *Shul with a Pool: The Synagogue-Center in American Jewish History* (Hanover, NH: Brandeis University Press, 1999).

88. Rogoff, *Down Home*, 209.

89. Hasia Diner, *Jews of the United States, 1654–2000* (Berkeley: University of California Press, 2004), 251.

90. Archibald A. Marx to Dr. I. M. Rubinow, February 3, 1931, B'nai B'rith, MS-900 B1h-7, folder 4, American Jewish Archives, Cincinnati, OH; Puckett, *Shadow of Hitler*, 25.

91. Judah Bernstein, "American Zionism on the Jewish Frontier, 1898–1948," paper presented at the Southern Jewish Historical Society Conference, November 4, 2017, Cincinnati, OH.

92. Jonathan D. Sarna, "Converts to Zionism in the American Reform Movement," in *Zionism and Religion*, edited by Shmuel Almog, Jehuda Reinharz, and Anita Shapira (Hanover, NH: Brandeis University Press, 1998), 196–98.

93. Puckett, *Shadow of Hitler*, 77; Michael A. Meyer, "Two Anomalous Reform Rabbis: The Brothers Jacob and Max Raisin," *American Jewish Archives* 68, no. 2 (2016):1–33.

94. "The Guiding Principles of Reform Judaism: 'The Columbus Platform'—1937," Central Conference of American Rabbis, accessed February 19, 2024, https://www.ccarnet.org/rabbinic-voice/platforms/article-guiding-principles-reform-judaism/.

95. Garland, *After the Gates Closed*.

96. Gurwitz, *Memories of Two Generations*, 315.

Chapter 14

1. "Afraid," sermon, March 3, 1933, Ferdinand Kilsheimer Hirsch Papers, folder 7, American Jewish Archives, Cincinnati, OH; Alison Collis Greene, *No Depression in Heaven: The Great Depression, the New Deal, and the Transformation of Religion in the Delta* (New York: Oxford University Press, 2016).

2. Greene, *No Depression in Heaven.*

3. Leonard Rogoff, *Down Home: Jewish Life in North Carolina* (Chapel Hill, NC: University of North Carolina Press, 2010), 230.

4. Dan J. Puckett, *In the Shadow of Hitler: Alabama's Jews, the Second World War, and the Holocaust* (Tuscaloosa: University of Alabama Press, 2014), 33–34; Jonathan Sarna, *American Judaism: A History* (New Haven, CT: Yale University Press, 2004), 257; Beth Wenger, *New York Jews and the Great Depression: Uncertain Promise* (Syracuse: Syracuse University Press, 1999).

5. Brith Sholom Beth Israel Budget Committee Report, 1929, quoted in "Statement of President," May 4, 1930, BSBI records, Mss 1068, Jewish Heritage Collection, College of Charleston Special Collections.

6. Puckett, *Shadow of Hitler*, 153.

7. Greene, *No Depression in Heaven.*

8. Greene; Sarna, *American Judaism*, 255; Caroline Light, *The Pride of Race and Character: The Roots of Jewish Benevolence in the Jim Crow South* (New York: New York University Press, 2014).

9. Independent Order of B'nai B'rith Records, MS-900, box D3-9, folder 1, American Jewish Archives, Cincinnati, OH; Alan M. Kraut and Deborah A. Kraut, *Covenant of Care: Newark Beth Israel and the Jewish Hospital in America* (New Brunswick, NJ: Rutgers University Press, 2007).

10. Greene, *No Depression in Heaven*, 78.

11. Leonard Rogoff, *Gertrude Weil: Jewish Progressive in the New South* (Chapel Hill: University of North Carolina Press, 2017), 192.

12. Greene, *No Depression in Heaven*, 139n20.

13. Sarna, *American Judaism*, 258.

14. Hasia Diner, *Jews of the United States, 1654–2000* (Berkeley: University of California Press, 2004), 238; Richard Breitman and Allan J. Lichtman, *FDR and the Jews* (Cambridge, MA: Harvard University Press, 2013); Laura Kalman, *Abe Fortas: A Biography* (New Haven, CT: Yale University Press, 1990).

15. Leonard Dinnerstein, "Jews and the New Deal," *American Jewish History* 72, no. 4 (1983):474; Marc Dollinger, *Quest for Inclusion: Jews and Liberalism in Modern America* (Princeton, NJ: Princeton University Press, 2000); Eric Goldstein, *Price of Whiteness: Jews, Race, and American Identity* (Princeton, NJ: Princeton University Press, 2006), 191; Diner, *Jews of the United States*, 238.

16. Natalie J. Ring, *The Problem South: Region, Empire, and the New Liberal State, 1880–1930* (Athens: University of Georgia Press, 2012), 133.

17. Greene, *No Depression in Heaven.*

18. Alan Brinkley, *Voice of Protest: Huey Long, Father Coughlin, and the Great Depression* (New York: Vintage Books, 1983); Greene, *No Depression in Heaven.*

19. Glenda Gilmore, *Defying Dixie: The Radical Roots of Civil Rights, 1919–1950* (New York: W. W. Norton, 2009).

20. Gilmore; "Amy Schechter, Daughter of Dr. Solomon Schechter, Held for Murder in Strike," *JTA*, July 23, 1929.

21. Joshua Parshall, "Yiddish Politics in Southern States: The Southern District of the Arbeter Ring, 1908–1949," PhD dissertation, University of North Carolina at Chapel Hill, 2017, 135.

22. Parshall, 155 (quote), 100.

23. Robert Ingalls, "Antiradical Violence in Birmingham During the 1930s," *Journal of Southern History* 47, no. 4 (1981):526. See also Mark Cowett, "Rabbi Morris Newfield and the Social Gospel: Theology and the Societal Reform in the South," *American Jewish Archives* 34 (1982):48.

24. Gilmore, *Defying Dixie*, 118–19. Scottsboro also inspired—as had lynching—a number of leftist Yiddish poets, who often drew parallels to European pogroms. See Amelia M. Glaser, *Songs in Dark Times: Yiddish Poetry of Struggle from Scottsboro to Palestine* (Cambridge, MA: Harvard University Press, 2020).

25. Leonard Dinnerstein, *Antisemitism in America* (New York: Oxford University Press, 1994), 185. See also Puckett, *Shadow of Hitler*, 19–20.

26. Goldstein, *Price of Whiteness*, 191.

27. *Chattanooga Daily Times*, March 10, 1930, 3.

28. Goldstein, *Price of Whiteness*, 163; Puckett, *Shadow of Hitler*, 24.

29. Helen Jacobus Apte, *Heart of a Wife: The Diary of a Southern Jewish Woman*, edited and with essays by her grandson Marcus D. Rosenbaum (Wilmington, DE: Scholarly Resources, 1998), 137.

30. Puckett, *Shadow of Hitler*, 28.

31. Puckett, 26.

32. Puckett, 118.

33. Rogoff, *Gertrude Weil*, 209.

34. Henry Cohen to Dorothy Greenman, September 5, 1939, Cohen Papers, MSS-263, box 1, folder 1, American Jewish Archives, Cincinnati, OH.

35. Puckett, *Shadow of Hitler*.

36. W. O. Saunders interview with S. Brill, folder 737, Federal Writers' Project papers #3709, Southern Historical Collection, Wilson Library, University of North Carolina at Chapel Hill.

37. Jerrold Hirsch, *Portrait of America: A Cultural History of the Federal Writers' Project* (Chapel Hill: University of North Carolina Press, 2004).

38. W. O. Saunders interview with S. Brill, folder 737, Federal Writers' Project papers #3709, Southern Historical Collection, Wilson Library, University of North Carolina at Chapel Hill.

39. Freda Ginsberg interview with Nathan Wild, folder 161, Federal Writers' Project papers.

40. Chlotilde R. Martin interview with Elizabeth Rabinowitz, folder 877, Federal Writers' Project papers.

41. Chlotilde R. Martin interview with Elizabeth Rabinowitz.

42. W. O. Saunders interview with S. Brill, folder 737, Federal Writers' Project papers.

43. Goldstein, *Price of Whiteness*, 169.

44. W. O. Saunders interview with S. Brill, folder 737, Federal Writers' Project papers #3709, Southern Historical Collection, Wilson Library, University of North Carolina at Chapel Hill; Chlotilde R. Martin interview with Elizabeth Rabinowitz, folder 877, Federal Writers' Project papers.

45. Chlotilde R. Martin interview with Elizabeth Rabinowitz.

46. Puckett, *Shadow of Hitler*, 199.

47. Helene Godchaux, "Report of President," 1939–40, National Council of Jewish Women, Greater New Orleans Section records, box 2, folder 1, Louisiana Research Center, Tulane University Special Collections, New Orleans, LA.

48. W. O. Saunders interview with S. Brill, folder 737, Federal Writers' Project papers #3709, Southern Historical Collection, Wilson Library, University of North Carolina at Chapel Hill.

49. Rogoff, *Gertrude Weil*, 237.

50. Rogoff, 233, 236.

51. Apte, *Heart of a Wife*, 170; Parshall, "Yiddish Politics," 169.

52. Deborah Dash Moore, *GI Jews: How World War II Changed a Generation* (Cambridge, MA: Harvard University Press, 2004), 112.

53. Puckett, *Shadow of Hitler*, 160. Seventy-seven Jewish soldiers were counted in Petersburg, Virginia: Louis Ginsberg, *History of the Jews of Petersburg, 1789–1950* (Petersburg, VA, 1954), 84.

54. Wendy Lowe Besmann, *A Separate Circle: Jewish Life in Knoxville, Tennessee* (Knoxville: University of Tennessee Press, 2001), 114.

55. Sarna, *American Judaism*, 259–60; Libby Garland, *After the Gates Closed: Jewish Illegal Immigration to the United States, 1921–1965* (Chicago: University of Chicago Press, 2014), 148–76.

56. Rogoff, *Gertrude Weil*, 219.

57. Bryan Stone, *Chosen Folks: Jews on the Frontiers of Texas* (Austin: University of Texas Press, 2010), 176; Puckett, *Shadow of Hitler*, 59.

58. Puckett, *Shadow of Hitler*, 66n98.

59. Puckett, 189; Gabrielle Simon Edgcomb, *From Swastika to Jim Crow: Refugee Scholars at Black Colleges* (Malabar, FL: Krieger, 1993).

60. National Council of Jewish Women, Greater New Orleans Section records, box 2, folders 1 and 4, Louisiana Research Center, Tulane University Special Collections, New Orleans, LA.

61. Helene Godchaux, "Report of President," 1939–40, National Council of Jewish Women, Greater New Orleans Section records, box 2, folder 1.

62. Helene Godchaux, "Report of President," 1939–40, and "Immigrant Adjustment Committee Report," n.d., National Council of Jewish Women, Greater New Orleans section, box 2, folder 1.

63. "Annual Report," Chairman of Service to Foreign Born, 1939–40, National Council of Jewish Women, Greater New Orleans section, box 2, folder 1.

64. "Port and Dock Committee Report," May 1943, National Council of Jewish Women, Greater New Orleans section, box 2, folder 4.

65. Franklin Delano Roosevelt, "State of the Union—January 4, 1939," American History from Revolution to Reconstruction and Beyond, University of Groningen, accessed February 20, 2024, https://www.let.rug.nl/usa/presidents/franklin-delano-roosevelt/state-of-the-union-1939.php; Andrew Preston, *Sword of the Spirit, Shield of Faith: Religion in American War and Diplomacy* (New York: Knopf, 2012).

66. Merl E. Reed, "FEPC and the Federal Agencies in the South," *Journal of Negro History* 65, no. 1 (1980):43–56; Kevin M. Kruse and Stephen Tuck, eds., *Fog of War: The Second World War and the Civil Rights Movement* (New York: Oxford University Press, 2012); Duncan Ryuken Williams, *American Sutra: A Story of Faith and Freedom in the Second World War* (Cambridge, MA: Harvard University Press, 2019).

67. Jessica Cooperman, *Making Judaism Safe for America: World War I and the Origins of Religious Pluralism* (New York: New York University Press, 2018); Ronit Y. Stahl, *Enlisting Faith: How the Military Chaplaincy Shaped Religion and State in Modern America* (Cambridge, MA: Harvard University Press, 2017).

68. Puckett, *Shadow of Hitler*, 191–92.

69. Puckett, 197.

70. Henry Cohen to Mr. Friedlander, June 10, 1942, Cohen Papers, box 1, folder 1, American Jewish Archives, Cincinnati, OH; Matthew Berkman, "Antisemitism, Anti-Zionism, and the American Racial Order: Revisiting the American Council for Judaism in the Twenty-First Century," *American Jewish History* 105, nos. 1/2 (2021):127–55; Thomas Kolsky, *Jews against Zionism: The American Council for Judaism, 1942–1948* (Philadelphia: Temple University Press, 1990); Kyle Stanton, "Hyman Judah Schachtel, Congregation Beth Israel, and the American Council for Judaism," *Southern Jewish History* 22 (2019):127–50.

71. "Statistics of Jews," *American Jewish Yearbook* 44 (1942–43):418–50, https://ajcarchives.org/Portal/Yearbooks/en-US/RecordView/Index/2561; Stone, *Chosen Folks*, 162–63; Myron Berman, "Rabbi Edward Nathan Calisch and the Debate over Zionism in Richmond, Virginia," *American Jewish Historical Quarterly* 62, no. 3 (1973):295–305.

72. Stone, *Chosen Folks*, 159–65; Allison E. Schottenstein, *Changing Perspectives: Black-Jewish Relations in Houston during the Civil Rights Era* (Denton: University of North Texas Press, 2021), 39–72.

73. Allan Tarshish to Mr. Tobias, August 9, 1947, Allan Tarshish Writings Regarding Zionism and Judaism, C Manuscripts Accession 2013-93, Jewish Heritage Collection, College of Charleston Special Collections, Charleston, SC.

74. Allen Krause, "Charleston Jewry, Black Civil Rights, and Rabbi Burton Padoll," *Southern Jewish History* 11 (2008):110.

75. Allan Tarshish, "The State of Israel, the American Council for Judaism, and I," Kahal Kadosh Beth Elohim Records, box 5, folder 4, Jewish Heritage Collection, College of Charleston Special Collections, Charleston, SC. For more on Tarshish's conflicts with KKBE over the American Council for Judaism, see KKBE Minutes, August 27, 1947, September 9, 1947, Presidential Report, April 30, 1950, May 2, 1950, April 25, 1954, box 5, folder 3, Jewish Heritage Collection; "Jewish Heritage Collection: Oral History Interview with Dorothea Shimel Dumas, Renée Shimel Frisch, and Jennie Shimel Ackerman," January 2, 1997, transcript, p. 38, Jewish Heritage Collection Oral Histories, Lowcountry Digital Library, last updated August 1, 2006, https://lcdl.library.cofc.edu/lcdl/catalog/lcdl:11819.

76. *For Those Who Live in the Sun* program, 1950, Kahal Kadosh Beth Elohim Records, box 54, folder 5, Jewish Heritage Collection.

77. Sarah Imhoff, "Hoover's Judeo-Christians: Jews, Religion, and Communism in the Cold War," in *The FBI and Religion: Faith and National Security before and after 9/11*, edited by Sylvester A. Johnson and Steven Weitzman (Berkeley: University of California Press, 2017), 121–33.

78. In 1949 an employee was fired from Atlanta's Federation of Jewish Social Service after testifying in support of a Communist Party organizer (Parshall, "Yiddish Politics," 102). In North Carolina a Sunday school teacher and B'nai B'rith youth counselor was fired after an informant in the Junius Scales trial identified him as a Communist (Rogoff, *Down Home*, 260).

79. Preston, *Sword of the Spirit*; Kevin M. Schultz, *Tri-faith America: How Catholics and Jews Held Postwar America to Its Protestant Promise* (New York: Oxford University Press, 2013).

80. Moore, *GI Jews*, 260–61, 263; Schottenstein, *Changing Perspectives*, 131–55; Rachel Kranson, *Ambivalent Embrace: Jewish Upward Mobility in Postwar America* (Chapel Hill: University of North Carolina Press, 2017).

81. Pete Daniel, "Going among Strangers: Southern Reactions to World War II," *Journal of American History* 77, no. 3 (1990):909.

82. For instance, Auschwitz survivor Joe Engel joined an aunt in Charleston in 1949; after several forays in New York, he settled down in the Lowcountry, where he operated a dry cleaning business that served a predominantly Black clientele: "Jewish Heritage Collection: Oral History Interview with Joe Engel," April 30, 1997, transcript, Jewish Heritage Collection Oral Histories, Lowcountry Digital Library, last updated August 1, 2006, https://lcdl.library.cofc.edu/lcdl/catalog/lcdl:11820.

83. David H. Onksy, "'First a Negro . . . Incidentally a Veteran': Black World War Two Veterans and the G. I. Bill of Rights in the Deep South, 1944–1948," *Journal of Social History* 31, no. 3 (1998):517–43; Tomiko Brown-Nagin, *Courage to Dissent: Atlanta and the Long History of the Civil Rights Movement* (New York: Oxford University Press, 2011).

84. Mary Dudziak, *Cold War Civil Rights: Race and the Image of American Democracy* (Princeton, NJ: Princeton University Press, 2002).

85. Aldon Morris, *Origins of the Civil Rights Movement* (New York: Free Press, 1984); "To Secure These Rights: The Report of the President's Committee on Civil Rights," p. 82, Harry S. Truman Library and Museum website, accessed February 20, 2024, https://www.trumanlibrary.gov/library/to-secure-these-rights.

86. Clive Webb, *Fight against Fear: Southern Jews and Black Civil Rights* (Athens: University of Georgia Press, 2011), 130.

87. Kari Frederickson, "'Dual Actions, One for Each Race': The Campaign against the Dixiecrats in South Carolina, 1948–1950," *International Social Science Review* 72, nos. 1/2 (1997):14–25.

88. Mark A. Raider, "'The Greater Sin': Jacob M. Rothschild's Yom Kippur Sermon on American Jews, the South, and Civil Rights, 1948," in *New Perspectives in American Jewish History: A Documentary Tribute to Jonathan D. Sarna*, edited by Gary P. Zola and Raider (Hanover, NH: Brandeis University Press, 2021), 269.

89. Carolyn Renée Dupont, *Mississippi Praying: Southern White Evangelicals and the Civil Rights Movement, 1945–1975* (New York: New York University Press, 2015), 57.

90. Babette Marx, "Annual Report," May 13, 1947, National Council of Jewish Women, Greater New Orleans Section records, box 3, folder 1, Louisiana Research Center, Tulane University Special Collections, New Orleans, LA.

91. National Council of Jewish Women, Charleston Section records, Mss 1038, box 2, Jewish Heritage Collection, College of Charleston Special Collections, Charleston, SC.

Chapter 15

1. National Council of Jewish Women, Greater New Orleans Section records, box 4, folder 2, Louisiana Research Center, Tulane University Special Collections, New Orleans, LA.

2. Minutes, November 16, 1952, South Carolina Association of B'nai B'rith Lodges records, Mss 1037, box 1, folder 1, Jewish Heritage Collection, College of Charleston Special Collections, Charleston, SC; Clive Webb, *Fight against Fear: Southern Jews and Black Civil Rights* (Athens: University of Georgia Press, 2011), 120–21.

3. Minutes, November 16, 1952, South Carolina Association of B'nai B'rith Lodges records, Jewish Heritage Collection; Kirsten Fermaglich, *A Rosenberg by Any Name: A History of Jewish Name Changing in America* (New York: New York University Press, 2018); Marc Dollinger, *Quest for Inclusion: Jews and Liberalism in Modern America* (Princeton, NJ: Princeton University Press, 2000).

4. Minutes, November 16, 1952, South Carolina Association of B'nai B'rith Lodges records, Jewish Heritage Collection.

5. Minutes, November 15, 1953, South Carolina Association of B'nai B'rith Lodges records, Jewish Heritage Collection.

6. Tomiko Brown-Nagin, *Courage to Dissent: Atlanta and the Long History of the Civil Rights Movement* (New York: Oxford University Press, 2011), 105; Dollinger, *Quest for Inclusion*, 164–65; Cheryl Greenberg, *Troubling the Waters: Black-Jewish Relations in the American Century* (Princeton, NJ: Princeton University Press, 2010), 164.

7. Leonard Bloom, "A Successful Jewish Boycott of the New York City Public Schools—Christmas 1906," *American Jewish History* 70, no. 2 (1980):180–88; Naomi Weiner Cohen, *Jews in Christian America: The Pursuit of Religious Equality* (New York: Oxford University Press, 1992).

8. Rabbi Julian B. Feibelman, "Petition to the Orleans Parish School Board," September 12, 1955, MS 94, box 29, folder 5, American Jewish Archives, in *American Jewish History: A Primary Source Reader*, edited by Gary Phillip Zola and Marc Dollinger, 306–8 (Waltham, MA: Brandeis University Press, 2014).

9. James L. Moses, *Just and Righteous Causes: Rabbi Ira Sanders and the Fight for Racial and Social Justice in Arkansas, 1926–1963* (Fayetteville: University of Arkansas Press, 2018); Matthew D. Lassiter, *Silent Majority: Suburban Politics in the Sunbelt South* (Princeton, NJ: Princeton University Press, 2006).

10. Webb, *Fight against Fear*, 147. See also Deborah Dash Moore, *B'nai B'rith and the Challenge of Ethnic Leadership* (Albany: State University of New York Press, 1981), 228–29; Faith Rogow, *Gone to Another Meeting: The National Council of Jewish Women, 1893–1993* (Tuscaloosa: University of Alabama Press, 1993). The North Carolina Association of Rabbis expressed "its whole-hearted support of the Supreme Court decision for the de-segregation in the Public Schools": Leonard Rogoff, *Down Home: Jewish Life in North Carolina* (Chapel Hill, NC: University of North Carolina Press, 2010), 288; see also Allison E. Schottenstein, *Changing Perspectives: Black-Jewish Relations in Houston during the Civil Rights Era* (Denton: University of North Texas Press, 2021), 102–30.

11. Report, September 26, 1954, South Carolina Association of B'nai B'rith Lodges, box 1, folder 1, Jewish Heritage Collection, College of Charleston Special Collections, Charleston, SC.

12. Moore, *B'nai B'rith*, 228–29.

13. Carolyn Renée Dupont, *Mississippi Praying: Southern White Evangelicals and the Civil Rights Movement, 1945–1975* (New York: New York University Press, 2015), 35, 78, 80.

14. Moses, *Just and Righteous Causes*.

15. Dupont, *Mississippi Praying*, 93.

16. Webb, *Fight against Fear*, 48n11

17. Webb, 49.

18. Anonymous, *A Jewish View on Segregation* (Greenwood: Association of Citizens' Councils of Mississippi, 1957).

19. Webb, *Fight against Fear*, 134.

20. Perry E. Nussbaum to Julian B. Feibelman, June 6, 1955, Perry E. Nussbaum Papers, MS-430, box 1, folder 6, American Jewish Archives, Cincinnati, OH.

21. G. T. Gillespie, *A Christian View of Segregation* (Greenwood, MS: Citizens' Council Educational Fund, 1954).

22. Aldon Morris, *Origins of the Civil Rights Movement* (New York: Free Press, 1984), 28–30.

23. Gary J. Dorrien, *Breaking White Supremacy: Martin Luther King Jr. and the Black Social Gospel* (New Haven, CT: Yale University Press, 2018).

24. Martin Luther King Jr., MIA Mass Meeting at Holt Street Baptist Church, December 5, 1955, MLKJP, GAMK, Martin Luther King, Jr. Papers (series I–IV), Martin Luther King, Jr. Center for Nonviolent Social Change, Inc., Atlanta, GA, T-18.

25. Seymour Atlas, *The Rabbi with the Southern Twang: True Stories from a Life of Leadership within the Orthodox Jewish Congregations of the South* (Bloomington, IN: Trafford, 2007).

26. Webb, *Fight against Fear*, 148.

27. William Malev, "The Jew of the South in the Conflict on Segregation," *Conservative Judaism* 13, no. 1 (1958):35–46, in Zola and Dollinger, *American Jewish History*, 313. Years later Rabbi Milton Grafman of Birmingham echoed this sentiment: "We, the Jewish community's leadership, believed that Jews, as such, ought to stay out of the desegregation fight on the grounds that it is a 'Christian problem' between whites and Negroes and not simply a racial problem" (Webb, *Fight against Fear*, 209n116).

28. Kyle Stanton, "Hyman Judah Schachtel, Congregation Beth Israel, and the American Council for Judaism," *Southern Jewish History* 22 (2019):127–50.

29. Lila Corwin Berman, *Metropolitan Jews: Politics, Race, and Religion in Postwar Detroit* (Chicago: University of Chicago Press, 2015), 150–87. See also Samuel D. Gruber, curator, *Synagogues of the South: Architecture and Jewish Identity*, Pearlstine/Lipov Center for Southern Jewish Culture and Jewish Heritage College, College of Charleston, synagoguesofthesouth.cofc.edu.

30. Congregation Shearith Israel, Diamond Anniversary Booklet, 1959, Dallas Nearprint, American Jewish Archives, Cincinnati, OH.

31. Rogoff, *Down Home*, 279.

32. Amy Milligan, "The Jewish Zealots of Tobacco Land," *Jewish Culture and History* 20, no. 1 (2019):62–79.

33. Goldberg to Perry E. Nussbaum, March 28, 1955, Nussbaum Papers, box 1, folder 6, American Jewish Archives, Cincinnati, OH.

34. David Weinfeld, "Two Commemorations: Richmond Jews and the Lost Cause during the Civil Rights Era," *Southern Jewish History* 20, no. 3 (2020):77–123.

35. Annual Convention Report, March 29–30, 1958, South Carolina Association of B'nai B'rith Lodges, box 1, folder 1, Jewish Heritage Collection, College of Charleston Special Collections, Charleston, SC; Webb, *Fight against Fear*.

36. Webb, *Fight against Fear*, 46.

37. Webb, 68. Annie Moore, whose father had been murdered in a house bombing noted, "No large sums of money were offered for information leading toward the apprehension and conviction of the ones responsible for this tragedy; no Governor spoke, no President urged the FBI to investigate to the fullest and report to him; no policemen stood on 24-hour guard over us who remained."

38. Janice Rothschild Blumberg, "Jacob M. Rothschild: His Legacy Twenty Years After," in *Dixie Diaspora: An Anthology of Southern Jewish History*, edited by Mark Bauman (Tuscaloosa: University of Alabama Press, 2006), 272.

39. Webb, *Fight against Fear*, 57.

40. Joshua A. Fishman, "Southern City," in *Jews in the South*, edited by Leonard Dinnerstein and Mary Dale Palsson (Baton Rouge: Louisiana State University Press, 1973), 317, 320.

41. Webb, *Fight against Fear*, 45.

42. A. O. Hero Jr., "Southern Jews, Race Relations, and Foreign Policy," *Jewish Social Studies* 27, no. 4 (1965):213–35.

43. Dupont, *Mississippi Praying*.

44. Rogoff, *Down Home*, 289.

45. Levi A. Olan to Perry Nussbaum, September 30, 1968, MS-430, box 1, folder 4, Perry E. Nussbaum Papers, American Jewish Archives, Cincinnati, OH. Bryan Stone, *Chosen Folks: Jews on the Frontiers of Texas* (Austin: University of Texas Press, 2010), 208. When a Black man who had converted to Judaism in Arkansas visited a congregation in another southern city, the rabbi felt compelled to ask the congregation's permission for him to join worship: Proctor, Schmier, and Stern, *Jews of the South*, 371. When the same issue was raised with a Black Jewish woman in Atlas's Montgomery congregation, the board president objected with derogatory language: Atlas, *Rabbi with the Southern Twang*, 67.

46. There were sit-ins at Jewish-owned stores like Weingarten's in Houston in 1960, which put new pressure on Jewish businessmen: Stone, *Chosen Folks*, 193; Webb, *Fight against Fear*, 88–113; Brown-Nagin, *Courage to Dissent*, 155–57.

47. Allen Krause, "Charleston Jewry, Black Civil Rights, and Rabbi Burton Padoll," *Southern Jewish History* 11 (2008):77. Merchant Edward Kronsberg responded to waves of protest by first hiring Black clerks and soon after firing them.

48. Congregational Meeting, April 29, 1962, Kahal Kadosh Beth Elohim records, box 6, folder 2, Jewish Heritage Collection, College of Charleston Special Collections, Charleston, SC.

49. "Foolish Thoughts in April," Burton L. Padoll Papers, Mss 1082, box 2, folder 2, Jewish Heritage Collection.

50. "Jewish Heritage Collection: Oral History Interview with Burton Padoll," October 21, 1999, transcript, Jewish Heritage Collection Oral Histories, Lowcountry Digital Library, last updated August 1, 2006, https://lcdl.library.cofc.edu/lcdl/catalog/lcdl:36578.

51. Jacob Rothschild, "No Place to Hide," *Southern Israelite*, August 1963, in Zola and Dollinger, *American Jewish History*, 308–10.

52. Rogoff, *Down Home*, 290. See also Kimberly Marlowe Hartnett, *"Carolina Israelite": How Harry Golden Made Us Care about Jews, the South, and Civil Rights* (Chapel Hill: University of North Carolina Press, 2015).

53. Kevin M. Kruse, *White Flight: Atlanta and the Making of Modern Conservatism* (Princeton, NJ: Princeton University Press, 2005); Lassiter, *Silent Majority*.

54. Adolph Phillipsborn to Perry Nussbaum, November 24, 1963, Nussbaum Papers, box 3, folder 3, American Jewish Archives, Cincinnati, OH.

55. Alexandra Zapruder, *Twenty-Six Seconds: A Personal History of the Zapruder Film* (New York: Grand Central, 2016); Danny Fingeroth, *Jack Ruby: The Many Faces of Oswald's Assassin* (Chicago: Chicago Review, 2023).

56. Webb, *Fight against Fear*, 95.

57. Martin Luther King Jr., "Letter from Birmingham Jail," April 16, 1963, Stanford University, Martin Luther King Jr. Research and Education Institute, accessed February 21, 2024, https://kinginstitute.stanford.edu/letter-birmingham-jail.

58. Harold E. Katz, "Memorandum on Racial Problems Affecting the Birmingham Jewish Community," n.d., Birmingham Nearprint, American Jewish Archives, Cincinnati, OH.

59. Milton L. Grafman Sermons, C-3338, American Jewish Archives.

60. Milton L. Grafman Sermons, C-3338.

61. Katz, "Memorandum on Racial Problems."

62. Joachim Prinz, speech, August 28, 1963, Joachim Prinz website, accessed February 24, 2024, https://www.joachimprinz.com/civilrights.htm.

63. Perry Nussbaum to Solomon K. Kaplan, October 28, 1963, Nussbaum Papers, box 1, folder 4, American Jewish Archives, Cincinnati, OH.

64. Webb, *Fight against Fear*, 80.

65. Debra L. Schultz, *Going South: Jewish Women in the Civil Rights Movement* (New York: New York University Press, 2001).

66. Marvin Braiterman, "Mississippi Marranos," in Dinnerstein and Palsson, *Jews in the South*, 351–59.

67. Paul Ellen, Nussbaum Papers, American Jewish Archives, Cincinnati, OH.

68. Gary Philip Zola, "What Price Amos?: Perry Nussbaum's Career in Jackson, Mississippi," in *The Quiet Voices: Southern Rabbis and Black Civil Rights*, edited by Mark K. Bauman (Tuscaloosa: University of Alabama Press, 2007), 248–49.

69. DuPont, *Mississippi Praying*, 172, 176.

70. Webb, *Fight against Fear*, 128.

71. Edward K. Kaplan, *Spiritual Radical: Abraham Joshua Heschel in America, 1940–1972* (New Haven, CT: Yale University Press, 2008).

72. Webb, *Fight against Fear*, 126.

73. Burton Padoll, "Strange Fire in Alabama," n.d., Padoll Papers, box 1, folder 5, Jewish Heritage Collection, College of Charleston Special Collections, Charleston, SC; Webb, *Fight against Fear*, 122.

74. David B. Ruderman, "Greenville Diary: A Northern Rabbi Confronts the Deep South, 1966–70," *Jewish Quarterly Review* 94, no. 1 (2004):643–65.

75. Arene and Perry E. Nussbaum to Friends, October 1, 1967, Nussbaum Papers, American Jewish Archives, Cincinnati, OH.

76. Congregation B'nai Israel (Little Rock, AR) program, November 19, 1966, SC-7319, American Jewish Archives.

77. John Dittmer, *Local People: The Struggle for Civil Rights in Mississippi* (Chicago: University of Illinois Press, 1995), 417.

78. Arene and Perry E. Nussbaum to Friends, October 1, 1967, Nussbaum Papers, American Jewish Archives, Cincinnati, OH.

79. P. Allen Krause interview with Perry Nussbaum, 1966, audio recording, website for *To Stand Aside or Stand Alone: Southern Reform Rabbis and the Civil Rights Movement*, edited by Mark K. Bauman with Stephen Krause (forthcoming), accessed February 25, 2024, standasideorstandalone.com/hear-the -interviews.

80. "A Former Jackson Resident" to Perry Nussbaum, November 24, 1967, Nussbaum Papers, box 3, folder 4, American Jewish Archives, Cincinnati, OH.

81. Marc Dollinger, *Black Power, Jewish Politics: Reinventing the Alliance in the 1960s* (Hanover, NH: University Press of New England, 2018).

Epilogue

1. Gary Richards, "Scripting Scarlett O'Goldberg: Margaret Mitchell, Tennessee Williams, and the Production of Southern Jewishness in *The Last Night of Ballyhoo*," *Southern Quarterly* 39, no. 4 (2001):5.

2. Logan Culwell-Block, "Parade Wins Best Revival of a Musical at 2023 Tony Awards," *Playbill*, June 11, 2023, https://playbill.com/article/parade-wins-best-revival-of-a-musical-at-2023-tony-awards.

3. Meg Kinnard, "Slavery Advocate's Statue Removed in South Carolina," Associated Press, June 24, 2020, https://apnews.com/article/us-news-ap-top-news-sc-state-wire-slavery-south-carolina -a88ad98372bbb810d1261d61acb5350f.

4. Rickey Ciapha Dennis Jr., "Historic Charleston Synagogue Remembers Enslaved Blacks Who Built the Sanctuary," *Post and Courier*, September 4, 2021, https://www.postandcourier.com/features/historic -charleston-synagogue-remembers-enslaved-blacks-who-built-the-sanctuary/article_a491b512-0a91-11ec -b049-07406797d88e.html.

5. Eli Evans, *The Provincials: A Personal History of Jews in the South* (New York, 1973) xi.

6. Eli N. Evans, *Judah P. Benjamin: The Jewish Confederate* (New York: Free Press, 1988); Eli N. Evans, *The Lonely Days Were Sundays: Reflections of a Jewish Southerner* (Jackson: University Press of Mississippi, 1993). Another important memoiristic account of southern Jews is Stella Suberman's *The Jew Store: A Family History* (Chapel Hill, NC: Algonquin Books, 2001).

7. Mark K. Bauman, "A Century of Southern Jewish Historiography," *American Jewish Archives* 57, nos. 1–2 (2007):3–78; Southern Jewish Historical Society records, Mss 1056a and 1056b, Jewish Heritage Collection, College of Charleston Special Collections, Charleston, SC; Southern Jewish Historical Society Nearprint, American Jewish Archives, Cincinnati, OH; records of the Goldring/Woldenberg Institute of Southern Jewish Life (ISJL) in Jackson, Mississippi; Museum of the Southern Jewish Historical Society Nearprint, American Jewish Archives.

8. Shari Rabin, "'Overlooked, Out There on the Rim, in the Southern Part of America': Eli N. Evans, Macy B. Hart, and the Project of Southern Jewish History (1987)," in *New Perspectives in American Jewish History: A Documentary Tribute to Jonathan D. Sarna*, edited by Gary P. Zola and Mark A. Raider (Hanover, NH: Brandeis University Press, 2021), 359–65; John Pope, "Museum of the Southern Jewish Experience to Open in New Orleans with Rooms Full of 'Meaning and Memory,'" *Times-Picayune*, May 17, 2021, https:// www.nola.com/entertainment_life/museum-of-the-southern-jewish-experience-to-open-in-new-orleans -with-rooms-full-of/article_5eb6a150-b26d-11eb-bdfa-9759b025ef52.html.

9. Cecilia Márquez, *Making the Latino South: A History of Racial Formation* (Chapel Hill: University of North Carolina Press, 2023); Uzma Quraishi, *Redefining the Immigrant South: Indian and Pakistani Immigration to Houston during the Cold War* (Chapel Hill: University of North Carolina Press, 2020).

10. Stuart Rockoff, "The Rise and Fall of the Jewish South," in *Jewish Roots in Southern Soil*, edited by Marcie Cohen Ferris and Greenberg, 284–303 (Waltham, MA: Brandeis University Press, 2006).

11. Nancy Hendrix, "A Demographic Study of the Jewish Community of Nashville and Middle Tennessee," p. 14, Council of Jewish Federations and Welfare Funds Demographic Surveys, Mss-585 box 3, folder 6, American Jewish Archives, Cincinnati, OH.

12. Matthew Frye Jacobson, *Roots Too: White Ethnic Revival in Post–Civil Rights America* (Cambridge, MA: Harvard University Press, 2006).

13. Eliza McGraw, "'How to Win the Jews for Christ': Southern Jewishness and the Southern Baptist Convention," *Mississippi Quarterly* 53, no. 2 (2000):209–23; Amy Weiss, "Billy Graham Receives the Ten Commandments: American Jewish Interfaith Relations in the Age of Evangelicalism," *American Jewish History* 103, no. 1 (2019):1–24.

14. Pearlstine/Lipov Center for Southern Jewish Culture and Jewish Heritage Collection, College of Charleston, "Holocaust Memorial," Mapping Jewish Charleston, accessed February 22, 2024, https://mappingjewishcharleston.cofc.edu/2020/holocaust-memorial/.

15. In 1989 he won a Republican primary for the statehouse. In 1990 he ran for the US Senate. Although he lost, he won the majority of the white vote and attracted considerable attention. Local Holocaust survivor Anne Levy confronted Duke and spoke out against him: Lawrence N. Powell, *Troubled Memory: Anne Levy, the Holocaust, and David Duke's Louisiana* (Chapel Hill: University of North Carolina Press, 2000).

16. Phyllis Leffler, "Insiders or Outsiders: Charlottesville's Jews, White Supremacy, and Antisemitism," *Southern Jewish History* 21 (2018):61–120.

17. Leffler, 76.

18. Adrienne Rich, "Split at the Root: An Essay on Jewish identity," in *Adrienne Rich, Poetry and Prose*, edited by Barbara Charlesworth Gelpi, Albert Gelpi, and Brett Miller (New York: W. W. Norton, 2018), 249.

INDEX

Page numbers in *italics* indicate figures and tables.

Abernathy, Arthur: *The Jew a Negro*, 151–52
abolitionism, 46, 52, 64, 73, 224n19
Abrahams, Emanuel, 31
African Americans: domestic workers, 114–15,
    139, 163, *163*, 181; Jews, 66–67, 135; murders of,
    94, 109, 114, 133–34, 149, 156, 160; labor, 136,
    142; political activity, 108–9, 122–23, 133, 171;
    interactions with white Jews, 111–12, 115, 136,
    147–49; spiritual autonomy of, 51. *See also* civil
    rights; slavery
Agudas Achim (Brotherly association), San An-
    tonio, 145
Ahavas Achus Society, New Haven, 121
Ahavath Achim (Brotherly love), Atlanta,
    145
Alabama: Anniston, 128; Adrienne Rich's parents,
    201; Bessemer, 162; B'nai B'rith, 121; border
    with Georgia, 37; Camp McClellan, 158; Clai-
    borne, 70; Dixiecrats, 181; Eighth Regiment
    (Confederate Army), 91; Father Arthur W.
    Terminiello, 178; House of Representatives
    election in, 108; indebtedness, 65; NAACP,
    outlawing of, 187; published histories of, 132;
    newspapers and the Holocaust, 172–73; seces-
    sion of, 75–76; Seligman and, 135; Stevenson,
    Rosewater in, 66, 75; Supreme Court, 111, 174;
    Temple Emanu-El, Dothan, 169; University of,
    176. *See also* Birmingham; Mobile; Montgom-
    ery; Scottsboro Boys; Selma
Alexander, Allen, Black politician, 108
Alexander II (Tsar), assassination of, 137
Allgemeine Zeitung des Judenthums (newspaper), 67
American Council for Judaism, 178–79, 188
American Jewish Committee, 149
American Jewish Congress, 186
American Red Cross, 162
American Revolution, 29–39
Anglicanism, 6, 9, 10, 15, 19, 21, 29, 33, 40

Anshei Galicia, Memphis, 146
Anshei Sphard (People of the Sephardic rite),
    146
Anti-Defamation League (ADL), 155, 184–86,
    188–89
antisemitism:, 135–37, 150, 151–52, 153, 161, 174;
    bombings at Jewish institutions, 188–89; eco-
    nomic, 65–66, 111, 136; in Europe, 159–60; legal
    exclusion, 10, 11, 42; pogroms, 141; rising global,
    168; social exclusion, 14, 135–6; stereotypes,
    65–6, 107, 111, 161; theology, 62–63; wartime, 36,
    89–92, 178, 232n18. *See also* Christians, descrip-
    tions of Jews, and Frank, Leo
Appomattox Court House, Confederate surrender
    at, 96, 100
Apte, Helen: on antisemitism, 153; on Germany
    inflamed with anti-Semitism and Hitlerism,
    172; on interest in going to temple, 165; on Leo
    Frank death, 157; theological providentialism,
    159
Arbeiter Ring, 146–47, 171, 180
Archdale, John, Carolinian official, 7–8
Arkansas: discrimination, 177; Jewish hospitals,
    170; Governor Faubus, 186, 196; politics, 115–16,
    119; Rabbi Rhine, 158; secession, 77; standoff at
    Little Rock High School, 186. *See also* Little
    Rock
Armistice Day, 159
Army of Northern Virginia, 88; desertion of
    immigrant soldiers, 91
Arnold, Isaac: desertion of, 91–92; Michelbacher
    in defense of, 92
Ashley Cooper, Anthony: Fundamental Consti-
    tutions of Carolina (FCC), 6; on slavery, 8
Association of Citizens' Councils, 186
Association of Southern Women for the Preven-
    tion of Lynching, 163
Atheists, 63, 106

Atlanta, 128, 136, 192, 198; Caroline Haas, 163; congregations, 146; David Macarov, 176; Decatur Street, 145, 150; electing Jewish officials, 200; Hebrew Christian Association, 136; Jewish orphan homes, 130, 148; Jewish women, 141; Jews in population, 114–15; Leo Max Frank, 153–55, 157; massacre of 1906, 150–51; newspapers, 127, 138, 143; Martin Luther King, Jr., 189; Rabbi David Marx, 130, 163; Rabbi Jacob Rothschild, 181; Rich brothers, 105, 129, 191; Russian Jewish immigrants, 147, 150; Temple in, 117, 159, 189, 244n49

Atlas, Seymour (Rabbi), "Brotherhood Week" radio broadcast, 187

Baker, David, on school desegregation, 184
Balfour Declaration, 158–59
Baptists, 9, 144
Barbados, 4, 5; Nidhe Israel (dispersed of Israel), 13, 20
Barney, William L., on motives for secession, 226n5
Barnston, Henry (Rabbi), Congregation Beth Israel, Houston, 178
Baruch, Bernard M., on father's Confederate uniform and Klan regalia, 110
Battle of Gettysburg, 91
Beekman, Rosalie, Natchez Civil War casualty, 87
Bell, Sherman, Black Senate candidate, 171
Benedix, Samuel: arrival to Savannah of, 39; leaders punishing, 40
Benjamin, Judah P.: Confederate government, 77; denigration of Jewish background, 90–91; in high political office, 63; praise for, 133; public office in Confederacy, 74
Benjamin, Lena, Leon Schwarz on, 115
Benjamin, Solomon A., charges for selling on Sunday, 63
Bentham, James, militia, 34
Bernard, Jacob, circumcision of sons, 225n38
Bevis Marks, London, 20
Bible, criticism of, 152
Bierfield, S. A., murder of, 110
"Big Chicken," landmark, ix
Bilbo, Theodore, on New Deal policies, 172
Bill of Rights, 40
Birmingham, Alabama: American Council for Judaism, 178; antisemitism, 178; civil rights movement, 187, 192, 193; divorce case, 174; Joseph Gelders, 171; Ku Klux Klan, 160; Milton Grafman, response to King and civil rights movement, 193; United Jewish Fund, 176;

World War II soldiers, 176; Zionism, 166. See also Newfield; Morris
Blatt, Solomon, on school integration, 184, 195
Bloch, Charles, 181; States' Rights, 186
"Bloody Sunday", 195
B'nai B'rith, 70, 130, 141; Anti-Defamation League (ADL) and, 155, 184–85; debate over Black civil rights, 183–84; donations for epidemic, 121; Grand District Lodge Number 7, 121; hospital for indigent persons, 170; raising money for epidemic, 120; South Carolina B'nai B'rith Convention, 185; wreath-laying ceremony with United Daughters of the Confederacy, 133
Board of Delegates of American Israelites, 70
Boltzius, Johann Martin: evangelizing Jews, 14; on German Jewish families, 22–23; on hate and persecution, 12
Bond, Horace Mann, childhood memories, 147
Borenstein, Sam, candidate for Tennessee governor, 171
Bragg, Thomas, Confederate attorney general, 230n86
Brenan, Jack, Klan march, 162
Brill, S.: denigrating religious Jews, 174; interview on dog Hitler, 173; Russian Jewish immigrant, 161
British Empire, 4, 38; experience of Jews, 26; Georgia as outpost, 3
Brooks, Allen, lynching of, 156
Brown, John, failed raid at Harper's Ferry, 73
Brown, Joseph E. (Georgia governor), letters to, 86
Brown v. Board of Education of Topeka, 184, 186
Buchanan, James, national day of fasting and prayer (January 4), 74
Bureau of Refugees, Freedmen, and Abandoned Lands, 101

Calhoun, John C.: death of pro-slavery senator, 63; monument of, 199–200
California, compromise of 1850, 64
Calisch, Edward N. (Rabbi), 130, 165
Camp Blue Star, 188
Camp Jacobs, Reform movement, 199
Cardozo, Francis L.: heritage of, 109; resignation of, 123
Cardozo, Isaac N., father of Francis Cardozo, 109
Carolina colony, 3; documentation of Jews in, 12; Fundamental Constitutions of Carolina (FCC), 6
Carolina Israelite (newspaper), 191
Carté, Katharine, on foreign Protestants, 210n37
Carvalho, Judith Nunez, birth of, 39

Carvalho, Solomon Nunes, painting of KKBE sanctuary, 53–54, 55

Cash, W. J.: on Jews refusing to assimilate, xiv; *The Mind of the South*, xii

Catholicism, 9, 10, 28, 40, 63, 150, 160, 169; Knights of Columbus, 157

Caucasian (newspaper), Democrat Weil and, 115

Cawhern, John, preacher, 151

cemeteries, southern Jewish, 43, 45, 49, 99, 132, 138

Central Conference of American Rabbis, Heller as president, 166

Chajes, J. H., on egodocuments as "diaries", 211n61

Chaney, James, murder of, 194

Charity, 15, 41, 44, 129–30, 142, 143–44, 170, 174, 177

Charleston, 7, 7; Brith Shalom, 139, 160, 169; exports, 24; Hebrew Orphan Society, 41, 49; Jewish migrants, 18; Jewish population in, 48; Jews in, 20–21, 42; Jews rebuilding synagogue, 54; Saint Philip's Church, 10; surrender to British, 34. *See also* Kahal Kadosh Beth Elohim

Charleston Courier (newspaper), 76, 107

Charles Town. *See* Charleston

Charlotte, North Carolina, 192; Jewish ladies of, 82; Harry Golden, 191; Lewis Leon, 80

Charlotte Observer (newspaper), 152

Charlottesville, Virginia: neo-Nazis march in, x; Isaiah Isaacs in, 45; Unite the Right, 201

Chestnut, Mary, on Judah Benjamin, 91

Christian Anti-Jewish Party, 189

Christianity, x, xii, 4–5, 36, 69, 160, 210n37; Anabaptists, 22; Arminian theology, 51; Christian Science, 165; Church of England, 6; Confederacy and, 90–91; denominational splits, 70; Elizabeth Parker's conversion to, 93; enslaved people, 73; evangelism of Jews, 14, 136, 165; freedom and, 26; fundamentalism, 152, 164; Huguenots, 9; Jewish conversion to, 23, 51, 56, 61, 93; Jewish critiques of, 94–95, 176; lynching, 156; revivals, 19, 20, 51, 88, 114; slavery, 73; Sunday closing laws, 63; trinitarianism, 20; United States, 57–58; whiteness and, xiii. *See also* Anglicanism; Baptists; Catholicism; Christians; evangelicalism; Lutherans; Presbyterians; Quakers; Unitarianism

Christians, descriptions of Jews, 36, 48, 152; ministers, 14, 15, 53; political leaders, 3–4, 15–16, 41, 107. *See also* Antisemitism

Christian View of Segregation, A (Gillespie), 187

Church of England. *See* Anglicanism

circumcision(s), 21; Jewish rite, 69–71

Citadel military academy, 139

City Emergency Relief Committee, 170

civil rights, 133–35, 163–64, 180–81, 183–86; activists for, 187–90; divisions in Selma, Alabama, 194–95; fight for desegregation, 190–92; Rabbi Grafman support for, 193–94. *See also* King, Martin Luther, Jr.

Civil Rights Act (1964), 194

Civil War, xiv, 42, 50, 72–99; American Jews after, 123–24; Jewish soldiers, experiences of, 88–89; memories of, 113, 114; Jews embracing Confederacy, 72–74, 77, 79–80, 82–83, 86; pain of familial division, 78–79; theological confusion of, 94. *See also* Confederate States of America; Unionism

Clansman (Dixon), 152

Clapp, Theodore, minister of Unitarian church, 51

Clark, Jim, Selma sheriff, 195

Cobb, Thomas R. R., on Judah Benjamin, 91

Code Noir (1724), 10, 27

Cody, Mary, Steinheimer's employee, 115

Cohen, Barnet A., enslaved people of, 44

Cohen, Eleanor H.: eulogizing Josh Moses, 99; transition to peacetime, 98

Cohen, Henry (Rabbi): on European situation, 173; Galveston, 130; Hebrew Union College, 178; Jewish Immigrants' Information Bureau, 143; son of, at Synagogue of Paris, 158; writing on Jews in Texas, 132

Cohen, Isaac, on inheritance of daughter Sarah, 49

Cohen, Isaac Barrett, Jewish cemetery recording fate of, 99

Cohen, Jacob, Jews Store, 37

Cohen, Marx E., Jr., Jewish cemetery recording fate of, 99

Cohen, Michael R., on cotton trade, 114

Cohen, Miriam Moses, on secession crisis, 78

Cohen, Moses: death of, 39; detail of gravestone of, 21, 22; KKBE congregation, 21; sons Abraham and Solomon, 26

Cohen, Sarah, David Cordoza and, 49

Cohn, David L., on race relations, 144

Cohn, Mathias Abraham: leading in local Jewish congregation, 116–17; local politics, 115, 116; Union of American Hebrew Congregations, 119

Columbia, South Carolina, 56, 70, 96, 184

Columbus, Georgia, 105, 133, 151, 157

Committee on Displaced German Scholars, 177

Communism, 159, 171, 172; opposition to, 180; accusations, 189

Confederate States of America, x; "the Lost Cause" and, 104–5; antisemitism within, 91; Christianity and, 90–9; Committee on Flag and Seal, 76; enslaved people, 232n30; Jews embracing, 72–74, 77, 79–80, 82–83, 86, 128; prayers for, 93

Confederate Union, 189

Conference of Rabbis of Southern Congregations, 132

Congregations: 40–41, 50, 69–70, 199, conflicts, 30–31; founding of 17–18, 37–8, 67, 116–17, 145–6; Reform Judaism, 130–1; Sunday schools, 56. See also synagogues

Conley, Jim, accusing Frank of Phagan death, 155

Conscription Act of April 1862, 84–85

Continental Association, creation of, 30

Cordoza, David, Sarah Cohen and, 49

Cornell University, 153

cotton trade, Cohen on, 114

Court of Claims, 102

Crisis (journal), 163

Crisp, Edward, "A Plan of Charles Town", 7

Cromwell, Oliver, on readmitting Jews to England, 5

Cursory Remarks on Men and Measures in Georgia (pamphlet), 36

DaCosta, Isaac: brother and nephew serving in militia, 34; burial of, 38; first Jewish mason, 26; fleeing to Philadelphia, 34; founding hazan of KKBE, 30; import-export businesses, 25; language and cause of liberty, 30; Olivera and, 18

DaCosta family, 22

Daily Forward (newspaper), 145, 147

Dallas, Texas,129, 156; Congregation Shearith Isarel, 188

Davis, Jefferson: Confederate memorial movement, 104; speech as "pretty warlike", 76

Declaration of Independence, 47

De Cordova, Jacob: account of Unionist past and present, 102; speaking on Texas, 64

Deists, 63

De La Motta, Jacob: dedication of Mickve Israel, 46–47; on organ as violation of Sabbath, 54; synagogue burning and rebuilding, 49

De La Motta, Sarah: death of, 39; Levi Sheftall and, 23

de Leon, David, Confederate support, 77

death, 23, burial, 17, 28, 29–30, 87, 89; cemeteries, 13, 26, 38, 43, 45, 50, 55, 61–62, 67, 68, 69, 138;

gravestones, 21, 49, 99, 138; wills, 17, 20, 44, 45, 49, 68, 103

DeLyon, Abraham, enacting British claims, 4; family of, 12

DeLyon, Isaac, Gratz and, 24

Democratic Party, 105, 106–7, 108, 109, 114, 122–23, 128, 160; Jews supporting, 73, 75, 108, 110, 113, 115–16, 119, 133, 170; Ku Klux Klan and, 109–10; opposition to civil right movement and, 181, 192

Didlake, "Aunt Martha", Schwarz on, 115

Didlake, "Uncle Henry", Schwarz on, 115

Dixon, Thomas, Clansman, 152

Dow, Lorenzo, visit to KKBE, 53

Dowdell, James Ferguson, on two classes of persons, 76

Dreyfus, Alfred, as cause célèbre, 136

Driving Miss Daisy (film), 198

Du Bois, W.E.B., The Souls of Black Folk, 136

Duke, David, campaigns for, 200–201

Duncan, Daniel, hanging for Lubelsky murder, 149

economic activities: 145–6, 168, 199–200, Civil War, 77, 82; Catholic colonies, 27; English colonies, 7, 23–25; merchants 37, 65–6, 111–12, 128–9, 147, 150, 191; peddling, 65, 148; social mobility, 114–15, 129

Eddy, Mary Baker, Science and Health with Key to the Scripture, 165

Edgeworth, Maria, and Rachel Mordecai, 48, 51

Ehrenreich, Bernard C. (Rabbi), 166

Einhorn, David (Rabbi), describing slavery, 74–75

Elzas, Barnett (Rabbi), books by, 132

Emancipation Proclamation, 88, 100

Emanuel African Methodist Episcopal Church, 52, 198, 200; Bible study massacre, ix

Emergency Quota Act (1921), 159

Engel, Joe, Auschwitz survivor, 256n82

Enlightenment, 5, 30, 39; Deism, 40; ideals, 50–51

Eplan, Leon, on being charitable to needy, 143

Epstein, D., donations for colonization of Russian Jew, 141

evangelicalism, 40, 51, 52, 62; attitudes toward charity, 170; missionaries, 165; public life, 41, 200

Evans, Eli, The Provincials, xi, 199

Ezekiel, Herbert: on antisemitism, 136; on idea of "return to Palestine", 146; on Jews and African Americans, 134

Ezekiel, Moses, B'nai B'rith commissioning, 122
Ezekiel, biblical book of, 87, 94

Fancy Sketch Book (Moïse), 56
Farmers Union News (newspaper), 150
Faubus, Orval E, (Governor): Congregation
    B'nai Israel, 196; Little Rock's Central High
    School, 186
Federal Emergency Relief Act, 170
Federation of American Zionists, Heller as presi-
    dent, 166
Fireman, Philip, describing satisfaction with
    Macon, 143
First Amendment, 40, 76
Fishblate, Solomon, on election, 134
Flegenheimer, Rosa, background of, 72; William
    and, 73
Flegenheimer, William: attending Lincoln inau-
    guration, 73; as prisoner by Prussian Army, 82;
    on Republican party's economic principles,
    109; Rosa and, 72, 73; transcription of Virginia's
    secession, 88; war experiences of, 98
Fleishman, Samuel: fleeing Confederacy, 84;
    murder of, 110–11
Florida, 7, 8, 167; census (1870), 111; Confederate
    military, 79–80; Helen Apte, 153; Rabbi Wise
    in, 71; representative, 91; Saint Augustine, 194;
    Samuel Fleischman, 84, 110; seceding, 76;
    Spanish, 19; University of, 203; West, 27;
    W. M. Lucy, 110
Floyd, George, murder of, 198–99
Fool-Killer, Abernathy's theory, 152
Foote, Henry, on Jews in Confederacy, 91
Ford, Henry, on Jewish world domination,
    159
Forrester, Nelly, Myers and, 46
Forrester, Richard Gustavus, Narcissa Wilson
    and, 46
Fortas, Abe, advisor to Roosevelt, 170
Fort Sumter, 77, 80
Frank, Leo Max: background of, 153–54; kidnap-
    ping of, 156; lynching of, ix, xv, 156, 157, 167;
    198; murder of Mary Phagan and, 154–56;
    portrait of, 154; Slaton (governor) commuting
    death sentence, 155
Frank, Moses, National Pencil Factory, 153
Frankland, Abraham Ephraim: recording fund-
    raising, 121; reporting epidemic deaths, 120
Freedmen's Bureau, 105, 110
Freedom Ride (1961), 194
Freedom Summer (1964), 194
French Louisiana, Code Noir (1724), 10

Frieden, Menachem Mendel, on means of "doing
    business", 144–45
Frink, Samuel, on liberty principles, 29
Fundamental Constitutions of Carolina (FCC),
    xiv, 6, 16; on Church of England, 9; on slavery,
    8–9

Gadsden, Christopher, gifting volumes to con-
    gregation, 41
Gallay, Allan, on colonial South, 16
Galveston, Texas, 119; cemetery, 61–62; circumci-
    sion rite, 70; Galveston Plan, 144; Henry
    Cohen, 130, 143, 173, 178; Jews of, 61, 64, 68, 127,
    143, 150; Rosanna Osterman, 77, 82
Gartenhaus, Jacob, Southern Baptist Home Mis-
    sion Board, 165
Gelders, Joseph: Communist-aligned civil liber-
    ties group, 171; memories of, 190
gender. *See* manhood; marriage; women
Genesis: creation in, 164; God's command to "be
    fruitful and multiply", 3
Georgia: British Empire, 3; constitution (1777),
    217n29; documentation of Jews in, 12; exports,
    24; House of Assembly, 29; Israelites, 33, 37;
    Jewish settlers in, 11; Jews in 1870 census, 111;
    Jews in colonial frontier, 3, 4; joining patriot
    cause, 31–32; patriotism of Jews in, 90; popula-
    tion of, 11–12; wartime antisemitism in, 89–91.
    See also Atlanta; Columbus; Macon; Savannah
German lands, 64–65, 85
Gerstmann, Simon: Court of Claims and loyalty
    of, 102–3; volunteer service leader, 86
GI Bill, 180
Gillespie, G. T., A Christian View of Segregation,
    187
Gilman, Samuel, Isaac Harby and, 51
Ginsburger, Max, personal check to Rabbi Heller
    for Russian Jews, 142
Glasser, Miriam, teacher at Shaw School, 149
Godchaux, Helene, National Council of Jewish
    Women, 177
Goldberg, David (Chaplain), on JWB-issued
    prayerbook, 158
Goldberg, Edgar, *Jewish Herald* (newspaper),
    156
Golden, Harry, advocating Black civil rights, 191,
    192
Goldenberg, C., performing circumcisions on
    sons, 69
Goldgar, Bernard, president of Sherah Israel, 147
Goldschmidt, Henry, on race, nation, and reli-
    gion, xii

Goldstein, Benjamin (Rabbi): memories of, 190; on Scottsboro Boys, 172

Goode, Joseph, on memory of 'Holy Rollers', 164

Goodman, Andrew, murder of, 194

Gotthelf, Bernard Henry: Jews of Vicksburg, Mississippi hiring, 104; on school boards, 133; Wessolowsky and, 127; yellow fever death, 122

Grady, Henry, New South prophet, 137

Grafman, Milton (Rabbi), response to King and civil rights movement, 193

Graham, Billy, preacher Ham converting, 161

Graizbord, Michael, on Jews and *judeoconver-sos*, 10

Grant, Ulysses S.: alleged hatred of Jews, 109; antisemitism of, 89; election of, 107–8; Lee's surrender to, 96–97; presidential campaign against Seymour, 107

Gratz, Barnard, DeLyon and, 24

Gratz, Rebecca, 79; Cohen writing to, 78; Jewish Sunday School, 56

Great Awakening, 19, 20; Little on revivals, 213n23; Second, 51

Great Depression, 168, 170, 180

Great Migration, 160

Grimké, Sarah and Angelina, call for abolition of slavery, 52

Gurwitz, Alexander: Balfour and, 158–59; Judaism and, 167; peddling experience, 147–48; working in San Antonio, 145

Gutheim, James K. (Rabbi), praying for Confederacy, 93

Haas, Caroline, as "first white child" born in Atlanta, 163

Hahn, Joseph, sheriff appointing Black deputies, 134

Ham, Mordecai F., Hirsch on sermons of, 161–62

Hamburg Temple, 50

Hammel Department Store, 163

Hampton, Wade (III), election in South Carolina, 123

Hampton Institute, 177

Hanukkah, 13

Harby, Isaac: Jewish worship, 50, 53; Samuel Gilman and, 51

Hart, Frances, Mordecai Sheftall and, 23

Hart, Macy B., Museum of the Southern Jewish Experience, 199

Hart, Philip, manumission of enslaved people, 44

Harvard University, restricting Jewish student admission, 159

Hayes, Rutherford B., presidential election of, 123

Hebrew benevolent societies, 41, 63, 67, 68, 170

Hebrew Ladies Memorial Association for the Confederate Dead, 104

Hebrew orphan asylums, 63, 170

Hebrew Southern Relief Association, 122

Hebrew Union College, 178; Cincinnati, 130; Hirsch and, 162; Rabbi Raisin and, 166

Heller, James (Chaplain), opening of JWB clubhouse, 158

Heller, Max (Rabbi): on "benevolence of separation" between races, 134–35; complaint during military speaking tour, 158; declaring self as Zionist, 166; Ginsburger's check for Russian Jews, 142; New Orleans, 130; Pittsburgh Platform (1885), 146

Hemings, Sally, Thomas Jefferson and, 45

Henry, Jacob, defense of religious liberty, 41–42

Herzl, Theodore, Herzl Zion Society, 146

Hirsch, Baron, Jewish philanthropist, 145

Hirsch, Ferdinand (Rabbi): career of, 162; on economic depression, 168; on Ham's sermons, 161–62; portrait, 169; Scopes "Monkey" trial in Tennessee, 164; southern Jews and Kiwanis Club members, 164

Hirsch, Isaac, on Second Battle of Bull Run, 87

Hitler, Adolf, on Jews as dangerous element, 172

holidays. *See* Passover; Rosh Hashannah; Shavuot; Sukkot; Yom Kippur

Holocaust, 197, 200; survivor, 261n15. *See also* Nazi Germany; World War II

Houston, Texas, 82; Congregation Beth Israel, 178–79; home to Herzl Zion Society, 146; *Jewish Herald*, 156; Jews advertising for *hazan* in *Israelite*, 104

Hunt, Brian, on colonists, 9

Hyams, Henry M., in high political office, 63

Illowy, Bernard (Rabbi): campaign for reimposing traditional Jewish law, 96; possible portrait of, 97; prayers of, 83; pro-slavery sermon of, 74

immigration, 5, 7, 11, 18, 37, 64–65, 68, 144, 147–50, 180, 199–200; from German lands, 62; from the Ottoman Empire, 145; from the Russian empire, 137–38, 141; "Hebrews" as racial classification in US, 149–50; to Galveston, 143; restriction, 159–60, 167; refugees, 176–77; women, 150, 163

Industrial Removal Office (IRO), 142, 143, 144

Industrial Workers of the World, 171

Inquisition, 16; Iberian Jews and, 12

Institute of Southern Jewish Life, 199

Isaacs, David, Nancy West and, 45

Isaacs, Isaiah: interracial relationships, 45–46; Jews Store, 37, 218n60; manumission of enslaved people, 44–45; settlement in Richmond, 27; Virginia tax documents, 219n7

Isaacs, Mark, on "deception" of "the so-called Synagogue", 117, 119

Isaacs, Myer S., Henry Jacobs on, 104

Islam, 9

Israel, land of, 42, 68, 200. *See also* Zionism

Israelite (newspaper), 70, 75, 104, 152; reporting on epidemic, 120–21

Jackson, 70, 194, 196; Rabbi Levitt of, 170; Rabbi Nussbaum of, 186, 194, 196

Jacobs, George (Reverend), 75, 79; funerals for soldiers, 99; pro-Confederate *hazan*, 104

Jacobs, Henry S.: as *hazan* in Augusta, Georgia, 104; on *Jewish Messenger*, 79; pro-Confederate minister, 85

Jefferson, Thomas: De La Motta sharing speech with, 47; Sally Hemings and, 45; *A Summary View of the Rights of British America*, 30

Jeremiah, referencing book of, 120

Jesus/Jesus Christ, 63, 157

Jew a Negro, The (Abernathy), 151

Jew as Patriot, Citizen and Soldier, The (Wolf), 79

Jew Bill, Maryland, 42

Jewish Herald (newspaper), 156

Jewish Immigrants' Information Bureau, Rabbi Cohen working with, 143

Jewish Ledger (newspaper), 127

Jewish Messenger (newspaper), 79, 104

Jewish Science (Moses), 165

Jewish Sentiment (newspaper), 143

Jewish South (newspaper), 127, 136, 151

Jewish Spectator (newspaper), 127

Jewish Theological Seminary, 171; Ehrenreich as graduate, 166

Jewish Tribune (newspaper), 127

Jewish View on Segregation, A (Association of Citizens' Councils), 186

Jewish Welfare Board (JWB), 157, 158, 178

Jews of South Carolina, from the Earliest Times to the Present Day, The (Elzas), 132

Jim Crow, xv, 138, 180; Nazi racism and, 172; norms of segregation, 173; racial division, 153; shadow of, 197; South, 150; uphill battle against, 160

John Birchers, Nussbaum on, 196

Johnson, Andrew, Amnesty Proclamation, 101

Johnson, Lyndon: Civil Rights Act (1964), 194; Voting Rights Act of 1965, 195

Johnston, Joseph Eggleston, Confederate memorial movement, 104

Jones, Samuel, manumission and bequests of, 45

Judeo-Christian nation, America as, 180

Judaism, xiii, 42, 45, 51, 77, 155; basics of, 62; Black man's conversion to, 258n45; Catholicism and Unitarianism, 63; Christianity and, 56–57; distinctiveness of, 61; evangelicalism and Unitarianism in competition with, 52; presenting as religious faith, 53; reform, 117; as source of spiritual power, 67; traditional, 173. *See also* Reform Judaism

Kahal Kadosh Beth Elohim (KKBE), 20, 21; Carvalho's painting of sanctuary, 53–54, 55; breakaway congregations, 37, 54; Charleston, 40, 96, 132, 166; Cohen of, 21–22; contributors of, 37, 38; DaCosta founding *hazan* of, 30; divorces and, 50; Levin of Charleston, 119; Lorenzo Dow's visit to, 53; plaque commemorating enslaved laborers, 199; Rabbi Padoll, 191; Reform, in Charleston, 50, 179; Simons attending, 67; synagogue burning to ground, 53

Kahn, Robert (Rabbi), serving overseas as chaplain, 178–79

Kaplan, Mordecai (Rabbi), building committee in Durham, 166

Kennedy, John F.: murder of, 192; Philipsborn and, 192

Kilmanjaro, John and Vicki, marriage in synagogue, 190

King, Martin Luther, Jr.: Ebenezer Baptist Church, 189; March on Washington, 193; praising journalist Golden, 192–93; Southern Christian Leadership Conference, 187; Union of American Hebrew Congregations, 193

King James Bible, 41

Kiwanis Club, 162, 164

Knights of Mary Phagan, 156

Knoxville, Tennessee, 69; Heska Amuna ("Graspers of faith"), 145–46

Koblentz, Morris, on distancing "Chattanooga Jewish citizens", 172

Ku Klux Klan (KKK), 179; ADL and, 189; antagonism in agenda of, 160–61; David Duke as leader, 200; Nussbaum on, 196; revival of, 156–57; secrecy of, 109–10; voter intimidation, 109

Kursheedt, Edwin, war experiences of, 88, 89

Kursheedt, Gershom, congregation organizer, 67

Lafair, Milli, Wessolowsky's domestic servant, 115

Last Night at Ballyhoo, The (film), 198

law: courts, 56, 63, 106; establishments of religion, 32–33, 40, 41–42; French and Spanish territory, 10–11

Lazarus, Aaron: enslaved people's involvement in Turner's rebellion, 52; fiancé of Rachel Mordecai, 48

Lee, Robert E. (General): Confederate memorial movement, 104; Leon writing about, 82; Michelbacher and, 83–84; Michelbacher in defense of Arnold to, 92; surrender to Grant, 96–97

Leeser, Isaac: describing Richmond's Jews, 103–4; *founding Occident and American Jewish Advocate*, 70; obituary of, 104

Lehman family, business of, 65, 114

Leibman, Laura, "Hakham" title, 213n28

Leibowitz, Samuel, defending Scottsboro Boys, 171–72

Leon, Lewis: capture and prisoner, 98; experiences of, 88; volunteering for Confederate army, 80; writing on Robert E. Lee, 82

Levin, J., as antiorgan dissenter, 54

Levin, Nathaniel, Kahal Kadosh Beth Elohim, 119

Levitt, Meyer (Rabbi), Yom Kippur sermon, 170

Levy, Anne, Holocaust survivor, 261n15

Levy, Ash, opposing secession, 77

Levy, Chapman, enslaved people of, 44

Levy, Isaac: Emma Mordecai eulogizing, 95–96; war experiences of, 88–89

Levy, Moses E., abolitionist pamphlet, 46

Levy, Sara, directions in will of, 44

Levy, William, advising students a Black college, 134

Life (magazine), 187

Lincoln, Abraham: assassination of, 101; Emancipation Proclamation, 88; inauguration of, 73

Lindo, Moses, inspector of indigo, 25

Little Rock, 115, 178; Congregation B'nai Israel in, 196; Rabbi Sanders in, 163, 184; standoff at Central High School, 186

Little Rock School of Social Work, Rabbi Sanders enrolling Black women, 163

Little, Thomas, Great Awakening revivals, 213n23

Locke, John: Fundamental Constitutions of Carolina (FCC), 6; on slavery, 8

Loewenthal, Henry, letter to *Israelite* (newspaper), 70–71

Long, Huey, on New Deal, 171

Lopez, David, first president of Hebrew Orphan Society, 49

Lopez, Sally, Jewish Sunday school, 56

Louisiana, 181, 201; Alexandria, 115; Baton Rouge, 70, 181; cemetery, 99; epidemic, 121; French, Code Noir (1724), 10; Huey Long, 171; Jews in, 10–11, 43, 63; Judah Benjamin, 63, 74; Lake Charles, 144; massacre in Colfax, 114; Natchitoches, 120; political offices, 63, 74; prayer, 134; Rabbi Hirsch, 162; seceding, 76; Spanish, 28; voting, 109; Whitecaps, 136. *See also* Baton Rouge; New Orleans

Lowenburg, Henry Frank, Mayer's hospitality to, 89

Lowenburg, Isaac, Mayer's hospitality to, 89

Lubelsky, Max: immigration to United States, 149; robbing and murder of, 149

Lubelsky, Rosa, immigration to United States, 149

Lucena, James, as avowed Anglican, 23

Lucy, W. M., murder of, 110, 111

Lushington, Richard, Charleston Jews serving under, 34

Lutherans, 9, 14

Lyons, Joseph: diary of, 51; on New Orleans, 63–64

Macarov, David, enlisting in US military, 176

Macon, 68; Arbeiter Ring, 147; candidate Sternheimer, 96; cemetery, 138; Congregation Beth Israel, 79; David Steinheimer, 114; Henry Loewenthal, 70; Isaac Marcusson, 130; Jews in, 105, 111, 142; Mark Isaacs, 117; Philip Fireman, 143

Macon Telegraph (newspaper), 137

Macy's department store, Straus as owner of, 105

Madison, James, De La Motta sharing speech with, 47

Majour, Costa Georga, Syrian immigrant, 150

Malev, William S. (Rabbi), arguing in favor of integration, 187–88

Manhood: 120, 166, mastery, 49, 100; military service, 82, 90, 92; religious duties, 18, 83, 130, 142. *See also* B'nai B'rith

Marcusson, Isaac (Rabbi): on antisemitism, 136; Macon, 130

marriage, 23, 49–50, 160, divorce and, 50; interreligious, 28, 45, 49, 50, 63, 69, 132, 172–73

Marx, David (Rabbi): Atlanta, 130; desegregation of city parks, 163; on Frank's lynching, 157

Masons, 15, 26, 42, 47, 162

Massell, Sam, elected Jewish mayor, 200

Mayer, John, hospitality to Lowenburgs, 89

Mayer, Maurice, *Allgemeine Zeitung des Juden-thums*, 67

Memphis Appeal (newspaper), 121

Memphis, 69, 75, 116; Abe Fortas, 170; congregations, 145–46; epidemic, 122; Israel H. Peres, 137; Max Samfield, 130; merchants, 120; newspapers, 127; representative, 119

Mendelsohn, Adam, Jews enlisted in Union Army, 228–29n50

Mercer, George Anderson, on Jews as the worst people, 90

Merlin, David, rebuilding the economic structure, 171

Messianism, 12–13, 14, 20, 35

Methodist(s): church, 52; evangelism, 40, 51, 144; John Wesley, 14; Lorenzo Dow, 53; meeting, 66; preacher, 162

Meyer, Jacob, guilty for selling on Sunday, 63

M. H. Lazarus Hardware, *148*

Michelbacher, Maximilian J.: prayers of, 83; pro-Confederate minister, 85, 86; on reputation of American Jews, 93; Robert E. Lee and, 83–84; writing Lee on Arnold's behalf, 92

migration, 26–27, 37, 43, 48–49, 65, 105, 176, 180, 200. *See also* immigration

Mikvah, 6, 14, 18

Miles, William Porcher, Confederate Committee on Flag and Seal, 76–77

Mincks, Samuel, selling enslaved man to Jewish merchant, 8

Mind of the South, The (Cash), xii

Minis, Abigail: enslaved people and, 25; Frances Sheftall and, 34; funding patriot cause, 32; grandson Dr. Philip Minis, 223n29; Sheftall and, 23

Minis, Abraham: attachment to Union, 101–2; colonial support, 15; death of, 23; enslaved people and, 25; mother Dina professing Unionism, 103

Minis, Dina, on seeing grandsons on both sides, 79

Minis, Lavinia, on news of war, 78

Minis, Philip: affair of honor, 223n29; funding patriot cause, 32

Minis family, women of, 36

Mississippi: Association of Citizens' Councils, 186; B'nai Brith, 185; groups, 8; Jews of, 65, 68, 200; Jewish Religious Association, 188; newspapers, 76; Oxford, Jewish federation, 200; public education, 109; Rabbi Abraham Ruderman in Greenville, 195; Rabbi Adolph Philipsborn, 192; Rabbi Max Heller, 130; Rabbi Nussbaum, 186,

194, 196; race relations, 144, 181; seceding on slavery issue, 73; senators, 172; summer of 1964, 194; vigilantes, 187; Whitecaps, 136. *See also* Jackson; Natchez; Vicksburg

Mobile, Alabama: Board of Delegates of American Israelites, 70; civil rights, 163–64; Isaac Monsanto in, 127; Joseph Proskauer, 170; philanthropy, 68, 172; post-World War II development, 180; synagogue construction, 70. *See also* Moses, Alfred Geiger; Schwarz, Leon

Moïse, Penina: "A Poetic Homily on the Late Calamity", 54; *Fancy Sketch Book*, 56

Moïse, Edwin Warren, in high political office, 63

Molette, Della, Schwarz on, 115

Molina, Moses, leaving money in will, 37

Monsanto, Benjamin, will of, 28

Monsanto, Isaac: documentation of, 27; enslaved people of, 27–28

Monsanto, Manuel, leaving funds to "quadroon named Sofia", 221n46

Montefiore, Sir Moses, Jewish philanthropist, 145

Montgomery, Alabama: bus boycott, 187; civil rights, 190; Lehman business, 65; philanthropy, 68, Wessolowsky visit, 128, 133. *See also* Ehrenreich, Bernard C.; Goldstein, Benjamin

Moore, Annie, house bombing killing father, 258n37

Mordecai, Abram, engaging in trade with Creeks, 37

Mordecai, Alfred: expressing opinion on slavery, 74; marriage of, 50; recruited to join Confederate side, 79

Mordecai, Benjamin: amnesty application, 101; *Charleston Courier* describing donation of, 76; description of, 66; donating to slavery cause, 73; funder of secessionist cause, 101; Simon Tuska and, 75

Mordecai, Emma: on enslaved man named Cyrus, 100–101; eulogizing friend Isaac Levy, 95–96; founding of Jewish Sunday School, 56; Lee's surrender to Grant, 96–98; on soldier on leave of absence, 84; support for war effort, 82

Mordecai, Jacob: marriage of children, 49–50; rededication to Judaism, 51; settling in Warrenton, NC, 43; Society for the Prevention of the Absconding and Abduction of Slaves, 52; son Alfred on slavery, 74

Mordecai, Rachel: baptism of, 51; on condition of the southern state, 53; on Jewish characters of Edgeworth's novel, 48, 51

Mortara Affair (1859), 68, 70, 225n38

Moses, Alfred Geiger (Rabbi): *Jewish Science*, 165; writing on Jews in Alabama, 132

Moses, Andrew Jackson: describing self as heavy loser by War, 100; sons Joshua Lazarus, Perry and Isaac Harby, 80; wife Octavia Harby Moses, 128, *129*

Moses, Clara Lowenburg, hiring Christian Science healer, 165

Moses, Franklin J., Jr., South Carolina governor, 109

Moses, Franklin J., Sr., South Carolina judge, 123

Moses, Isaac Harby: photograph with brothers, *81*

Moses, Joshua Lazarus: death of Fort Blakely, 98–99; serving with brothers, *81*

Moses, Mordecai, public office of, 133

Moses, Myer: complaints against, 31; militia, 34

Moses, Octavia Harby: Confederate booster, 128, *129*; sons Joshua Lazarus, Perry and Isaac Harby, 80

Moses, Perry, serving with brothers, *81*

Mosler, Henry, *Portrait of a Hazan* or Rabbi, 97

Moultrie, William, consecration ceremony of KKBE, 41

Museum of the Southern Jewish Experience, 199

Myers, Abraham Charles, Confederate support, 77

Myers, Gustavus Adolphus, Nelly Forrester and, 46

Myers, Samuel, on slavery, 46

Nashville: Jews in, 69, 89, 128, 135, 189, 200; US Army in, 87

Natchez, Mississippi: congregation, 96; Greek revival building in, 117; Jews, 128; John Mayer of, 89; representatives, 119; Rosalie Beekman, 87

Nathans, Moses N.: exhorting Galveston Jews, 61–62

National Association for the Advancement of Colored People (NAACP), 163–64, 184, 187

National Association for the Advancement of White People, David Duke as founder, 200–201

National Conference of Jews and Christians, founding, 162

National Council of Jewish Women, 142, 174, 177, 181, 183, 185

national day of fasting and prayer, January 4, 74

National Guardsmen, 171

National Origins Act (1924), 159, 160

National Pencil Factory, 153

National States' Rights Party, 189

Native Americans, ix, 3–4, 6, 8, 30, 31, 32, 61; Christianization, 5, 9; Creeks, 11, 24; enslavement in Carolina, 210n25; religious traditions, 9, 40; Samuel Nunes, 36–37; Yamasee, 7–8, 11

naturalization, Jews, 9, 15–16, 18, 26, 40

Naturalization Act (1790), 40

Nazi Germany, 172–73; in civil rights discourse, 192–93; US criticizing treatment of European Jews, 177; war against, 178

Nazi Party, in the United States, 172

Negro, a Menace to American Civilization, The, 151

Nehemiah, biblical figure of, 93

Neiman-Marcus, department store in Dallas, 129

Nelson, Joseph, witnessing murder of Fleishman, 110–11

New Deal, 170–71

Newfield, Morris (Rabbi): sermon "Hitler and the German Jew Situation", 172; Reform Judaism and, 158; warning congregation, 245n73

New Orleans: Bernard Illowy, 83, 96; circumcisions in, 69; Code Noir (1724), 27; conflict in, 78; congregations in, 51, 67–68, 70, 74, 117, 132, 146, 165; epidemic in, 121–22; interracial relationships in, 45; Jewish orphan homes, 130; Jewish population in, 49, 178; Jews in, 11, 27–28, 43, 46, 49, 57, 83, 199; marriage of Jewish men settled in, 50; Max Heller, 130, 134, 158, 165; multicultural, 63; National Council of Jewish Women, 174, 177, 183, 185; Netzufot Yehudah (Dispersed of Judah), 67; newspapers, 127, 135; occupation of, 93; public school integration, 184; replacing Charleston as economic hub and Jewish center, 63–64; Shangarai Chasset, 49, 67; slavery, 66, 181; Temple Sinai, 117, *118*; United Hebrew Benevolent Society, 142; United States forces in, 87, 89, 93

New Orleans Association for the Relief of Jewish Widows and Orphans, 225n38

New Orleans Daily Democrat (newspaper), 135

New South, 127, 136, 137, 155

New York: Jewish population in, 49, 142; Shearith Israel (remnant of Israel), 13, 20

newspapers, Jewish, 70–71, 75, 79, 104, 113, 120–22, 127, 191–92

North Carolina: Alfred Mordecai, 74; Arthur Abernathy, 151–52; Black Jews, 190; Board of Delegates of American Israelites, 106; Charlotte, 82; Elizabeth City, 173; Elizabeth Parker, 93; Gertrude Weil, 170, *175*; Greensboro, 149, 190–91; Jacob Henry, 41; Jews in, 168; mob in Williamston, 160–61; new vision of citizenship,

106–7; rabbis in, 188; Republicans in, 106; summer camp in, 166; US troops, 77; Vance as wartime governor, 106–7, 133; Warrenton, 43, 48; William and Rosa Flegenheimer, 72; Wilmington, 129, 134. See also Charlotte

Nunes, Moses: children with "Mulatto Rose", 45; living among Creeks, 24; trader, 36

Nunes, Samuel, lawsuit against Mordecai by, 36

Nuremburg laws (1935), 172

Nussbaum, Perry (Rabbi): bombing of synagogue and home, 196; Jewish Religious Association, 188; participation in interracial activism, 195–96; on Union of American Hebrew Congregations, 194; on views of members, 186–87

O'Brien, Michael, exploring "modernity's provincial emergence, trajectory, and impact", xi

O'Connor, Flannery, on South as "Christ-haunted", xii

Oglethorpe, James, on Jewish residents in Georgia, 11

Old Jewish Cemeteries of Charleston, S.C., The (Elzas), 132

Olivera, David, son of Jacob, 18

Olivera, Jacob: beneficiaries of, 17–18; on last will and testament, 17, 25; religious life of, 19; sale of woman (Flora) to son-in-law, 25; Sheftall and, 20

Olivera, Judith: daughter Leah, 13, 17; husband Jacob, 13, 17; women's immersion in "living water", 13–14

organs: Charleston houses of worship, 54; opponents of, as violation of Jewish law, 55–56

Oriental Hebrew Association Or Ve Shalom (Light and peace), 145

Orphan's homes, 130, 148, 154

Ossoff, Jon, election of, 200

Osterman, Rosanna: donating to hospitals, 82; Galveston Jews consecrating burial ground, 61; "hopes, prayers, and wishes", 77; posthumous generosity of, 103

Oswald, Lee Harvey, Ruby killing, 192

Ottelenghe, Joseph, Society for the Propagation of the Gospel, 23

Ottoman Empire, 13; immigrants from, 145

Padoll, Burton (Rabbi): on Jewish case for desegregation, 195; Kahal Kadosh Beth Elohim (KKBE), 191

Panic of 1873, stock market crash, 114

Parade (musical), 198, 201

Parker, Elizabeth, conversion to Christianity, 93

Parks, Rosa, city bus boycott, 187

Passover, 88, 133, 139

Pearl Harbor, December 1941 attack, 176

Pearlstine, Hyman and Esther, photograph of Passover seder, 139, 140

Pember, Phoebe, supporter of Confederacy, 82

Peres, Israel H., 137; service on Memphis school board, 137

Petersburg, Virginia, 42, 43, 70, 164; Brith Achim, 146

Phagan, Mary, Frank and murder of, 154–56

Philips, Eugenia Levy, imprisonment of, 93

Philipsborn, Adolph (Rabbi), on integration, 192

Phillips, Eugenia Levy, supporters of Confederacy, 82

Pittsburgh Platform (1885), 146, 151

Platt, Ben, actor portraying Leo Frank, 198

Plessy v. Ferguson, 184

politics. See Democratic Party; law; Public Office; Republican Party; socialism, zionism

Portuguese Jewish identity, 5, 38

Poznanski, Gustavus, consecration of new synagogue, 57

Presbyterians, 22; Scottish, 9

prohibition, Jews and, 150–51

Proskauer, Adolph: Confederate military service, 239n21; election to Alabama House of Representatives, 108; fighting Sherman's army in Georgia, 94; Nat Strauss and, 242n6

Proskauer, Joseph, advisor to Roosevelt, 170

Protestantism. See Christianity

Protocols of the Elders of Zion, The (infamous forgery), 159

Provincials, The (Evans), xi, 199

Prussia, 82, 83

Psalm 39, "A Poetic Homily on the Late Calamity" by Moïse, 54

Psalm 119, 35

Public Office, Jews in, 25, 31, 37, 74, 106, 108, 113, 115, 133, 134, 200, 210

Publications of the American Jewish Historical Society (journal), 132

Quakers, 9, 15, 22, 34

Rabbis, 68, 85, 119, 130–33, 165, 188; activism, 134, 151, 161, 184; chaplains, 157, 158; civil rights, 190, 193–94; slavery, 74

Raisin, Jacob (Rabbi): Hebrew Union College, 166; racial justice, 134; Reform Kahal Kadosh Beth Elohim, 179

Rankin, John, on New Deal policies, 172
Raphall, Morris (Rabbi): George Jacobs and, 75; public address to national day of fasting and prayer, 74
reconciliation, 104–5, 113–14, 119–23
Reconstruction, 100–122; Bureau of Refugees, Freedmen, and Abandoned Lands, 101; Jewish life at end of, 113; Republican Party and, 108
Reconstruction Act (1867), Congress passing, 105–6
Reformed Society of Israelites, 53, 54
Reform Judaism, 117, 119, 123, 131–32, 164–65; complaint against Rabbi Newfield, 158; National Federation of Temple Youth, 166; Union Prayer Book, 130. See also Central Conference of American Rabbis; Hebrew Union College; Union of American Hebrew Congregations
Rehina, Zalma, on freedom in new nation, 42–43
Republican Party, 105, 108, 109; alliance of support for Reconstruction, 108; Grant of, 107; Hayes of, 123; Jewish support of, 108, 109, 110, 115–16; Lincoln of, 73; North Carolina, 106
Rhine, Abraham Benedict (Rabbi), on assimilated families and faith, 158
Ribeiro, Samuel Nunes: colony of Georgia, 11; son Moses Nunes, 24
Ribeiro, Zippora Nunes, Shem Noah as servant to, 12
Rich, Adrienne, feminist critic, 201–2
Rich, Richard, reputation for racial liberalism, 191
Richmond, Virginia: Ashkenazi congregation, 67; Beth Ahabah, 145; Beth Shalome, 40, 42; cemetery, 43; Civil War, 72, 77–79, 82–85; congregations, 40, 51, 56, 67, 145; Edward N. Calisch, 130, 165, 178; Emma Mordecai, 95–98; George Jacobs, 75, 99, 104; Hebrew Ladies Memorial Association, 104; Isaiah Isaacs, 27, 44; Jacob Cohen, 37; Jews in, 44, 46, 52, 57, 68, 70, 103, 144, 188; Michelbacher to General Lee, 92; newspapers, 85, 90, 127; school board, 133; Thalhimer Brothers, 129
Richmond Dispatch (newspaper), 85
Richmond Enquirer (newspaper), 90
Richmond Grays, Whitlock volunteering for service, 80, 82
Richmond Light Infantry Blues, 42
Rich's, department store in Atlanta, 129
Riggins, John, lynching of, 156
Robinson, Lucy, Steinheimer's cook, 115
Robinson, Thomas, Steinheimer's farmer, 115
Roobin, A., gravestone, 138

Roosevelt, Franklin Delano: declaring South "the Nation's No. 1 economic problem", 170–71; eliminating racial discrimination, 177; March 1933 bank holiday, 168; Rabbi Levitt's letter to, 170
Rosenberg, Samuel, on southern Jews' racism, 163
Rosenfeld, Jacob, Benai Berith Jacob, 86
Rosenwald, Julius, funding Black colleges, 163
Rosewater, Edward: diary entries on secession of states, 75–76; diary of experience, 66; working in War Department, 87–88; writing on secession, 77
Rosh Hashanah, 41, 193
Rotary Club, 162
Roth, Dora, United Jewish Fund, 176
Rothschild, Jacob (Rabbi): alliance with King, 189–90; on bombings of Jewish institutions, 189; on segregation, 191; Yom Kippur sermon, 181
Rothschilds, European Jewish banking family, 65
Rubin, Isaac David and Sarah, photograph commemorating Jewish New Year, 139, 140
Rubinowitz, Elizabeth: identified as "Orthodox Jew", 174; on religious feeling, 173
Ruby, Jack, killing Oswald, 192
Ruderman, Abraham (Rabbi), on Greenville as "oasis of liberalism", 195
Rush, Benjamin, De La Motta and, 47
Russell, Richard B., Bloch and, 181
Russia, 84, assassination of Tsar Alexander II, 137; Jewish immigration, 141; revolution (1905), 144
Rutledge, John, Williamson's letter to, 31

Sabbath: Christian, 15, 33, 94, 137; Jewish, 18, 23, 32, 54, 145, 170, 177, 180, 188; Sunday closing laws, 41, 63; Sunday services, 131
Saint Philip's Church, Charleson, 10, 38
Salvador, Francis, patriot politician, 31
Salvador, Joseph: leaving money in will, 37; on religion in South Carolina backcountry, 40
Samfield, Max (Rabbi): consolation amid yellow fever epidemic, 121; indifference of Southern rabbis, 242n3; Memphis, 130; portrait, 131; serving on school boards, 133
Samuel, Rebecca: criticizing northern cities, 46; idea of Jewish exile, 57; on isolation in Petersburg, VA, 43; on Jews living in Virginia, 42
San Antonio, Texas, 145, 166
Sanders, Ira (Rabbi): Little Rock School of Social Work, 163; on school desegregation, 184–85

Sanger, Alex, Jewish merchant, 161
Sasportas, Isaac, on slavery, 46
Savannah, 4, 8, 127; Benai Berith Jacob, 86, 102–3;
    cemetery, 46; Constitution, 76; cotton losses,
    102; D. Epstein, 141; George Anderson Mercer,
    90; Jewish congregation, 29, 54; Jews in, 12,
    14–20, 22–24, 30, 32, 36–38, 43, 102; Joseph
    Lyons, 51; marriages, 37; Mickve Israel, 12–13,
    16, 20, 39, 40–41, 47, 117; Moses Nunes, 45;
    pioneers in, 57; Nathan Wild's wife, 173; picket-
    ing shopkeepers in, 191; political divide, 78;
    Rabbi Solomon, 166; revolutionary forces,
    33–35; Simon Gerstmann, 86; synagogue burn-
    ing down, 49; trade in, 26. See also Minis;
    Sheftall
Schechter, Amy, agitating for radical change, 171
Schechter, Solomon, Jewish Theological Semi-
    nary, 171
Schoenberg, Marx: Confederate military service,
    239n21; death in clash at ballot box, 108
Schorsch, Jonathan, on sacramental and salva-
    tional status, 215n64
Schwarz, Augusta, community activity, 113
Schwarz, Leon: Black musicians and workers, 115;
    Congregation Mishkan Israel church dedica-
    tion, 117; JWB office in Paris, 158; on Klan in
    memoir, 161; Mobile, Alabama Democrat
    mayor, 113
Schwarz, Reuben: bankruptcy of, 114; commu-
    nity activity of, 113
Schwerner, Michael, murder of, 194
Science and Health with Key to the Scripture
    (Eddy), 165
Scopes "Monkey" trial, Hirsch responding to,
    164
Scottsboro Boys, Leibowitz defending, 171–72
Second Battle of Bull Run, Hirsch on, 87
Second Great Awakening, 51
Sehat, David, term "moral establishment", 41
Selig, Lucille, Leo Max Frank and, 153
Seligman, Joseph, experience of anti-Semitism,
    135–36
Selma, Alabama: civil rights, 194–95; Leon
    Schwarz, 113; Louis Gerstmann, 242n6;
    newspapers, 108, 117; refugee resettlement
    in, 177; synagogue, 113, 117; Wessolowsky
    visit, 128
Sephardic Jews, 3, 5, 11, 12, 13, 17, 21, 26, 31, 38
Seven Years' War, 27, 30
Seymour, Horatio, presidential campaign against
    Grant, 107
Shavuot, 133

Sheftall, Benjamin: documentation of Jews in
    Savannah, 12, 13; naturalized citizen, 26; slavery
    and, 25; sons Mordecai and Levi, 18, 23; Union
    club, 26
Sheftall, Frances: closeness of Jewish community,
    34–35; writing to imprisoned husband, 34
Sheftall, Levi: correspondence with Washington,
    39–40; death of and will, 44; on healing be-
    tween Great Britain and colonies, 32; president
    of Mickve Israel, 39; on recording birth of
    children, 37; reporting on coming and going of
    Jews, 34; slavery and, 25; wartime experiences,
    35; writing under "Real Citizen", 36–37
Sheftall, Mordecai: death of, 41; funding patriot
    cause, 32; gravestone of, 46; ground donation
    of, 30; prayers for daughter of, 40; slavery and,
    23, 25; working to clear brother's name, 35–36
Sheftall, Sheftall, son of Mordecai, 32, 35
Sheftall diaries, 38; records of David Leion and
    wife Hannah, 222n14
Sherman, William Tecumseh: occupation of
    Savannah, 102; Proskauer fighting army of, 94
Simons, Billy, attending Kahal Kadosh Beth
    Elohim, 67
Six-Day War (1967), 196
Sixteenth Street Baptist Church, Birmingham,
    193
Slaton, John M., commuting Frank's death sen-
    tence, 155
slavery: biblical argument for, 51; emancipation
    of enslaved people, 100; Fundamental Consti-
    tutions of Carolina (FCC), 8–9; Jews' partici-
    pation in, xiv–xv, 43–46; laws and amendments
    abolishing, 105; rabbinic perspectives on,
    74–75; "three-fifths clause", 43; within Jewish
    families, 23, 25–26, 66–67
Socialism, 147. See also Arbeiter Ring
Social Security Act of 1935, 170
Society for the Prevention of the Absconding and
    Abduction of Slaves, 52
Society for the Propagation of the Gospel in
    Foreign Parts, 9; missionary Ottelenghe of
    the, 23
Solomon, Clara, on occupation of New Orleans, 93
Solomon, George (Rabbi): on lack of interest in
    synagogue, 165; opening summer camp in
    North Carolina, 166
Souls of Black Folk, The (Du Bois), 136
South Carolina: ADL's chapter, 189; B'nai B'rith
    Convention, 183–84, 185; Christian Protestant
    religion, 33; constitution, 32–33, 227n24; di-
    vorce in, 50; Episcopalians, 41; exports, 24, 30;

South Carolina (*continued*)
Franklin J. Moses Jr. as governor, 109; Grimke sisters, 52; interracial marriage in, 132; Jewish men in forces, 34, 80, 99; massacre in Hamburg, 123; mercantile occupations of Jews, 111; politics of, 181, 183–84, 195; Provincial Congress, 31; religion in, 40, 52, 56–57, 63, 70, 76, 173; seceding on slavery issue, 71, 73; slavery, 44, 66, 100; Supreme Court, 56, 123; voter intimidation, 109, 122; white militiamen murder of Black residents, 122. *See also* Charleston; Columbia; Sumter

South-Carolina Gazette and General Advertiser (newspaper), 36

Southern (American) Jewish Historical Society, 188

Southern Baptist Home Mission Board, 165

Southern Christian Leadership Conference, Martin Luther King Jr. as president of, 187

Southern Claims Commission, 102

Southern Israelite (newspaper), 174

Southern Jewish Historical Society, 199

Soviet Union, 180

Spiegel, Marcus, war experiences of, 89

States' Rights (Bloch), 186

Steinheimer, David, Black labor and economic viability for, 114–15; fleeing Confederacy, 84–85; peddler observations, 65

Stephens, Alexander, celebrating new Constitution, 76

Stern, Malcolm, book labeled "diaries", 211n61

Sterne, Ernestine, public office of, 133

Sternheimer, L. Z., Confederate currency and, 96

Stono Rebellion, 19, 24

Straus, Lazarus, Macy's department store, 105

Strauss, Nat: Proskauer and, 242n6; ridiculing Christianity, 96; on theological confusion, 93–95

Sukkot, 133

Summary View of the Rights of British America, A (Jefferson), 30

Sumter, 107, 161–62

Suriname, 26

Sylvester, James Joseph, University of Virginia, 63

synagogues, 165–6, 190, attendance, 48, 67, 84, 93, 95, 158, 173; buildings, 98, 138; consecration 47, 57, 117; construction, 41, 54, 49, 68, 70, 117, 188; damage, 53, 96, 189, 196. *See also* congregations, Reform Judaism

Talladega College, 177

Tarshish, Allan (Rabbi), American Council for Judaism, 179

Tattnall Guards, 90

Tennessee, 69, 77, 133, 200; Grant's General Orders Number 11, 89, 107; Oak Ridge, 176; S.A. Bierfield, 110; Sam Borenstein, 171; Scopes Trial, 164. *See also*, Knoxville, Memphis; Nashville

Tepper, Sol, Clark and, 195

Terminiello, Arthur W., on Jews as self-interested agitators, 178

Texas, 61, 64, 76, 99, 102, 121; Charles Wessolowsky, 130; El Paso, B'nai Zion, 146; Greenwood, 120; Jews of, 132, 138, 143–44, 153, 167; Kennedy in, 192; Klansmen, 160–61; public office, 134; Waco, 130; William Levy, 134. *See also* Dallas; Galveston; Houston; San Antonio

Texas Jewish Herald (newspaper), 172

Thalhimer Brothers, department store in Richmond, 129

Thomasville, Georgia, resolutions of, 89–90

Thurmond, Strom, Bloch and "Dixiecrats" nominating, 181

Till, Emmet, murder of, 187

Touro, Judah, 67; benefactor of Unitarian church, 51; death of, 68; Ellen Wilson and, 46; moving to New Orleans, 43; posthumous generosity of, 103; will of, 225n36, 235n19

Touro Monument Association, 68

Trivellato, Francesca, Sephardic Jews in Europe, 26

Truman, Harry S., Civil Rights Committee, 180–81

Trump, Donald J., Charlottesville protests, 201

Turner, Nat, rebellion of, 52–53

Tuska, Simon, on public attack on Jewish honesty, 75

Tweed, Thomas, on "religion," xi

Uhry, Alfred, *Parade*, 198

Union Army, Mendelsohn on Jews enlisted in, 228–29n50

Unionism, Jews professing, 101–3

Union of American Hebrew Congregations (UAHC), 119, 131–32, 188, 193; prayers for, 119–20

Union of Congregations of the South and West, Wise allied with leaders for, 119

Unitarianism, 51; Catholicism and, 63; evangelicalism and, 52

United Confederate Veterans, 133

United Daughters of the Confederacy, 133

United States Bureau of Immigration, 149

United States Constitution, 40; Congress passing Reconstruction Act (1867), 105–6; First Amendment, 76; "three-fifths clause", 43

University of Alabama, 176

University of Virginia, 63

Valentine, Isaac D., Jewish cemetery recording fate of, 99

Valentine, Simon: joining Huguenots, 9; purchase of enslaved man, 8

Vance, Zebulon B.: death of, 133; Jews as idealized other, 152; North Carolina's wartime governor, 106–7

van Moses, Philadelph, description of Moses, 109

Vesey, Denmark, failed revolt of, 52

Vicksburg, Mississippi: Jewish immigrants, 68, 104, 144; Rabbi Philipsborn of, 192; representatives of, 119; Reverend Gotthelf of, 104, 122; US Army and, 91; Wessolowsky in, 127–28

Virginia, 5; African Americans in, 133, 163; General Lee surrender, 96; Isaac Hirsch, 87; Jews in, 4–5, 43, 89, 144; Leeser on, 70; Ordinance of Secession, 72; Racial Integrity Act, 160; Readjuster Party, 133; religion in, 33; revolt in, 52; Suez Crisis, 188; University of, 63; US troops, 77, 87–88, 91. *See also* Charlottesville; Petersburg; Richmond

Vladek, Baruch Charney: account published in *Daily Forward*, 146–47; African Americans and Jewish immigrants, 149; Jews serving Black clientele, 148

Volskovitz, Samuel, on existence as "Black Jew", 135

von Dohm, Christian Wilhelm, on Jewish citizens, 40

Voting Rights Act (1965), 195

War of Jenkin's Ear, 16

Washington, Booker T., encouraging the hiring of Black workers, 137

Washington, George, correspondence with Sheftall (Levi), 39–40

Watson, Tom: Leo Frank case, 172; newspaper spewing anti-Frank vitriol, 155

Weekly Louisianan (newspaper), 116

Weil, Edouard: leading in local Jewish congregation, 116–17; local politics, 115, 116; Union of American Hebrew Congregations, 119

Weil, Gertrude: bringing European relatives and friends to US, 176; on Christianity's idea, 175–76; on listening to radio for world happenings, 173; portrait, 175

Weil, Lee B., describing antisemitism, 178

Weis, Julius, on enslaved people, 66

Wesley, John, evangelizing Jews, 14

Wessolowsky, Charles: Black workers of Confederate veteran, 115; capture and prisoner, 98; notions of bravery and belonging, 90; travels of, 127, 128, 130, 138

West, Nancy, David Isaacs and, 45

Weston, Lydia, mother of Francis Cardozo, 109

Whitefield, George: founding congregation, 20; series of revivals, 19; on synagogue on island of Gibraltar, 14

Whiteness, 4–5, 40, 46–7, 49, 52, 57–58, 66, 76–7, 107, 135, 137, 147–50, 155–56, 162–63, 179, 183, 189

Whitlock, Philip: memories of cousin's forced conscription in Russia, 84; volunteering in Richmond Grays, 80, 82; war experiences of, 89

Wild, Nathan, on Jewish observance, 173

Wilkinson, Horace, on custody of child in divorce, 174

Williamson, Andrew, letter to Rutledge, 31

Wilmington Concordia Society, 129

Wilson, Ellen, Judah Touro and, 46

Wilson, Narcissa: child of Touro and Wilson, 46; Forrester and, 46

Winner, Lauren, on slaves of Jewish families, 66–67

Wise, Isaac Mayer (Rabbi): *American Israelite* (newspaper), 122; American Judaism of, 178; death of, 131; on descendants of immigrant Jews, xi; founding *Israelite* (newspaper), 70–71; George Jacobs and, 75; Hebrew Union College, 130; on Jewish prisoners of war, 92; on Michelbacher, 232–33n36; Union of Congregations of the South and West, 119

women, Jewish, 36, 49, 106, 130; activism, 56, 69, 104–5, 121, 141–43, 162, 170, 174–75, 177, 181, 183, 185; economic activity, 24, 68; Helen Apte, 152; immigrants, 150, 163; Judaism and, 13–14, 18, 50; wartime, 34, 78, 82, 98; Unionism, 103

Wolf, Simon, *The Jew as Patriot, Citizen and Soldier*, 79; records of groups of brothers, 229n55

Worker's Circle. *See* Arbeiter Ring

World War I, 153, 157–59, 180

World War II, 176–78, 179, 182

Wright, James, seeking to prevent Jews from residing in Georgia, 34

Yale University, 137

Yaschik, Henry, on Supreme Court, 184

yellow fever epidemic: of 1878, 121–22; Jewish communities and, 120–21

Yom Kippur, 84, 120, 133, 158, 170, 181

Zapruder, Abraham, Kennedy death and, 192

Zevi, Shabbatei, suspected messiah, 13

Zionism, 146, 166, 178, 188, 197

A NOTE ON THE TYPE

This book has been composed in Arno, an Old-style serif typeface in the classic Venetian tradition, designed by Robert Slimbach at Adobe.